Globalisation:
The Missing Roads of Tribal's

Globalisation:
The Missing Roads of Tribal's

Spark from Bidisa – Vol. IX

Edited by:

Vijay P. Sharma

Pradip K. Bhowmick

Palash Chandra Coomar

KALPAZ

ISBN: 978-93-5128-186-3

Price: ₹ 1250

First Published, 2016

Published by

Kalpaz Publications
C-30, Satyawati Nagar,
Delhi – 110052
E-mail: kalpaz@hotmail.com
Ph.: 9212142040

Printed at: G. Print Process, Delhi

Cataloging in Publication Data—DK
Courtesy: D.K. Agencies (P) Ltd. <docinfo@dkagencies.com>

International Seminar on Globalisation and Tribal (2014 : Bidisa, India)
Globalisation : the missing roads of tribal's : Spark from Bidisa - Vol. IX / edited by Vijay P. Sharma, Pradip K. Bhowmick, Palash Chandra Coomar.
pages cm
Papers presented at the International Seminar on Globalisation and Tribal, held on 6-7 December 2014 at ISRRA, Bidisa, West Bengal.
ISBN 9789351281863

1. Globalization—Social aspects—India—Congresses. 2. Tribes—India—Social conditions—Congresses. 3. Tribes—India—Economic conditions—Congresses. I. Sharma, Vijay Prakash, 1954- editor. II. Bhowmick, Pradip Kumar, 1955- editor. III. Coomar, Palash Chandra, 1956- editor. IV. ISRRA (Organization)host institution. V. Title.

HN690.Z9G56 2014 DDC 303.4820954 23

Contents

Contributors

1. Abhishek Chauhan, Faculty M.A in Rural Development Course, (Dept. Of Anthropology) Ranchi University, Ranchi Jharkhand (India).
1. Ala Udin, Associate Professor, Department of Anthropology, University of Chittagong, Chittagong 4331, Bangladesh.
2. Anindita Gupta, Research Scholar,Department of Lifelong Learning and Extension, Rural Extension Centre,Visva-Bharati (A Central University, Sriniketan – 731236,Birbhum, West Bengal
3. Anindya Mitra, Research Scholar, Department of Lifelong Learning and Extension, Rural Extension Centre, Visva-Bharati (A Central University), Sriniketan, Birbhum, West Bengal.
2. Arup Bera, Department of Anthropolgy, Mahishadal Girls' college, Purba Medinpur-721628.
3. Ashok Pandey, UGC-SRF (D.PHIL. SCHOLAR), Department of Anthropology, University of Allahabad, Allahabad-211002
4. B. Sarkar, Assistant Professor, Dept. of Education, Kalyani University.
5. Bigitendriya Debsharma, Research Investigator, Cultural Research Institute, Backward classes Welfare department, Govt. of West Bengal.
6. Biva Samadder, Lecturer, Dept. of Sociology, Surendranath College, Kolkata.
7. Chandan Kumar Panda, Assistant Professor of Agricultural Extension.Department of Agricultural Extension, College of Agriculture, Tripura,P.O.- Lembucherra, Dist.- West Tripura, State- Tripura, PIN – 799 210.
8. Debashis Debnath, Indian Institute of Forest Management, Bhopal.
9. Debasis Mondal Research Scholar Centre for Journalism and Mass Communication Visva-Bharati University Santiiketan-731235.
10. Debotri Chakraborti , Research Scholar, Department of Anthropology, Visva-Bharati University, Santiiketan-731235,
11. Dr. Barnali Maity, Asistant Professor and Head, Department of Sociology, Ramnagar College,of Vidyasagar University, Midnapore, West Bengal.
12. H.K. Bhat, Retired Professor of Anthropology, University of Mysore, Mysore.
13. Juganando Medok, Dept. of English, Kherajkhat College, Lakhimpur. Assam.
14. K M Rezaul Karim, Assistant Professor, Department of Sociology, Govt. BL College, Khulna-9202, Bangladesh.
15. Kaushik Chattopadhyay, Assistant Professor, Dept. of Sociology, Prof. Syed Nurul Hasan College, Farakka, Msd.

16. Mantu Hazarika, Asstt. Professor, Dept. of Sociology, Kherajkhat College, Lakhimpur. Assam.
17. Md. Intekhab Hossain Guest Faculty, Department of Sociology, Aliah University, Kolkata, West Bengal, India.
18. Nilakantha Panigrahi, Associate Professor, Department of Anthropology and Tribal Development, Guru Ghasidas University (A Central University) Bilaspur, Chattishgarh.
19. Pradip Kumar Mandal, Assistant Professor, Department of History, Manbhum Mahavidyalaya.
20. Rimi Sarkar, Research Scholar, Department of Sociology, University of Kalyani, Nadia, W.B.
21. Salina Ahmed,Associate Professor, Sociology Discipline, Khulna University, Khulna-9208, Bangladesh
22. Samita Manna, Professor, Department of Sociology, University of Kalyani, Nadia, W.B.
23. Sayan Dutta, Field Supervisor of Cohort Study, National Institute of Bio-Medical Genomics, Kalayani, Nadia.
24. Shailendra Prasad Sinha is Senior Lecturer, Department of Anthropology, Ranchi University, Ranchi-834008.
25. Sourajit Roy, Assistant Professor, Department of Sociology,St. Joseph's College, Lebong Cart Road,North Point, Darjeeling.Pin- 734104.
26. Srikrishna Mondal, Faculty member, Deptt. of Anthropology, Mahishadal Girls Collage.
27. Subhrendu Maiti, Former Faculty, Dept of Anthropology, Bongaon College, WB.
28. Sudip Bhui, Assistant Professor, Department of Anthropology and Tribal Studies, S K B University, Purulia.
29. Sujit Kumar Paul, Associate Professor, Department of Lifelong Learning and Extension, Rural Extension Centre,Visva-Bharati (A Central University), Sriniketan, Birbhum, West Bengal.
30. Suman Kalyan Samanta, Asst Professor and Head, Dept. of Anthropology, Mahishadal Girls College, Purba Medinipur.
31. Swapan Kumar Kolay, Associate Professor & Head, School of Anthropology & Tribal Studies, Bastar University, Jagdalpur- 494001.
32. Swarup Kumar Jana, Assistant Professor, Dept. of Commerce Ramananda College , Bishnupur, Bankura, Pin-722122. West Bengal.
33. Syed Abul Hafiz Moinuddin, Professor and Head, Department of Sociology, Vidyasagar University, Midnapore, West Bengal, India.
34. Vandana Kumari, Research Associate (Cultural), Anthropological Survey of India, NWRC, Dehradun.
35. Prabhat K. Singh, Deparment of Anthropology, Ranchi University, Ranchi-834008

Preface

This volume is an outcome of selected papers presented in the International Seminar on "Globalisation and Tribal" by Learned speakers. There are 28 articles in this volume that contains discussions and deals with views on globalisation and presents wide ranging knowledge about globalisation and its impact on Tribes.

An attempt has been made here to understand the concept of Globalisation in a literal sense, as international integration. It can be described as a process by which the people of the world are unified into a single society. This process is a combination of economic, technological, socio-cultural and political forces. One can be sure that virtually every one of the 2822 academic papers on globalisation written in 1998 included its own definition, as would each of the 589 new books on the subject published in that year.The sociologist, Anthony Giddens, defines globalisation as a decoupling of space and time, emphasising that with instantaneous communications, knowledge and culture can be shared around the world simultaneously.

A Dutch academic who maintains a good website on globalisation, http://globalize.kub.nl/ Ruud Lubbers, defines it as a process in which geographic distance becomes a factor of diminishing importance in the establishment and maintenance of cross border economic, political and socio-cultural relations.

Left critics of globalisation define the word quite differently, presenting it as worldwide drive toward a globalised economic system dominated by supranational corporate trade and banking institutions that are not accountable to democratic processes or national governments.

Globalisation is an undeniably capitalist process. It has taken off as a concept in the wake of the collapse of the Soviet Union and of socialism as a viable alternate form of economic organisation. In other words, Globalisation is the rapid increase in cross-border economic, social, technological exchange under conditions of capitalism.

Simon Reich also explores this question in a working paper for the Helen Kellogg Institute for International Studies at the University of Notre Dame. Many see it as a primarily economic phenomenon, involving the increasing interaction, or integration, of national economic systems through the growth in international trade, investment and capital flows.

However, one can also point to a rapid increase in cross-border social, cultural and technological exchange as part of the phenomenon of globalisation.

When did globalisation begin? There is no agreed starting point, but understanding of globalisation is helped by considering the following.The first great expansion of European capitalism took place in the 16th century, following the first circumnavigation of the earth in 1519 to 1521.

There was a big expansion in world trade and investment in the late nineteenth century. This was brought to a halt by the First World War and the bout of anti-free trade protectionism that led to the Great Depression in 1930. Some see this period as an interruption to the process of globalisation commenced in the late 19th century.

A sense that the world was united was generated by the establishment of the International Date Line and world time zones, together with the near global adoption of the Gregorian calendar between 1875 and 1925. During that period, international standards were also agreed for telegraphy and signalling. The end of the Second World War brought another great expansion of capitalism with the development of multinational companies interested in producing and selling in the domestic markets of nations around the world. The emancipation of colonies created a new world order. Air travel and the development of international communications enhanced the progress of international business.

The fall of the Berlin Wall and the collapse of the Soviet Union ended the cold war between the forces of capitalism and socialism with capitalism triumphant. The development of the internet made possible the organisation of business on a global scale with greater facility than ever before.

Economic globalisation -Economic globalisation has had an impact on the worldwide integration of different cultures. For example: a steel plant in the United Kingdom owned by the Indian company Tata Group. Globalisation, as a term, is very often used to refer to economic globalisation that is integration of national economies into the international economy through trade, foreign direct investment, capital flows, migration, and spread of technology.

The word globalisation in what Noam Chomsky calls a doctrinal sense is also used to describe the particular neoliberal form of economic globalisation. Global is commonly used as a synonym for "international", however such usage is typically incorrect as "global" implies "one world" as a single unit, while "international" (between nations) recognizes that different peoples, cultures, languages, nations, borders, economies, and ecosystems exist.

Recent evolutions-Globalisation in the era since World War II was first the result of planning by economists, Business interests and politicians who recognised the costs associated with protectionism and declining international economic integration. Their work led to the Bretton Woods conference and the founding of several international institutions intended to oversee the renewed processes of globalisation, promoting growth and managing adverse consequences. These were the International Bank for Reconstruction and Development (the World Bank) and the International Monetary Fund. It has been facilitated by advances in technology which have reduced the costs of trade, and trade negotiation rounds, originally under the auspices of GATT, which led to a series of agreements to remove restrictions on free trade. Since World War II, barriers to international trade have been considerably lowered through international agreements - General Agreement on Tariffs and Trade (GATT). Particular initiatives carried out as a result of GATT and the World Trade Organisation (WTO), for which GATT is the foundation, have included: Promotion of free trade; Reduction or elimination of tariffs; construction of free trade zones with small or no tariffs; Reduced transportation costs, especially from development of containerisation for ocean shipping; Reduction or elimination of capital controls; Reduction, elimination, or harmonisation of subsidies for local businesses; Restriction of free trade: Harmonisation of intellectual property laws across the majority of states, with more restrictions. Supranational recognition of intellectual property restrictions (e.g. patents granted by China would be recognised in the United States)

Effects of globalisation: Globalisation has various aspects which affect the world in several different ways such as: Industrial (alias Trans nationalisation) - emergence of worldwide production markets and broader access to a range of foreign products for consumers and companies

Financial - emergence of worldwide financial markets and better access to external financing for corporate, national and sub national borrowers.

Economic - realisation of a global common market based on the freedom of exchange of goods and capital.

Political - political globalisation is the creation of a world government which regulates the relationships among nations and guarantees the rights arising from social and economic globalisation. Politically, the United States has enjoyed a position of power among the world powers; in part because of its strong and wealthy economy. With the influence of Globalisation and with the help of The United States' own economy, China has experience some tremendous growth within the past decade. If China continues to grow at the rate projected by the trends, then it is very likely that in the next twenty years, there will be a major reallocation of power among the world leaders. China will have enough wealth, industry, and technology to rival the United States for the position of leading world power.

Informational - increase in information flows between geographically remote locations Cultural - growth of cross-cultural contacts; advent of new categories of consciousness and identities such as Globalism - which embodies cultural diffusion, the desire to consume and enjoy foreign products and ideas, adopt new technology and practices, and participate in a "world culture"

Ecological- the advent of global environmental challenges that can not be solved without international cooperation, such as climate change, cross-boundary water and air pollution, over-fishing of the ocean, and the spread of invasive species. Many factories are built in developing countries where they can pollute freely.

Social - the achievement of free circulation by people of all nations Transportation - fewer and fewer European cars on European roads each year (the same can also be said about American cars on American roads) and the death of distance through the incorporation of technology to decrease travel time.

Technical/legal - Development of a global telecommunications infrastructure and greater transborder data flow, using such technologies as the Internet, communication satellites, submarine fiber optic cable, and wireless telephones. Increase in the number of standards applied globally; e.g. copyright laws, patents and world trade agreements.

Examining the Impact of "Globalisation on Tribals in India", B. Ezhilarasu, (Economics, VOL. 4, 2014) attracted attention with following observations. "The new economic policies have serious impact on the adivasi lives whose right over access to natural resources, livelihood opportunities, right to primary education and health, protection from atrocities and human rights abuses and the right to uphold their traditional and customary practices, are under series threat due to the changes in laws and policies. The most serious threat to the adivasi people on the country today is the pressure on the Fifth Schedule. Both Central and Several state governments are seriously making efforts to amend the laws prescribed under Fifth Schedule and their corresponding state láws in order to allow private and corporate players to take over tribal and forest lands. Violation of the Fifth Schedule has occurred in many states like in Andhra Pradesh where the Land Transfer Regulation Act was ignored while giving mining leases in scheduled areas to private companies. Private mining has been taking place in Rajasthan, M.P, Odhisa, Maharashtra and other Fifth Schedule states. One of the ways of globalisation in India is disinvestment or privatisation. Many Public sector Enterprises are being sold off to private sectors with the objective of raising revenues to meet the fiscal deficits and to improve efficiency. Profit making enterprises like BALCO, which are in the tribal belt, have been privatized. Public Sector Enterprises in the tribal belt were beneficial to tribal people giving them employment and livelihood. Privatisation of these enterprises will adversely affect the tribal people and disturb the regional balance in terms of industrialisation. The new Industrial policy paved the way for Tribal Land alienation. These results in the alienation of tribal lands for various purpose like construction dams, mining projects, setting up of wildlife sanctuaries, construction of government infrastructure and encroachments by non tribals. While the adivasis have been displaced and pushed into the fringes of globalisation, the natural resources were victim to large scale destruction directly for industry purposes and indirectly by the non tribals. As a result the tribals ended up as debris in the globalised policies unable to access the resources which were their life sustaining forces or to compete with the mainstream society to be absorbed into alternate economies. Those absorbed in the new industries and projects were minimal compared to the extent of displacement and the destruction of traditional livelihood. Conclusion Tribals are part of the Indian society, at the same time they are different. Age old exploitation and repression of the tribals, have cut them off from the main stream of socio-economic development of the country as a whole. The tribal population is identified as the aboriginal inhabitants of our country. They are most vulnerable section of our society living in natural and unpolluted surrounding far away from civilisation with their traditional values, customs and beliefs. The gains of globalisation have so far accrued to those who already have education and skill advantage, easier market access and possession of assets for use as collateral to access credit. For the tribals, globalisation is associated with rising prices, loss of job security, lack of health care and tribal development programmes. Globalisation may also weaken the constitutional protections, in terms of education and job reservations given to tribals. Hence the Government should frame Special policy and programmes that are required to address the issue". (B. Ezhilarasu 2014, Economics, VOL.4)

The participants in this seminar collectively shared the followings:

In the globalisation process the Indian tribals are prone to exploitation and have been making vulnerable, the efforts have to be made so that vulnerability would be stopped.

Besides the processes of social change like westernisation, modernisations, there is an impact of globalisation by disarticulating and disturbing the tribal social institutions, the efforts of the globalisation are to be directed towards the institution building, social or cohesive bondage, institutional mechanism, value system- based in the tribal social system.

Globalisation has been impacting the tribals' subsistence economy in the name of income generation. The international financing system such as World Bank, IMF and the other donor agencies are funding the major or mega projects in the name of sustainable development, which has far reaching results, in the end of day project will be withdrawn leaving the tribal on the verge of destroyed economy. Instead the projects are to be designed in the tribal lands for reducing poverty by producing quality forest and tribal products on bio-resources and bio-diversities based, making value added and to get the market linkages.

Due to construction of large-scale irrigation projects, infrastructural establishments, industrial complexes, disruption, displacement and migration of large number of peoples in these mega projects have been taken place. Those affected people are neither compensated nor resettled properly. So rehabilitation-cum- resettlement policies have to be implemented as policy objectives and decisions, specially focussing on indigenous integrated farms and exploring of the perception of the tribal peoples.

The globalisation is to be associated with combating climate change with the introduction of the sustainable and clean technologies to attempt the 'go-zero and zero-emission' with the reduced carbon emissions for ecological sustainability.

The promotion of the indigenous knowledge specially indigenous technologies is to be made for the community well being linking electronic technology after the research and development on bench-marking for the local market gaining.

In the information and communication technologies e-governance is to be strengthened to disseminate the information of the development opportunities and the identification of the problems and issues.

The globalisation requires electricity for production and daily consumption due to up-gradation of the life standards. More emphasis is to be given for producing non-conventional alternative energies like solar, wind or hydro-electricity by providing with electricity and supplying the energy giving materials by cultivating the bio-fuels.

The tourism sector has to be developed with development of nature tourism, rural tourism and eco-tourism for bio-diversity management, community livelihood development and imparting environmental education.

Ethno-eco tourism site is to be established with the promotion of ethnic foods, ethno-medicines or ethnic dresses in the indigenous lands.

The foreign direct investment is to be made towards afforestation and reforestation for the development of livelihoods and income-flow and also mitigating the carbon emission.

The utility of mobile phones are to be made by providing the information of the job market and product market.

Micro-finance has to be developed to develop small and micro-enterprise development.

Globalisation is world-wide drive for domination of the corporation or corporate sector, which is to be mobilised towards accountability in the democratic process with more development of corporate social responsibilities.

The human capital development in the tribal areas. is to be strengthened by giving quality education or knowledge management in the ICT sector and also professional management system.

There is large impact of industrialisation of modern pharm industries on the tribal health Health care measures are to be taken by introducing of ethno-medicine and follow up health tourism based making in association with culture and traditions on the natural products. Some diseases like HIV/AID are found prevalent in the tribal belt as the impact of globalisation, which should be removed by developing the awareness.

Shift from manufacturing to the service sector encourages weakening at the labour unions and exploiting people in the labour wages.

In the globalisation process tribals are subjected to capitalistic exploitation as large section of the tribal population work as unskilled workers and they are forced into low paid labour sections.Union Government Or state govts. in India, should ensure through policy and legislations that minimum harm would be taken place as tribals are at the mercy of the employers.The processes of globalisation are to be made on the theme- 'Think globally and act locally'. So at the local level the civil societies are to be formed into self-help groups at the village levels and subsequent federations from block to the divisions or districts for the entrepreneurial activities and for the community empowerment.

We hope, readers will enjoy many more interesting ideas emerging from the articles in this volume. This book will be beneficial to Anthropologists, Economists, Sociologists, Social Workers and Administrators.

Vijay Prakash Sharma

Pradip Kumar Bhowmick

Palash Chandra Coomar

1

Birhors' Ways of Life in 21st Century: A Micro Study in a Few Villages of Hazaribag District, Jharkhand

Rimi Sarkar and Prof. Samita Manna

Introduction

Tribal communities in general are considered as the simple and nature based society. There are about five hundred tribal communities in India who are at different stages of economic and socio cultural levels of developments (Das, 1991). Many of them still retain their own ways of life through certain modifications due to acculturation and assimilation.

The Birhor is one of the primitive tribal groups in India. Since Independence there have been continuous efforts on the part of Central and State Government for uplifting the tribal communities and to bring them at par with the mainstream population. Along with these, several development programmes are done by the voluntary organisations who are also working actively for the uplift of these downtrodden people. In spite of this, even today the Birhors have not been able to receive any benefit from these development programmes. The Birhors of Jharkhand originally belong to the Mundari group and they consider themselves as the descendants of the Sun. The word Birhor etymologically signifies the *dwellers of jungles*. This primitive tribe is found in the hilly areas of Central and East India.

In Jharkhand Birhors are found in Palamu, Garhwa, Daybed, Singhbhum, Giridih, Lohardaga, Ranchi, Hazaribagh, Gumla etc. The Birhor settlement is known as *tanda* and their houses where they live called *Khumbhas*. Clan is the most important kin group in Birhor communities which is known as *Killi*. It is an exogamous group.

Table 1: Clan of the Birhor Respondents

Sl no.	*Clan*	*Meaning*	*Frequency*	*Percentage (%)*
1.	Maghaiya	Nilgai (Blue Bulls)	45	30.00
2.	Hemrome	Supari (Betel-Nut)	18	12.00
3.	Marandi	One type of Grass	60	40.00
4.	Indur	Idur (Rat)	27	18.00
	Total		**150**	**100**

Figures in the parentheses indicate percentages.

The above Table 1 shows the different types of clans of the Birhors. The origin of almost all the clans have been found in some hills or mountains, which are now regarded as sacred places of their ancestral spirits. In this study there are four clans - Maghaiya, Marandi, Hembram and Indur found in the Birhors. Among all the clans of Birhor, the majority of respondents belong to the Marandi clan (40.00%).

II

For the present study, five blocks in Hazaribag district of the state of Jharkhand have been selected. From these blocks, seven villages under seven panchayats are studied and 150 families of the Birhors have been selected from the Hazaribag district of Jharkhand.

Table - 2: Distribution of Birhor Households in Different Panchayats and Villages

District	*Block*	*Panchayat*	*Village*	*Total Birhor House-hold*	*Sample Birhor House-hold*
Hazaribag	Churchu	Churchu	Churchu	20	16
	Muffasin	Balsagra	Jhumri Mahua	10	06
		Morangi	Demotarn	31	26
	Barhi	Khodahar	Kewal	50	47
	Katkamsandi	Katkamsandi	Katkamsandi	15	10
		Kandsar	Kandsar	34	30
	Dumron	Ichak	Sijhua	20	15
Total	**05**	**07**	**07**	**180**	**150**

Table.2 describes the distribution of Birhor households in different panchayats and villages. In case of Birhor communities of Jharkhand, the maximum numbers of sample households have been found in Kewal village under Khodahar Panchayat in Barhi Block. Again, from the Kandsar village under Katkamsandi block, a good number of data have been gathered.

All the data have been collected through direct interview method with the help of a structured scheduled consisting of a number of open-end and close-end questions, along with participant observation. The data collection was started from March, 2012 and it ended in June, 2012.

III

Birhors: The Ways of Life in 21st Century

Globalisation has brought a radical change in our daily life in 21st century. Due to the impact of industrialisation, modernisation and globalisation people of the whole world have been enlightened. With the process of globalisation the world has been transformed into a *Global Village*. After Independence many changes are noticeable in every aspect of tribal societies. But primitivism still persists in Birhor community. Till today they suffer with the problem of isolation, poverty, lack of education, lack of opportunities etc. in their day-to-day life processes.

Language

The Birhor people speak *Birhori* language which belongs to the Mundari group of language. It is important that while they communicate with other tribes and castes they fluently speak Hindi dialect. But in their everyday life they interact with each other in their own language which is only understandable by their own community members. Till today they maintain their 'language solidarity' within themselves.

Occupation and Income of the Birhor

Their primary earning sources for maintaining their livelihood usually come from their nearby forest. Their relation with the jungle is direct. The Birhors are nomadic hunters, food gatherers and rope makers. They always like to settle not far away from the villages of peasants, because they sell their rope and forest products to the villagers in near by market, which is called *Hatt*. Food items, medicine, firewood, fodder, leaves, and branches are the chief articles which are collected by the Birhors for maintaining their livelihoods from the forest. Forest plays a vital role in their life. They have great specialisation in making ropes from different types of creepers and bark of trees. They hunt by nets and they also trap pig, rabbit, squirrel, rat etc. It has been observed from the study that 43.21% people are engaged with the hunting gathering process. All the men, women and even capable children depend primarily on hunting-gathering economy. So if sometimes they fail to hunt in this situation they have to live without food or in starvation for a few days. As a result, all the traditional settlements of the Birhors have been found near forests.

Picture-1 Picture-2

Picture 1 & 2: Birhor men and women engaged in rope making

The next most important livelihood for the Birhors is wage work. At present Birhors work in nearby fields as agricultural labourers, or as wage labourers on brick-kilns or in government tender-works. From this study, it has been observed that 22.48% Birhor are engaged with the agricultural activities and 9.30% Birhor are labourer. Women also work as daily wagers. However, wages paid to women are almost always lower than those paid to men. However, their male folk are always accompanied with the women folk not only to work in the fields of the other people as a daily wager but also in other non-agricultural activities too. Generally, a Birhor woman is paid Rs 70- 80 for a day's work while the Birhor man earns Rs 90 per day. Very few Birhors are employed as skilled labourers, and most of them (13.18%) are tractor drivers. In spite of all these, the collections of forest resources are actually the primary source of income for maintaining their life. The Birhor economy presents a mixture of forest economy, agriculture and labour. At present the government has arranged to provide 35 kg of rice and Rs 400 per family of the Birhor for every month. Besides, some arrangement has been made to provide salt, kerosin, oil etc. at a reduced price-rate from the government for improving their life style. Also, the Jharkhand government has been providing one paccka house for every Birhor family. But they did not maintain it properly. As a result the condition of these houses is very dire. Thus the environmental factors and the changing conditions are compelling the Birhors to modify their traditional ways of life to a considerable extent. But till today this tribal people for their livelihood, have to depend traditionally on nature. But now the natural resources of the Birhor in forest region are gradually reducing. So they are facing lots of problems in their everyday life. In recent times, our government has taken many serious steps for uplifting these PTG group and many of the schemes have already been started to make the vision successful. But their economic condition fails to justify their development till today. For Birhors, forest is still the main earning source for maintaining their society and culture.

Education of the Birhor

Illiteracy is extremely high among the Birhor tribe due to their forest living economy. But now our government's educational schemes, many primary schools have been opened to provide the primary level of education to them-those who are living in various *tandas*. Generally these tandas are the villages which are developed for their rehabilitation by our government. But the study reveals that the Birhors are very reluctant to send their wards to school for education as they are not familiar with it.

Among the Birhors the level of education is very less. It has been observed from the study that 88.00% of the members are illiterate. At present those who go to school are the *First Generation Learners*. Most of the young girls read up to the stage of primary level. As a whole, the literacy level of education in this tribe is alarming. Some educational schemes of the government have been introduced in Birhor areas but the schemes are not responding properly. In many cases for regular school attendance of the students mid-day-meal schemes have already been launched but it has been observed in many cases that the students only go to school for food but not for education. The study has revealed that the severe existence of primitivism, backwardness and illiteracy prevail among the Birhors since the date of Independence. This PTG group are not well aware about the positive goal of education. Till today they belong to the under privileged section of the society. As a primitive tribe the Birhors are still in dark without availing the light of education.

Marriage Pattern of the Birhor

The Birhors believe that marriage is significant and important for reproduction of children. Naturally marriage within the same clan is prohibited, but now-a-days their rule of exogamy is not followed properly. After marriage the newly married couple forms a separate house (*Orha)*. From this study it has been seen that child marriage is practiced in their society where the age of the bride is below 14 years. As a result, they are married before their puberty. For the lack of social awareness the age limit of the marriage is lower in this tribe. In many cases, due to their low age of marriage they die during the time of child-birth or their babies die due to malnutrition. It is found that 50.00% of respondents' marriage has taken place at the age of 14-17 years. But sometimes adult marriage is also practiced in this community when girls attain puberty, which is known as *Bekar*. It has been observed that 36.00% marriage takes place between the ages 18-21 years. The common way of acquiring a groom in the Birhor is by the bride price. In their society there is no restriction to negotiate marriage among the kin groups but the members are not allowed to go for marriage within their own *tanda*. The society is also very open regarding remarriage as there is no restriction on the remarriage of a deserted male or a female or a widow.

Birth and Death Ceremony

The birth of a child is an enjoyable occasion for the couple-family of *tanda* and the community. The marriage is considered as successful when the couple is blessed with child. It is a joyous occasion for the family. The maximum (82.00%) birth takes place in their houses. According to Sahu (1995), *Chhathi* is the final purification of Birhor. The female members of the community are invited to bless the child and the mother. The pregnant woman gets a social position in their society. In this period the woman has to maintain some taboos for maintaining her sound health for upholding the baby. There is no special preference or treatment for either the girl or the boy. The food, care, different facilities and love are equally extended for all children. Purification related to rituals like *Chatthi* and *Munhjutthi* are held for both the boys as well as the girls. Still now women follow many superstitions during the period of pregnancy or before pregnancy. The pregnant women put *joributi* (some preventive measures through herbal roots, leaves etc.) during their pregnancy period and to get male child or female child they are advised to carry *Premjori* and *Hathjori* respectively by their medicinal experts. They also use *joributi* as contra septic device. The Birhors are not aware of family planning. According to the Census data, as the number of Birhor tribes are gradually decreasing, the Jharkhand government has not taken any step to control the birth rate of the Birhors. So the hospital officials do not provide any suggestion for ligation of mothers. Almost all the Birhor women are unaware of the sexually-transmitted diseases.

The Birhor also believe that the spirits of their ancestors move around their huts till the end of the death rituals. Death naturally involves some supernatural beliefs and demands some rituals to be performed. Cremation is the general practise among the Birhor, but the dead bodies of the children and pregnant women are buried. After the death of a person all the used materials of the deceased are seemed to be polluted and thrown away and new materials are replaced in it.

Religions and Festivals

The religious life of the Birhors is coloured with different deities and sprits. They think that the whole universe is created and controlled by Sing Bonga. Sing Bonga is regarded as their supreme deity which is extremely powerful. Besides this, there are other deities which are *Devi Mai* (Earth God), *Kando Bonga* (Benevolent) *Hapram Bonga* (Ancestral Spirit) etc. who possess benevolent power to protect the society and the people of the Birhors. Except these deities, they believe in different spirits whose effects caused good or bad in their society and their daily life. The main sacred head among the Birhor is *Naya*. Birhors celebrate a number of festivals throughout the year. Among them a few festivals are important like *Karam (a karam branch is planted at the courtyard in the month of August – September for the welfare of the community), Dasai (a festive day performed by the community members for the welfare of the family in the month of September – October), Fague* (holi in the month of March), *Sankrant* (last day of the Bengali year that is March - April) etc. These festivals break the monotony and cheer them up with new sprit and life.

Conclusion

In recent time, some schemes have been initiated by Jharkhand government for the Birhors. *Mukhyamantri Khadya Yojna* is now available for all Birhors living in various tandas. Each family receives free supplies of food of 20 kg of rice and 10 kg of wheat for every month from the government. Besides, the *Annapurna Yojna* has already been sanctioned for the Birhors who are entitled to receive NOAPS (old age pension). But still now it is under process. But as supplement the old people have already been provided 10 kg rice per month till the implementation of that project.

For the development of Birhor community some rehabilitation facilities are also provided through the state and central government of India. Under rehabilitation scheme each family receives 5 (five) acres of land and 10 (ten) decimals for house erection or home stead land. In spite of these facilities, no remarkable change has been noticed in their society; till now they are facing the problem of drinking water, nutritional food and sanitation. The study reveals that in the dawn of 21st century the Birhors like to maintain their traditional ways attached with forest based believes, rituals and sentiments. Even today they practice many activities related to their cultural traits as they are known as primitive jungle men and want to live in isolation for restoring their primitive culture.

Reference

Dasgupta, S. & Kiely, R. (2006). Globalisation and After. Sage Publication. New Delhi.

Dasgupta, S. (2004). The Changing Face of Globalisation. Sage Publication. New Delhi.

Manna, S. (2000). The Fair Sex in Tribal Cultures: Problems and Development. Gyan Publication. New Delhi.

Ray, U. K. (1991). Birhor - A Semi Nomadic Tribe of West Bengal. (In) Das et al. (ed.) Cultural Research Institute. Calcutta.

Roy, S.C. (1925). The Birhors: A Little Known Jungle Tribe of Chotanagpur. Ranchi.

Sahu, C. (1995). Birhor Tribe – Dimensions of Development. Sarup Book Publishers Pvt. Limited. New Delhi.

http://humanexperience.stanford.edu/thinkingtwice-globalisation.

2

Globalisation and Inclusive Development: Status of Tribal Communities in Odisha

Nilakantha Panigrahi

Introduction

India is one of the few countries in the world with large concentration of tribal population. Tribal societies are organic components of Indian nation state. Tribes inhabit in almost every region of India, but their concentration is largely found in central India and north-east India. The tribal population in India is heterogeneous from demographic, socio-economic, cultural, ecological and, socio-economic exploitation, strong faith in religion and magic and lack of aspirations and developmental perspectives. They are the oldest settlers of our country but since time immemorial they have remained backward in their living standard than the non-tribal populations. Illiteracy, technological backwardnessaptitudes to innovate are some of the major reasons of their backwardness. Tribal backwardness and their exploitation by the non-tribals have drawn the attention of the administrators, missionaries, social reformers and anthropologists since the British regime in our country.

Objectives

The paper first gives a conceptual meaning of the term globalisation and inclusive development. Secondly, an overview of tribal population of Odisha and the dichotomy of poverty in the north and south Odisha is attempted. Finally, it presents a changing historical accounting of tribal livelihood basket and based on the growth of Odisha the paper analyses the socio-economic implications of neo-liberal economic reforms on tribal people who are basically living in the natural resource rich inaccessible geographical regions of the state. The paper argues that the current development scenario in Odisha has brought a sizeable quantum of fund for the development of the tribal communities and created new platforms for them, but there are some areas where the state is still to achieve the welfare promises made by the Constitution of India.

The paper is basically based on secondary data. However, authors own experiences accrued while working in different research projects relating to tribal life and livelihood issues in Odisha helped him to substantiate the analysis. The annual reports of the ST SC Development Department, Govt of Odisha, 10th and 11th Five Year Plan documents, Economic Survey reports of different years have been reviewed for the purpose.

Globalisation: An Anthropological Understanding:

This section tries to make an anthropological understanding of the term 'globalisation'. The word 'Global' is over 400 years old (OECD 1989), but the common usage of similar words such as 'globalisation', 'globalize', and 'globalizing' did not begin until about 1960. In 1961 the Webster became the first major dictionary to offer definitions of 'globalism' and 'globalisation'. Globalisation is a package of transnational flows of people, production, investment, information, ideas, and authority. The proponents of globalisation look at it as a symbol of progress. Globalisation is also considered as a means to destroy environment, corrupt the political processes, and to yield cultural lags in the development processes.

It is no doubt that the discipline of economics has contributed a lot in shaping of this concept (Wallerstein 1974a & b), but sociologists (Robertson, 1992:13) emphasized on 'cultural globalisation'. The sociological concept of globalisation centres on the concept of 'global whole' in terms of a global order (Ibid: 25). This refers to the concept of 'global village', 'Global Super Market' and 'Super Church' (Turner 1994:80) which is the product of continuous global-local interactions.

Anthropological debates for last two decades centre around 'Others', 'Primitives', 'Traditional', in contrast to 'Us', 'Civilised', 'Moderns'. Thus, the anthropological concern with globalisation in the 80s and 90s was closely related to the perceived crises of the discipline that was sharply brought to the fore in the ethnographic writing and in the deconstruction of the traditional anthropological object of the "Primitive".

In the nineties the Swedish anthropologist Ulf Hannerz proposed 'macro-anthropology of culture' (1992:218), which tried to study the cultural flow of meaning within four different frames like 'form of life', 'market', 'state', and 'social movement'. Anthropologist like Appadurai (1997:33) pointed out that the global cultural economy is a disjunctive order that cannot any longer be understood in terms of existing centre-periphery models'. He introduced different dimensional models of global cultural flow consisting of 'ethno-scapes', 'techno-scapes', 'finance-scapes', 'ideo-scapes', which connotes the fluid and interpenetrating boundaries between the contemporary cultures.

Many argue that globalisation has resulted in a global culture which basically defines culture on the lines of similar lifestyle, consumption patterns and societal values. The cosmopolitan culture has forced a section of people to think globally and to act locally. However, this is not an universal definition. Many scholars argue that globalisation is a diffusion process of Western institutions across the world, in which other cultures are crushified (Gidden, 1990). The Western media and popular TV programmes and Hollywood films have inundated the world, seeking to refashion and remodel the taste and aspirations of the middle class order across the world. The attempt of homogenisation and commodification of cultural processes are the major concern before the globalisation in Indian context. In this dynamic process the tribal people are no way free from loosing indigenous cultural identities and the processes of marginalisations.

In the context of globalisation in contemporary anthropological studies certain basic questions have been raised regarding the dialectics between the local and the global. More specifically it is time to see how local diversities are seen under globalisation processes? Whether globalisation has differential effect on different space and communities? Whether we can treat globalisation as an unequal process? Should a global ethics that applies equally to all those involved in world affairs be imposed on Third World countries, and particularly on the tribal communities?

Inclusive Development

11th Planning Commission, Govt of India defined inclusive development as a form of 'Growth process which yields broad-based **benefits** and ensures **equality of opportunity** for all'. World Bank has defined Inclusive development to both **pace and pattern** of growth. Mahamta Gandhi has defined inclusive development as 'Universal Upliftment' or 'Progress of All'

With the paradigm shift from "Development Approach" to "Inclusive Growth Approach", the Tribal Sub Plan for the 11th Five Year Plan period a the following objectives.

- It aimed at tribal centric, tribal participative, and tribal managed development process, with a conscious attempt from dependence and under effective adopted official delivery system to an overall empowerment of the tribal people.
- It promised to accelerate the reduction in the incidence of poverty and unemployment and there by reduction in income inequalities, human resource development by providing economic and health services and development of the confidence among people through intensive educational efforts, development and strengthening of infrastructure base for further economic exploitation of the resources (Physical and human both) of tribal areas,

- And, provision of physical and financial security against all types of exploitation.

In this context, the introspection in the eve of Twelfth Five Year Plan with respect to find out the mechanisms to reduce the dichotomy is praised worthy. Twelfth Five Year Plan also talks of 'Inclusive Growth'. The philosophies, and mechanisms adopted in Eleventh Plan for 'Inclusive Growth', have contributed some amount of benefits in minimizing the present state of poverty stricken life and living of the poor living in certain regions across rural-urban and coastal-inland which were neglected. However, the challenge of Twelfth Plan seems to be the crises in world capitalism which cannot be ignored and will have a visible impact in the planning and implementation in India in coming years.

II

Tribal Communities of Odisha:

Odisha has large concentration of tribal population in the country. Out of 427 Scheduled Tribes of the country, Odisha has 62 tribal communities who constitute around 22.21per cent of State's population (Census of India, 2001). The tribal communities living in the State range from small communities like *Chenchu, Bonda, Juanga, and Didayi* to large communities like *Munda, Santals, Kondh, Oraon, Saora and Bhuiyan.* Almost 44.21 per cent of the total land area of the State has been Constitutionally declared as Scheduled Area[1], which covers most of the districts except the coastal districts and few in-land areas. The districts largely dominated by Scheduled Tribes are Malkangiri (58.51%), Mayurbhanja (57.87%), Nawarangpur (55.26%), Rayagada (54.99%), Sundargarh (50.74%), Koraput (50.67%), Kondhaland (50.13%), Keonjhar (44.62%), Gajapati (47.88%), and Jharsuguda (33.31%) (Ibid). The tribal communities of the State can be categorized as hunter-gatherer-nomads living in hilly and forest areas, hunter-gatherer and shifting cultivators, simple artisans, settled agriculturists, industrial and urban unskilled and semi-skilled workers.

In Odisha out of 62 Scheduled Tribes, 13 tribal communities have been declared as Particularly Vulnerable Tribal Groups[2]. These communities are: *Bonda Paraja, Chuktia Bhunjia, Didayi, Dongaria Kondha, Hill Kharia, Juanga, Kutia Kondh, Lanjia Saora, Lodha, Mankiridia, Birhor, and, Paudi Bhuiyan, and Saora* (Govt. of Odisha,1998-99). These communities have differences with each other, which are reflected in their political, economic and socio-cultural life. Few vulnerable communities like *Birhor, Kondh and Paudi Bhuiyan* are also found beyond the State boundaries and are distributed in the States of Jharkhand, Chhatishgarh, Assam and West Bengal. Many of these communities are belonging to the Austric sub-family of Austro-Asiatic language family. Their economic life pre-eminently centres on collection of various forest produces, practice of shifting cultivation[3], and hunting and gathering. Some of these communities over the time have adopted terraced cultivation, settled agriculture; however, more or less they still adhered to the collection of minor forest produces. Many of these communities have successfully adopted rope making, basket making, wage labour, horticulture etc. All of these communities are patrilineal, partilocal, patriarchal and posses both nuclear and extended form of families, patri-lineages and clans. For them marriage by negotiations is always considered as socially approved and most prestigious, however, they also follow other ways of acquiring mates, such as marriage by capture, marriage by exchange and marriage by service. Since these tribal communities are tradition bound and have limited worldview, clans or similar organisations like *Birinda* (practised among the *Saoras*) basically regulate their social organisations and marriages. Any breach of customary practices by the members results in social excommunications and imposition of fines. The secular and sacerdotal village functionaries known differently among different communities perform the role of village head, priest, medicine man, shaman etc. and look after their politico-jural and religious functions. The ethnic identities of these communities are reflected through their dress pattern, housing structure, ornaments, god, goddess and spirits of both benevolent and malevolent nature.

III

Livelihood Resources of Tribal Communities:

(a) Forest Resources

In post-independent period the first National Forest Policy of 1952 attempted to redefine the forest policy and the traditional rights of the forest dwelling tribes. It converted certain concessions (enjoyed by tribals for long) by withdrawing the release of forestland for cultivation, controlling free grazing, and discouraging tribals to do away with the practice of shifting cultivation. The National Commission on Agriculture (NCA) 1976 revised the National Forest Policy which recommended that forests be managed efficiently for commercial purposes and for the maximisation of forest productivity, but NCA remained silent about the traditional rights of the tribals. Gaining over experiences, the Govt. of India under 42nd Amendment of the Indian Constitution deleted forest from State list and entered it under Concurrent list in 1976. The Indian Forest Bill 1980 again vested powers with forest officers to arrest and for the seizure of goods. This policy also reflected the colonial legacy, which did not treated *adivasis* as the friend of forest and empowered the State Government to declare any reserve forest as non- reserved and also allotted forest land for non- forest purposes. The National Forest Policy 1988 talked more on environmental stability through the preservation of forest by replacing contractors in place of tribal co-operatives, gave concessions to the ethnic minorities, and provided suitable alternatives for the shifting cultivators. But in practice the official draft did not follow the letter and spirit made in the resolution.

Forest Management Policies

All the forest policies promulgated in post-Independence periods have been directly implemented in the State. As a result, the tribal communities were steadily isolated and segregated from appropriating the forest resources the only viable and sustainable source of their livelihood. The traditional rights of tribal communities over the time have been transferred to concessions and controlled under various State policies. The implementation of these policies during different plan periods has drastically affected the economic, social and cultural life of the tribal people. There is some micro level evidence to the effect that JFM is functioning better in the northern region. A good indicator of this is the extent of institutional and community-based management of forests under JFM to the extent of 478325 hects during the year 2005 against the total government forest area of 9981 sq.km. Thus the extent of forest area protected by Vana Samrakhyana Samiti (VSS) and Community Forest Management (CFM) is much higher in the north compared to the south (PCCF,Ibid). Much before the introduction of Joint Forest Management in the State, it was seen that around 3 to 10 percent of all reserve and protected forest lands of Odisha were under informal community protection (Ghosh, 1996) and the tribal people of Odisha seen to have shown remarkable performance in managing their land resources. Perhaps for this reason Govt. of Odisha has felt that for successful forest preservation the local community should be fully involved and made responsible for the prevention of illicit felling, theft of forest produces and encroachment in reserve forest (GOI, 1997).

Roy Burman Committee (1982) has pointed out the commercial viability of around 300 NTFPs, explained the close linkages between the tribals and forest; and the potential of prosperity of different traders to trade forest produces at various levels. With the 73rd Amendment of Indian Constitution, which gave power and revitalised the Panchayati Raj Institutions, Govt. of India extended this special power through the Panchayats (Extension to the Scheduled Areas) Act 1996. Later on, Govt. of Odisha has also announced and formed the Odisha Panchayati Raj (Amendment) Act of 1997 and extended the Central Act 40 to the Scheduled Areas of the State. Government of Odisha (2000) have considered these special provisions and involved the local communities as partners in the management of degraded forests and the members of the Vana Samrakshyan Samiti (VSS) have been entitled to share the use of forests. Considering this, GoO have handed over 75 NTFP items during 2000 to Gram Panchayats as regards their procurement and marketing at local level (Govt. of Odisha, 2000).

Extent of Forest Degradation and Effective Forest Cover

Data with respect to the availability of closed forest area as per cent of total forest area (which is the reciprocal of the extent of degradation of forests), and closed forest area as per cent of total geographical area (a measure of effective forest cover), for the northern and southern regions, shows that the extent of degradation of forests is relatively less in the northern region since close forest in northern region tune to the extent of 64.35 per cent against 48.09 per cent in southern region (PCCF, 2005). Effective forest cover i.e close forest area as per cent of total geographical area is also relatively higher to the extent of 21.59 per cent in the northern region against 17.50 per cent in southern region (Ibid). In addition, there is a much greater concentration of closed forest area in the northern region to the extent of 42.9 per cent, as compared to the southern region having 31.40 per cent.

(b) Land Resources:

The land utilisation pattern in Odisha has undergone sea change. The data reflect that since 1980-81 the forest coverage has declined. The change of forest area during 1960s and 1970s might be due to the inclusion of barren land, uncultivable land and cultivable waste into the forest fold, whereas, the decline in 1980s and 1990s might be due to conversion of forest land for non-forest use. The land systems of tribal people in Odisha vary from region to region due to historical and topographical factors. A good number of tenancy regulations have been formulated in Odisha at different time periods. Concerned about the extent of land alienation and the plight of the landless tribals, Government of Odisha has passed two regulations to restrict alienation of tribal land and to restore back the alienated tribal land. They are the Odisha Scheduled Areas Transfer of Immovable Property (By Scheduled Tribes) Regulation 2 of 1956 and the Odisha Land Reform Act, 1960. The Regulation 2 of 1956 is applicable to the Scheduled Areas as specified by the Government of Odisha with immediate effect to exercise powers conferred by sub-Paragraph-2 of Paragraph–5 of Fifth Schedule of the Constitution of India. Similarly Odisha Land Reform Act, 1960 i.e. Odisha Act of 1960 (Act 2) protects the interest of the S.Ts in respect of unauthorized occupation of the whole or part of a holding of ST persons within any part of the State other than Scheduled areas. It also deals with the distribution of wasteland for agriculture and for homestead, and distribution of ceiling surplus land to ST households.

Extent of High Land

The data reflect that the southern region has relatively higher proportion of high land (64.2%) of the total cultivated area, and lower proportion of low land to the extent of 13.9 per cent, when compared with the northern region situation which has 50.00 per cent high land and 20.4 per cent low land in the total cultivated area (Government of Odisha, 19970. This indicates a lower agricultural productivity in general in the south because of lower moisture retention capacity of high land soil. Both in the short and long run, one finds a higher rate of soil erosion in the southern region due to greater extent of degradation of forest. This also reflects the quality of land, cropping pattern, yield rate, adoption of technology, and overall contribution of agriculture to their livelihood basket and household economy.

Decline in Tribal Land Holding:

The Agriculture Census Report of the State for the year 1980-81, 1985-86 and 1990-91 reported a fall in the size of holdings of the Scheduled Tribes. More specifically, the average size of holdings of marginal and small farmers among the STs have increased overtime, while medium and large holdings have declined both in absolute numbers and the area covered. For example, for the period 1980-81 to 1985-86 the number of ST households working on land increased from 9.18 lakh to 9.65 lakh. However, the total operational area of these households has declined from 15.79 lakh hectares to 15.47 lakh hectares. This clearly indicates a decline in ST holdings by 32,000 hectares. Another study was conducted by the Board of Revenue (1990-91), Government of Odisha, which substantiates the fact that the number of small and marginal farmers registered an increase because of the distribution of ceiling surplus and agricultural land by the State. Change in the tribal land holding is also observed due to the impact of Government policies on the distribution of wasteland to the tribals and restrictions imposed on the alienation of tribal lands. The land holding pattern among the tribals of the state reflects that around 24.26 per cent were belonging to small holding groups, 30.30 per cent belong to semi-medium category, 30.10 per cent belonging to medium holding and only 26.66 per cent belonging to large holding groups (Govt of Odisha,1999-2000). The Odisha Land Reform Act 1960 (OLR Act) emphasizes on the distribution of wasteland for homestead and agricultural purposes. The data during 1980-81 to 1998-99 indicate that distribution of wasteland among the tribals, is less when compared with the SC households. The implementing authorities have deviated from the basic principle of the policy that such land is to be distributed according to their population strength. Secondly, the difference in the number of households benefited from their distribution in different years perhaps indicate the absence of any time-bound programme adopted by the Government for distribution of land.

Alienation of Tribal Land:

The impact of Odisha Scheduled Areas Transfer of immovable Property (By Scheduled Tribes) Regulation 2 of 1956 in the Scheduled Areas of the State when analyzed since its inception and till 1999-2000, the data reveal that 86,999 cases of land alienation were instituted of which 84,721 cases have been disposed of and these have benefited 46,439 tribal households through restoration and distribution of 42,497.16 acres of land (Annual Administration Report, Govt. of Odisha, 1999-2000). Another process of land alienation from tribal communities is observed through legal transfer either made to private parties or to Government in the name of development projects. An analysis of the data during the period 1996-97 reflect that 9,743 tribal households in different districts of Odisha have been legally permitted to transfer 8,550 acres of land reported mainly in the districts of Koraput, Rayagada, Nawarangpur, Sundergarh and Mayurbhanj (District Collectorates, 1997). Alienation of tribal land for individual appropriation, resettlement of colonies and establishment of mega-development projects have been made either through forceful eviction or through legal permission from competent authorities, is reported more in case of undivided Koraput district (Pathy, 1987; Behura and Panigrahi 2001). Looking at the seriousness of the problem of land alienation among the Scheduled Tribes living outside the scheduled areas and understanding the importance of distribution of surplus land to the land less S.Cs and S.Ts, to preserve their land based interest, the Odisha Land Reforms Act of 1960 popularly known as OLR Act of 1960 was introduced in Odisha on 1.10.1965. This new law while protecting the interest of the S.Cs and S.Ts speaks that any illegal transfer of land from these Scheduled groups residing outside the Scheduled Areas can be cancelled. The 12 years rule regarding the adverse possession of the Limitation Act of 1963 was modified to 30 years for S.Cs and S.Ts. The payment of *salami* was also waived out since 1985 and the settlement of Ceiling Surplus Land in favour of S.Cs. to be done according to their population strength which cannot be transferred within 10 years of its settlement.

Since 1991 Odisha, which is historically affected by severe poverty has enthusiastically endorsed the neoliberal ideology in development approach. Since then the state has adopted mining and industry as one of the major approaches to State development. In 80s the growth of the mining sector in Odisha was 8.3 per cent, while during 90s it became 12.7 per cent and 13.7 per cent in the first five years of the 21st Century. The push in mining activities in Odisha is clearly evidenced in the analysis of forest resources. The forest area diverted for non-forest use, in fact, showed an average annual increase of 43% between 1993-94 and 2003-04, with mining accounting for one third of this diversion. The details of diversion of forest area for non-forest use and number of projects in Odisha from 2000-01 to 2009-10 is given in Table-1. Except 2002-03 and 2008-09 in all other years quite a sizeable forest area is diverted for non-forest use. A sectoral distribution of forest area shows that irrigation and mining projects have taken the largest share (PCCF, Aranya Bhawan, Odisha, 2009-10). The whole picture seems to suggest that the role of Odisha as a provider of raw materials in the all-Indian scenario is strengthened with liberalisation. The revenue collected from various forest produces in Odisha shows that kenduleaf, timber, bamboo and sal seeds are the major products. For example the total sale value of kenduleaf in Odisha was Rs 413.77 crores in 2011, Rs 364.26 crores in 2010, Rs 326.64 crores in 2009, Rs 301.96 crores in 2008, Rs 259.32 crores in 2007, Rs 248.55 crores in 2006. Similarly, the revenue generated from the sale of timber in Odisha has generated Rs 29.62 crores in 2008-09, and Rs 40.68 crores in 2009-10 (Table-2) (PCCF, Aranya Bhawan, Odisha, 2009-10).

Table No-1 Diversion of Forest area for Non-Forest use in Odisha in different years

Year	*No of Projects*	*Forest area diverted for Non-Forest use (In Hect)*
2000-01	27	1219.06
2001-02	10	1711.74
2002-03	15	508.18
2003-04	23	1493.71
2004-05	9	1274.39
2005-06	28	2207.23
2006-07	17	911.83
2007-08	20	1802.56
2008-09	14	723.74
2009-10	13	1008.68

Source: PCCF, Aranya Bhawan, Odisha, Bhubaneswar.

Table No-2 Production and Revenue collection from Forest Products by OFDC (Revenue in Crore)

Items	*2008-09*			*2009-10*		
	Production	*Sold Quantity*	*Revenue collected*	*Production*	*Sold Quantity*	*Revenue collected*
Timber and Timber products (In Cum)	29101	24160	29.62	21396	26001	40.68
Fire Wood (MT)	20352	23118	3.60	23163	23065	4.45
Bamboo (SV)	77510	77510	5.81	61915	61878	5.62
Kenduleaf (Qtl)	428868	427979	304.76	NA	NA	326.49

Source: PCCF, Aranya Bhawan, Odisha, Bhubaneswar.

Over the time the extent of land settled in favour of the tribals is less than that of the non-tribals. More particularly, in case of the vulnerable tribal communities of the State, who are basically residing on the hill slopes beyond 9-degree slope, the State has failed to measure their lands through Cheaper Plane Table Method of Cadastral Survey. Government has felt that non-conferment of *rayati* rights to persons cultivating land in the hill slopes within 30 degrees is one among other reasons for the unrest of the tribal communities. Only recently the Government of Odisha after careful consideration, decided to carry out special surveys of unsurveyed hill slopes in scheduled areas (except Kashipur Tahasil of Koraput district and Kalahandi district) and to confer *rayati* rights to the tribals (GoO, 2000). Land rights has become an issue whenever the State has attempted to establish a mega-project in the resourceful tribal regions ignoring the corporate rights of these vulnerable communities over their community land and forest based resources enjoyed by them for generations together.

Magnitude of Poverty and its impact:

The Head Count Ratio (HCR) of Odisha during different time periods shows that it was 63.16 per cent during the year 1993-94 which reduced to 60.83 per cent during 2004-05, but substantially reduced to 39.19 per cent during 2009-10. While poverty in rural Odisha by social group's analysed one finds the HCR during 1993-94 was 82.14 per cent. Creation of employment was 84.52 per cent during 2004-05 and 66.03 per cent during 2009-10 (Panda, 2012). With the help of poverty measurement tools like HCR, Poverty Gap Ratio and Sen Index the poverty analysis shows that the poverty in Odisha has declined consistently for all social groups except scheduled castes. For the SCs poverty increased significantly between 1993-04 and 2004-05 and then declines (Ibid). Decline of poverty in Odisha is much higher when compared with Indian scenario from the period 2003-04 to 2009-10 (Table-3).

Table No-3 Poverty comparison: Odisha and All India (HCR)

Region		*Regions* *1993-94*	*2004-05*	*2009-10*
Rural	Odisha	63.16	60.81	39.91
	India	65.79	41.83	33.81
Urban	Odisha	34.76	37.58	25.91
	India	39.09	25.74	20.88

Source: Economic Growth Inequality and Poverty in Odisha, 1993-2010. S.C.Panda, Delhi School Of Economics, New Delhi.

Educational Achievements

Educational achievement is one of the indicators which influence the living conditions of the people. Therefore, an attempt is made to assess the changes in the literacy level of the tribal people in particular and Odisha in general. The data indicate that the literacy rate in Odisha during 1991 was 49.09 per cent which becomes 63.61 per cent in 2001 and 73.45 per cent in 2011. The detail achievement in literacy during post-globalisation period in different census years between male and female literacy is more in Odisha (28.41%) when compared with the all India scenario (24.84%) in 1991 and 24.98 per cent in Odisha while it is 21.69 per cent in India during 2011. The literacy rates in different districts of Odisha show that none of the tribal dominated districts literary range from 74.42 to 87.51 per cent. Sundargarh, Mayurbhanj, Keonjhar and Kandhamal are covered under medium range educational achievement, having literacy rate between 61.31 to 74.41 per cent. The low literacy rank districts with 48.2 to 61.30 per cent literacy rate include districts like Malkangiri, Koraput, Rayagada, Nawarangapur, Gajapati and Kalahandi (Table-4) (Census Report, 2011).

With respect to the rural-urban gender gap in literacy rate of Odisha during 2001 the data indicate that the rural male literacy was 73.57 per cent and the female literacy was 47.22 per cent. In urban region the male literacy was reported to the tune of 73.57 percent while that of female literacy was reported to the tune of 72.68 per cent. In Nawarangapur district the female literacy is least (21.02%) and in Malkangiri district the male literacy is lowest (41.21%). Literacy status in all tribal dominated districts is below the state aver rage. The data with respect to the distribution of the literacy rate during 2001 and 2011 census years in tribal dominated districts shows that during 2001 in all the districts the literacy rate is almost 50 per cent less, while in case of rural areas of Nawarangapur, Koraput and Malkangiri districts the literacy rate during 2001 was little less then the state average. During 2011 census survey the status of literacy in these three districts has slightly improved both in rural, urban and for total persons.

Table No-4 Distribution of Literacy rate a comparison of 2001 and 2011 Census year

State /District	*Literacy Rate 2001*			*Literacy Rate 2011*		
	Total	*Rural*	*Urban*	*Total*	*Rural*	*Urban*
Kalahandi	45.94	43.54	74.39	60.22	58.30	82.28
Rayagada	36.15	43.54	72.23	50.88	45.45	79.20
Nabarangpur	33.93	31.34	73.71	48.20	45.65	75.68
Koraput	35.72	27.30	74.90	49.87	43.27	81.54
Malkangiri	30.53	27.86	65.30	49.49	47.19	74.70
Odisha Total	**63.08**	**59.84**	**80.84**	**73.45**	**70.78**	**86.45**

Source: Census Reports, 2001 and 2011 (Provisional).

Coming to the literacy status of the female in the tribal dominated districts of Kalahandi, Bolangir and Koraput region (Popularly known as KBK) districts, the data for the Census year 2001 reflect that for the rural areas the literacy status of the female in the districts of Nawarangapur, Koraput, Kalahandi, Rayagada, and Malkangiri are much less then the state average, while for total female the literacy rate in these districts are also almost 50 per cent less except Kalahandi. However, during the Census year 2011 there is a sizeable improvement in each district in the literacy status of the women both for rural areas and for the total female (Census Report, 2001 and 2011 (Provisional). In newly formed Koraput, Rayagada and Nabarangpur districts the rise in the literacy level in 2011 ranges from 14 to 15%, but in Malkangiri it is 19 per cent against 10.73 per cent for state average. For rural region the increase in the literacy position ranges from 14 to 19 per cent against 10.94 per cent for the whole state. So literacy development in these districts is much better than overall state position. In case of the literacy position of the tribal women in Koraput, Rayagada, Nabarangpur and Malkangiri districts, one finds an increase of 15 to 18 per cent against the State average of 13.55 per cent in 2011 Census, while for the rural area female literacy in 2011 ranges from 16 to 19 per cent compared to the state average which increased in women literacy by 14.44 per cent. Along with other factors literacy of women in inland districts have contributed to reduce the IMR from 124 during 1991 to 61 during 2010, also reduced the MMR from 346 during 1997-98 to 258 during 2007-09, CDR from 12.8 during 1991 to 8.6 during 2010. The Life Expectancy at Birth has increased from 56.5 years during 1991-95 to 59.6 years during 2011.

Employment Creation:

At this point it is relevant to draw attention to the intrinsic limits of the modernizing vision of the Odishan state. It is worth mentioning that in 2005 the number of people employed in sponge iron production was fewer than 50,000 (Satapathy 2005). Therefore, process of mining privatisation appears to be unable to generate significant employment opportunities. This data is even more meaningful when read against the context of the pervasive poverty which continues to affect Odisha where, in the overall scenario, the rate of poverty reduction has slowed significantly with liberalisation. Let us recall here that during the period 1983 to 1987-1988 the estimated population living below the poverty line had dropped by nearly 10.0 per cent (from 65.3% to 55.6%). However, during the period from 1993-94 to 2004-05 the estimated population living below the poverty line remained nearly unvaried (from 48.6% to 46.6%) (Panda 2008). A look into the generation of employment in Odisha due to mining activities from the period 2004-05 to 2009-10 shows that except 2005-06 in none of the year the rate of increase of employment has crossed 50,000 (Table-5).

Table No-5 Number of Workers directly employed in Major Mineral activities :

Sl. No.	Minerals Ores / Districts	Employment / Years 2004-05	2005-06	2006-07	2007-08	2008-09	2009-10
1.	Bauxite - (Koraput, Sundergarh)	775	839	866	678	634	664
2.	Chromite - (Dhenkanal, Jajpur, Keonjhar)	6607	8236	8452	9816	6528	7826
3.	Coal - (Angul, Jharsuguda, Sundergarh, Sambalpur)	17624	14500	13985	17747	13467	13875
4.	Dolomite & Lime Stone (Bargarh, Bolangir, Koraput, Sundergarh)	1626	2378	1822	1843	2206	2312
5.	Iron Ore - (Jajpur, Keonjhar, Mayurbhanj, Sundergarh)	19592	20782	16677	18912	16838	14679
6.	Manganese ore – (Keonjhar, Sundergarh, Rayagada, Bolangir)	1513	1505	2612	2655	2294	2538
7.	Others (China day, Quartze, Graphite, Minerals and, Gems Stone, etc)	2100	7524	2962	2525	2200	1811
	Grand Total	**49837**	**55764**	**47376**	**49176**	**44167**	**43705**

Source: Directorate of Mines, Odisha

With respect to the employment created in Odisha in SSI/MSME Sector (Micro, Small and Medium Enterprises) the data from 2000-01 to 2009-10 shows that a total of 2,06,935 number of employment has been created during a period of 10 years with an average of 20693 per annum (Directorate of Industries, Odisha). Employment created in SSI/MSME sector during 2009-10 when analysed their distribution as per ethnic categories one finds out of 23195 employment, STs have been benefitted by 2950 (12.71%), SCs have been benefitted by 3142 (13.54%), and other caste groups benefitted with 73.73 per cent. In terms of percentage distribution of employment in MSME as per different social categories during the year 2010 the data reflect that STs with a population share of 22.21 per cent share 15,39 per cent of employment while SCs who share 16.53 per cent of population share 13.46 per cent in the employment. In total both STs and SCs who share 38.66 per cent of population in Odisha share 28.85 per cent of employment under the MSME of the state (Ibid).

Tribal Welfare Programmes:

Considering the dispersed nature of tribal population, the concept of Tribal Sub-Plan approach was introduced in Odisha in 1979 where Integrated Tribal Development Projects (ITDP) was launched. Presently Odisha has 118 Tribal

Development Blocks distributed over 21 ITDPs and/or Integrated Tribal Development Agencies for both planning and execution of tribal development programmes. In addition to, Odisha has 17 Micro Projects for 13 Particularly Vulnerable Tribal Groups to bring them into the mainstream, which covers 61,240 households in 537 villages distributed over 20 C.D. Blocks in 12 districts. Looking at the backwardness of these tribal communities the planners realised that these communities under Tribal Sub-Plan approach require special care and holistic attention for their development. The gamut of development activities under these projects covers various sectors like agriculture, horticulture, soil conservation, health, education, animal husbandry, communication, provision of drinking water etc. These Micro Projects have been formulated for these communities with 100 percent subsidised fund flow under Special Central Assistance (SCA).

Further, Government of India with the assistance of IFAD set up a special tribal project on 14th May 1988 for a period of 14 years in two phases with a budget approval of Rs 31.70 crores. The project aimed at all round development of tribal people of Kashipur block of Koraput district with 447 villages covering a population of 51,385. This by and large could achieve limited objectives but generated good experiences in this regard. Government of Odisha with assistance from IFAD-DFID-WFP is implementing a special development project in 32 Blocks of southern districts called as 'Odisha Tribal Empowerment and Livelihood Programme' (OTELP). Different evaluation studies reflects the changes in the qualitative living of the tribal people shows the positive impact of this special project (ST SC Development Department, Government of Odisha, 2012).

In spite of, XI Five Year Plan rightly pointed out that tribal people have not been properly included in the development processes. Therefore, the concept of inclusive development is adopted which is committed for their inclusion in the development in following manner.

- To provide access to resources and to raise the income level of the asset less tribal people
- To ensure support for the survival, protection, and development of the PVTGs.
- To secure forest rights and development of forest dwellers
- To bridge the critical gaps in economic and social infrastructure of tribal people
- To provide basic health services and to reduce IMR/MMR and control of malaria
- To increase the literacy status particularly primary education.
- To ensure the implementation of protective regulations like – OSATIP, OLR, PESA, FRA, Prohibition of Money Lending, Abolition of Child Labour, Atrocity Act, PCR Act.

Fund flow for Tribal Development Programmes

With respect to the fund flow for tribal development in Odisha here attempt is made to highlight the investment so far made for the tribal development programmes during 10th and 11th Five Year Plan period in Odisha. The financial support for tribal development in the State generally comes from three different sources viz: State Plan, Special Central Assistance (S.C.A.) and Central and Centrally Sponsored Schemes (C.C.S.P.). In the 8th Five Year Plan TSP funds were used more purposively to improve the socio-economic conditions of tribal people. ITDA level plan preparation and suitable administrative structure were prioritized. The 10th Five Year Plan adopted a multi-pronged approach for the development of tribal people through educational development and economic empowerment through income and employment. The 11th Five Year Plan also focused the slogan of 'Inclusive Growth of the STs'. A scrutiny of the budgetary resources for the STs during 10th and 11th Five Year Plan period raises serious concerns. Gaps are observed in the budget allocation between the promises as per the guidelines and realities as in the implementation. Since 2002-03 the budget allocation at Central Government level reflects a high performance by allocating more than 8 per cent of the total budget under TSP. In Odisha similar trends are observed only in 11th Five Year Plan period with respect to the budget allocation in proportion with the population strength of the tribal people (Iable-6 and 7). During 11th Five Year Plan State Plan for TSP has increased by 8.70 per cent when compared with 10th Plan period. The Central Plan during this period has reduced, while allotment under Central Sponsored Plan was almost double in 11th Plan period. Except Central Plan allocation for TSP has increased in Odisha.

Table No-6 Fund Flow to Tribal Sub Plan (TSP) Area in Odisha in different years. (Rs in Cr.)

Year	*State Plan*	*TSP out of State Plan*	*Central Plan (CP)*	*TSP out of CP*	*CSP*	*TSP out of CSP*	*Total Plan Size (SP+ CP+CSP)*	*SCA to TSP*
2002-03	2438.67	315.96	205.50	56.92	145.51	23.03	3185.59	16.54
2003-04	2393.95	309.20	290.39	66.80	135.53	21.60	3217.47	35.00
2004-05	2614.96	391.53	250.95	66.50	144.63	21.97	3490.21	89.73
2005-06	2535.00	385.75	272.54	68.21	295.06	50.59	3102.59	150.24
2006-07	3543.24	482.52	312.11	88.49	396.03	76.39	4251.39	145.47
2007-08	5828.38	1249.28	383.66	107.82	850.04	177.70	7062.09	132.75
2008-09	7375.85	1653.40	447.39	133.96	1118.89	264.29	8942.13	143.35
2009-10	7214.13	1569.83	373.21	85.41	1324.62	331.64	8911.96	159.80
2010-11	10010.48	2131.56	649.12	94.68	1116.20	267.50	11775.81	409.40
2011-12RE	12004.81	2585.71	855.73	125.73	1967.97	455.91	14828.51	244.88

Source: Demand for Grants, Different Years, Government of Odisha.

Table No 7 Fund Flow to Tribal Sub Plan in Odisha from various sources during 10th and 11th Five Year Plan

(Rs in Cr.)

Plan Period	*Fund Flow to TSP out of*				*G.Total*
	State Plan (SP)	*Central Plan (CS)*	*Central Sponsored Plan (CSP)*	*Special Central Assistance (SCA)*	
10th Five Year Plan (2002-03 to 2006-07)	1884.96 (65.86)	346.92 (12.12)	193.58 (6.77)	436.98 (15.27)	2862.44 (100)
11th Five Year Plan (2007-08 to 2011-12)	9189.87 (74.56)	547.60 (4.44)	1497.04 (12.14)	1090.18 (6.64)	12324.69 (100)

Source: Demand for Grants, Different Years, Government of Odisha.
(Figures in the bracket are per cent to total)

With respect to the flow of funds to TSP in different sectors the data indicate that in 9th Five Year Plan period out of 38 Department's Irrigation and Flood Control, Energy, and General Services have allotted less than the required per cent of fund for the TSP as per its norm. In 10th Five Year Plan period similarly the department of Rural Development, Irrigation and Flood Control, and General Economic Services has allotted fewer funds then the population size of the STs or the TSP norm in Odisha. In 11th Plan period as many as six departments like Agriculture and Allied Activities, Energy, Industry and Minerals, Science, Technology and Environment. General Economic Services and General Services have allotted fewer funds then the population size of the STs or the TSP norm in Odisha (Table-8). The table shows that the State Plan to TSP in 11th Plan period has increased almost six fold when compared with 10th Plan period. In 10th Plan period the allocation for TSP out of State Plan was not as per the population criteria of the TSP guideline for fund allocation.

Table No-8 Fund Flow to TSP Area in Odisha in different plan periods (Rs in Cr.)

Year	*Total State Plan*	*State Plan to TSP*	*Per cent of Flow*
9th Five Year Plan			
1997-98	2684.0	576.6	21.5
1998-99	2071.2	643.9	31.1
1999-2000	2488.9	627.9	25.2
2000-01	2906.7	818.0	28.1
2001-02	2906.7	818.0	28.1

Cond...

10th Five Year Plan			
2002-03	2438.67	315.96	12.95
2003-04	2393.95	309.20	12.90
2004-05	2614.96	391.53	14.99
2005-06	2535.00	385.75	15.22
2006-07	3543.24	482.52	13.64
11th Five Year Plan			
2007-08	5828.38	1249.28	21.43
2008-09	7375.85	1653.40	22.41
2009-10	7214.13	1569.83	21.76
2010-11	10010.48	2131.56	21.29
2011-12RE	12004.81	2585.71	21.54
2012-13BE	15204.14	3386.09	22.27

Source: Demand for Grants, Different Years, Government of Odisha.

Growth in Odisha:

Growth story of Odisha can be measured through certain indicators like incidence of poverty by social groups, State Domestic Product, growth rate, sectoral contribution of the Net State Domestic Product, and Sectoral Contribtuion to GSDP etc. A look into the sectoral contribution of the Net State Domestic Product (NSDP) both in pre-and post-reform era in Odisha shows that agriculture and allied sector was contributing 51.72 per cent during 1980 to 1992, which reduced to 34.53 per cent during 1992 to 2005 and to 19.35 per cent in 2009-10. Industry which was contributing 17.03 per cent raised to 20.41 per cent per cent during 1992 to 2005 and increased to 26.25 per cent in 2009-10. Similarly, the service sector was contributing 31.25 per cent which increased to 45.05 per cent in 1992 to 2005 and to 54.40 per cent during 2009-10 (Odisha Economic Survey, 2009-10) Table No-9).

The data with respect to the poverty reduction shows that it is more among the SCs than the STs. The reduction of poverty among the STs is almost half of the state average. A regional look into the poverty status as per NSS round also shows a decline in the reduction of poverty among different social groups both in south and north Odisha. Among STs Poverty reduction is 13.9 per cent in south Odisha, while it is 15.14 per cent in north Odisha and even above the state average (10.31%) of poverty reduction for the tribal people. A regional look into the poverty reduction through the measurement with the help of HCR in Odisha shows a decline of 23.97 per cent in rural area, while it is 31.98 per cent in the country during 1993-94 to 09-10. In urban area the poverty reduced by 8,85 per cent in Odisha while it is 18.21 per cent in urban India during the period. Decline in poverty in Odisha between 2004-05 and 2009-10 is above the all India figures (Table-9 and 10).

Table No-9 Incidence of Poverty in Rural Odisha by Social Groups

Social Groups	*1993-94*	*2004-05*	*Poverty reduction during 1993-94 to 2004-05*
ST	71.33	64.3	7.01
SC	49.79	38.6	11.19
OBC	–	24.5	
Others	40.23	15.6	24.63
Total	**49.81**	**35.53**	**14.28**

Source: Odisha Economic Survey, 2009-10

Table No-10 Social Group-wise and Region-wise Poverty (Head Count Ratio) Estimates based on Pooled Data, NSS Round Rural Odisha

Method	*Social Groups*	*Coastal*	*Southern*	*Northern*	*All Total*
61st Round (2004-05)	ST	50.63	76.42	59.39	64.32
	SC	26.99	59.52	42.85	38.55
	OBC	13.52	45.26	33.58	24.48
	Others	11.71	41.38	22.52	15.57
	Total	18.38	62.5	43.69	35.54
66th Round (2009-10)	ST	47.15	62.52	44.25	54.01
	SC	22.69	49.8	28.28	34.46
	OBC	10.48	30.77	15.56	18.79
	Others	14.63	17.61	12.67	14.93
	Total	16.57	47.03	25.07	29.65

Source: Odisha Economic Survey, 2011-12

A look into the State Domestic Product (SDP) in Odisha since 1994-95 to 2009-10 shows that there was a high growth during the year 1994-95 (14.4%). 2003-04 (14.06%), 2004-05 (13.1%) and 2006-07 (12.6%). However, the growth rate during last couple of years is above the national average. A look in the sectoral contribution to the GSDP in Odishain different decadal period show that during 1950-51 the primary sector was contributing 67.31 per cent which reduced to 42.04 per cent during 1990-91and 25.50 per cent during the year 2009-10. The contribution of the secondary sector was 6.94 per cent during the year 1950-51 which increased to 15.59 per cent during the year 1990-91 and to 23.52 per cent during the year 2009-10. When one looks at the contribution of the tertiary sector to the GSDP it was 36.12 per cent in the year 1990-91 which increased to 51.28 per cent during 2009-10 (Ibid).

Reduction in the extent of poverty among different social groups during different time period in Odisha shows that during 1993-94 the magnitude of poverty among STs was 71.31 per cent which continued almost also during the year 1999-2000 and reduced to 64.3 per cent in the year 2004-05 with a poverty reduction of 7.01 per cent in 11 years. Among the SCs the reduction of the poverty during the above period was 11.19 per cent. In total poverty reduction in the state during the period was by 14.28 per cent (Odisha Economic Survey, 2009-10). The measurement of poverty with the help of HCR among the STs of rural Odisha shows a reduction of 16.11 per cent during the period 1993-94 to 2009-2010. Likewise the poverty gap has reduced by 6.52 per cent during the period. Among the SCs poverty reduced by 15.71 per cent and the poverty gap became 6.67 per cent during the period. This shows a positive impact of the development processes during the reform. The growth rate in Odisha (9%) approx after 2003-04 has been well above the national average and is found to be statistically significant. Agriculture, Manufacturing and Hotels/Restaurants contribute significantly to this growth in the state. Manufacturing has been major contributor to Odisha particularly after 2003-04. The above data justifies that inequality in rural Odisha shows a decline whereas in urban Odisha it has risen. There has been significant reduction of poverty between 2004-05 and 2009-10, which has been roughly the period of high growth in Odisha (Panda, 2012). This justifies that higher growth along with government intervention in social welfare schemes is the solution to reduce poverty in Odisha.

Conclusion:

The growth rate in Odisha (9%) approx after 2003-04 has been well above the national average and is found to be statistically significant. Agriculture, Manufacturing and Hotels/Restaurants contribute significantly to this growth. The upward movement starts around 2003-04, indicating that benefits of liberalisation was exploited by the state relatively late, particularly in manufacturing. Inequality in rural Odisha shows a decline whereas in urban Odisha it has risen. There has been significant reduction of poverty between 2004-05 and 2009-10, which has been roughly the period of high growth. The data shows that there is a high income difference between rich and poor districts (3.5 times). Rich districts are growing faster. The poverty reduction is slow among SCs and STs till 2004-05 but reduced very fast afterwards. Poverty among the ST & general groups in coastal region has gone up.

In the context of the Tribal Sub-Plan approach for integrated tribal development is indeed laudable. It is operative since the Fifth Five-Year Plan period. ITDAs are good nodal implementing agencies, but their delivery system needs a lot of strengthening in many respects. The administrative control over various line departments by the ITDAs need to be increased.

At the State level, in the context of tribal welfare, the role of ST SC Development Department need to be strengthened in the similar manner to ensure the required earmarking of the funds for tribal welfare programmes in due proportion of tribal population. It is understood that investment in tribal welfare is less as it is not in accordance with the ratio of tribal population of the State. This is one of the reasons for the persistence of the gap at the levels of development of tribal people in tribal areas and outside. This is perceptible in the fields of literacy and education. The per capita income of STs has been low as compared to the per capita income of general population. Similarly, the net irrigated area to the total cropped area is less in the TSP area, whereas it is more in non-TSP or plains areas.

The simplistic idea of trickle down approach cannot be over relied any more believing that growth and equity will operate simultaneously. Growth is a necessary but not sufficient condition to create conditions for delivery of higher quality services by the state. The process of change in the institutional environment in TSP areas have started in south Odisha where the OTELP with the assistance of IFAD is functioning is needed so as to make tribal people more obligatory and also ensures their access into welfare services provided by the state. The political capital and administrative capabilities are also the prerequisite conditions 'to begin development at home and it must come from within'. In other words globalisation should be considered as a part of the development strategy, but not the ultimate means to achieve the goal of welfare state in India and thus in Odisha a federal state.

Notes

1. Scheduled Area in Odisha: Mayurbhanj, Sundargarh, Koraput, Rayagada, Nabarangpur and Malkangiri districts in whole, Kuchinda Tahasils of Sambalpur district, Keonjhar, Telkoi, Champua. Barbil Tahasils of Keonjhar district, Khondamal, Balliguda and G.Udayagiri Tahasils of Khondamal district, R. Udaygiri tahasils, Gumma and Rayagada Block of Parlekhemundi Tahasils in Parlekhemundi Sub-division and Suruda Tahasils of Ghumsur sub-division in Ganjam district, Thuamul Rampur and Langigarh Block of Kalahandi district and Nilagiri block of Balasore district. The total area of the Scheduled Areas of the State contains almost 70% of the forest areas of Odisha even though they form only 44% of the State area.
2. The concept of Particularly Vulnerable Tribal Groups adopted in 11th Fiver Year Plan period who were earlier known as Primitive Tribal Groups in India. They are identified on the basis of certain criteria like pre-agricultural level of technology, low level of literacy and stagnant or diminishing population. Out of 62 tribal groups Odisha has declared 13 groups as most vulnerable groups. There are 17 Micro Projects working for the socio-economic development of these groups started since the Fifth Five Year Plan period. The funds for these projects are allocated from Special Central Assistance (SCA) of Government of India.
3. Shifting cultivation in Odisha is known differently in different names among various tribal communities. The practice is known as *dangar, bagad, toila, rami, dabi, biringa cultivation.* This cultivation is largely practiced by 11 tribal communities living in the districts of Kandhamal, Keonjhar, Sundargarh, Rayagada, Gajapati, Koraput and Kalahandi. The tribal communities practicing

shifting cultivation are *Bonda, Didayi, Koya, Gadaba, Paraja, Kutia Kondh, Dangaria Kondh, Lanjia Saora, Malua Kondh, Pengo Kondh, Desia Kondh of* Kandhamal and Kalahandi , the Juanga, and *Pauri Bhuiyan* of Keonjhar district. This cultivation is essentially a mixed cropping where 10 to 20 varieties of cereals, millets like *ragi* (*elucive corocema*), *kodo* (*Paspalam scrobiculatum*), *swnua* (*Echinochloa frummeta cea*), bajara (*pennisetum typhoidessno*), jawar (*Sorghum vulgara*), maize (*Zea mays*), pulses, oilseeds, vegetables and perennial crops are cultivated.

References

Appadurai, A. (1996). Modernity at Large. Cultural Dimensions of Globalisation, Delhi: Oxford University Press.

Behura, N. Panigrahi, N. (2001). Functioning of the Fifth Schedule in the Constitution of the State of Odisha. Report submitted to ICSSR New Delhi by NCDS Bhubaneswar.

Census of India (1991). Primary Census Abstract, Scheduled Tribe Population, Series-1, Part II-B (iii).

———(2001). *Final Population Tables*, Series 22, Paper 2, Directorate of Census Operations, Odisha.

——— (2001). *Primary Census Abstract: Scheduled Tribe Population,* Series 1, Part II B(iii).

———(2011). Houses, Household Amenities and Assets (All Indicators), Directorate of Census Operation, Odisha.

Giddens, A. (1990). The Consequences of Modernity, London: Policy Press, P.175.

Government of India. (2002) Orissa Development Report. Planning Commission. New Delhi.

———Planning Commission. (2006). National Mineral Policy: Report of the High Level Committee. New Delhi: Government of India.

Government of Odisha (1961). Shifting Cultivation in Odisha, Agricultural Department of Social Conservation Organisation, Odisha. Govt. Press.

———(1980-81 to 1985-86). Report on Agricultural Census of Odisha, Agricultural Census Commissioner, Govt. of Odisha.

———(1980-81 to 1995-96). Report of the Annual Administration of Scheduled Areas of Odisha (Concerned years), Welfare Department, Govt. of Odisha.

———1997. *Odisha Agricultural Statistics: 1995-96*, Directorate of Agriculture and Food Production, Bhubaneswar.

———2002. *Statistical Abstract of Odisha*, Directorate of Economics and Statistics, Bhubaneswar.

———(2002-03). Annual Report, SC and ST Development Department and Minority and Backward Communities Welfare Department, Government of Odisha, Bhubaneswar.

———2005. Office of the Principal Chief Conservation of Forests, Aranya Bhawan, Bhubaneswar.

———(2005). Economic Survey 2004–05. Directorate of Economics & Statistics and Planning & Coordination Department. Bhubaneswar: Government of Orissa.

———(2007). Economic Survey 2006–07. Directorate of Economics & Statistics and Planning & Coordination Department. Bhubaneswar: Government of Orissa.

———(2008). Economic Survey 2007–08. Directorate of Economics & Statistics and Planning & Coordination Department. Bhubaneswar: Government of Orissa.

———(2007-08). Annual Report, SC and ST Development Department and Minority and Backward Communities Welfare Department, Odisha, Bhubaneswar.

———(2008-09). Annual Report, SC and ST Development Department and Minority and Backward Communities Welfare Department, Odisha, Bhubaneswar.

———(2010). Economic survey 2009-10. Directorate of Economics & Statistics and Planning & Coordination Department. Bhubaneswar: Government of Orissa.

———(2011-12). Outcome Budget 2011-12, ST and SC Development, Minorities and Backward Classes Welfare Department, Odisha, Bhubaneswar.

Organisation for Economic Co-operation and Development. 1989. Interdependence and Co-operation in Tomorrow's World, OECD: Paris.

Pathy, J. (1987). 'Ethnic minorities and processes of their development' (mimeo). Report submitted to UGC, New Delhi.

Roy Burman B K. 1982. Report of Committee on Forest and Tibals in India, TD Division, Ministry of Home Affairs, Govt. of India.

Singh, K. & Kalirajan, K. 2003. A decade of economic reforms in India: The mining sector. Resources Policy, 29, 139–151.

Turner, Bryan (1994). Orientatalism, Potmodernism and Globalism. London: Routledge.

World Bank (2005). 'Odisha Policy Notes 2005: Vulnerability in Odisha: Diagnosis and Approach,' (Mimeo), Prepared for the Planning and Co-ordination Department, Government of Odisha.

3

Globalizing Perspectives of Tribal Life: A Sociological Understanding

Sayan Dutta and Dr. Kaushik Chattopadhyay

Introduction

An anthropologist proposed a game to the children of an African Tribe. He put a basket of fruit near a tree and told the kids that the first one to reach the fruit would win them all. When he told them to run they all took each others' hands and ran together, then sat together enjoying the fruits. When asked why they ran like that, as one could have taken all the fruit for oneself, they said, *UBUNTU* ---- a philosophy of African tribes that can be summed up as 'I am because we are'.

Including other things, this example exposes social processes of two different cultures. One is from *civilised*, and the other is from *lesser civilisations*. Here the concept of '*civilisation*' can be linked to creation of *order* (laws, rules and regulations), *organisation* (political and social), and *efficiency* (least loss of effort due to disorder and disorganisation, time savings from good infrastructure and order, mass production, etc.). On the other,those who have tribal beginnings, and have less experience in organised (established) cities and permanent settlements, they, with tribal roots, can be regarded as '*lower or lesser civilisations*' (Diamond, 1999). This lesser part exposes more solidarity, homogeneity and a sense of belongingness.

First Wave: Globalisation's Innovative Child

Tribes understood their environment: vegetation, insects, mammals, birds. They knew which plants could be used as medicines and which were poisonous. Knowledge was site-specific. In most cases, it was difficult to apply elsewhere; but locally, it allowed many groups to sustain a quality of life that should not be undervalued. It was devalued through the contact in between the so called civilised and the tribal folk in the Middle Ages. Historically, the application of local knowledge, indigenous research with new innovative economy, population growth, migration and new settlement pattern has mobilised through the process of deforestation. Deforestation has started and the tribal roots begin to wither away.

Detribalisation as a result of deforestation was continuous throughout the Bronze Age. Its occurrence during the late Bronze Age was a consequence of the reorganisation of the economy of the Thracian tribes between 1000 B.C. and 800 B.C. in the production of iron and population movements into metal producing zones and pastures of mountain regions (Chew, 2006; Stefanova, 1995: 29). But it was not a generalised phenomenon. In North America, parts of the Caribbean, and some areas of South America, Asia, and Africa, the primitive communal mode of production predominated among indigenous tribes. These societies were classless and stateless; they relied on hunting, fishing, gathering, and some early forms of horticulture for their subsistence. In these deeply religious societies, economic life is regulated by moral and religious norms. Lack of a substantial surplus and relative distance from aggressive empires prevented them from evolving toward a tributary mode through the emergence or imposition of a parasitic state (Berberoglu, 2003). These formations remained intact until the arrival of the European colonizers in the early sixteenth century, which brought about major transformations in tributary and tribal societies throughout the New World.

Second Wave: Globalisation's Industrial Child

What was new in this transformation? In one word, it was a shift from barter to a mercantilist economy or from a reciprocity and redistribution to a market exchange. Moreover, the center of ancient economic life largely covers other forms of organizing the economy. Clan societies, various forms of small groups and of course hierarchical social-economic formations have also been in contact with other tribes or clans to trade. This suggests that economic dependence,between one group and another, is reproduced in history. Though trade was not global, actors were not rational, and though early social formations were by and large able to sustain themselves, trade was an integrated part of life. Later with further division of labour, between different societies, actors also came to see products that they could not produce themselves as "essential," which increased the dependence between groups of people located in different places (Maffesoli, 1988). The history of economic development cannot be separated from the history of trade and the web of commerce helped to create a civilisation as Fernand Braudel has discussed in his three-volume work *Civilisation and Capitalism*. We leap forward to the period in which nations, in a modern sense were developed in relation to each other, and in struggle with each other, to the period in economic history called mercantilism.

In a global scale, this nexus compels to develop an international risk management. The most obvious risks from contact with the tribes of strangers was probably plunder, theft and violence. If the risks of these were assessed as high, one obvious risk management method was to keep one's own tribe armed at the ready. Increasing sophistication in international relationships and trade identified different potential risks, often closely connected with increasing travel. These included the spread of new and dangerous ideas, which break the cultural homogeneity and the spread of disease – the latter by animals and goods as well as people.

In an organisational role structure a tribal society is based on commonalities, collective rituals and shared emotions. Urban Tribes with their sub-cultures form various new social groups. They remain common in their faith, but in practice they form ephemeral interest groups (Watters, 2003). Their new life styles were constituted by shifting forms of identification within these fragmented groups. These various micro-groups were emerging in modern society who shared a common dialect but shallow informal culture. Although these 'tribes' were fleeting, their members shared a common emotional bond that was very different from the cold, bureaucratic ties of formal organisations within which they born, grow up and pass away.

Third Wave: Globalisation's American Child

With the growth of world-wide urbanisation and the rise of global mega-cities, social life is thought to be increasingly fragmented, giving rise to urban settlements, alienated minorities, the inner-city no-go areas and violent youth sub-cultures (Debo, 1940). The idea of the 'lonely crowd' and the 'inner-directed personality' paints a picture of passive and isolated urban dwellers glued to their tribal identity.

If we think globalisation as a process of inter-connectedness in between a world metropolitan life with an indigenous tribal identity, then the problem is not helped by the gradual decrease in farming surpluses, necessary to feed the cities. In some countries, even the farmers are having difficulties feeding themselves. Another important cause of the overconcentration of people in cities is the migration and resettlement of "refugees of war" (such as in Angola, Mozambique, and Somalia). Unfortunately, there are neither jobs nor services for the millions moving to urban areas, and conflicts between the various nations or tribes are becoming more frequent, pushing many African and Asian societies into a chronic crisis situation.

When globalisation is identical with Americanisation then, firstly, from the skeptical position, it is argued that the neo-liberal globalizing age is one of fragmentation, disintegration, malaise, meaninglessness, a vagueness or even absence of moral parameters and societal chaos; and secondly, from the affirmative position, there is a more hopeful, optimistic view of the globalizing age (Outhwaite, 2006). This second type perspectives are either open to positive political action (struggle and resistance) or content with the recognition of visionary, celebratory personal nondogmatic projects that range from 'New Age' religion to 'New Wave' life-styles and include a whole spectrum of post-modern social movements. The perspectives of the first type tend to speak of the death of society or, as we shall see, of the social; those of the second type tend to accentuate the positive: the emergence of new forms of sociality – what we may call the dionysiac or the neo-tribal.

Conclusion: Struggles for Survival and Well-being

We realize world-systems as inter-societal networks in which the interactions (e.g., trade, warfare, intermarriage, and information) are important for the reproduction of the internal structures of the composite units and importantly affect changes that occur in these local structures (Chase-Dunn and Hall, 1997). Because the boundaries of non-state social groups (e.g., "bands" or "tribes") are often empirically fuzzy, and because the term 'society' can too easily imply a clearly bounded social group.

Globalisation of human rights, primarily in terms of cultural diffusion and from the intersections of universalizing conceptions of rights, restructures local cultures. The non-governmental organisations, consisting of human right activists, have humanitarian agendas in various tribal areas of the world. This globalisation process in its organisational and institutional forms helps raising the movement as one of "activists beyond borders" by which human rights culture is spread on a global scale and reshapes age old tribal traditions and customs in its new forms and contents. While, its existence is not a sufficient condition for democracy, it is essential for new democratic life.

From an inclusion-exclusion debate, the changing processes of cultural practices may examine. Assimilation, accommodation, acculturation and such other processes can explore the inclusion pretence of consumerist culture in a global scale on one hand, and ethnic conflict, violent movements, displacement and imperial hegemonic structure of development can expose the exclusion inevitability on the other hand. Cultural globalisation does not go through such perspectives. Here studies have been overwhelmingly concerned with the impact of the internet on global transactions, interactions and interconnectedness. These studies have been less concerned with claims about the end of grand narratives – in part because globalisation is itself a grand narrative. The debate about cyberspace, cyborgs, and postmodern culture was, we might suggest, concerned with two questions – is society changing and do we need new methods and epistemologies to capture those changes? In its bleakest moments, globalisation theory asks not what type of society might exist, but whether society is possible at all in a global village without water and a serious decline in basic commodities (such as oil, rice and soyabean). If there are not enough resources to support existing populations, the outcome will be 'new wars' or low intensity wars about borders and water, or hot wars around access to oil (such as the emerging conflict around oil deposits in the South China Sea). The war on terrorism has diverted attention away from discussions of simulation and representation to a focus on borders, border conflict, refugees, and fundamentalism which intern holds a process toward retribalisation.

The ideas about social fragmentation, liquid modernity, and representation began simultaneously to influence science fiction and social theory around the themes of cyberspace and cyberpunk. The new community of hackers and the technologically literate cybertribes who were socially disaffected and searching for social forms that could express the connectivity made possible by computerisation. The new possibilities might overcome the 'electronic industrial ghettoes' that characterized postmodern society.

References

Berberoglu, B. (2003). *Globalisation of Capital and the Nation-State: Imperialism, Class Struggle, and the State in the Age of Global Capitalism.* New York: Rowman & Littlefield Publishers, Inc.

Chase-Dunn, Christopher, and Thomas D. Hall. (1997). "Ecological Degradation and the Evolution of World-Systems," in *Journal of World-Systems Research,* 3: 403–431.

Debo, A. (1940). *And Still the Waters Run: The Betrayal of the Five Civilised Tribes.* Princeton, NJ: Princeton University Press.

Diamond, J. (1999). *Guns, Germs, and Steel: The Fates of Human Societies.* New York: W.W. Norton.

Maffesoli, M. (1988). *The Times of the Tribes.* Paris: Méridiens.

Mohapatra, S. (1986). *Modernisation and Ritual Identity and change in Santal Society.* New Delhi: Oxford University Press.

Outhwaite, W. (2006). *The Future of Society.* Oxford: Wiley-Blackwell Publishing.

Saren, G. (2013). 'Impact of globalisations on the Santals: A study on migration in West Bengal, India,' in *International Journal of Humanities and Social Science Invention,* 2: 29-33.

Sing Chew, (2006). 'Ecological Crisis Phases, Globalisation, and World-System Evolution,' in Andrew Jorgenson and Edward Kick (eds.), *Globalisation and the Environment.* Boston: Brill.

Stefanova, I. (1995). 'Studies on the Holocene History of Vegetation in the Northern Pirin Mountains,' in T. Bozilova (ed.), *Advances in Holocene Paleoecology in Bulgaria.* Sofia: Tonkov. Pp 9–37.

Watters, E. (2003). *Urban Tribes: A Generation Redefines Friendship, Family and Commitment.* London: Bloomsbury.

4

Effects of Globalisation on the Ethnomedicinal Practices of Lepchas in the Darjeeling Himalaya

Suman Kalyan Samanta

Introduction

Each and every community has an own history and heritage about their status of living, process of daily livelihood maintenance, social-cultural features and traditional practices. In most of the time it is observed that these communities are utilizing their surrounding ecological resources to attain their daily requirements. From the perspective of health and disease most of the local and indigenous people are using their traditional knowledge and using various types of folk medicines. On behalf of that they took various ethnomedicinal substances. Although in time being their traditional knowledge and practices have been changed by maintaining very slow and continuous process that, may be the ultimate result of globalisation and modernisation. According to World Health Organisation there are approximately more than 80% indigenous population in the developing countries are mainly depending on the traditional medicine for primary health care needs. A major portion of these involves the use of medicinal plants (Bennerman et.al., 1983).

There are many examples of medicinal ethno botanical surveys conducted in India in the past that have recorded many ethno-botanical remedies among many aboriginal groups: Malasars(Pandi Kumar, 2007); Malamalasars (Yesodharan, 2007); Malayalis(Viswanathan, 1989); Irulas(Ramachandran, 1991); Gonds(Ramnath, 2002); Kanikar(Ignacimuthu,1998); Todas, Kotas(Abraham, 1981); Kattunayakas (Balakrishnan, 2003); Apatani(Kala, 2005); Chellipale (Udayan, 2005).

In this connection it can be mentioned that due to some external and internal causes presently the people's dependency on these traditional medicinal treatment systems become changed. Globalisation, media and marketisation as well as modernisation have a very strong effect and influence on these traditional ethnomedicinal treatment systems. Darjeeling Himalaya is one of the nurture houses of several types of traditional ethnomedicinal practices. Presently these traditional practices are in serious threats that may be patent of various Indian ethnomedicinal resources by various multinational companies of abroad or lack of interest of the younger generations or any thing others.

Modern medical facilities available in the Darjeeling Himalayas and its adjoining areas

When considering the availability of infrastructural facilities specially in terms of medical facilities it is observed that Darjeeling District has a quite poor standard in comparison to the other districts of West Bengal. There are only 24 Health Centres in the district where as number of Allopathic Dispensaries are 136, number of Public Health Centers are 26 and number of Public Health Sub-centers are 135. As per the need concern the number of various types of medical and paramedical centers and hospitals are very minimum. Along with number of doctors, nurses, other stuffs, beds and necessary medical equipments and instruments are very nominal (Statistical Hand Book West Bengal, 2010). The doctor to people ratio is 1: 4892 that is a negative indicator of good health condition of any area.

Availability of ethnomedicinal resources in the areas of Darjeeling Himalayas

In most of the cases it is observed that various ethnic groups are traditionally much more interested in the said treatment system. In the present study areas there are several ethnic groups those have been living since time immemorial. The major ethnic groups of the region are the Nepalese, Lepchas and Bhutias (Tibetans). The tribes of this Himalayan region also have rich ethnomedicinal traditions for which a few literatures are available (Biswas, 1956; Yonzone et al., 1984; Venu et al., 1990; Rai et al., 1998; Das and Mandal, 2003)

Methodological considerations

Study area

The study has been conducted in the foot hills areas of Darjeeling Himalaya because these areas are of plenty of ecological resources specially of ethnomedicinal elements as well as ethnomedicinal practices. The topic based field survey has been conducted mainly in the Lolegaon and its adjoining areas of Darjeeling district. Due to positional advantage and eco-geographical features the study area has been selected. Although other Lepcha dominated areas also have been visited for the purpose of the study but prime importance has been given on the above mentioned study areas. Not only that the availability of forest based various medicinal plants and herbals is the another cause for the selection of the study area.

Study community

There are so many communities living in the foot hills region of Darjeeling Himalaya. Among these communities there are several ethnic groups those have been residing in the areas since time immemorial. The major ethnic groups of the region are the Nepalese, Lepchas and Bhutias (Chhetri, et. al., 2005). Lepchas in remoteness from modern facilities of the world got adapted to develop skills required to withstand difficult conditions of nature. Lepchas have become carrier of enormous understanding on the use of plants descended upon them through use of traditional medicinal cure to various ailments (Pradhan & Badola, 2008). In the present study first and foremost importance has been given on the traditional ethnomedicinal practice of the Lepcha communities of the above mentioned study areas and role of globalisation and modernisation on that traditional treatment system. From ethnic point of view the Lepchas have their own history of ethnic origin, social cultural practices, customs and traditions. Lepcha is a Mongolian tribe of Sikkim, western Bhutan, eastern Nepal and Darjling. The Lepchas numbered 3952 in 1987 and 202 in 1881 in the district of Darjeeling (Risley, 1891).

Methods used

In the present study the primary focus has been given on the ethno medical practices among the Lepchas of Darjeeling district specially in the foothills of Darjeeling Himalaya. In the present study, door to door information has been collected as well as individual level data were also given same importance. Data mainly have been collected from senior and knowledgeable family members as well as aged persons of the neighboring areas. Several methods have been used with due importance. Mainly the paper is based on in-depth interviews, observation and case study method. Data have been collected both from personal and family level. The traditional herbal specialists, local quack doctors and nearest Govt. and non Govt. medical and paramedical personals have been interviewed with due importance. Not only that medical shopkeepers specially of allopathic, homeopathic, ayurvedic and grocery shops are also interviewed because they can be able to highlights the recent trends of urgency and dependency of the people on different medicinal, cosmetic and other selling materials from their shops. And on the basis of that a preliminary assumption can be developed about the variation of dependency of people on traditional ethnomedicinal materials and modern market oriented products as per time concern.

During the study special emphasis has been given on some matters like as from the traditional healers various types of information have been collected like as high prevalence of disease in the study area, mode of treatment as accepted by the local people in past and present, availability of various types of traditional and modern medical facilities in the areas, cost effectiveness for the treatment, availability of various medicinal plants and herbals in said area and their medicinal qualities, level of success of these treatment. People's world views regarding use and acceptance of traditional and modern medical facilities also have been considered with due importance.

Major areas of changes

Presently it is an already established fact that due to the effects of globalisation, development of modern medical system, spread of western education system, extinction of various medicinal plants, herbs and any other ethnomedicinal elements due to various man made and other environmental causes most of the people have gradually lost their interest to use various ethnomedicinal elements. This is a serious threat to the said traditional system. It is a very serious matter of concern as per the glorious past of Indian traditional ethno-medical treatment system and Ayurvedic treatments. So it is needed to study with immense importance.

Discussion

Plant herb used	Traditional purpose of use	Effects of globalisation and modernisation
Swertia chirayitab (Gentianaceae)	As the most frequently used and highly extracted species (whole plant) for its applicability in many common diseases, such as, fever, cold, cough, diarrhoea, stomach-ache. Infusion of the whole plant (50–60 ml) taken one time daily in empty stomach for 2 weeks.	Now it is considered as one of the critically endangered species as per habits of use of the villagers. Most of the people of the surveyed areas have expressed their opinion that they have a quite little time to collect this plant and to process it than it would be easier to them to collect allopathic or homeopathic medicine from neighboring market. As a result they are able to given more time in their profession.
Aconitum ferox,	Traditionally use for fever, skin diseases, cough and gout.	Used in past but owing to distance of availability, severely declined populations and loss of knowledge amongst youngsters, the majority of respondents did not mention them as under current use rather they are much more depending on market oriented products.

Usnea sikkimensis	It is beneficial as a remedy for lung troubles, hemorrhage and asthma, and also the massaging scalp with plant powder helps strengthen head hair of the people. It is also used for *stops* nose bleeding, prevents or treats foot blisters.	However, such uses of plants are not so sound amazing and interesting to the present generations. Presently they use various allopathic medicines along with iodine, butadiene losson, various types of cream, bandate etc.
Oroxylum indicum (Gentianaceae)	Generally it is observed that among the Lepchas of Darjeeling Himalaya it having common utility for folk as appetizer and to treat dysentery and throat pain.	In present situation they are much more depending on the metronidazole-tinidazole compound purchasing from local medical shop. Not only that now a days they are much more depending on preventive and curative measures like as use of boiled, saline and purified water, maintaining cleanness.
Pandanus nepalensis	This was a very useful medicine to the local people specially to giving the relief from snake bite. It is generally placing or tying up of young or tender leaves on the skin at the place of snake bite that helps reduce the pain caused.	Presently the local people are interested in going to the Govt. hospitals rather than to go to any herbal specialist or traditional medicine man. In such circumstances in most of the cases they should try to hospitalize the patient to the Govt. hospital at Kalimpong as early as possible. Now a days they have a good faith on the intravenous serum injection rather than traditional herbal medicine specially to use in case of snake biting. Although the Lepchas have their own traditional medical systems but now a days they became gradually depended on modern medical system.
Berberis aristata; Abroma augusta; Girardiana heterophylla; Stephania glabra; etc.	Primarily used as the curative medicine to diabetic patients. The local people have collected the medicinal plants from the neighboring hilly forest areas. They have extracted root bark (5–10 ml) taken twice daily (after breakfast and dinner) for 1–2 weeks.	In the past they used these medicinal plants in a more better way and have an extreme dependency on these medicinal plants as a process of remedy from diabetes mellitus. From the case study based information it can be said that now a days the people are not fully depending on these types of medicine rather they have been used it as the alternative subsidiary medicine. In this connection it is also mentioned here that in the surveyed areas there are more than 87% people depending on the allopathic medicine that means they have more faith on the western medical systems.

Aconitum heterophyllum (Ranunculaceae); *Dactylorhiza hatagirea; Nardostachys jatamansi; Panax pseudosinseng; Picrorhiza kurrooa* (Scrophulari-aceae) etc	All these plants have been used at an excessive level by the local people for peculiar medicinal properties specially in fever, cough and cold situation. In the past they have collected these medicinal plants from the neighboring hilly and forested areas of Darjeeling Himalaya.	Although these species were used for ethnomedicine in the past but in a changing circumstances owing to distance of availability, severely declined populations and loss of knowledge amongst youngsters, the majority of respondents did not mention them as under current use. The younger generations are not so faithful on these traditional medical systems.
Adhatoda zeylanica	Generally fresh tender leaf extracted is given to the children mixed with sugar molasses to cure diorrhoea. The medicine should be given 3-4 times in a day.	In the ancient days this medicine was very popular to protect normal descentry of growing child. Now a days at the preliminary level of the descentry the mothers served this medicine to their children. But in the critical condition they generally have not taken any risks and admitted the patients to the neighboring Kalimpong hospital or remain under treatment of any medical practitioner.
Clematis (bucha-nanianam Ranunculaceae)	In the foot hills of Darjeeling the plant is locally known as 'Pinasay lahara', considered very effective for sinusitis and nose blockade, headache due to nasal blocked, is another very popular plant among local folks. From the case study based information it is observed that the older generations have a very soft heart to this medicine.	The younger generations now a days have been preferred various nasal drops to get remedy from these problems. Although this traditional medicine has been regularly used by the aged people.
Bergenia ciliate (Saxifragaceae) *Eupatorium cannabinum* (Asteraceae); *Pteris biaurita* (Pteridaceae) and *Aloe vera* (Liliaceae)	These plants are very famous for its powerful medicinal properties in the surveyed areas. The local people have used these medicines specially for the treatment of cut and wounds and thus reveal the long conserved ethnobotanical knowledge of the community people.	These plants become rare as per its existence in the region so due to scarcity of these plants the collection of said plants at that argent moment is quite impossible. In this connection most of the villagers put forward their opinion that now a days they are much more depending on the allopathic or homeopathic medicines. Generally in any ill health condition they go to the local quack doctors or medical shopkeepers of the area and observing the symptoms they prescribe the respective medicine.

Artemisia vulgaris L. [Asteraceae]	Locally the plant is addressed as 'Titepathi'. The traditional medicine man of the study area has told that total portions of studied plant have the medicinal property. The local people have been using the said plants specially as a curative medicine to different diseases like as in skin diseases, ulcer and nose bleeding, gout and rheumatism, mosquito and insect repellent.	This plant is very commonly useful to all purpose. Medicinal plants have a very higher popularity but presently a tremendous scarcity has been observed as per its availability in the region. In an illegal way some of the intermediaries have sold these plants in a very higher price rates. In such circumstances the cost effectiveness for that medicine is very high; so people are generally motivated to allopathic treatment. Because to them few allopathic tablets or capsules can be able to giving them very quick relief as a result their regular activities do not hamper where as the ethnomedicinal treatment is quite a time lagging process.
Helianthus annuus L.[Asteraceae]	In case of bronchial asthmas the villagers have been depending too much on these medicines specially, lung diseases, cough, cold and bronchitis.	In the minor level problem the villagers have been using these medicinal plants but in the serious and chronic cases the villagers have been generally taking the help of western medical systems. According to the old villagers in their younger stage they took help of only ayurvedic medicine but now a days they have admitted the patients in the Kalingpong Sub-divisional hospital or North Bengal Medical Collage Hospital.
Phyllanthus emblica L. [Euphorbiaceae]	Local people addressed it as 'gumla' they treat as an all purpose medicine. Generally they have used it in the dysentery, indigestion, gonorrhea, with honey cures leucorrhoea, relieves pain during menstruation and menopausal stage. The local medicine man has prepared different medicine from leaves, barks, stem, and fruits and that medicine has been used for various purposes.	From the field based data there are more than 80% of young mothers who have preferred modern medical system as per its very quick action. In most of the cases in any gynecological problems of the mothers at the preliminary stage they took some traditional medicine but in any fatal condition they always have preferred modern medical systems that means they have carried off the patient to medical practioner or Kalimpong Sub-divisional Hospitals.

Effects of globalisation on the traditional medical practices

On the basis of the field based experiences it can be said that due to the positional disadvantages, the Lepchas lack agricultural recourses most of the Lepcha families of the survey areas are depending on the various types of occupation. Not only the adult male member but the other female, child and aged members also spread up their hands of help and co-operation to strengthen their family economy specially in production of handicraft materials, marketing, carry-on and carry-out materials to markets or homes, daily maintenance of family. As a result almost all the members of the family remain very busy throughout the day and even throughout the year. In these circumstances they have a very little time to collect various ethnomedicinal substances from the forest to treat any ill health condition or diseases. Generally they have purchased it from the neighboring shops of Lolegaon but due to unavailability of the product in these shops they have collected it from Kalingpong or Lava and even from Darjeeling. It is also observed that presently they are much more depending on the modern medical systems and more specifically to say that they are quite depending on the allopathic medical systems. Sometimes they also prefer homeopathic treatment.

Conclusion

The Lepcha tribal community is one of the dominating communities in the foot hills region of Darjeeling Himalaya. They have a very rich heritage about their some social and cultural features. The traditional ethno medicinal system of the Lepcha community is another remarkable feature of the area. Lepchas are one of the primitive tribes to have used their surrounding plants and animals for their health and sustenance. Since exploitation of natural plant resources is in full swing in the entire Darjeeling Himalayan region and many of the medicinally useful plant species have been depleted drastically, their conservation has become need of the hour. But in reality it is observed that the process of globalisation and modernisation have a very sound effect on traditional ethno medicinal practice of the Lepchas. Now a days they become more and more dependent on the modern medical systems rather than traditional ethnomedicinal practices. Although the numerically dominant portion of the Lepchas are still now depending on their traditional ethnomedicinal treatment system but a very rapid change has been observed within them due to the effect of globalisation and modernisation.

References

Bennerman. R., Burton, J. & Chen W.C. 1983. *Traditional Medicine and Health Care Coverage*, WHO, Geneva.

Pandi Kumar P, Ayyanar M, Ignacimuthu S: Medicinal plants used by Malasar tribes of Coimbatore district, Tamil Nadu. *Indian J Trad Knowl* 2007, 6(3):579-582.

Yesodharan K, Sujana KA: Ethnomedicinal knowledge among Malamalasar tribe of Parambikulam wildlife sanctuary, Kerala. *Indian J Trad Knowl* 2007, 6(3): 481-485.

Rengalakshmi R: Folk biological classification of minor millet species in Kolli hills, India. *J Ethnobiol* 2005, 25(1):59-70. .

Viswanathan MB: Ethnobotany of Malayalis in the Yelagiri hills of Vellore district, Tamil Nadu. *J Econ Taxon Bot* 1989, 13:667-671

Ramnath M: Gonds, Linnaeus and botanical techniques: Plants and conservation in tropical forests. *Nat Resour Forum* 2002, 26:314-319.

Rama Rao N, Henry AN: *The ethnobotany of Eastern Ghats of Andhra Pradesh.* India. Kolkata: Botanical Survey of India; 1996:1-238.

Ignacimuthu S, Ayyanar M, Sankarasivaraman K: Ethnobotanical investigations among tribes in Madurai district of Tamil Nadu, India. *J Ethnobiol Ethnomedicine* 2006, 2:25

Ignacimuthu S, Sankarasivaraman K, Kesavan L: Medico-ethnobotanical survey among Kanikar tribals of Mundanthurai Sanctuary. *Fitoterapia* 1998, 69: 409-414.

Abraham Z: Ethnobotany of the Todas, the Kotas and the Irulas of Nilgiris. In *Glimpses of Indian ethnobotany.* Edited by Jain SK. New Delhi: Oxford & IBH Publishing Co; 1981:308-320.

Balakrishnan V, Narayanan MKR, Kumar NA: Ethnotaxonomy of Dioscorea among the Kattunaikka people of Wayanad District, Kerala, India. *Plant Genet Resour Newsl* 2003, 135:24-32.

Kala CP: Ethnomedicinal botany of the Apatani in the Eastern Himalayan region of India. *J Ethnobiol Ethnomedicine* 2005, 1:11.

Udayan PS, Sateesh G, Thushar KV, Indira B: Ethnomedicine of Chellipale community of Namakkal district, Tamil Nadu. *Indian J Trad Knowl* 2005, 4:437-442.

Viswanathan MB: Ethnobotany of Malayalis in the Yelagiri hills of Vellore district, Tamil Nadu. *J Econ Taxon Bot* 1989, 13:667-671.

Ramachandran VS, Manian S: Ethnobotanical studies on the Irulas, the Koravas and the Puliyas of Coimbatore district, Tamil Nadu. *Indian Bot Rep* 1991, 8(2):85-91.

Ganesan S, Suresh N, Kesavan L: Ethnomedicinal survey of lower Palni hills of Tamil Nadu. *Indian J Trad Knowl* 2004, 3:299-304.

Chhetri, D.R., Basnet, D., Chiu, P.F, Kalikotay, S., Chhetri & Parajuli, S. 2005. Current status of ethnomedicinal plants in the Darjeeling Himalay. *Current Science*, VOL. 89, NO. 2.

O'Malley, L. S. S., *Darjeeling District Gazetteer*, Gyan Publishing House (reprinted), New Delhi, 1907.

Mitra, S. & Mukherjeee, S.K. 2010. Ethnomedicinal uses of some wild plants of North Bengal plain for gastro-intestinal problems. *Indian Journal ofTraditional Knowledge*, Vol. 9(4). Pp 705-712.

Biswas, K., 1956. *Common Medicinal Plants of Darjeeling and Sikkim Himalaya.* Bengal Government Press, West Bengal, Calcutta.

Rai, P.C., Sarkar, A., Bhujel, R.B., Das, A.P., 1998. Ethnomedicinal studies in some fringe areas of Sikkim and Darjeeling Himalaya. *Journal of Hill Research* 11, 12–21.

Yonzone, G.S., Yonzone, D.K.N., Tamang, K.K., 1984. Medicinal plants of Darjeeling district. *Journal of Economic and Taxonomic Botany* 5, 605–616.

Venu, P., Kumar, V., Bhasin, M.K., 1990. Human activity and its impacts on vegetation: a case study in Sikkim Himalayas. *Journal of HumanEcology* 1, 27–38.

Das, A.P., Mandal, S., 2003. *Some Medicinal Plants of Darjeeling Hills*, WWF-India. West Bengal State Office, Kolkata.

Chhetri, D.R., Parajuli, P. & Subba, G.S. 2005. Antidiabetic plants used by Sikkim and Darjeeling Himalayan tribes, *India. Journal of Ethnopharmacology* 99 (2005) 199–202.

Risley, H.H. 1891. *The Tribes and Castes of Bengal*. Calcutta: Bengal Secretariat Press.

Pradhan, B.K. & Badola, H.K.2008. Ethnomedicinal plant use by Lepcha tribe of Dzongu valley, bordering Khangchendzonga Biosphere Reserve, in North Sikkim, *India. Journal of Ethnobiology and Ethnomedicine, 4:22. (Retrieve on 30.03.2012,* http://www.ethnobiomed.com/content/4/1/22)

McKay, A. 1997. *Tibet and the British Raj: The Frontier Cadre, 1904-1947,* Richmond, Curzon Press.

5

Modernisation Blooms New Fragnance in Santal Culture

Sujit Kumar Paul and Anindita Gupta

Introduction:

India has vast geographical area with diversified ecological,cultural and linguistic zones. The tribal form a significant population of India as, the country have given shelter to more than five hundred tribal community constituting 08.6per cent of total population. The term 'Adivasi' is implied to the tribal people. The term *Adivasi*has become known to many people. The ILO has classified them as indigenous people and they are living in this subcontinent from unrecorded period.They settled mostly in ecologically marginal areas of hills, forest and other places isolated from the main stream population and are characterised by theirdistinct dialects, culture, folklore, geographical isolation as well as their subsistence economy.The Santals form one of the largest tribal groups in eastern India concentrated mainly in Bihar, West Bengal, Orissa and Tripura.Birbhum districtof West Bengal,comprise nearly 6.74 per cent of total population and 89 per cent of tribal population. This district is situated in the eastern side of the SantalPargana district of present Jharkhand.The Santals are the major tribal group concentrating in Birbhum district. They are locally known as 'Majhi'.Some authors as Hunter, Dalton, Risely and the administrators Mc. Alpin of eighteen century portrait Birbhum as the Homeland of the Santals. In 1872 Santal population in Birbhum was 6954 and it increases to 242484 in 2011. Being amore adaptive community, the lifestyle of the Santal here is not so primitive.

The Santal of this region have come in contact with the non-tribal and urban lifestyle. The impact of this exposure can be seen in the field of culture, language, traditions, occupation, customs etc. As a result of exposure to modern way of life and economy, thisSantal have come close to modern forms of life, institutions and values that have encouraged socio-cultural transformation in their society. They are influenced by the new cultural traits, practices and systems which they come across at the place of settlement, academic institutions, and employment.Thereafter; it would be interesting to understand the impact modernisation on the Santal. In order to do so, attempt has been made to address the transition of traditional culture of Santal of this region to its modern platform. The study also reveals the benefits of modernisation which has aided the Santal from being in a back footed position, in the social ladder, as well as has provided them with better living condition including education and health care and empowerment of women. The modern process of change, have brought a change in tradition and cultural modification among Santal of this region. Santal ancestors possess own religion, strong cultural heritage and traditional village political structure which are at stake today. The reason is particularly due to acceptance of modern culture as well as the changing taste of the Santal through awareness from different sources. This study is confined among the Santals residing in Bolpur-Sriniketan Block of Birbhum district, West Bengal. Present study is an outcome of field based work. It includes focused group discussion, intensive interview, interaction with key persons, and informal discussions withSantal people. Secondary sources of data are also used in writing the paper. The study focuses on the presentation of the qualitative analysis for better understanding of the cultural change.

Inter-relationship between tribal and non-tribal

The Santals in this district is mostly from rural areas, illiterate or poorly educated.The development of infrastructural facilities as well as construction of roads, better communication systemled change in socio cultural status of the Santals of this region.Inter-regional disparities are being observed to be in a declining state in all sphere of their life. Cultural diffusion and acculturation are the resulted fruits of interaction with other non-tribal people which is bringing changes in long term process. Changes in a drastic manner have been noticed in food habits and their use of material culture. In early days the Santal of this region had their traditional institution through which enriched their cultural heritage. In post-independence period several programmes taken by the government, non-government organisations as well as Christian missionaries imparted education and awareness among the Santal which introduced them to the exterior modern world. It was after independence that the government paved attention on the welfare of Scheduled Castes and Scheduled Tribes. The Constitution took special care and these weaker sections were provided with a number of safeguards for the promotion of their interests, including educational. Special mention, in this connection, must be made of the Article - 46 of the constitution in which it has been made one of the Directive Principles of State Policy to promote with special care, inter alia, the educational interests of weaker sections of the people, particularly the

Scheduled Castes and the Scheduled Tribes. The bliss of reservation policy in academic sector, employment sector etc. together with these programmes, taken by government result in their up gradation, changing their socio cultural life to a huge extent. Inter-relationship between tribal that is Santal of this region as well as the non-tribal communities transformed the traditional image of tribal society gradually to a modern society. Along with the socio-cultural changes through adaptation of the different habits and opening of a number of employment opportunities another interesting transformation that has been noticed is in the field of religion. The Santal are inclined to Hindu pole or are converted to Christianity.

Occupational diversification

The tribal economy can be catalogued as subsistence type of mixed economy with mutual dependence among them. Tribal, which acts as single body, makes its economic dealings in periodical markets without having a profit making motive in it. Co-operation and collective endeavours acts as strong developing pillars of their economy with less rate and scope of innovation and specialisation. It can be also characterised as absence in access of technological aids. The mode of production and earning is "domestic" among the tribal. Traditionally they are found to be absorbed in majorly two different kinds of economic activities namely as agricultural labourers as well as through forest oriented activities.The life of the tribal is closely knotted with nature. Forests and tribal are in separable as it is the common thread in all respects of their life starting from birth, marriage, livelihood and death. Forest is the pillar in case of contribution to the tribal economy. This ethnic race, Santal, was originally hunters and gatherers. Non Timber Forest Product (NTFP) are used in the form of food, fodder, fibre and household articles, medicinal and ornamental forms and supplement their income, especially during lean seasons, besides providing religious and aesthetic needs (Vidyarthi and Gupta 2001).Tribals are hugely dependent on the forest-based economy. The Santal of this region are of no exception. The Santal uses edible NTFP for direct consumption, like root, fruits, flower, seed, honey, mushroom and small animals like pigeon, cock, wild hen, hares, pigs etc. Other than consumption their economy is also dependent on forest in the productive sector that is handicrafts. A huge section of the Santal population here subsisted on crafts and cottage industries such as basket making, spinning and weaving, matting, bamboo work, as well as Sal leaf-plate making etc. The entire raw materials which are required for these productions are derived from the forests as well. Other than these they practised agriculture to some extent. But with the reckless cutting of trees, deforestation, consumptionpattern and supply of forest products reveal that there has been a significant pressure on the forest with the increasing population growth, urbanisation, and high rate of economic growth, pollution and over exploitation. The degrading circumstance of forest resources threatens sustainable economic development as there has been a huge economic and social impact of this loss on the Santal of this region. The working on handicrafts which once was notices to be a prime occupation among a section of Santal here is now observed to be a subsidiary one or for self-utilisation. The study has noticed a gradual steady inclination of the Santal inhabitants of this region towards professions other than their traditional one that is forest-based or agriculture.The reasons also vary for this change like being introduced to education and higher education have paved the way of opportunities for employment towards urban and industrial fields for white collar jobs in public or private sectors.. They have made a mark in government sectors as well. Some Santal families of this region, for their livelihood do possess white-collar jobs like in different offices, hospitals, factories, clerks, official assistants, teachers etc. Santal inhabitants having low or no educational background do also have changed their profession owing to shortfall of traditional resources or for better openings in other sectors. They are found to be entertained by professions like construction workers, domestic workers in others households, workers in restaurants, as beauticians, driver, moreover little educated are found be cook of mid-day meal and Anganwadi Centres.MGNREGA on the other hand is a gem which emerged in their life, delivering the assurance of guaranteed work with a replacement of better remuneration for less laborious work. Moreover the periodical small markets of this community are presently linked with the bigger markets; therefore this has introduced a number of new innovative occupations in the Santal economy. A huge concentration can be given on the commercial attitude of the Santalwhich is developed as the fruits of modernisation. This is observed to be a major cause of occupational diversification. Income among this section of people is not restricted to self-sufficiency any more. They have stepped in the world of new technology and luxury that demands for a higher range of income diversifying the traditional occupations to modern economic activities.

Socio-CulturalChanges

The change in traditional socio-cultural issues is the resulting fruits, of the changing taste of the Santal of this region. Adoption of modernisation is the requirement of time. Though modernizing the thoughts of Santal would be helpful to their society, but erosion of their rich cultural heritage which has been passing on from ages by tribal ancestors from one generation to other, in the process of modernisation is undoubtedly a very costly phenomena. They are experiencing a phaseof cultural crisis in the present century as a result of this modernisation. The dramatic changes in the economic and political environment of Santal population have had a profound influence on their social life as well. Many Santal still live in clusters of villages in interior forests or in areas, with less accessibility and influence of the town,with an approximate homogeneous population, do still retain their culture to some extent. But today changes have been noticed in areas whereaboriginal population have been split up and came in contact with numerous populations of different caste and culturalbackground. The social and cultural order which was in practice, while they interacted withSantal belonging to the same traditions, started to decline with the connection of people distinct from those of their indigenous population. This disturbance was caused by this admixture of the Santal with the other caste people who are economically and politically more powerful than the former ones. Thereby, in a naturalway they inclined to fall in adopting the social customs and practices of the so called higher caste people to acquire the similar position in the society. The pace of social change is noticedto be faster among the Santalhere, who were in frequent interaction with their settled neighbouring peasant communities and in some cases with the urban population. Such tribal communities were certainly ahead of others that are; the primitive tribal communities who still reside in interior either in forests or far of places from cultural contact of other caste people.The latter are more vulnerable, and do have less opportunity of interaction with the advanced communities. So, when analysis is done regarding the range of changes of the tribals then interestingly they are found to be at different positions owing to different levels of acculturation. The effectiveness of traditional systems of the Santalhas sharply declined because of the increasing dependence on externaleconomic forces as well as their settlements surrounding the other caste people. Emergence of education and self-awareness for development from different sources are also mentioning criteria responsible for the encouragement of their modern adaptation.

Education

Santals are generally illiterate. But the picture has been observed to take different colour in this present century to some extent. Awareness regarding education has been observed since two generations of the Santal community to a higher range. Parents are sending their children to anganwadi centres and schools. Most fascinatingly in this region Santal girls are also encouraged for higher education.Improvement in literacy level has positively effected in changing the economic and sociocultural life of the Santal as well as this will restrict them to be exploited in the hands of other people. Government as well as non-governmental sectors has immensely contributed in high reaching the literacy and creating awareness regarding the need for education. The development programmes for improvement of educational level together with reservation policy in different types of job by the government have helped the Santal youth to change the occupation pattern for betterment of their living. The Ministry of Social Justice and Empowerment and Ministry of Tribal Affairs, Government of India have taken some measures for economic development. These are: ITDP, LAMPS, and AMSY under NSTFDC (income generation scheme). The Development programmes act as the accelerating force in the producing an opportunity of higher education and better employment which is grabbed by the present generation Santal of this region. National Scheduled Tribes Finance and Development Corporation introduced education loan scheme in the name of AdivasiShiikshaRrinnYojana in which an eligible person can get concessional loan for professional and technical course to PhD conducted by government or government sponsored colleges or institution.A new trend of tutorial arrangement for the children has been observed in the study area. These tutorials are often run and guided by young educated Santali girls imparting the light of education among their juniors. Various programmes and schemes like Post-Matric Scholarships (PMS), Pre-Matric Scholarships, Hostels for ST students studying in middle schools, higher secondary schools, colleges and Universities, Coaching and Allied scheme, up-gradation of merit, Top Class education for meritorious ST students in reputed educational institutions for higher/technical education, Rajiv Gandhi National Fellowships for M.Phil and Ph.D courses, many State level educational promotion schemes of free text books, uniforms, bicycles, merit scholarships, etc. have been implemented by both the Central and State Government. Many students of the locality are availing the benefit of the government schemes for their educational development.

Marriage

Santal marriage can be sketched as pure and sacred which is practised following their traditional customs, and is identifiable through its joyful activities of singing, dancing, in the rhythm of drums and flute. Bride price is an integrated custom of this tribal marriage. 'Raibar' locally named as 'Ghotok' plays a significant role in conducting Santal marriage. Child marriage is a dominating phenomenon here with a number of reasons. Though there prevails the influence of the rigid and deep-rooted traditional culture, it has been observed that acceptance of modern views are the emerging trends of Santal society. With awareness generation, impact of education and social changes, the present generation views certain changes in their thinking process, which is depicted in the marriage ceremony of the Santal of this region. In upcoming generations it has been observed that focus on higher qualification of girls is made. It may be in a very limited and rare case but girls are observed to receive such opportunities in few families which can be set as an example for the future generations. Some people desired, but fail to save their daughters from being victimised of child marriage. Findings of the study have portrayed a new phenomenon among Santal marriage of this region. In the recent years advent of transaction of dowry has been observed among Santal marriage. Marriage is being conducted on fulfilment of the pre settled demands of the bridegroom's father by that of the bride's. This custom is found among the higher caste people of the society. Such practise did not persist in the traditional cultural orbit of Santal marriage. But with sanskritisation and modernisation since recent years dowry transaction has become a strong part of Santal marriage in this region. Bride price on the other hand, which is regarded as the part of marriage do merely remain as a custom. Added to these, certain slow but steady changes are noticed in the study area. Previously girl-bride had no voice regarding her marriage. But present scenario do gives an opportunity to women to voice for their age at marriage and authority of choice of partner. As far as the celebration of the ceremony is concerned in earlier times Santal marriages had no conception of offering food meals that is lunch or dinner to the invitees or relatives of the bride or bride-grooms family. But recently a changing trend is being observed in the study. Now-a-days preparations are made by ordering caterers to serve food to the invitees. Interestingly inter caste marriages is an emerging trend among the Santals of this region. In this case majorly, marriage is found to be conducted among Santal and the higher caste Hindu family. The concept of legal separation that is divorce is also found to be practiced in this community. In earlier times couples were separated for personal preference or with mutual consent, and remarried accordingly. But presently they are inclined towards legal approval of marriage and separation. Thereafter demand for marriage registration and divorce is in practise.

Family Pattern

The advent of urbanisation has changed the pattern but family do retain its importance in the Santal society.Family may be broadly defined as a unit of two or more persons united by marriage, blood, adoption, or consensualunion, in general consulting a single household, interactingand communicating with each other (Desai, 1994). The joint families in present century have broken to nuclear families. It is observed that the family structure in Santal society is majorly nuclear. There are many reasons which accelerate these changes like occupation in areas outside the village or town, opting for higher education, mal adjustment with elder family members, migration for jobs, inclination towards city lifestyle etc.The children of such nuclear families as seen do develop early independence with added responsibilities. The elder children do take up their unavoidable imposed responsibilities of rearing their siblings. Often in Santal nuclear families it is found that the maintenance of the family is carried out by the female member or the mother. Father being capable of earning either doesn't work of spends his earning on gambling and intoxication. Therefore majorly these broken nuclear familiesof single parent responsibility are poorand cannot adequately meet their children's needs. Moreover migration for economy puts stress on child's education and health as well. The residential changes of families among the youth in towns and cities from their traditional lands have deprived their children from being a part of their joint families and this created gap between generations do place them away from their orbit of origin.

Health Practices

Santals are characterised with challenges like poverty, malnutrition, ignorance towards health-care and lack of awareness, poor sanitary and living condition, poor maternal and child health services, which are contributing factors for miserable health conditions of their community. An individual is usually considered to be ill or affected with some diseases if he/she is incapable of performing his routine work. The pattern of consumption to a large extends plays a vital role is malnourishment of the Santal children. Reproductive health is also found to be poor among the Santal families. Difficulties during pregnancy, lack of nutrition, prone to anaemia, premature pregnancies and giving born to mal nourished children as well as infant mortality and maternal death are some of the common illness found in health status among Santalwomen. The physiological vulnerabilities, present among the girls are much more likely to result in maternal death during child birth. It has been also noticed that primarily the young Santal mothers are not concentrated upon for medical check-up which leads to complications in advanced pregnancy. These young brides, during pregnancy, do even lack the knowledge regarding their regular health check-ups, immunisation, and other services provided by the government under ICDS, which is a significant sing of negligence towards their health awareness. Moreover tuberculosis, *kala-jar*, skin infections are a few common findings of disease among the Santal here. From ancient times Santal do believe on *Ojha*, their traditional health practitioner and consumes medicines from medicinal plants as given by him. Increasing level of education and health awareness are found to decline the dismal health condition among the Santal families. The spread of information about the importance of proper nutrition, good health and various birth control measures, in addition to general health check-up have grown in acceptance of medical practitioners and allopathic and homeopathy medicines. As a consequence, presently Santal have developed a belief and have become dependants on health centres, even for minor illness like cold and cough, they prefer to visit health centre rather than seeking opinion from traditional practitioners. Further, during child delivery, majority of Santal women of this region are getting admitted to the nearby health centres. Moreover, Santal female folk have become well aware of family planning and women from this community go for ligation operation at times beyond the positive concern of husband and his family. Consumption of external liquor and excessive smoking are also responsible for their ill health.

Food habits

Food habit is another indicator which represents the changing of the Santal. Interaction with non-tribal not only changed the outlook but its effect is also dramatically visualised in the taste and consumption of food. Since the Santal of this region are daily labourers thereafter their consumption restricts to rice, potato, some leafy vegetables and puffed rice. Only in occasions they are found to consume meat. But with enhanced education and generating awareness regarding the nutritive value of different food items and vegetables, a gradual change in the *consumption pattern* can be noticed. They have started to consume different cereals (dal), and vegetables at times through kitchen garden. On the other hand preference of fast food has a growing rate among the youth of Santal of this region. Even among children snacks like chips, kurkure, magi, are very popular. It has also been noticed that a number of fast food stalls have developed in this region which run in a good manner. Changes have been noticed in their drinking behaviour also. The Santals of this region especially the youths are found to be inclined to consume local liquor other than or parallel to their traditional home made drink. Only during their festive seasons they majorly concentrate on their traditional drink. Other than that throughout the year they are found to purchase and consume local liquor.

Expenditure pattern

Previously the expenses of the Santals covered their food, clothes, and other daily requirements. But with awareness generated from different sources, they have become health conscious and are gradually realising the importance of education. So, now the expenditure pattern has made space for these two areas as well. As far as health is concerned it has been previously discussed that Santals has now grown a belief towards medicines other than from medicinal plants given by *Ojha*. They do visit health centres, even in need they are spending on private practitioners as well as medicines. They are observed to have developed the habit of staying healthy and this has resulted to open the door of expenses for treatment starting from minor to major issues of mal health of the family members especially children. Another area also draws importance in the list of expenses upon is education. Parents are sending their children even girl child for higher studies in college and universities. In addition to these parents do spend on private tuitions for children so that they do not face difficulty in studies since either their parents are illiterate, less educated or they lack time, being overloaded with work, for teaching their children. New trends of expenditure also include modern clothes and cosmetics to keep oneself update and presentable with the outside world. Expenses on fast food have been also observed even in regular basis.Santal youths of this region are found to expend on local liquor to a large extend which was previous absent since they majorly consumed their home made traditional drink.

Wealth Making

Traditionally tribal were not of a character to be conscious about wealth making or securing and saving the same. They were not commercial in nature in their economic sphere that is it can be observed that there is absence of profit making motive in economic dealings. A new trend has been noticed that Santals in this area have developed a tendency of accumulating wealth or making property. They have inclined towards a habit of saving from their income which was completely an alien concept for them previously. They are now found to visit banks, create bank accounts, and save as per their capability. Reasons for savings as conveyed by respondents were for marriage of girls, education of children, constructing house, cattle business, future use etc. The Santal who are educated, have white collar jobs or earn well through business or other services do save to increase their wealth and property. They are in a tendency to be rich and established in terms of house, property, education and lifestyle to secure an equal position and status like the non-tribal in the society. theyare of an opinion that through wealth consumption resulting in changing life style, they can make a better standard for themselves in the society. The greed and desire for lúxury have opened hands for savings and developing commercial attitude.

Self-presentation

Self-presentationis an indicator,as considered by the Santal youth, to present their state of modernisation that accelerates their acceptability in the wider society.They wear modern dresses like jeans (by both young girl and boy), shirt, skirt-top, salwar-kurta, as well as they wear modern jackets of jeans and foam in winter season. Santal boys are also found to use fashionable covered shoes and fancy sandals in case of girls.The Santal girls and women use facial cosmetics to a large extend like fair and lovely, kajal, lipstick, fashionable hair pins which they believe do enhance their beauty and places them in equal standard with the other non-tribal girls or women in the society. Apart from white metal jewellery, the santal female folk of this region do wear other metal and junk ornaments. Wearing wrist-band or iron bangle is also a presentation of modernisation. The self-presentation of present day Santal youth is similar to the non-tribal of the society.

Language

Language is another important aspect which deserves a special mention in the list of changes owing to modernisation. Santal, whether men or women is capable of speaking Bengali, the regional language of this area, very fluently. This has been possible owing to coming in contact with the non-tribal people who either resides as neighbours, in employment background, or in educational institutions. The study reveals that to a huge extent the Santal of this region do avoid to speak in their mother tongue in group meetings or places where other non-tribal are present. Astonishingly this is found among the children of present youth as they find that would discriminate them and lower their standard among others. Even the parents of present generation do not want their children to speak in Santali resulting to the fact that a mentionable section today and the complete Santal population of tomorrow would be unknowing their mother tongue. Children of so called Elite class that is the one who belong from a little rich and educational background are fluently speaking English and Hindi but are restricted to speak in their mother tongue since being unknown to them as attempted by their parents.

Housing pattern

Housing pattern is also a visual change of culture degradation among the Santal of this region. House-hold pattern was cultural identification of the Santal. The colourful decorations through paintings and art on the mud walls at outdoor was the representation of their creativity and their traditional art. But present day these are found to rare among the community. The rich elite class people do construct their house out of the village. The study has observed certain households of elite among the Santal having bungalow decorated with beautiful garden with expensive plantation. They are well furnished and equipped with modern equipment.

Regular Usages

Adoption of modern articlesis observed in this region. The Santals do use a wide range of modern articles whicheither were absent or not popularly known among the Santal forefathers. From the beginning to end of the day, presents us a number of articles which they have adopted with time and with residential opportunities near urban areas. The study has revealed a wide range of articles which has been replaced with modern ones to large extend. But certain articles do persist which is new adoption of the Santali culture of this region.

Reading newspaper either in household or maximum times, in glossary shops nearby, in others house, or in group meetings is a new emergence. Other than this the usage of mobile phones and internet deserves special mention in the discussion.At a glance, usage of a multimedia mobile phone which is available in low cost increases the standard and style statement of the person. Household have been found to be decorated with modern equipments like colour television, water filter, aqua guard, water heater, refrigerator, sofa-set, rod-iron beds etc. Here the study places certain articles which have been replaced with its modern ones by most of the Santal of this region.

Traditional items	Replaced modern articles
Neem leaves	*Tooth-brush*
Neem leaves	*Tooth –paste*
Clay and traditional soap	*Popular branded soaps*
Ritha or some seed of a plant	*Shampoo*
Utensils made of kasha	*Utensils made of steel, aluminium, bone china, glass.*

Cond...

Earthen pots and jars	*Filter*
Mud ovens and fuel by dried leaves and branches	*Gas oven*
Local sandals of plastic	*Branded shoe*
Lanterns	*Emergency lights (electronic)*
Plastic handmade raincoats	*Raincoats*
Mud pots for water consumption	*Aluminiumcontainers*

List of modern articles replaced by the traditional ones among Santal

Religious Belief and Rituals:

The ritual focal point was the roll of drums and rhythmic tunes of flutes. Open fire were the source of light. These were accompanied with singing and dancing, but there was no other music or external intrusion of source of entertainment than these in the celebrations by tribal ancestors. Today the scenario of celebration of any kind of ritual is found to have taken a very different shape from its previous mode. Village and the surrounding areas are filled with shops, tea stalls, and make-shift restaurants with small wooden benches thatgrow up on the eve of the celebrations. Loudspeakers blare out film music at an interval of small distances. There are construction of stage found to conduct programmes with musicians, singers and aurcestra. Santal girls are found to perform on famous Hindi and Bengali film music. A transformationhas been observed from a tribal gathering devoted to theworship of their deities and traditional celebration to a great fair attended by numerous of non-tribal which reflects the submergence of pure Santal culture in the ocean of Hindu practices.

Attitude towards their own rituals is found to be differing in the present generation than their ancestors. They find traditional celebration to be ancient practises and are not getting attracted towards them. They do celebrate the festivals in their own manner with their friends or loved mates. Haria consumption which had been the part of the ritual since their forefathers has been replaced with modern external alcohol by the youth. Side by side their ***attitude towards other caste rituals*** as the study depicts is a phenomenon of interest, well acceptance and adoption of the same as well. Such as the youth of Santal community do celebrate Durga puja, Saraswati puja, Viswakarma puja, Holi and Diwali parallel with the non-tribal. The interest of the study increases on the findings relating to their ***attitude towards modern celebrations.*** Modernisation has led the Santal youth to step on the foot prints of the non-tribal youth in modern celebrations like birthday, marriage day, Valentine's Day, etc.

Conversion of religion

Conversion of religion is by sided in case of Santal. Certain section of them has inclined to Hindu pole by adapting the religious ceremony, rituals and customs and a huge section have converted to Christianity. It is observed in the study that the Santals are converted to Christianity majorly with the objective to receive the desired benefits rather than being devoted towards their religious beliefs. Expansion of Christian Missions and educational institutions having Santalbeneficiaries are tending to increase the impact for accelerating the process of conversion among the Santal. It is generally observed that when the household head becomes converted, other members are also likely to follow the trend. Moreover the Christian Mission run schools where Santals get free education and sometimes other subsidiary benefits such as, books, hostel accommodation etc. In times of economic crisis like house repair, money needed for treatment, schooling of the helpless children Missions often help them in kind or with cash. They also distribute blankets among the poor Santals. In addition to these they make routine visits to different Santal villages, inquire about their difficulties and advise and help accordingly. Thereafter the received benefits, humanitarian behaviour and desire of development accelerate the conversion of Santal to Christianity.

Santal Society and Elite class

There has been created a new section of population that is, the so called Elite class among the Santal community as a result of the introduction of the different dimensional facts, such as, contact and interaction with other caste people, adopting their culture, customs, habits etc. In addition to these are opting for higher education, awareness from different sources, modernisation and their enhanced economy due to the said factors. This class though origin from Santal community at presents neglects their identification of being so as they consider the Santal of village inhabitants to be backward and inferior in compare to them. The Santal Elite is capable to put his society in the light of greater exposure to the outside world in terms of declining their backwardness through spread of education, transmitting knowledge about their constitutional rights, awareness regarding other aspects etc. But result slows a difference. The new identification and status acquired from higher education and better economic standardthrough advanced occupations and lifestyle restricts them in participating in their own rituals and ceremony which they have been previously celebrating with their forefathers. The higher social standard similar to other non-tribal in the society is been gladly accepted by this elite class at the cost of sacrificing their own origin.

It has been found through different replies, the Santal are gradually getting convinced that their backwardness can be removed only with the spread of education. They also emphasise in the context that their children should opt for higher education and join different occupational sectors for the betterment of their living condition. Moreover in addition to these they consider Elite class as their role model since they have acquired a special position in the society through their individual capacities and qualities. They expect that the elite would become catalytic agent of change in their society. The respondents convey that it is walking on their footsteps the future generation can acquire socio-economic and political development. On the other hand though have a positive attitude towards these people, they do also express their grief that most of the Elite persons and their families gradually with time do generally cut off their roots from their village.

Political Organisation

In general view there exist no societies which do not persist political activities. There after Santals of this region was also of no exception. They have their own traditional political structure as selected by the concern of other members which would look after the village disputes maintaining the social prestige of the community. The internal disputes after discussion and hearing for case of both the sides are resulted with punishment of the guilty as decided by the structure. But influence of recent external political structure and their residing with the non-tribal have weakened if not dismissed their traditional governing body. Legal cases do not remain restricted to their own boundary, they are now judged by the legal body of the region as well. Parallely the Santal people here are joining hands of the new established local government Panchayati raj institutions along with their traditional governing body. They are found to participate in gram sansad and gram sabha meeting, gram Panchayat elections, development programme and in decision making process also. Women are also coming in front for their development. Moreover responses are found where community themselves have approached to judiciary for judgement.

Multi-dimensional changes of women-folk

The term "tribal women" itself is pointer to the fact that it is an ambiguous label and has value mainly in terms of official discourse in India(Beteille, 1986). Though Santal women enjoyed a freedom, concentration was least given on their views and voices of tribal women. The fact is that they are found to be very hard working through references. But with modernisation, awareness and spread of education support from government and non-government organisations Santal inhabitants of this region are found to concentrate on the development of female child also. Santal girls of this region have adopted modern views in terms of education, attitude and behaviour, self-presentation and desire for employment in a mentioning manner. Beside, shouldering the household responsibilities, the present Santali women youth have desires and efficiency of higher education, employment and having an equal standard in the society as the non-tribal woman.They have succeeded in this march to a huge extent. The female youth are observed to have a keen interest in gaining qualification at least till class-X or class-XII since this can fetch them some employment opening in future. They are found to be employed in sectors like as beautician, domestic workers, restaurant workers, health workers, as mason and working in self-employed small business of garments and Sal leaf plate making. Educated Satali girls along with the opportunity of reservation have received employment in white-collar jobs, as teacher, office clerk; receptionist etc. young educated girls have also started to impart education among their juniors in tutorials. Slowly they are also voicing against the early age of marriage (though not succeeded in all cases) as they have a aspiration to complete their education and create a self-identity. Respondents are found to convey that they do not want to repeat the same dark future of their daughters like them owing to child marriage. This realisation has emerged owing to the boon of education and awareness of development among them as fruits of modernisation. Santal girls and women do form Self Help Groups (SHG) and run them which have enriched their skills, developed confidence and a habit of savings. References have been found that SHG has contributed a lot in the spheres of literacy, skill development from gaining trainings from panchayat and personality development as a whole. Apart from thesethe study also depicts a change in the colours of culture of women youth. They have adopted completely modern fashion in terms of dressing, facial make-up, and ornaments and so on. Moreover these advanced Santali women not only differs in self-presentation but also in pursuing a sense of self-confidence, and a capacity to place ones opinion in social gathering as well. Which is found to be absent in case of the ones who are still to come in the orbit of modernisation. The present trend also participates in the mainstream political sphere. With the reservation in political bodies, the Santali girls are gradually making an entry into the political structure of the society. Thesparkling achievements of these women folk of this region acquired through their desire, efficiency, hard work and co-operation of their family are setting example in front of the entire community giving the other girls an inspiration to follow their footsteps.

Case study: I

JitendranathMurmu, age 28 years lives in exterior area of Fuldanga village. He is Madhyamik qualified and at present is employed in Calcutta Police since 14 years. He is married to a Santal girl from Purulia who can't speak Santali at all. Thereafter conversation between them is in Bengali. His wife is madhyamik qualified as well. Jitendranath is owner of a two stored well decorated and well-furnished bungalow. He has two daughters. One study in class-II in Happy Home School (English medium) and the other is younger and thereafter visits anganwadi centre. Both the parents are of opinion that they will give higher education to their daughters so that they can lead a better standard of living in their future. Jitendranath is of opinion that the tribal community is lagging behind owing to their lack in hold on English language. Thereafter he has admitted and planned to continue his daughters' education in English medium schools. This family is culturally different from their traditional tribal culture and have adopted themselves and their upcoming generations on the footsteps of regional Bengali culture. He considers his traditional activities to be backward as well as his birth place Khejurdanga village to be interior. So he rarely visits his birth place and house he was born and brought up his children are completely unaware of Santali culture as they never received the opportunity to come in contact with them. Their mother-tongue Santali is a foreign language to them since they do not interact in this language even with their parents. The dressing pattern, food habits and regular activities of this family is so, that, at a glance they represent the modern culture of the society. Children of Jitendranath are very fond of Chinese food which is a foreign item in Santali culture. Moreover they possess bank account, use gold jewellery, have utensils made of steel, glass and bone china. Even they greet people by saying "hello" or "namaskar" instead of "Johar-Johar". Children shake hands with new comers. Wife of Jitendranath is comfortable in wearing salwar-kamiz, and kurtas. She has no experience of wearing two-part traditional Santali dress in her lifetime. She insists her children to watch Hindi programmes so that her daughters can shade off the tag of being Santal, as this community people in general is not accustomed with this language. The family do not use their surname while telling their names until they need to do so as they are not comfortable in showcasing their tribal identity. Moreover,Jitendranath is very happy with his present employment structure and finds his service to be a better option than agriculture or cultivation in terms of both economy and social prestige. As far as Santali rituals and festivals are concerned, respondent conveyed that he and his family do not have any interest and time to visit and participate in those occasions his children like other Bengali children neither knows the folk songs nor have seen the rhythms of folk dances on flutes and drums. On the other hand they have hole heatedly adopted the modern celebrations like birthday, marriage day etc. They also celebrate the Hindu caste festivals like Durgapuja, Saraswati puja etc. in a grand way. Thereafter this is a picture of impact of modernisation on Santali culture. Adoption of modern activities and sanskritising the Hindu culture is realised to be modern or up to date by this family to receive equal standard as the non-tribal in the society. This has lead to, the changing taste of Santal, in the effort of becoming modern at the cost of eroding the deep rooted, age old culture and traditional customs of their origin.

Case study: II

This incident is of a village in Birbhum district, West Bengal. A girl named ParbatiMurmu of 24years is a pass graduate from a renowned college Girls College of Birbhum district. She is trained in technical works like mobile repairing, basic computer training, and health education. She acquired a tremendous support from her family to continue her studies, especially from her mother. This opportunity has led her to complete her studies, acquire trainings which will help her to achieve a good job, will give her economic independence and a security as well. Not only that her personality and outlook has developed and parallel she has also developed speaking different languages other than Santali that is regional language Bengali, English as well as Hindi to some extent and received training in computer as well, which has enriched her profile. She has also adopted the new modern fashion of dressing and wearing in terms of clothes, hairstyle, facial makeup and ornaments and she admits that this helps her to be well accepted in the society among non-tribal. Parbati is strict to her principle that she will marry on being employed. Today this graduate girl is economically independent as she earns through giving tuitions and works as health worker in a village. She also imparts tuitions to her juniors. At present she has set an example in front of the Santal community. Following her example her sister a few girls and other also walks her footsteps which is an achievement of their village, and community on a broader perspective.

Conclusion

Tribes are integral parts of Indian society and their culture encompasses an important element of Indian civilisation.The impact of modernisation is manifested in their day to day activities. A Santal youth is ought to be different from his ancestors, as the processes of modernisation have lead them to learn about new food habits, language, dress pattern, use of modern equipment, learn habit of savings etc. Interaction and coming in contact with the non-tribal communityfor residence, employment background or in educational institutions etc. have accelerated majorly their understanding for the need of education of their children and were exposed to modern health practices. Thepresent paper reveals that the transformation by adoption of modern activities is disintegrating the homogeneity of the Santals. They are experiencing a transitional phase in terms of socio-cultural and economic backgrounds. If this process of cultural transformation continues, it can be said that they will retain no distinct socio-cultural identification of their own in near future. With the benefits of advancement and development modernisation tends to mark an end to the original fragrance of Santal culture. The upcoming generations would be mere the people walking on the foot-steps of Bengali Hindu culture or converted Christians. With time it is evident that people is required to shape up themselves with the current trend and technology. But in doing so, abolishing individuals own identity, the customs and rituals, neglecting the practises of origin would undoubtedly, not be an acceptable incident in the history of Santal civilisation.

Reference

Beteille, A., 1986, "The Definition of Tribe with Reference to India".*European Journal Sociology*, Vol.27.

Chaudhuri, A.B., 1987,*TheSantals Religion and Rituals*, Ashish Publishing House, New Delhi.

Chaudhury, K.Sukant and Patnaik, Mohan Soumendra (eds), 2008, *Indian Tribes and The Mainstream*, Rawat Publications, New Delhi.

Deva, Indra, 1982, "Culture and Development". Paper presented in the seminar on *Development: Socio-cultural Dimensions*, 15-17 February. Chandigarh: Department of Sociology, Punjab University.

Desai, M. (1994).*Concept and conceptual frameworks for understanding family. Enhancing the role of the family as an agency for social and economic development* (Unit for Family Studies Report, pp.16-41). Bombay, India: TISS.

Ghoosh,Prasasti, 2013, Development Programmes And The Tribal: A Study On The Santals Of Birbhum District, *IOSR Journal of Applied Geology and Geophysics (IOSR-JAGG)*, Volume 1, Issue 5, Nov. – Dec. 2013.

Hembram, P.C., 1988, *Sari-Sarna (Santal Religion)*, Mittal Publications, New Delhi.

HossainKaziTobarak, The Santals of Bangladesh: An Ethnic Minority in Transition, http://anthropology-bd.blogspot.in/2008/07/santals-of-bangladesh-ethnic-minority.html.

Majhi, A.S., 2010,*Tribal Culture, Continuity and Change*.Krishan Mittal for Mittal Publication, New Delhi.

PamechaRenuka, 1985, *Elite In A Tribal Society,* Pritwell Publishers, Jaipur.

Paul, Sujit Kumar (2005). Tribal Agriculture and Modernisation - The Change and Continuity.Daya Publisher, New Delhi.

Saren,Gurupada, 2013, Impact of globalisations on the Santals: A study on migration in West Bengal, India, *International Journal of Humanities and Social Science Invention,* Volume 2, Issue 7, July 2013.

Sharma A.N &Tiwari P.D, 1989, Tribal Ecosystem and Malnutrition in India. Retrieved on April 27, 2013 from books.google.co.in/books?

Vidyarthi L.P., RaiBinay Kumar, 1976, *The Tribal Culture of India*, Concept Publishing Company, New Delhi.

6

Challenges of Resettlement of Displaced Tribal Population: A Study of Kaptai Dam

Dr. K M Rezaul Karim[1]
Dr. Selina Ahmed[2]

Introduction

More than 5000 indigenous people live in about 90 countries of the world. They are about 3 crore 70 lakh in number, consisting of more than 5% of world population.[i] Among 143.3 million population of Bangladesh, majority are Bengalis, and approximately 3 million are indigenous peoples belonging to at least 57 different ethnic groups. According to population census 2011, the total number of tribal population in the country is 1586141 (1.10% of national population). Among them 797477 (50.28% of tribal people) are male and 788664 (49.72% of tribal people) are female.[ii] The indigenous peoples are concentrated in four regions of Bangladesh. The regions are north-east including Chittagong Hill Tracts (hereafter CHT), North-west, Mid-north and the districts of North Bengal.[iii] Among them 36 communities live in plain land and rest in hilly areas of CHT with their own languages, alphabets, numerical systems, cultures, religions and civilisations.[iv] According to the census of 1991, the total population of tribal community is about 1.2 million, which constitutes about 1.13% of the country's total population.[v] In fact, the tribal population might be more than the figure given in the census report.[vi] In 1960, the British colonial rulers annexed the CHTs to the then province of Bengal. They granted a certain degree of autonomy to the region and limited access to outsiders. The Pakistani administration abolished this special status and started encouraging migration of non-tribal and exploiting its natural resources.

Denial of the land rights of indigenous peoples of Bangladesh has long historical background that started with the appropriation of the forest commons of the indigenous peoples by the colonial Forest Department in the 1870s. With the construction of the *Kaptai* Dam[vii] in 1960, more than 1 lakh people were uprooted.[viii] A vast reservoir of some 550 square miles came onto being which inundated most of the fertile *Karnafully* valley and large parts of the *Chengi*, *Kassalong* and *Maini* valleys containing lush paddy fields and vegetable gardens. A large number of frustrated *Chakma* farmers migrated to Arunachal Pradesh of India where they still remain as stateless refugees.[ix] The migration into the CHT of an estimated 2 lakh to 4 lakh landless Bengali farmers from several districts outside CHT in 1979. The early 1980's through a Government-sponsored program led to the dispossession of thousands of acres of lands (including forests) previously belonging to indigenous peoples, which are yet to be recovered. In accordance with the 1997 CHT accord and subsequent legislation, a commission on land has been formed to resolve disputes over land, which is yet to start working.[x] However, the instances of land dispossession suffered by the indigenous peoples of the plain land are perhaps even more widespread than in the case of CHT.

Statement of the problem

The *Kaptai* dam is the only hydro-electric power source in Bangladesh. The dam was supposed to provide benefits in terms of hydropower, flood control, irrigation and drainage, navigation and enhanced forest resource harvesting. Most of these objectives have been served in various degrees except irrigation and drainage. Lately commercial such as cultural and recreational activities have been introduced in the lake. This, however, is part of the story. During construction, the dam flooded an area of some 655 km, which included about 22000 ha of cultivable land, 40% of all such land in the CHT. The lake took away the homes of 18000 families and displaced around 100000 tribal people. Among them the majority (70%) were *Chakma*-which accounted for more than a quarter of the total population of the CHT and inundated more than 54000 acres or 40% of the best plough lands of the CHT.[xi] They lost their ancestral homesteads along with horticulture, plants, domestic animal, kitchen gardens, cultivable lands as well as kinship relation and social network.[xii] The dam also flooded the original *Rangamati* town and the palace of the *Chakma* Raja.

The construction of *Kaptai* Dam led to the first crisis of internal displacement in the CHTs and threats of assimilation with majority culture of Bangladesh. It provided fuel to the armed conflict that ensures. The devastating effect of the *Kaptai* dam is still deeply felt as alienations factor and the tribal populations. A rather casual attempt was made to rehabilitate that large group of people (nearly 25% of the local population). Officially, the majority of the displaced people were rehabilitated on the upper reaches of the rivers *Kasalong* and *Chengi* during the early phase of the project.[xiii] In reality, the newly created 'environmental refugees' were resettled in the low-lying areas of *Langdu*, *Barkal* and *Bhaghaichari*. Much of the resettlement area had gone underwater as the reservoir gradually filled up, causing many to be displaced for the second time. This had naturally aggrieved the tribal population as they received few if any of the benefits of the dam.

Many of the displaced people left the country; some estimates say that about 40,000 of them went to the sparsely populated areas of Mizoram, Tripura, Assam and Arunachal province in India where the majority remains today as stateless persons. Another 20,000 may have gone to Myanmar.[xiv] This event and a series of administrative and legislative actions taken since the emerge of Pakistan had ultimately led to the 22-year-long violent and armed confrontations between the Bangladesh Government and the tribal people that began in the mid-1970s and lasted till accomplishment of the peace treaty in 1997. Some provisions of the treaty have not been implemented yet and these remain as the source of discord between the two parts. The content of issue resettlement is articulated in objectives of the study clearly.

Objective of the paper

The present paper has been prepared with a view to achieve the following objectives:

1. To analyse the type, nature and extent of the losses caused by the construction of *Kaptai* dam;
2. To examine the nature and scope of resettlement and rehabilitation program taken for tribal uprooted population.

Methodology

The paper is based on information collected from the secondary sources of Government statistics, individual researchers' findings, research reports, Task Force Reports, population censuses, articles, journals, edited books, academic publications, magazines and dailies.

Study Area

Chittagong Hill Tracts is located in the south-east part of Bangladesh. The British created the region in 1860 under the 22nd Adm. Act. At that time, most of it was densely forested and inhabited by tribal people.[xv] The district was created in recognition of its unique natural and cultural characteristics. The CHT is comprised of three administrative districts: *Rangamati*, *Khagrachhari* and *Bandarban*. The total area of the CHT is 13148 sq. km, which is about 10 percent of the land area of Bangladesh. Roughly around 1.2 percent of the population is indigenous living in the CHT's and in the plain lands. Currently, the population of the CHT is evenly composed of Bangalis (50%) and tribal communities (50%). The *Chakma* are the largest tribal group, constituting about 24% of the CHT population. The other major tribes are the *Marma* (14%) and the *Tripura* (6%).[xvi]

Review of literature

All over the world, there are more than 15000 large and numerous other small dams that have displaced some 60 million people from their homelands. The construction of dams on rivers to store water for power generation is well-known for its adverse effects on the environment and forced population displacement. Those persons affected by the projects rarely receive any compensation. In the recent past, Turkey has built the Ataturk dam in the Kurdish region, where some 60000 people were displaced. Another project in this region, the Illisu dam, will affect about 75000 people of the Kurdish region. Such encroachments on the resources and rights of the people of the land are not isolated—the Narmada in India, the Three Gorges in China, the Nam Theun II in Laos and the Itoiz in Spain are just a few examples of such violations. Unfortunately, a large part of the population displaced by dams has come from the underclass and the tribal communities. In India, a dam built under the Subarnarekha Multipurpose Project in Jharkhand, Bihar State submerged 120 villages and thousands of acres of agricultural land. About one lakh people, mostly tribal, were forced from their land and turned into development refugees. In India, about 40% of the people displaced by dams have been low castes or tribal people, even though they make up less than 6% of the Indian population.[xvii] The story looks very similar in Bangladesh. It is about time that the government and the affected groups worked out a peaceful and mutually agreeable solution in a democratic way and through a properly designed institutional framework. This would go a long way in ensuring the security and prosperity of the CHT region in the new millennium.

Brief History of CHTs

The tribal people have been living in the CHTs for a long time, but they are not the original settlers in that area. Most of the tribal people of CHTs was not inhabited or was barely inhabited by people till the large-scale in-migration in the 17th and 18th centuries. The *Chakma*'s moved into the CHT with their king when the *Marma* king of Arakan drove him out. Later on, the Mughals drove the *Marma* people out of Arakan in 1756.[xviii] Other tribes of CHT have a similar history. According to Thomas Herbert Lewin[xix] "a greater proportion of the hill tribes at present living in CHTs undoubtedly came about two generations ago from Arakan. This is asserted both by their own traditions and by records in Chittagong Collectorate. Accordingly, the claim often made by the tribal people that they are the 'sons of the soil' is not valid in the sense of being original settlers in CHT. Bengali settlers lived in parts of the CHT long before that time, albeit in small numbers. The different tribal communities of the CHT have lived separately from the beginning and have distinct linguistic, cultural and anthropological features. Over the course of about 300 years, these tribal communities have gone through a series of interventions sometimes protecting and sometimes undermining their interests. It is evident from the series of events that the displacement of tribal people due to the *Kaptai* dam was almost inevitable, as their control over the region was gradually being curtailed, which culminated with the annulment of the tribal area status of the CHT in 1964. The issue of resettlement of the displaced people was handled poorly for a number of reasons. There was a general lack of understanding of the tribal culture by the government of Pakistan and the donor agencies.[xx]

They thought that these were 'nomadic' hill-people practicing *jhum* cultivation and it was unnecessary to design a permanent resettlement program for them. In reality, the tribal people did move from hill to hill. But they had a long cycle of *jhum* cultivation. Before the inundation of the *Karnafuli* valley, the average cycle of *jhum* cultivation was 7-10 years, and in some cases 10–15 years. After inundation of the river valleys, which took away 40% of the fertile agricultural land, this cycle became reduced to only 3-5 years as thousands of local people were forced back to *jhum* cultivation. This pressure on land was further intensified by the rapid population growth that took place during the 1960s and 1970s in the entire CHT area. The collective outcome of those developments was intensive agriculture both in the remaining plain lands and in the hills, leading to soil erosion, productivity loss and water pollution caused by increased use of fertilizer and pesticides. The other important reason for not having an adequate relocation scheme was simply the lack of adequate budgetary provision. Initially, some compensation was paid for the loss of land, trees and structures but there was little money available for rehabilitating 100000 people. The majority of them were taken to the *Kasalong* valley, where a reserved forest was partly cleared to create land for those people. When the water level of the reservoir rose after completion of the dam in 1962, much of that land went underwater and the government simply gave up all efforts to resettle those people again.

Resettlement and Rehabilitation Program of Kaptai Dam

The resettlement and rehabilitation of the affected people has become an important issue in present days and hence an integral part in project planning formalities.[xxi] Usually Government offers compensation in cash or other kinds. But there are number of issues involved in the process of resettlement and rehabilitation. Issues such as site selection, compensation, future occupation, health, education etc. require intense knowledge and expertise.[xxii] There were several inadequacies of the resettlement and rehabilitation program due to *Kaptai* in CHT. The construction of the *Kaptai* dam led to the first crisis of internal displacement in the CHTs and, combined with loss of control over natural resources and threats of assimilation with the majority culture of Bangladesh, provided fuel to the armed conflict that ensued. The devastating effect of the building of the *Kaptai* dam is still deeply felt as an alienating factor among the tribal population.[xxiii] Every Government has policies, laws and regulations requiring compensation for the people losing assets, yet these might not be sufficient to restore livelihoods and living standards. There was a commitment from the then East Pakistan Government for rehabilitation and compensation, but most of the evictees were deprived of such compensation. The government could not keep its promise to compensate for the lost arable land with similar land elsewhere. Firstly, not enough arable land was available in the region; each family was given a maximum of 10 acres of land even though they owned more land in the project area. Secondly, fertile land in the river valley was compensated by hilly lands, which was of no immediate use to the people, who had got accustomed to the plain land farming introduced in the CHT by the British from the early 20th century. Thirdly, monetary compensation was too small: for example, the displaced people received only Taka 500–700 per hectare as compensation whereas they had to pay Taka 5000 per hectare to buy similar arable plain land in other areas where some of them eventually settled. According to the Acquisition Ordinance, compensation is the…market value of the property at the date of publication of the notice…." informing the property owner of acquisition "…the deputy commissioner shall take into account the average value, to be calculated in the prescribed manners, of the properties of similar description and with similar advantages in the vicinity during the twelve months preceding the date of publication of the notice…."[xxiv]

The government of Pakistan had made a rather late attempt in 1968–69 to rehabilitate some 11000 families in 51 *moujas* surrounding the lake. A total of 66000 hectare of land was allocated for this purpose. As per the plan, each family received on average 2.4 hectare of land for growing fruits, in addition to fruit saplings, fertilizer and pesticides. Agriculture extension officers arranged training in horticulture and initially the resettled people participated in the program enthusiastically. Unfortunately, the plan did not work well in the end because little or no attention was paid to the storage and marketing aspects of the production. People grew mango, jackfruit, pineapple and lemon but did not receive a fair price for the products. In fact they feel prey to exploitation by the middlemen. Moreover, over the years the productivity of the land has fallen significantly, rendering the program less effective now.

The large-scale displacement of the tribal people caused by the *Kaptai* dam is certainly one of the important factors that have contributed to the worsening of the relationship between the tribal and Bengali population in the CHT. The rate of influx of the Bengalis increased due to the setting up of some major industrial infrastructures such as the *Karnafuli* pulp and paper mill and administrative offices of various departments of the government.

According to the CHT Accord 1997 Section (D) Article (1) a Task Force will be made for the proper rehabilitation for the affected persons of CHT.

The government re-assures through the CHT Accord its commitment to give back their dispossessed lands and support their *Kaptai* dam is still deeply felt as an alienating factor among the tribal population. The region has also seen a phenomenal increase of the Bengali population. Government-sponsored resettlement of more than 400000 landless Bengalis from the plains between 1979 and 1984 dramatically altered the demographic balance as well as amplified resource constraints. According to 1991 population census, the total CHTs population then amounted to approximately one million, the tribal population making up a little more than 51% and the remaining 49% being overwhelmingly Bengalis. The population census-2001 showed a total population of 1.3 million, but a breakdown by ethnicity is still not available. While the tribal population might have been understated in 1991, the massive influx of Bengali settlers since then has probably made the tribal population a minority in the region. Migration of Bengalis from the plains continues unabated.[xxv]

Summary of the findings

It has been mentioned earlier that with the construction of *Kaptai* dam in 1960s, more than 100000 indigenous people were forced to leave their ancestral properties. Many of them were forced to take shelter either in forest lands or with the Bengali community people that aggravated the vulnerability of indigenous people to a greater extent. In exchange, an inadequate amount of monetary compensation was paid out and hardly one-third of the lost lands were replaced. A large number of *Chakma* migrated to India. Of those who remained, which included both plough cultivators and jum cultivators or jumias the majority were forced to initially take up jhum cultivation, although a significant number of them later took up horticulture.[xxvi] Socially they became isolated, economically they lost the means of livelihood and culturally they were denied their traditional and conventional means of recreation, festivals, ceremonies, rituals, folkways and mores. Even the evictees were not allowed to have any land rights and other basic services like healthcare, sanitation, drinking water, education and employment, Therefore, most of the evictees became the refugees in the process of economic, social, cultural, political and environmental exclusion.

A Task Force Committee has been constituted on 20 January 1998 and selected Mr. Dipankar Talukdar, the member of parliament of the *Rangamati* hill district as the chairman with nine (9) members. However, till now except the definition of the internally displaced persons no progress has taken place. The Task Force accepted definition of Internally displaced persons is as: "In the time from 15 August 1975 to 10 August 1992 due to the conspicuous unstable and commotion situation of the CHTs the tribal people who compelled to abandon their own village, *Mauza*, area and has gone or compelled to go others within the country will be considered as Internally Displaced Person."

Task Force accepted the above definition and the definition is clear that the Jumma people will be the only Internal Displaced Persons of CHT but the Government has one-sidedly included the Bengali Muslim settlers who are illegally given settlement in CHT. The PCJSS and Jumma Refugee Welfare Association has protested against the inclusion and as a part of the protest boycotted the Task Force Meeting held on 22 September 1999. The government has not responded about it whereas announced 38,156 settler families as Internal Displaced Persons. The Governments point of view is that there is no identification that only the Jumma people will be counted as Internal Displaced Persons in the Terms of Reference of Task Force. The Government's Special Affairs Division also circulated an ordinance to consider the outsider settlers as Internal Displaced Persons on 19 July 1998.[xxvii]

Displacement causes socio-economic and cultural disruption of the lives of the affected people.' No trauma can be more painful for a family than to get uprooted from a place where it has lived for generation and to move to a new area. A feeling of helplessness and alienation is often engendered in those who are displaced especially when entire communities are uprooted from ancestral homes. The largest and first occurrence of displacement of conflict induced displacement is found in the CHT due to *Kaptai* dam. The dam adversely affected the self-sufficiency of the tribal society, culture and economy. Moreover, it failed to create employment opportunities for the hill people, as envisaged. Until today a large number of the displaced people have neither obtained adequate compensation nor been properly rehabilitated. It is not therefore difficult to believe that dissatisfaction with the *Kaptai* Dam and its aftermath was one of the major causes behind the present unrest in the CHT.

Conclusion

The construction of *Kaptai* Dam not only devastated the livelihood of indigenous people, also created a political conflicts that led to the massacre of hundreds of people, provided further fuel to the armed conflict between the indigenous people and major ethnic people. The devastating effect of the building of *Kaptai* Dam alienated the indigenous population from their own culture. The root of the problems emanating from the *Kaptai* dam lies in not recognizing the rights of the indigenous people and in the lack of willingness on the part of the authorities to communicate with them. The government encouraged the tribal people to take up new occupations such as fishing or horticulture but the response was poor, mainly due to lack of necessary skills and cultural shock. Such skills and knowledge are not part of their heritage.[xxviii] There was virtually no consultation with the tribal people in the 1960s during construction of the *Kaptai* dam. Now the consequences can be seen: both the Bengalis and the tribal people have paid a high price for the problems created by the dam and the displacement of one hundred thousand people.

Notes

1. Assistant Professor, Department of Sociology, Government BL. College, Khulna-9202, Bangladesh.
2. Associate Professor, Sociology Discipline, Khulna University, Khulna-9208, Bangladesh.

Refferences

1. *Literacy Bulletine*, August 2013, Vol. 231, P. 1.
2. BBS, *Population and Housing Census 2011*, Dhaka: BBS, 15 March 2011.
3. Ramakanto Singh, *Ethnic People of Bangladesh*, Dhaka: AHDPH, 2001, pp. 40-41.
4. Meghna Guhathakurta and Suraiya begum, Bangladeshe Avantarin bastuchuto baktibargo (Internal displaced persons in Bangladesh), *Samaj Nirikhan* (social studies), Vol. 96, January and March 2006, p. 60.
5. But the actual populations of indigenous communities are considerably higher as peoples of these communities who have been converted into other Christians or Hindu, are excluded from the account of indigenous populations.
6. Philip Gain(ed.) *Bangladesh: Land, Forest and Forest People*, Dhaka: SEHD, 1998, p. 12.
7. Kaptai dam is the only hydropower source in Bangladesh, Commissioned on 30 March 1962, the dam initially had two hydropower units with a total capacity of 80 MW. Presently, it has five units with a total capacity of 230 MW. It produces approximately 5% of the electricity consumed in Bangladesh.
8. Barkat and Huda, Politico-economic Essence of Ethnic Conflicts in the Chittagong Hiil Tracts of Bangladesh, *Social Science Review*, Vol. V, No. 2. December 1988, Dhaka University.
9. Subir Bhaumik et.al. (eds) *Living on edge: Essays on the: Chittagong Hill tracts*, South Asia Forum for Human Rights, Kathmandu, 1997.
10. Abul Barkat et.al. Life and Land of Adibashis: Land Disposstion and alienation of Adibashis in the plain districts of Bangladeh, Dhaka: HDRC and Pathak Shamabesh, 2009, p. 29.
11. Mahfuzul Haque, 'Development Disasters: The Role if Indigenous Knowledge and Practices', in *Indigenous Knowledge Development in Bangladesh: Present and Future* (Edi: Paul Sillitoe), 2000, p. 38.
12. Khondoker Mokaddem Hosssain, The State of Indigenous People in Bangladesh, *Indigenous People and Bangladesh Environment*, BAPA, BEN, 2007, p. 33.
13. The Construction of the dam began in October 1957.
14. Saleem Samad, *State of Minorities in Bangladesh: from Secular to Islamic Hegemony*, 2000, p. 13.
15. Less than 5% of the population were Bengalis from the plain lands.
16. Bangladesh Bureau of Statistics, *Statistical Yearbook-1995*, Dhaka: BBS, August 1995.

17. Debasish Kundu and Mahfuzul Islam, Searching the Indigenous Agenda: *Indigenous Peoples and Bangladesh Environment*, Dhaka: 17-19 December, 2007, p. 68.
18. Hutchinson, 1906
19. A soldier-cum-administrator of British India's north-east frontier (Lewin, 1869).
20. *S. Parveen & I. M. Faisal* funded by USAID.
21. Osman Gani. *The Problems of the Charlands and Probable Solutions.* Dhaka: Social Institute, 1997. p. 1.
22. A. Rahman Sheikh, Development Induced Displaced in Pakistan, *Refugee Watch*, No.5, (Sept., 2001), p. 11.
23. Kundu and Islam, *Indigenous Peoples and Bangladesh Environment*, December 17-18, 2007, Dhaka, p. 69.
24. *The Acquisition and Requisition of Immovable Property Ordinance* (Dhaka: Ministry of Land, GOB, 13 April 1982), p. 5.
25. Care, 2004, 2005.p. 6.
26. Philip Gain(ed.) *Bangladesh: Land, Forest and Forest People*, Dhaka: SEHD, 1998, p. 61.
27. Reff. No. SLB-78/98/185
28. R I Chowdhury et.al.(edi), Tribal Leadership and political Integration: A Study of Chakma and Mongs Tribes of Chittagong Hill Tracts, Chittagong: Chittagong University, 1979.

7

The Continuing Conflict: Critical Transition to Peace in the Post-Conflict Chittagong Hill Tracts of Bangladesh

Ala Uddin

Introduction

This paper is concerned with the indigenous people living in the Chittagong Hill Tracts (CHT). The CHT is an extensive hilly area located in the southeastern Bangladesh comprising 5,089 square miles.[1] This isolated region shares its border with northeast Indian states of Tripura and Mizoram, and eastern Myanmar (Burma) state of Rakhine. The mountainous belt, which is geographically distinct contains very limited cultivable land (3.2 percent), most of which are of low quality, in contrast to the fertile multi-cropped alluvial plains of rest Bangladesh. Other than the *Bangali* (Bengali) settlers, 11 heterogeneous groups[2] live in the hills. Although internally diversified (through resources of culture e.g. dress, language, religion, etc.) collectively they are called as *Pahari* (hill people). However, the Pahari maintain cultural separateness from the Bangali in terms of race, language, religion, economy and other socio-cultural organisations. The region has been the site of much contention between the hill tribes (Pahari) and the state during the colonial period (1757–1947) that continued even after the creation of Pakistan (in 1947), and independence of Bangladesh (in 1971).

The British conquered the entire region winning in the *Palashir Juddha* (Battle of Plassey) in 1757 still they did not begin to rule the hill region directly until 1857, which was known as *Kapas Mahal* (Cotton Territory, now CHT). Until then the hill tribes (Pahari) had managed to maintain traditional life-ways in the *terra incognita* (now known as CHT). Following the *Sipahi Biplab* (Sepoy Mutiny) in 1857, the British took over the power from East India Company in 1860, and began direct rule annexing it to the colonial empire (van Schendel et al. 2000).

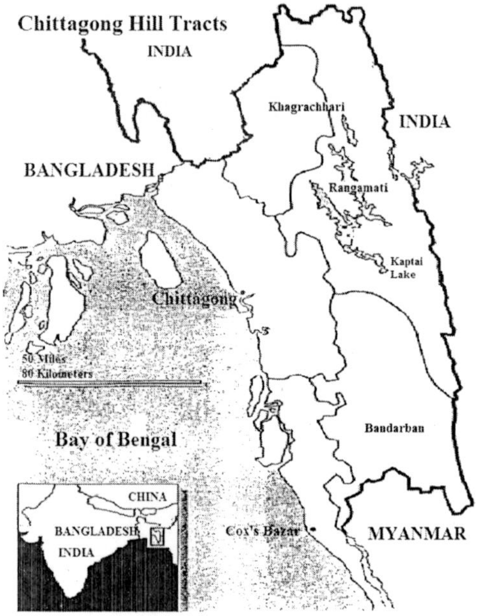

Map 1: The Chittagong Hill Tracts

Although in the very beginning economy was not observed as primary concern, soon they gave attention in increasing revenues from the hills. In the beginning they used to collect tax in the form of cotton, they began collecting tax in cash (money) rather than kind (cotton) from 1789. The British also evolved market economy, and encouraged the people to give up *jum* (shifting cultivation) for plough cultivation. For obvious reasons, the monitorisation went against the interest of the Pahari who had no experience of dealing with money, bazaar or market economy (see for details, Mohsin 1997; Lewin 1869; Mey 1984). Since the Pahari had no experience of plough cultivation, the British ruler and Chakma raja (circle chief) hired some nearby Bangali farmers to teach the ways of plough cultivation in scarce plain lands. Eventually some Bangalis settled in the river-valleys, who later engaged in plough cultivation, trade, and intermediaries of the colonial rulers. Like plough cultivation, bazaar has been a remarkable induction in the hills that brought significant transformation in traditional social system. Reasonably, the bazaar exchange was totally unknown to the Pahari, which remains elusive and unmanageable to them. Thus, the British paved the path of migration of the Bangalis to begin formal trading in the hills.

Following the end of colonial rule (1947 onward), the post-colonial Pakistan government planned to harness the river and water resources of the hills to strengthen the industrialisation of Pakistan ironically in the name of "national development" and "national integration" (Dewan 1991; van Schendel et al. 2000; Tripura 2001; Mohsin 1997; Bertocci 1996). Accordingly, the Pakistan government constructed a hydroelectric dam on the Karnaphuli river *sans* local consultation that occupied some 256 square miles in Rangamati district. Immediately, the dam not only submerged nearly 54,000 acres (84.375 square miles) of best cultivable land (40 percent), it displaced almost 100,000 Paharis (mostly Chakmas) from their lands (Roy D. 2003; Shelley 1993; Mohsin 1997; Roy, C. 2000; Sopher 1963; 1964). Since the displaced Paharis had no formal titles to land (i.e. formal document of land registration), they were not well treated in the rehabilitation program staffed mainly by the Bangalis; as a result, most of them remained homeless and about 40,000 Paharis had to drive out to India and another 20,000 to Burma (Sopher 1963).

Although by the early 1970s most of the land was under occupation (Mohsin 1997); in the end of 1970s the Bangladesh government decided to send landless Bangalis into the hills as by then the plain districts became over populated while the CHT was 'erroneously' supposed to be 'empty'. The military government decided to solve the population problem of the plains evicting the Paharis from their lands. Accordingly, about 400,000 landless Bangalis were sent to the hills by 1984 that immediately displaced about 100,000 Paharis from their lands. Displaced Paharis who used to reside in the river-valleys moved into the steep high hills to reside. Eventually the cultivable lands further decreased so as the fallow period for jum cultivation. In consequence of low fertility, now they do not get sufficient crops as before. Consequently, the Paharis who were already in duress because of land scarcity caused by the dam (in 1960s) faced further survival problem caused by the transmigration program of the government (began in 1979).

In this situation, the indigenous Pahari began resisting the influx of the Bangali settlers in the CHT. In response to the resistance, the government deployed a huge number of military and other armed forces to foil the "insurgency". In consequence, many incidents of massacre, attack and reprisal attack, indiscriminate arrest & torture, killing, sexual violence, religious conversion, forced marriage, and abduction took place, often committed by the armed forces and settlers. However, a couple of initiatives led to a long-awaited accord in 1997 (widely known as "peace accord") which formally ended the two and half-decade-long bloody conflict in the hills. Still the CHT is neither a peaceful nor a secured region to its people though 15 years have elapsed since the signing of the accord. Still local bear fear in their mind both at home and outside, both at day and night. They spend time in fear of being evicted and tortured.

The "peace accord" although opened a window of opportunity toward peace, it failed to resolve conflict and violence between the Bangali and Pahari. Moreover, it pushed the Pahari into intra-Pahari (JSS-UPDF) violent conflict.

Many vital clauses of the accord are yet to be implemented. As a result, to the local, the post-accord CHT is "neither secured nor peaceful" (Mohsin 2003). Other than the employment of some Paharis, and some infrastructural development, the said "peace accord" in fact, brings no significant impact toward ensuring peace and communal harmony. Although to some commentators, the post-accord CHT is less fearful compared to Pahari and Bangali conflict; however, a new form of "fratricidal" violent conflict represents the region as a conflict zone. Under the circumstances, the present paper attempts to offer an insight into the ongoing conflicting situation, and critical transition toward peace in the CHT.

This paper is based on local perception comprehended through an anthropological investigation conducted in Rangamati district of the CHT from 2008 to 2013 using purposive sampling method. In line with the above-mentioned objectives, research tools, such as *life history*, *in-depth interview, case study, group discussion, key-informant interview* and *observation* were properly employed to grasp the native point of view. Secondary sources were also used to supplement the primary information. Data analysis by the author was supplemented also by the local's interpretations. To comprehend the dynamics of the region—continuing conflict and critical transition toward peace, this paper has been organised as follows: section one explores the root causes of conflict between the Pahari and Bangali and between the JSS and UPDF (discussed above); section two elucidates the routes to the accord; section three presents the resultant situation of the accord; section four stresses the implementation and peace process; and finally, the conclusion condenses major points of this study.

Route to Peace and its Pathways

Similar to conflict, peace does not occur automatically. Literature on peace studies suggests a number of conditions for effective peace processes. Political negotiations between a state and an insurgent group most often occur when interparty material and perceptual (military, political, social, economic, symbolic, legal, etc.) asymmetry shifts so that both adversaries recognize the other's ability to frustrate their chances of success (Dudouet 2011). Zartman (1996) calls this as a 'mutually hurting stalemate', allied to the concept of 'ripe moment': that brief moment when the playing field is acceptably level for both sides and talks become possible (Miall, Ramsbotham & Woodhouse 1999; Dudouet 2011). Therefore, armed group's interest in negotiation tends to increase when power relations shift in their favor, as it opens the possibility for bargaining on a more favorable political solution. By contrast, persistent asymmetries in favor of the state tend to impede negotiated approaches, as bargaining outcomes will necessarily reflect the interests and concerns of the more powerful side (Hopmann 2001).

The accord 1997[3] is the successful negotiation following many unsuccessful initiatives taken by different regimes since the late 1970s. Since 1975 (following the killing of Sheikh Mujibur Rahman, first prime minister of Bangladesh) successive military governments ruled Bangladesh until 1990. Negotiations between the JSS and those military governments did not progress because of lack of mutual trust, goodwill, terms of reference, mandate and scope. A negotiation becomes successful when both parties trust each other, which was materialised in 1997 between thc JSS and BAL (Bangladesh Awami League), the then ruling party. Like the, Sheikh Mujibur Rahman (the then president of BAL, the BAL government that voted to power in 1996 (after 21 years) recognised the CHT as a distinct region, which required special attention. Like Sheikh Mujib, Sheikh Hasina (daughter of Sheikh Mujib, and prime minister (1996–2001) also did not recognize the Paharis as indigenous and did not recognize their rights in the constitution for what they have been waged struggle since 1972.

Sheikh Mujib tried to persuade the Paharis that they were no more "tribes" (others/non-Bangali), and thereby he called upon them to become *Bangali* and join the mainstream population and enjoy the citizen's rights. The *father* of the Bangali nation perhaps could not perceive the spirit of the ethnic identity who devoted his entire life only to the cause of freedom of the Bangali. He had very little scope for thinking about identity of other's within Bangladesh. Following the 23-year long struggle against Pakistan and just within one year of independence of Bangladesh, it was difficult for him to pay attention to the non-Bangali while he was a nationalist leader who spent most of his time for the Bangali *jati* (nation) and Bangla *bhasha* (language). Scholars also opine that, either Pahari demand for local autonomy was untimely (earlier), or Mujib was too nationalist to make room for the non-Bangali immediately.

However, following the assassination of Sheikh Mujib engineered by a section of young military officers, and a series of coups and counter coups, Major General Ziaur Rahman[4] (as President of Bangladesh) attempted to constitute a forum named "Tribal Convention" in 1977 that continued till 1978 but failed because of lack of mutual trust. After the assassination of Ziaur Rahman, also by military officers, Lt. General H.M. Ershad (as President) took few steps toward negotiation until 1988. In the meantime, many people (Pahari, Bangali, and security forces) were killed in the armed conflict between the *shanti bahini* (military wing of JSS) and security forces during 1978 and 1988. Nevertheless, the JSS leaders, although hesitant, responded positively and put forward the following five point demands to Ershad:

- Autonomy for the CHT, including establishment of its own legislature, renaming of the region as *Jummaland*, and constitutional recognition of the Jumma nation's right to self-determination;

- Removal of Bengali [Bangali] settlers who had entered the CHT after August 1947 (the year when the CHT was annexed to Pakistan);
- Withdrawal of Bangladeshi security forces from the CHT;
- Retention of the CHT Manual of 1900 and a constitutional provision restricting any amendments to it; and
- Deployment of UN peacekeeping force.

The JSS demands were entirely been rejected by Ershad arguing that the demands were beyond the framework of the Bangladesh Constitution. The JSS also refused to alter its position on the charter of demands. Consequently, the attempts failed even before substantive negotiations could begin (Chakma 2008). However, Ershad formed the three Hill District Councils (HDCs) in CHT for the overall socio-economic development of the less developed people of this region. The HDCs are administered mainly by the Paharis as chairmen and majority members (mainly by Chakmas, Marmas and Tripuras).

Following the step-down of Ershad in the face of democratic movements, BNP was voted to power under the leadership of Khaleda Zia (widow of Ziaur Rahman) in 1991 and her government formed a nine-member multi-party Parliamentary Committee to conduct negotiation with the JSS. The JSS was very positive toward the initiative of the democratic government and announced unilateral ceasefire in August 01, 1992. Getting assurance from the Committee, JSS leaders submitted its revised five point demands. The revised JSS demands were:

- Regional autonomy for the CHT with a regional council recognised by the Constitution;
- Restoration of land rights of the tribal people with a ban on allocation of land to the Bengalis from the plains;
- Withdrawal of security forces from the CHT;
- Constitutional recognition of ethnic minorities and a guarantee that their rights would not be altered without their consent; and
- Withdrawal of Bengali settled in the CHT after 17 August 1947.

The BNP government also rejected the demands. However, following its predecessor's footsteps, the BAL that was voted to power in 1996, continued negotiations with the JSS for a settlement of the conflict and constituted a twelve-member national committee to that end. After seven rounds of grueling negotiations, an agreement was finally signed in 1997 (Chakma 2008). The motivating factors and conditions that had contributed to the accord 1997 are as follows:

- Both the GoB and JSS realised the futility of armed conflict;
- The end of Cold War in the late 1980s and geopolitical arrangement among the South Asian and East Asian countries;

- Changed role of the international organisations;
- Pressure from the donor organisations;
- Revitalised relationship between two bordering countries (Bangladesh and India);
- Relationship between the ruling Indian congress and BAL;
- Withdrawal of support from India for JSS/shanti bahini;
- JSS trusted BAL government as they used to believe in secularism.

The much talked about accord consists of major four sections:

- Recognizing the CHT as a "tribal inhabited area" first section deals with commitments to pass legislation and sets out details of the composition of a committee to oversee the implementation of the Accord.
- The second section, entitled "Hill District Local Government Councils/Hill Districts Councils," details proposed legal amendments to strengthen the District Councils' existing powers and to extend their jurisdiction to include new subjects.
- The third section, entitled "Chittagong Hill Tracts Regional Council" lays down the composition of a new unit of regional authority to be constituted and styled as a Regional Council incorporating the three hill districts. In the case of both the Regional and the District councils, the chairpersonship and two-thirds of the seats are to be reserved for "tribal" people.
- The fourth section, entitled "Rehabilitation, General Amnesty and Other Matters" addresses a wide range of issues, including the rehabilitation of international refugees, internally displaced persons and indigenous fighters, and the grant of amnesty to the guerillas and other people involved in the armed struggle (Roy 2003:9).

The Accord 1997: A Window of Hapless Hope

In order to put an end of the two and a half decades old bloody conflict, the JSS and the GoB signed the accord on 02 December 1997, which opened a new window of hope for peace, freedom, stability, and development. Unsatisfactorily, in the last 15 years that hope has not only remained unfulfilled, instead it has backfired with the potential for a new era of instability and likelihood of a future conflagration that intensified ethnic tensions even within the Paharis.

15 years already have elapsed; many questions and suspicions have arisen as to whether the accord is a failure. Conflict between the two main erstwhile protagonists, Pahari and Bangali still holds. Although the Bangalis or security forces have not been attacked by the Paharis the reverse is not true. Adversely,

the post-accord CHT witnesses the rise of a new form of violent conflict that threatens the spirit of the accord between erstwhile allies from among the Pahari autonomist activists (JSS-UPDF). Consequently, over the years, many Paharis met violent death in armed fights between these two opposing groups, known locally as the "pro-accordists" (JSS) and the "anti-accordists" (UPDF).

The commissions and omissions of the police and other government security forces regarding this conflict have led locals to believe that although these forces are ostensibly neutral, they are not interested in applying the law when the victims of the conflict are Pahari, whoever the perpetrators of the conflict might be (Roy 2003). According to the locals, the reason of such role may be the ethnic identity of the security personnel; hardly any of them belong to the local smaller ethnic groups (Pahari). In a recent case in Matiranga (03 August 2013), spreading a rumor that the Paharis kidnapped a Bangali, the Bangali settlers burnt to ashes more than 35 households of the Paharis, and another 277 houses were looted and ransacked. As the tension spread among the villagers, more than 900 families from 13 villages left the villages to take shelter in the no man's land in Indian territory. A two-month-old Chakma girl died after the horrific attack. During the hideout in the jungle, she became ill after being exposed to the heavy rains. According to the Paharis, it is a conspiracy to uproot the Paharis from their land. "It is a part of the drama that was staged mainly to grab the cultivable and livable lands of the Paharis. This rumor is nothing but a preplanned story to give birth to incidents like that." Most Pahari also believe that bias and discriminatory attitude on the part of the government help perpetuate this conflict (see, Roy 2003:6).

Complaints of non-implementation of the accord are numerous. The Bangladesh government claims that most part of the accord has been implemented, while the JSS considers this not more than ten percent; however, according to the UPDF the accord does not maintain the interests of the Paharis. On the other hand, according to many Bangali settlers the accord is a political deal between the BAL and JSS, which does not uphold the interest of the Bangalis, and of sovereignty of Bangladesh state. They also complain that the JSS and UPDF are responsible for creating conflict and killing of innocent people in the post-accord hills. Interestingly, Jyotirindra Bodhipriya Larma (J.B. Larma), known as Santu Larma the President of JSS, also Chairman of RC, who signed in the accord on behalf of the CHT people, has time and again been complained of non-implementation of the accord in no unclear terms. He recently has warned the government that if the government does not implement the accord soon they may take arms again to establish their right on their lands.

However, as stated by many locals, the accord did not address the underlying causes of conflict. Amena Mohsin writes in this regard, "While the CHT accord was meant to resolve the armed conflict between the insurgents of the CHT and the government of Bangladesh, it did not address the underlying complaints of the hill people and is thus unlikely to establish peace until the government seriously addresses these grievances" (2003:13). This is somewhat true that the accord has ended frequent armed conflict and massive violence between the two antagonists, the Pahari and the Bangali, but it satisfied none of the both. Furthermore, it instigated armed conflict within the Pahari. Indifference to the implementation or even non-implementation of the accord in the last 16 years dashed whatever hope the accord generated among the people.

The flaws of the accord in addressing the basic issues of conflict and the failure of the GoB to live up to its promise have led the peace process nowhere but to implant the seed of a more complex conflict in the future (Chakma 2008:13). Realizing the reality and consequences of the accord, within one year of the accord, Mohsin claimed that, "[the] seeds of insecurity, discontent, inequality and further polarisation are inherent within the peace accord" (1998:107). However, unlike other pessimistic scholars, Chakma *raja* (circle chief) Devasish Roy thinks:

> "Like many other accords, the CHT accord too has many shortcomings, but since political processes are always ongoing, one may hope that its shortcomings may be corrected in the future through visionary and dynamic politics. However, until such a conductive atmosphere presents itself, the most important priority for the CHT people is to have the accord implemented, especially its provisions on rehabilitations, self-government, land, demilitarisation, development and law and order" (2003:7).

Despite some flaws of the accord, still many Paharis believed, once the accord is fully implemented peace is inevitable in the hills. However they no more hope; because, 16 years have already elapsed. Moreover, the BAL government (1996–2001) which had signed the accord is passing its second term (2009–2013) soon. Only few months are left, they did not bring any significant development toward the implementation of the accord. The most important issue of land disputes remained unsolved. Still the Pahari did not get their rights on their lands; rather they have been displaced from their lands without any protection from the government/security forces. As seen in the recent incident at Matiranga (August 2013), the government security forces were reluctant while the Bangalis were evicting the Paharis from their lands and homes. In addition, although in the aftermath of the accord, conflict between the Pahari and Bangali is occasional, the regular one is violent conflict between the JSS and UPDF that killed at least 600 Pahari youths by 15 years. Therefore, one can say that on the one hand, the accord could not establish communal harmony between the Pahari and Bangali; on the other hand, it instigated violent conflict within the Pahari (JSS-UPDF).

The Accord 1997: State–JSS *sans* the Local

The "peace accord" 1997 was signed between the GoB and the JSS; on behalf of the government, chief whip of the parliament, Abul Hasnat Abdullah (as the convener of the National Committee on CHT Affairs) and on behalf of the inhabitants of CHT, Jyotirindra Bodhipriya Larma (the president of JSS) singed in the accord. The accord has been portrayed as "peace accord" nationally and internationally despite the fact that there was no place for the word, 'peace' in the whole text. Although different regimes since the late 1970s took a number of initiatives for a negotiated settlement of conflict, except few Paharis, the issue of negotiation was not consulted among the locals. The JSS is the sole organisation that merely was informed about this. Local participation and opinion was thus not ensured. Therefore, according to many Paharis, the accord was not representative, and did not reflect the opinion of the locals. Besides the UPDF who oppose the accord, some other Paharis also opine that, "the accord was signed between the BAL government and JSS; both the BAL and the JSS are fundamentalists; and political interest and power politics are their main concern."

The JSS also agreed with the accord where the Pahari of the CHT was declared as "tribal" instead of "indigenous" or "*adibashi*".[5] A Pahari says,

> "The JSS compromised our long-waged struggle with the Regional Council that has been seen as a power house for the JSS leaders."[6] "If they could convince the government to declare the Paharis as 'indigenous', among others, the land disputes would have been resolved through customary laws within the 15 what is still almost unaddressed, while land is the crux of all conflicts."

More aggrieved are the non-Chakma Paharis. To them, "it does not ensure the interest of all Pahari, the accord benefits only the JSS leaders, more particularly the Chakma." They argue, since the Chairmen of the Regional Council (RC) and District Councils (DCs) are Chakmas, and absolute majorities of these office staffs are Chakmas, non-Chakma Paharis have no capacity to avail of the facilities. In most cases, JSS members are the only 'eligible' to avail all supports and facilities allotted for the Paharis. A Tripura says, "If we see the staffs of the regional council, it seems to be second JSS office as it is staffed mostly by the JSS people." Thus, the non-Chakma, non-JSS Pahari do not find this office as their own office for what they waged about twenty-five years disregarding their own lives.

Absence of third party (national or international organisation) is also another limitation of this accord, which could oversee and mediate or arbitrate disagreements or disputes during the process of implementation of the accord. The relative success of certain peace and autonomy agreements that are strongly entrenched, such as in Mizoram, India, Italy, and South Tyrol suggest that the presence of the entrenchment clauses may provide sustainability to peace processes.[7] Given the situation, now, steps toward the implementation or non-implementation of the accord are totally on the desire of the government. Presently, in fact, the JSS or Pahari have no "real" space; for example, the Chairman of RC is not informed in major decisions, such as army pullout and brigade withdrawal. He speaks out repeatedly, but the state does not heed him. His men, the UPDF, also question his role and representation. Division and conflict within the Pahari (JSS-UPDF) weaken the demand for implementation while the government uses this advantage.

Post-Agreement Dilemmas among the Pahari

Regarding the accord a Pahari says, "The accord has destroyed our mutual harmony and peace, it boosted competition and clash of interest". He further explains, in pre-Bangladesh period, the CHT never witnessed kidnap, killing, rape, deception, and the like, and even amid these all odds, we had no internal competition for resources, or job and never got involved in armed conflict within us. In the aftermath of the accord, the region has been witnessing armed conflict, killing, extortion, corruption, and public competition within the Paharis. Clash and mistrust between Chakma, Marma, Tripura, and other groups are evident now. In the pre-accord period, the Pahari were worried about the attacks by the settlers or security forces, but now, one Pahari group are frightened by another group (e.g. JSS-UPDF tension).

The conflict among the Pahari first became known on 10 February 1998 when, led by JSS president, combatants of shanti bahini surrendered to the then prime minister, Sheikh Hasina in Khagrachhari stadium. Immediately, a breakaway faction of Pahari student and youth groups hitherto allied to the JSS—unequivocally condemned the accord as a 'sell-out" to "reactionaries" (Roy 2003:100). To them the accord was "against the interest of the Pahari, against the spirit of the Jumma nationalism and it was a compromise between government and JSS" and vowed to continue its struggle for "complete autonomy" that later formed the UPDF in 1998. They also criticized the accord for not having provisions on constitutional safeguards, for being unclear on land rights and for absence of provisions on the withdrawal of the military personnel and the repatriation of transmigrated Bangali settlers outside the hills.[8] Since then, conflict between the JSS and UPDF has been a common contesting issue in the hills. Many Pahari have been killed by Pahari in "fratricidal" clashes. Attack, counter-attack, killing, counter-killing have become common phenomena in the hills. As a result, in every month Paharis kill Paharis in JSS-UPDF violence. In first six months of 2013, at least twenty Paharis (mostly from among the Chakma) from both factions were killed, hundreds were kidnapped and hurt.

Thus, the reason behind the conflict between the JSS and UPDF has its roots in the accord 1997. Many Paharis even believe that the security forces assist the UPDF. They patronize the UPDF by giving arms and cover to demoralize and weaken the JSS, so that, JSS lost its absolute power to press the government to implement the accord. The reason behind peoples' perception is so, that the UPDF has been committing incidents against the JSS staying at a close distance to the army camps. Some people also opine, "Where the JSS is weaker than the UPDF, army assist the JSS against the UPDF, and where the UPDF is weaker, they get the army's support against the JSS". Local believe that, the security forces, especially the military forces want the continuation of conflict and violence in the hills in order to justify their deployment. The security forces, particularly the military forces enjoy the absolute power and facilities.

Besides the JSS-UPDF conflict, competition for job, business, and education are among the conflicting issues even within the Pahari. Non-Chakma Paharis complaint, the Chakma occupy the maximum facilities in job and education sectors. There are some "tribal" quotas in government jobs and educational institutions (college, university), where almost all posts have been occupied by the Chakma. Since their literacy rate is higher than other Pahari groups, and they have their own people in all sectors, they manage to avail all advantages of the quota system. For example, the non-Chakma blame that, there are very few fortunate non-Chakma students who got approval to avail the scholarship from Rangamati in the "Australian Development Scholarship for Indigenous candidates from the CHT": in 2009, out of 20, 16 students were Chakmas, 02 Marmas, 01 Tanchangya, 01 Bawm and none from the rest 9 groups.

The Paharis are not sure which era was/is good for them: pre or post accord. They cannot differentiate qualitatively. They do not know the future of accord and their survival. They even do not know what the BAL has been doing with them. They are in dilemma whether they should lose hope or try again to gain indigenous rights. They are not sure whether they will be able to take arms against the state security forces; many think, it would "difficult" indeed. Many leading Paharis have been assuming power, money and politics that got positions in RC, HDC, CHT development board, parliament and ministry. Therefore, it would be difficult to get back them from the mainstream power politics and involve in jungle war.

Bangali Perception about the 1997 Agreement

Like the Pahari, the Bangali have also mixed reactions about the accord; however, the substance of agreement and disagreement regarding the accord is not necessarily the same. Like the Pahari, old Bangali (also known as *adibashi* Bangali) are happy with the accord hoping that it might resolve the existing crisis and establish harmony and peace, and there would be no intervention by army or shanti bahini. They both want peace, harmony and uninterrupted life. However, while some Pahari opine that the accord failed to ensure the representation of all Pahari, almost all Bangali settlers oppose the accord. To them, the accord is "discriminatory" against the Bangali interest. Moreover, in pre-accord rime, they had many means of livelihood like fishing, wood/bamboo collection. They used to maintain these by give and take relationship (paying dues to) with shanti bahini. In the aftermath of the accord, they are to maintain the relation (paying dues) with both JSS and UPDF, and sometimes even with some other armed "gangs".

According to the Bangali settlers, "During the pre-accord time the Paharis used to maintain a relationship with us so that we do not harm or attack them, but, in the post-accord time, we observe behavioral changes (anti-Bangali) among them; they possibly think that the CHT would be separated from Bangladesh, and settlers would be ousted from the hills." They also state, "The Pahari are enjoying almost all facilities; nobody oversees our situations. Since the accord, many national, regional and international NGOs have been functioning in the hills; almost all NGO staffs are from among the Pahari, and their activities highlight only the welfare of the Pahari. In international NGOs, like, UNDP, WFP, DANIDA, salaries vary from Taka 40,000"100,000, whereas with very good academic records Bangali are doing jobs with salaries between Taka 5,000"20,000. Given the situation, most Bangalis do not support the accord and protest against the NGO activities that give preference only the Pahari, not the poor and vulnerable.

Although, among the plain land Bangali, some intellectuals, progressive persons and progressive political parties, are in favor of the accord; national political parties, such as BNP, Jamaat, Islamist parties, and even BAL maintain reservation about it. To many Bangali settlers, the accord signed by the BAL government was "too conciliatory" toward the Pahari; and "unnecessary and self-destroying" for the Bangalis who have been settled there under a government-sponsored population transfer program. To the Bangali settlers, their issues were not addressed in the accord, when they hear that the government is serious to implement the accord, they fear whether they would be ousted from the hills, when they hear that military would be withdrawn, they fear whether the Paharis would kill them.

In protest against the accord, the settlers also formed few organisations to establish their "citizen rights". *Samo Adhikar Andolon* (Equal Rights Movement) is one of them whose main patron is Abdul Wadud Bhuiyan, a Bangali leader who was also a Member of Parliament (MP) from Khagrachhari constituency on BNP ticket and later he became the Chairman of Chittagong Hill Tracts Development Board (CHTDB) during BNP rule (2001"2006). Among the Bangali settlers who are supporter or activists of BAL though do not support the accord by heart; however, do not protest against it. Although the BAL government signed the accord, many believe that they are also not serious to implement the accord. They do not want to lose electoral support of the Bangalis who now constitute 50 percent of the total population of CHT. The implementation process, speed and other related activities and attitudes also maintain this view.

Politics of Peace, and Pending Peace

The historic accord was warmly welcomed throughout the world and the then Prime Minister of Bangladesh was awarded the UNESCO Peace Prize (in 1998) for the "Peace Accord"; however, the fact is that, the accord itself has no significant impact on the lives of the Pahari even after 15 years of its signing. Moreover, mere implementation of the accord cannot bring about significant changes regarding the establishment of peace, especially given the polarisation that has emerged within the Pahari, and where the mainstream political parties are markedly divided on the accord.

In 1997, when the BAL government and the JSS reached to the accord, it was not accepted by the opposition parties such as the BNP, Jamaat and others though the BNP government had many meetings with JSS aiming to reach an agreement while they were in power (1991"96). However, following the political culture of Bangladesh, like all other issues, the accord was rejected by the then opposition party BNP and some other Islamist parties. During the BAL regime, the BNP called strike to cancel the accord, but during its own tenure (2001"06), they did not cancel or withdraw it. Indeed, it implemented a few aspects of the accord. It indicates that, the BNP also wants same kind of accommodation with the Pahari.

However, following the imposition of the state of emergency (2007"08), BAL again came to power in 2009. In its election manifesto, they promised that if voted to power, it would implement the accord fully.[9] Assuming the power, the BAL government formed an "Agreement Implementation Committee". This committee already has taken few visual steps toward the implementation of the accord. It declared (in July 2009) withdrawn of a brigade and few temporary camps from the hills. BNP, Jamaat and a few other parties as well as settlers groups protested against the decision. A land commission was also formed to resolve the land disputes. The committee also cancelled some illegal leases in accordance with the accord. That's all. They already have passed their tenure (2009–2013); however, failed to show any effective measure aiming to implement the unimplemented clauses of the "peace accord". They are rather embittering the Pahari by refusing to recognize them as "indigenous people" in the constitution. Although in the manifesto they mentioned the Pahari as indigenous people (adibashi); however, the BAL government officially proclaimed that there are no adibashi in Bangladesh but some "small ethnic minorities". Thus, the "peace accord" remained contested and peace remains pending in the hills– an ongoing issue for politicisation.

Critical Transition to Peace

The problem in the hills is not new. It had old historical roots; new dimensions were added to them during the Pakistan and Bangladesh periods (Chowdhury 2002). The existing crisis has been nurtured by the politics of *nationalism*, politics of *ethnicity*, and politics of *peace*. The disparity against the Pahari has been created from the *above*. Hostile state policies, attitude of the political parties, and activities of the security forces—all have been contributed to the continuation of the crisis.

Throughout the actions and reactions of different stakeholders, we see a complex situation in the CHT. At least 50 percent inhabitants (most Bangalis and some Paharis) of the CHT are discontented with the accord and post-accord development programs. Although it is true that Pahari-Bangali conflict reduced apparently in the aftermath of the accord, still peace does not exist in the hills as 'absence of violence is not peace'. The impressions of different section of people and stakeholders given below indicate the critical transition in the hills.

- **Bangladesh government**: The accord 1997 was signed between the JSS and Bangladesh government. At that time BALwas in power, they already passed 8 years in power after the signing of the accord (1996"2000; 2009"2013); however, could not bring significant changes toward peace in the hills. Vital issues remain unimplemented such as land issue, which has been considered as the crux of hill problems. According to many, the BAL government signed the accord for political benefit and international recognition. They are not serious about the implementation of the accord. They inspired much hopes but people became hopeless at the end. On the other hand, BNP and Islamist parties had protested against the accord, but did not cancel it when they were in power (2001"2006). When BNP and Islamist parties come to power most Pahari displease since they (BNP and Islamist parties) protested against the accord and did nothing for the betterment of the Paharis in accordance with the accord. However, the settlers feel happy as they were settled in the hills assisted by the military government in 1979 while Ziaur Rahman (founder of BNP) was President of Bangladesh. The Paharis became hopeful while the BAL assumed power in 2009 but later disappointed with the reluctance of the government.

- **The Pahari**: The Pahari were consolidated until 1980s; however, until 1997 they hoped for a democratic and autonomous CHT, but disappointed soon. In the aftermath of the accord 1997, the minority groups consider of being deprived and discriminated by the dominant groups. There exist two violent factions even in the dominant group Chakma: JSS and UPDF. In effect, we observe mixed actions and reactions among the Pahari. The JSS who signed the accord 1997 and supported wholeheartedly, has threatened the government to implement the accord to avoid further armed resistance in the hills. Although already 16 years have passed, according to the JSS, not more than 10 percent of the accord was implemented. On the other hand, the UPDF, which was born as a response to protest the accord, not only protest against the accord, are involved with violent conflict with the JSS. In effect, JSS-UPDF conflicts have become an everyday matters began in 1998, continues increasingly and violently. The Paharis that even do not support the UPDF, and are not dominant among the Paharis (e.g. Bawm, Mro, Pangkhoa) consider of being ignored and deprived. They believe that in the name of interests of the Paharis, the dominant groups (i.e. Chakma, Marma, and Tripura) avail all facilities. In consequence, besides the inter-ethnic (Pahari-Bangali) conflict, intra-ethnic (dominant vs minority indigenous groups and and JSS Chakma vs UPDF Chakma), and other groups keep the region as a conflict zone.
- **The Bangali**: There are two sections among the Bangali in the CHT: *adibashi* (indigenous/old) Bangali (who settled before 1971), and the settler Bangali (settled after 1971, largely through the population transfer program began in 1979). The adibashi Bangalis want restoration of peaceful coexistence in the hills while being the majority the settlers want power and supremacy over the Pahari. They do not support the accord because as they believe once the accord is implemented the Pahari will be given back rights on their lands already occupied by the settlers. Some BAL supporters support the accord as a political weapon; however, the supporters of BNP and Islamist parties do not support it saying that the accord was signed against the interest of the Bangalis and sovereignty of Bangladesh state.
- **Civil society**: In fact, many people in the plains do not know much about what have been going on in the CHT. Most of the Bangali do not know more than three ethnic groups' name (i.e. Chakma, Marma, and Tripura). Many know the Paharis as Chakma or shanti bahini who oftentimes used to "kill" the settlers. Many Bangalis

believe if the accord was implemented fully and if the military forces were withdrawn from the hills, they will be killed or ousted from the hills. The supporters of BNP and Islamic parties do not support the demands of the Paharis. The supporters of BAL support the accord politically, but do not support other demands of the Paharis. Both the BNP and BAL consider the impression of the 50 percent people of the CHT, the Bangalis. However, some civil society people support the Pahari for their indigenous rights e.g. leftist politicians, journalist, intellectuals, and university teachers. They take part in various programs called by the Pahari in the hills and plain districts (Dhaka/Chittagong).

- **Military forces**: One of the major factors in the CHT is the presence or withdrawal of the military and other security forces. Although there is a clause for gradual withdrawal of military forces from the hills still the militaries are the main authority in the hills, still the military operation has been functioning in the hills. The military forces do not want to come back from the hills in the name of security and peace. However, most Paharis believe that the army do not want to go back to barrack because they can enjoy the absolute power in the hills. While almost all Paharis want the withdrawal of the military forces from the hills, the Bangali do not support this, they want army for their safety. According to the Pahari unless the military forces were withdrawn from the hills their life would be fearful. Here it is noteworthy to mention that the military forces wish to work in two lucrative places: one is the UN peace mission, and the other is the CHT. As stated by many Paharis, the military forces are like the "king of the jungle" in the hills. "They will not leave CHT. For their own interest (money & power), they want conflict to be continued to justify their stay as "king".
- **Implementation of the accord 1997**: If we look into the accord, we see no significant progress toward peace. Land issue remains unsolved; settler Bangali issue remains uncertain. In the last 16 years, the land commission failed to give back the rights of the Pahari on their ancestral lands. In fact, except some structural and visible changes, the accord has no significant achievement in the hills.

Throughout the study it contents, transition to peace in the hills is not only critical but also very difficult. No sign has been seen for the recovery from the existing predicaments.

Concluding Remarks

Although the accord already has passed 16 years since it was signed, many vital issues are yet to be addressed. Although it officially has ended armed conflict between the Pahari and the security forces (including Bangalis); nevertheless, it cannot be said that peace exists in this region; because, 'absence of violence is not peace'. Still, people are living there in fear, where fear became 'a part of their life'! In effect, the post-accord CHT is still not a peaceful region for its inhabitants. Some studies precisely shows, fundamental causes were not addressed in the accord (Roy 2003), while some other studies adds that slow pace of implementation or even non-implementation has dashed whatever hope the agreement generated (Chakma 2008); however, the local dynamics remained unaddressed.

Based on the findings, this paper indicates that the following issues are responsible for the continuing conflict in the hills that eventually make the transition critical:

(a) flaws in the accord; (b) non-acceptance of the accord by a section of the Pahari; (c) continuous displacement; (d) intra-Pahari (JSS-UPDF) conflict over domination/supremacy; (e) military intervention; (e) lack of political will from the GoB; (f) non-implementation of vital clauses of the accord; and (g) mistrust and hatred between the two antagonists (Pahari and Bangali).

As mentioned before the accord was signed *sans* the local. Both the Pahari and Bangali were uninformed about it. The underlying issues of conflict were also not adequately addressed in the accord, for example, land disputes, punishment of the people who violated the human rights, and the like. Most importantly, the accord is ambiguous about the military and settler issues; though today, the Bangali are about 50 percent of the hill population their issues were not addressed in the accord: whether they would be repatriated to plain districts; if not, how they would be coexisted with the Pahari. Mutual distrust and hatred between the Pahari and Bangali could not be removed until and unless a comprehensive measure is taken to resolve the crisis and to establish communal harmony. As a result, the roads to peace have become more difficult, as elucidated by Amena Mohsin (2003).

Throughout the study it contents that, the continuing conflict in the hills is evident as peace stays far from the hills, still people bear fear in their mind; and thus, fear has become part of their everyday life. Clearly, the accord 1997 failed to bring significant changes toward peace and freedom. Therefore, there are two equal possibilities: (a) going back to ethnic conflict or continuation of the conflicting situation, and (b) toward peaceful coexistence. First possibility is inevitable if proper measures are not taken for the second one. The ongoing predicaments will continue if necessary initiatives are not taken timely and properly; and, the transition will remain critical or difficult. In order to go with peace, many appropriate measures are pre-requisite to implement involving people from all sectors: JSS, UPDF, ordinary Paharis, security forces, adibashi Bangalis and settler Bangalis. The peace deal should be comprehensive and holistic; politico-economic as well as minority issues must be included in the process.

Notes

1. Ten percent of the total land area of Bangladesh; but population is about one percent (1.6 million out of 160 million). The CHT comprises three administrative hill districts: Rangamati, Bandarban and Khagrachhari.
2. Although 11 ethnic groups (Mongoloid) are recognised as ethnic groups or "tribe" in the hills (according to estimated size): *Chakma, Marma, Tripura, Mro, Tanchangya, Bawm, Pangkhoa, Chak, Kheyang, Khumi,* and *Lushai;* there are two unrecognised groups: *Gurkha* and *Ahom* who have been living in the hills since the British colonial period. The mainstream population Bangalis have joined by transmigrations largely arriving since the late 1970s; together they now form the largest ethnic group in the region (Mohsin 2003; Roy 2000; Roy 2003).
3. The accord 1997 was signed between the GoB (Government of Bangladesh, National Committee on CHT Affairs) and the JSS (on behalf of the inhabitants of CHT).
4. Founder of Bangladesh Nationalist party (BNP), also founder of Bangladeshi nationalism in place of *Bangali* nationalism.
5. The Pahari prefer to call them indigenous people (*adibashi*) while the state and Bangali are against of calling adibashi, as they believe that Pahari are not *adibashi*, they are rather immigrants. To Bangali, Pahari are "tribe" (*upajati*).
6. JSS president J.B. Larma (popularly known as Santu Larma) has been Chairman of the Regional Council since 1998 with the status of State Minister. Among the four members of the council (three from JSS) one from Chakma, one from Marma, one from Tanchangya, and one from Bangali.
7. The Mizoram agreement is constitutionally protected by a "double entrenchment" clause, which safeguards against changes other than through an amendment to the Indian Constitution (requiring a specific majority in parliament) and without the contest of the Mizoram State Assembly (see, Nunthera 2002). In the case of the South Tyrolean autonomy, it is protected by a bilateral treaty between Italy and Austria (see, Woelk 2003). See also, Roy 2003:22.
8. Proshit Bikash Khisha, UPDF leader, Interview published in *Earth Touch* (No. 4, March 1998, SEHD, Dhaka, Bangladesh, 1998) 10-11.
9. The government led by the BAL (1996-2001) was quick to hail it as a "historic accord", repeatedly invoking it as one of its major success stories (Roy 2003:1516).

References

Ahmed, Aftab. "Ethnicity and Insurgency in the Chittagong Hill Tracts Region: A Study of the Crisis of Political Integration in Bangladesh", *Commonwealth & Comparative Politics* 31 (3) 1993: 3266.

Chakma, Bhumitra. "Assessing the 1997 Chittagong Hill Tracts Peace Accord", Asian Profile 36 (1) 2008: 93106.

Dudouet, Ve'ronique. Nonviolent resistance in power asymmetries. In: Beatrix Austin, Martina Fischer & Hans J Giessmann (eds), *Advancing Conflict Transformation: The Berghof Handbook II*, pp. 237–264. Opladen: Barbara Budrich. 2011.

Dudouet, Ve'ronique. *From war to politics: Resistance/liberation movements in transition*. Berghof Report 17. Berlin: Berghof Foundation. 2009.

Dudouet, Ve'ronique. Dynamics and factors of transition from armed struggle to nonviolent resistance. *Journal of Peace Research* 50(3) 2013:401–413.

Gurkha, Manju Rani. "Disappearing Gurkhas", *Dhaka Courier* (August 7) 1998:39.

Hopmann, P Terrence. Bargaining and problemsolving: Two perspectives on international negotiation. In: Chester A Crocker, Fen O Hampson & Pamela Aall (eds), *Turbulent Peace: The Challenge of Managing International Peace*, pp. 445–468. Washington, DC: USIP Press. 2001.

International Work Group on Indigenous Affairs (IWGIA). *The Indigenous World: 2000-2001*. Copenhagen: IWGIA. 2002.

Lewin, Thomas H. *A Fly on the Wheel, or How I Helped to Govern India*. London: Constable. 1912.

Mohsin, Amena. *The Chittagong Hill Tracts, Bangladesh: On the Difficult Road to Peace*. Boulder, London: Lynne Rienner Publishers. 2003.

Mohsin, Amena. "Chittagong Hill Tracts Peace Accord: Looking Ahead", *The Journal of Social Studies* AugOct 1998:104117.

Mohsin, Amena. *The Politics of Nationalism: The Case of the Chittagong Hill Tracts*. Dhaka: The University Press Limited. 1997.

Majumdar, Chandrika Basu. *Genesis of Chakma Movement in Chittagong Hill Tracts*. Kolkata: Progressive Publishers. 2003.

Miall, Hugh; Oliver Ramsbotham & Tom Woodhouse. *Contemporary Conflict Resolution: The Prevention, Management and Transformation of Deadly Conflict*. Cambridge: Polity. 1999.

Nunthera, C. "Peace Accords as Instruments of Conflict Transformation: Arrangements that Work and Arrangements that Don't (Mizo Accord, 1986, Assam Accord, 1985, Bodo Accord, 1993)". Paper presented at the workshop on Dimensions, Dynamics and Transformation of Resource Conflicts between Indigenous Peoples and Settlers in Frontier Regions of South and Southeast Asia, held in Mont-Soleil, Canton of Berne, Switzerland, on 2529 September, 2002.

Roy, Rajkumari Chandra. *Land Rights of the Indigenous Peoples of the Chittagong Hill Tracts, Bangladesh*. Copenhegen: Internation Work Group for Indigenous Affairs (IWGIA). 2000.

Roy, Raja Devasish. "The Discordant Accord: Challenges Towards the Implementation of the Chittagong Hill Tracts accord of 1997", *The Journal of Social Studies* Vol. 100 (June) 2003: 457.

Roy, Raja Devasish. Challenges for Judicial Pluralism and Customary Laws of Indigenous Peoples: The Case of the Chittagong Hill Tracts, Bangladesh", *Arizona Journal of International and Comparative Law* 21(1) 2004: 180.

Shelly, Mizanur Rahman. *The Chittagong Hill Tracts of Bangladesh: The Untold Story.* Dhaka: Centre for Development Research. 1992.

Sopher, D.E. "The Swidden/Wet-Rice Transition Zone in the Chittagong Hills". *Annals of the Association of American Geographers* Vol. 54, 1964:101122.

van Schendel, Willem et al. *The Chittagong Hill Tracts: Living in a Borderland.* Bangkok: White Lotus. 2000.

van Schendel, Willem. "The Invention of the 'Jhumma': State Formation and Ethnicity in South Eastern Bangladesh", *Modern Asian Studies*, Vol. 26 (1) 1992:135173.

Woelk, Jens. "From Compromise to Process: The Implementation of the South Tyrolean Autonomy Arrangement". Paper presented at the Expert Meeting Kreddha and UNESCO, Catalunya, Barcelona, 913 May, 2003.

Zartman, I. William. *Elusive Peace: Negotiating an End to Civil Wars.* Washington, DC: Brookings Institute. 1996.

8

The Impact of Globalisation on Industrialisation process in Tribal areas with special reference of Mising tribe of Dhemaji district in Assam

Juganando Medok and Mantu Hazarika

Introduction.

Mising in the distance past were dwellers of present day Arunachal Pradesh in the valley Siang River for long time. As they migrated towards lower valley, they were known as 'Miri'. They have migrated in search larger area of fertile land for cultivation. The 'Adi' and the Mising have strong affinity in cultural and linguistic aspects. So, it is believed that they migrated to the Brahmaputra valley in distant past, of which there is no historical record. As per from holy 'Kritan-ghosha' a devotional poetic works, of Great saint Sankerdev, there is mention of 'Miri', along with Khasi, Kachari, and Garo tribes of north-east. Even he had Miri disciple named Paramananda. During the reign of Ahom in Assam, historical records show that there was armed conflict between Ahom and Miri in 1615, 1655, 1685, so on.

Misings tribe is one of the indigenous tribes of Assam. They belong to Tibeto-Burman Family of Mongoloid group. The Misings are mainly found in eight district of Assam namely, Sonitpur, Golaghat, Jorhat, Sivasagar, Dibrugarh, Tinisukia, Lakhimpur and Dhemaji. They are enlisted as schedule tribe (plain) in Assam. They are second largest tribes of Assam after the Bodo tribe.

According to the census report of India, 2001, the total population of the Mising in the state of Assam was 587310, of which 299895 (male) 51.60 percent and 287410(female), 48.94 percent. About 98.2 percent of the Mising population dwell in rural area and negligible 1.77 percent dwells in urban area. The Mising tribes constitute 17.8 percent of the total schedule tribe population of Assam. The same census reveals that 517170 (88%) is speaks Mising language as their mother tongue and remaining 12% have switched off to Assamese language. In case literacy rate 60.1% of the population is literate and male/female differentiation goes as 71.4% and 48.3% respectively.

This paper would try to analyse the impact of globalisation on industrialisation process in tribal areas with special reference Mising tribe of Dhemaji district in Assam in the following way.

Industrialisation

In today's fast changing world, every communities of the state is seen to coping with the dynamic motion. Mising community is of no exemption. Mainly small scale industries are seen set up in various part of inhabitant of the people. Handicraft of their own dress is one unique features of the women community of Mising. Home spun clothes for whole house hold members preferred by the people. In every household there is seen a handlooms mechanism on which the women of the family weaves when they feel a leisure time. Mising have their own cultural dress and they are much concern about it. As seen in their festival, Ali-Ayeng Ligang, each and every one of the society dress up in their own tradition way. Because of its uniqueness in embroidery there is vast demand in the market of Assam scenario. As now a day many actress and actors of Assam prefer the traditional dress of Mising in their shooting.

Many of the youngsters now seen to taking up the production of the traditional dress and market them in various part of Assam. One of them is Mrs. Sangeeta Mili, who is running a industries in the Dhemaji town. Engaging about 34 girls who are also pursuing their higher education in Dhemaji College, Dhemaji Commerce College, Dhemaji Girls College and Dhemaji higher Secondary School etc.Mrs Sangeeta's is seen to and fro to various parts of the country for marketing her products in various handlooms and textile expos. Also in the subdivision Jonai, border area of Assam there is various small scale industries for production of the traditional dress seen set-up by the Mising people. It also covers various parts of Arunachal Pradesh, As there is close affinities with the Adi tribes.

Above this, there is now growing a picture of rearing of cattle for business purpose. Rearing of goats, cows, oxen, buffaloes, pigs ducks chicken (domestic and broiler) and even setting- up various tanks for fish framing. Fish and pig has a great religious importance. Because almost every household puja or ceremonial programme they always scarifies a pig or hen or fish. For this purpose there is great demand for these things among the community. Ox and buffaloes are also reared for agricultural. Demand of milk to the various town of district is fulfilled by Mising people. Rearing of cattle in large is the chance to contribute milk as per the demand. Now people have taken to rear hybrid cows for more production of milk.

Business Aspects

Business is one of the source livelihoods in modern world. Business umbrella is the one that give one a personal status and dignity. Business was a night-mare for Mising around fifties of the last century, while referring to the mentioned district. Communication barrier was the main inconvenience on this account, as there was no developed road infra-structure in the district. Being record as one of the backward district of India till the date is lacking behind in various way. Railways in various part of the country is experiencing super-fast track but the said district is seen building broad-gauge line today. Though having this hurdles before them, people are striving themselves to walk in shoulder to shoulder with changing world.

There are few energetic young men who all are challenging in taking up entrepreneurship and establishing one own business opportunity. Numol Pegu, form Gorpara village of the district, has set-up own rice mill and market the rice to various parts of the district. He, not only, run the mill but also cultivates large area of paddy. The said person is a LL.B from Guahati University. Moving away from his track went to make one own's fortune in business. Presently, his assets are around 50 (fifty) lacs. As informed from his end, he could not have made the said assets by going to court or opt for government Job.

Next Mr. Binod Doley of Gogomukh, a fast growing town of the said district, has made considerable assets for being a government registered contractor. He runs many buses and small cars/transports as his business. Above this he has large fish framing tanks in scientific methods. For this he always keep close contact with government fishery department of the district. As he informs that he has acquired subsidised schemed loans from the department. He has built around twenty rooms for business purpose at Gogomukh town itself. So, this individual set-up business is rarely seen among the Mising community.

In various towns of the district, many youngsters are seen to set-up grocery shop or pork selling shop for their livelihood. In olden days these ways of livelihood was a negligible for the people. The changing scenario of this society is admirable step. This was because of the illiteracy among the society. Now, education umbrella have brought to eye and intellect the way of living, which they have taken to their heart and execute their own business.

Agricultural Aspects

Mising is one of the indigenous tribe of Assam who depends on agriculture for livelihood. Impact of industrialisation in the field of agriculture is reflected in using of tractors and other machinery equipments ploughing and harvesting.

Average people are stilling depending on the traditional way of framing. But new phase development in agro-sector has reached to interior part of Mising people. As people are using tractors for ploughing for quickness and better yield of the corps. Being seclude tribes of Assam, they are benefitted by govt subsidy to attain the machineries.

Pesticides use on corps was ignorance to these people till the last decades but time had led them learn how and when to use. Before they think that use of pesticides and minerals/organic manure make the soil less fertile. They were not aware well product in using the said materials. They only use cow dung as manure in the field. Mainly paddy is staple food of them. But being riverside their abode mustard oil corps cultivation is produced to large extends for financial benefits. Some cereals are also produced along with the other corps.

Recently in various part of the district, people have taken-up the plantation of rubber, jetropa, and tea plantation as their occupation. Mr. Bhupen Patir, of Jonai sub-division needs mention in connection rubber plantation. An area of about 15 acres of rubber plantation has done individually. It is really a bold step by him and he deserves to be innovator rubber plantation among the Mising people in the district. Following his step another planter namely, Mr. Jugendra Medok of Dhemaji sub-division also took up the same process of plantation. He too, is building good benefits from the plantation. Large people are taking up this benefit in small scale. There are many small tea planters in the district from the community. Of which, Mr. Robin Permey, is significant one. Being government service holder, he has large tea estate as his assets. Earning from the estate bring him more benefits than the service. Mr. Jukta Kumbang ailing from Silapather, has also large tea estate as assets. He is political leader and due to the political advantage he has acquired large area land from the government.

Cultural Aspects

Culture is the identity of a society. Each society has its own identical culture and of which Misings is of no exception. In this case we can say of the Mising folk-song namely oi:nitom, is now popular among the Assamese people. Noted singer of Assam like Zubeen Grag, Manash Robin had picked up in Mising Language and released album of them. Next,comes the Mekhela-Sadar(traditional dress for women) is popuplar among the other culture.It is because of its unique embroidery, colour combination and differentness in flower embroidery mark out it. So, it is seen that many women and girls of the village is producing the said Mekhela-sadar and sells it financial benefits. Therefore, it is seen that various community people is setting up small-scale industries for production of said cloth as per demand. It uniqueness in handicraft mark its demand.

Environmental Aspects

Misings people from the remote past prefer river valley as its abode. For which, flood is one of the common problem face by them. The people were not accustomed to cleanliness or proper sanitation in old days. But for the blessing of modern education and information technology, there is seen a changing scenario in the villages of Misings. Thatched-roofed house are seen to change to concrete one. Mising people use to collect river water for drinking in remote time. Today, Government scheme for pure drinking water have reached to the people. There is a customary way of drinking Apong (rice-beer of Mising people), along with lunch and dinner by the people. Some changed have occurred. Many of the youngsters are avoiding it for good. The adults are also seen limiting its use in both house-hold purpose and even in religious purpose. Gambling with card was also one characteristic of many villagers. Today, that is rarely pictured. This change is due to the influence of the other society and educational globalisation. Many N.G.O.s and government programme have help a lot in up-rooting these illness of the society.

Education Aspects

Mising people are based on agriculture for their livelihood, which were less aware of the blessing of education. Most of elderly people prefer their children to work in field rather than going to school. Till the date, many villages of Mising dominated area is deprived from a lower-primary school within its boundary. Though it may shock to intellectual group but it's a true fact.

Today, their world is changing. As by the influence of the other progressed society and government's scheme for free and compulsory education has brought drastic change. Many doctors Engineers, M.B.A.s, Graduate, and post graduate has been produced in large scale. People now becoming learned have took jobs in different sectors and various part of the country. Accumulating with education and experiences these people come back to their native place, impart their contribution in industrialisation and betterment of the people. The strong touches to their near and dear ones of the people do help in great extend in the development of the society.

Political Aspects

India is one of the largest democratic in the world. Mising, being people of this umbrella, is not out of politics. But in remote days they were totally ignorant of government policies and benefits of politics. They have, very lately, granted autonomous status in the state. Now they run their own people under Mising Autonomous Council, its head quarter at Gogamukh, in Dhemaji of Assam. New generation is well aware of the benefits of the politics, as many of them are seen to take up politics as profession. So, some of them are Member of Legislative Assembly of Assam. Many of them had joined various political parties (national and state) and holding dignified position. These people have brought various schemes to the village like building community hall, cultural auditorium, setting-up state dispensary, drinking water programme, development of village playground and graveyard etc.

The aforesaid council is keen in taking up various measures for developing industrialisation. It provides fund for setting up small-scale industries like handloom-textile, piggery farming, fishery farming, banana plantation, grilling industry etc.

Conclusion

From the above discussion we can conclude that impact of globalisation on industrialisation process of the Mising tribe of Dhemaji district of Assam. it has presented about the initial development in the said sector. Though various small-scale industries setting-up are mentioned but in true sense it can't be said as the latest development. But for a backward community, the initiative led by the mentioned people is really a admirable step and the community need to count.

Reference

Taid Tabu Ram. 2010- A Dictionary of the Mising Language, Anundoram Borooah Institute of Language, Art and Culture, Assam.

Kulkarni, M.G. 1974- Problems of Tribal Develoment, A case Study, Praimal Prakashan Aurangabad.

Allen, B.C. 1926 – Assam District Gazetteer, Lakhimpur vol. III.

9

Impact of Globalisation on Tribal Life and Culture

Swapan Kumar Kolay

Introduction

Globalisation has been in existence since the rise of trade link between Sumer and Indus Valley Civilisation in the third millennium B.C. (Frank, 1998). In India, the New Economic Policy that was globalisation initiated in 1991 under the leadership of the Congress Party led P. V. Narsimha Rao Government. Impact of Globalisation both theoretically and practically, can be observed in different economic, social, cultural, political, finance and technological dimensions of the world (Pratheep, 2010). Over the last decade, the open market policy of the Indian Government has resulted in increased privatisation, huge lay-off of labor, rise of corruption and heavy debts on the nation. The benefits of development touted under globalisation have not reached the poorest sections of the society. The disparity between the rich and the poor has widened. Its disturbing impact on family and the drastic erosion of traditional social life is a main concern.

The Indian situation is very complex and complicated as we enter the new millennium. Sixty four years of independence did bring some changes but not to the larger poor and the marginalised sections of the society. Politically, the situation is very unstable and by and large, people have little faith in organised political parties. Corruption and lack of integrity have exposed national leaders and ordinary people are in real confusion as to their political role. The emergence of communalism in its new forms has undermined national unity along with regionalism and linguistic problems. The women still remain marginalised. Environmental issues have taken a prominent place in the agenda of the social activists but the modern develop-mentalists are advocating interference with nature and building up of dams etc., as the only way for the development for India.

The compulsions of international competition have created greater pressures to exploit the natural resources that India has. There is an impetus towards greater concentration of these resources and moves towards concentration accumulation. The victims of this accumulation are the small landholders, in other words, the Dalits, Adivasis and the members of Other Oppressed Castes. Agriculture has, under the new auspices, acquired corporate logic. Traditional methods of sustainable farming are threatened today.

The withdrawal of the State from welfare and public services spheres also has deleterious impacts, especially on the weaker sections. Their food security is affected adversely, their access to health care services, education and employment has become even more restricted, housing and transport facilities have gone beyond their reach. With liberalisation, the problem becomes complex as rapid economic growth unaccompanied with a social safety net increase disparity as only a small section of society benefit. Today the process of Globalisation and its impact on culture, both local and national, give it a new urgency (Singh, 1994).

In the post independent era, prime importance was given to mega infrastructure projects in India to build it up as an industrially developed nation in the world scenario. A number of developmental projects in the form aluminum, iron and steel plants, reservoirs, large hydel and irrigation projects have been launched in the last six decades. Several international agencies have also extended their hand to the national organisations in order to make these programmes successful and sustainable.

Mega development projects, be it irrigation, power, mining, steel, alumina, ports, railways or irrigation land to large scale displacement. Acquisition of private land for different developmental projects creates involuntary displacement by the affecting people's life in a very painful ways. They lose their home and heart and also snatch away the only source of their livelihood. "Both displacement and rehabilitation processes be set with risk factors like landlessness, homelessness, joblessness, marginalisation, food insecurity and social disarticulation which often culminate in material impoverishment and social disintegration of displaced families (Cerena, 1988; 1996)". "Development versus displacement" has become a debatable issue in recent years.

Land is the basic input for any development project. But the land acquisition, which leads to displacement, immediately shatters the social, economical and environmental scenario of the people in the project area. Displacement brings about profound changes in the life process of displaced persons. In numerous case studies the economic, psycho-social and cultural impacts of displacement have been vividly depicted (Asthana, 1996; Thukral, 1992; Reddy, 1992). It is very difficult to quantify the psycho-social and cultural loss due to displacement. But the economic impact of displacement can be quantified; attempt has been made to measure the economic gain and loss of oustee households.

There is a scarcity of uninhabited area due to rapid urbanisation and industrialisation which necessitates acquiring private land in inhabited area to establish a development project. It is an imperative in such cases to prepare and implement a suitable rehabilitation and resettlement plan, so that there will be no negative change in the standard of living of the Project Affected Persons (PAPs).

The paper to assess the socio-economic status and its impact on development of project affected persons of Baxide mine area of the Rayagada district of Orissa. Moreover, to measure on the utilisation of compensation amount received and the impact of the development activities undertaken by UAIL/ URDS.

In the last decade, the state of Orissa has witnessed rapid industrialisation. Mega, steel, power, aluminum projects have come up by different companies in different location of the state. Utkal Alumina International Limited (UAIL) is one among them. UAIL is a joint venture of Indian Aluminium Company Ltd. (INDAL), ALACAN, Canada and Hydro Aluminium as (Hydro) of Norway. It is coming up in Kashipur Block of Rayagada district. The project has acquired 287 hect. of Govt. land, 872.3 hect. Private land and 76 hect. of forest land and in process displacing 148 number of families and affecting nearly 1600 number of families by acquiring their cultivable land.

Sampling Methodology

As it is intended to cover each and every project affected family through the study instead of sampling a census approach of collection of data is adopted. Apart from individual household survey a village wise resource data is gathered through a structured village schedule.

Openion of people's representatives and local leaders/ knowledgeable persons of village were also interviewed at the time of study. There was also an interaction with the project implementing authorities whose suggestions and views were also duly considered for the purpose of the study. Different Government Officials viz. Block Development Officers, CDPO, Veterinary Assistant surgeon, Medical Officer, District Agriculture Officer, School Inspector, Para-medical workers were contacted to get a clear picture of the study area.

Study Area

The study area consists of 24 inhabited villages and one uninhabited under 5 Gram Panchayats of Kashipur Block of Rayagada district. The total area of the block is 481.86 sq. km. The area is dominated by "*Kondh*" tribes followed by *"Dombo"* one of the scheduled castes. There is also a minor concentration of "Paikas" and "Gaudas" who belong to socio-economic backward class.

Majority of population speak *"Kuvi"* which originally a Dravidian groups of language of Kondhs. As per 2001 Census Kondh among the 62 tribes of Orissa are the largest tribal group of the state, numbering about two millions. Planned and sub-planned developments programme since the British rule have failed to understand the indigenous socio- cultural inter relations of this tribe and finally left them deprived of their minimum needs. Few of the demographic features of the block are given below:

Table 1: Rayagada District at a Galance

Geographical Area	7584.7 Sq. Kms.
No. of Sub-divisions	2
No. of Blocks	11
No. of Tahasils/ Town	4
No. of Municipality	1
Police stations including Mahila P.S.	12
Assembly Constituencies	04
Panchayats	171
Villages	Inhabited-2445, Uninhabited- 222
Population, 2001 Census	Total – 8,23,000 ; SC-1,17,524 (14.28 %);
(Provisional)	ST- 4,61,209 (56.04 %); OC- 2,44,266 (29.68%)
Decennial Growth Rate (Percentage) 1991-2001(P)	15.27
Sex Ratio (Females per '000 males) 2001 (P)	1029
Population Density (per Sq. Km.) 2001 (P)	116
Literacy Rates 2001	Total 35.61, Male 47.35, Female 24.31
Rain fall	Normal rainfall (M.M)-1521. 8, Actual rain-fall 2000 (M. M)- 876.8
Irrigation Potential created (upto 1999-00) in '000 hect	Major & Medium: 10.80, Minor (Flow): 25.37, Minor (Lift):21.07
Land utilisation Pattern 1999-2000 ('000 hect.)	Forest Area – 281; Mis. Tree permanent pas-ture, Land put to Non-Agrl. Use, Barren &

	uncultivable land – 197; Cultivable Waste- 12; Current Fallow- 31; Other Fallow- 14; Net area sown- 172; % of forest area of the district to state total- 4.84; % of forest area of the district- 39.76
Education (1999-2000)	No. Primary Schools: 1482, No. Middle Schools: 186, No. Secondary Schools: 83, No. General Colleges: 19
Industry (1998-99)	Registered reporting factories - 26 Total employees – 4240 Productive capital – 6294352000, Net value added by manufacture (Rs In lakh) – 4287
Percentage of village Electrified	54.23
Communication 2000-01 (in Km.)	State Highway 399, Major District Road 130, Other District Road 69, Forest Road- 183, Railway Route length- 208, No. of Railway stations- 14
Area of Agriculture (Hect.)	Cultivable land-184014 Hect., major food crops- 147170 Hect., major millets/course cereals- 45867 Hect., pulses- 34100 Hect., Oil seeds- 27500 Hect..
Total farming families in the District	140000
Irrigated lands in Hect.:	Khariff- 42115 Hect., Rabi- 11360 Hect.
Forest (Area in Sq. Kms)	Reserve Forest-771.62, Demarcated Protected Forest- 1147.19, Unclassified Forest Area- 0.96, Other forest- 892.56
Classification of Workers	Cultivators- 118395, Small and Marginal Farmers- 86188, Agricultural Labourers- 121147, Artisans- 8510, Cottage Industries House holds- 3636, Allied Agro Activities- 4260, Other Workers- 38574
Banking Network	State Bank of India- 17, Indian Overseas Bank- 8, Andhra Bank- 1, Indian Bank- 1, Koraput Panchabati Gramya Bank- 20, Koraput Central Co-operative Bank- 03, Mini Banks (LAMPs)- 14.

Source: District Statistical Hand Book- 2007

Fig. 1: Map of the Study Areas in Orissa

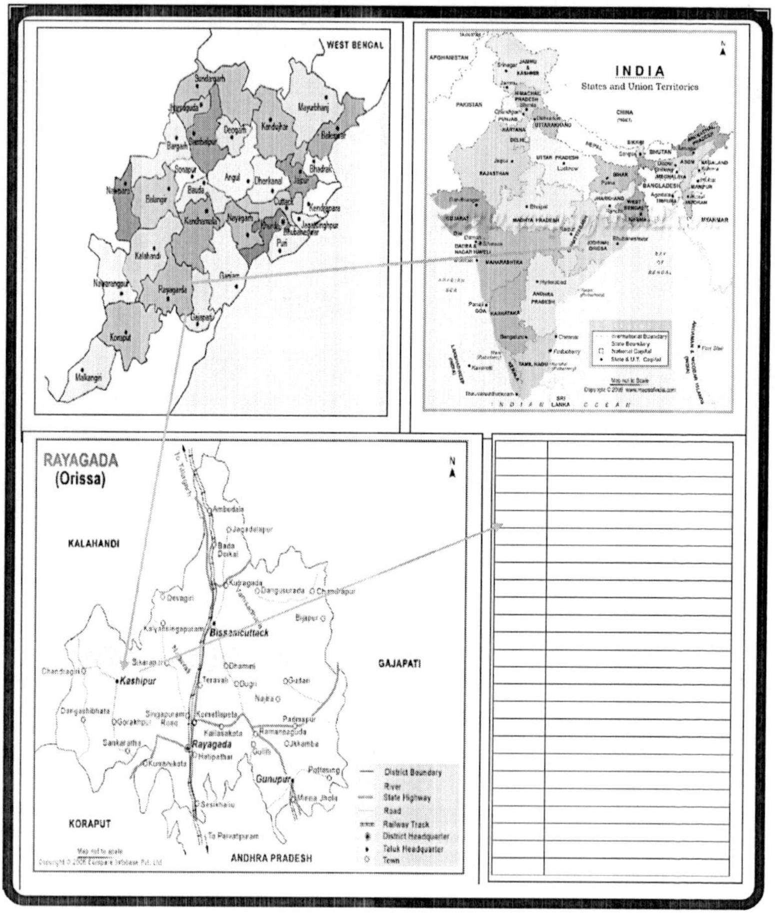

Result and Discussion

Socio-economic Condition a mong the Project Affected Persons (PAPs)

In the present study, the total number of project affected persons (PAPs) of Baxide mine area is estimated at 1953.These PAPs inhabit in 38 numbers of villages in and around the project area, though their land has been acquired from above mentioned 25 villages for the purpose of the project. The number of households in which this project affected persons is residing in 1538.

In terms of land acquisition (Table 2), highest number of PAPs i.e. 356 people have lost their land in D. Koral village followed by Dwimundi and Ramibeda villages also a considerable number of PAPs land has been acquired which stands at 247 and 212 respectively. These four villages comprise of 50% of the total project affected persons (as per record of rights). From the point of view of project affected persons (PAPs) in the villages from which the land acquisition is made, these four villages can be categorized as the most affected villages.

It has also been attempted (Table 3) through the study to analyse the project affected persons (PAPs) on the basis of their village inhabitation. As it is mentioned earlier, though most of the PAPs have lost their land in the same village in which they reside, some of them have lost in villages other than their village of inhabitation. It has also been where on PAPs has lost his land in more than one village. Except in 22 inhabited villages from where the land has been acquire PAPs also found in 16 numbers of other villages. In terms of inhabitation, D. Karol village also have the highest number of project affected persons (PAPs) i.e. 242. Also Bhitormuchkuni, Dimundi and Tikarpada villages have 188, 158 and 124 numbers of PAPs respectively. These villages are considered as the most affected, as constitute 42% total PAPs.

Table 4 reveals that a caste wise analysis of project affected persons reveals that majority of them are schedule tribes followed by schedule castes. Out of these PAPs, 947 are scheduled tribes, 577 are schedule castes and 370 belong to general caste.

As evident from Table 4, reviewing the ratio of male and female among the PAPs, it is estimated that nearly 32% of the total PAPs are females. A majority of PAPs i.e. 68% are male, it is because most of the land records are in the name of the male member of the family. Among the female PAPs most of them are married daughters having right over parental property.

Occupation persuaded by the PAPs is studied and presented in Table 5. A total 740 PAPs do not have any occupation or are non workers. Nearly 58% of the total working population are cultivators and earn their livelihood from agriculture. Therefore, cultivation, nearly 48% of the total working population are engaged as agriculture labourer. Thus agriculture is the main stay of the PAPs in the project area. More than 80% of them are either directly or indirectly engaged in it other than agriculture, allied activities like dairy, fishery, poultry, forestry etc. also fond to be pursued by a small proportion (2.1%) of PAPs. A negligible proportion (1.2%) is also engaged in non-farm activities. A look into the PAPs engaged in different artesian activity emerged to 0.7% who are potters and other traditional skilled workers.

It is also attempted Table 6 through the study to real the status of dwelling house where the PAPs reside. 64.9% of them reside in *Kaccha* house with thatched roof while 32.8% in *Kaccha* house with tile roof. Only 2.3% have *pucca* house with RCC roof.

A detailed probe into the size and type of family of project affected persons revealed following facts. Nearly 70% of PAPs have 3 to 5 members in their family, while 16% and 14% having below 3 and above 5 members in their family respectively.

Availability of safe drinking water is regarded as one of the major social index for any population. So, it has been attempted through the present study to gauge the availability of potable drinking water to the PAPs. Most of them use tube-well for the purpose of fetching drinking water, while a minor proportion still depend on open well, stream and/ or other unhygienic source like ponds, river, *nullah* etc. Practice of sanitation among the PAPs is also probed. It is assessed that boring few almost all PAPs have a habit of open defecation. Only a minor percentage answered that they use latrine for defecation purpose.

Nearly 31.6% of PAPs often visit nearest health centre for treatment, where as it is found that still 68.4% of them depend on quacks, witchcraft, herbs for treatment of common ailments like cold, fever, diarrhea etc.

In assessing the status of educating children of PAPs family, it is reported that though attendance in local primary schools have been increased over the years and there is a substantial decrease in the drop out rate, still a large number of school going age children are deprived of attending school.

Land Acquisition and Compensation of Project Affected Persons

The quantum of land loss by the project affected person is analyzed is details and described. It is revealed from (Table 7) the fact that most of the small land owners are loosing their land to an extent of one acre. Nearly 18% of total have lost their land in a range of 1-2 acres and 25% lose in a range of 2-4 acres. 404 numbers of PAPs have lost 100% of their land. The details of PAPs by extent of their land loss in percentage is given in Table 7. An attempt has also been made to analyse the proportion of land loss by the project affected persons (PAPs). It is noteworthy to mention here that 19.5% of total PAPs have lost their total land holding are treated as 100% land losers. 21.5% of the total PAPs have lost their land in a range of 51-70% of their total landholding. Land loss in a range of below 25% of the total land holding and 26-50% of the total land constitutes 15.8% and 18.7% of the total PAPs (21.5%) have also their land holding in a range of 76- 99% of their total land holding. Tikarpada village constitute maximum (163) number of 100% land losers followed by Ramibeda and D. Koral village in which the number of the same stands at 61 each.

In reviewing the status of land loss by type of land, it reveals that most of the PAPs have lost *"Atta"* land followed by *"Berna"* and *"Mala"*. The per capita quantum of land loss in *Berna* and *Mala* category is found to be high in Tikarpara village in comparison to other villages. In village Ramibeda per capita land in *Bahal* category is found to be considerably highest in respect to other affected villages. The status of private land acquisition is in Table 8.

Owing to land acquisition most of the PAPs have been shifted from upper land holding status to lower land holding status. Even some of them become land less (having no operational land holding) after acquisition. About 20% of the total PAPs have lost their total cultivable land by the way turning landless. Most of them were marginal farmers or Small farmers prior to land acquisition. Bearing a few, all most all the large farmers having more than 10 acres land holding prior to acquisition have been shifted to medium, small and marginal farmers category. A sizeable of them have also become landless in the village like Dwimundi, D. Koral, Remibeda and Tikarpada etc. Nearly 22% of total medium farmers have been shifted to landless category followed by 29.5% and 22.8% to small farmers and marginal farmers respectively. The picture is almost same in small farmers and marginal farmer category. The details picture is in Table 9.

A study is also made to find out the position and use of Govt. land needed to be requirement out of which about 50% is classified as uncultivable waste, where shifting cultivation is practiced. 30% of this consists of forest. Table 10 provides the details requirement of Govt. land. In 70% of this land *podu* cultivation is practiced. Among the *podu* cultivators 40% are landless, 40% are PAPs and 20% are non-PAPs having own agricultural land.

Village wise amount of compensation received by PAPs analysed and presented in Table 11. Nearly 5% of the PAPs are yet to receive compensation in 5 affected villages. In all other villages 100% PAPs have accepted the compensation amount. The number of PAPs not received compensation is highest (79 PAPs) in Ramibeda village followed by 18 in Koral village. PAPs are distributed according to the range of compensation amount above Rs One lakhs. A majority (28.2%) of PAPs have received compensation below Rs 5000/- followed by 27.4% of them have received compensation in the range of Rs 10, 001- 30, 000/-. Nearly, 15.4% of total PAPs have received compensation amount in a range of Rs 5,000/- - 10,000/-. Only 10.4% of the total PAPs have received it in a range of Rs 50, 000/- - 1, 00,000/-. It is important to note here that a highest proportion (32) of PAPs have got compensation about Rs 1,00, 000/- in Dwimundi village followed by 22 in D. Koral village. In 8 project affected villages more than half of the PAPs received compensation amounting below Rs 5, 000/-. Nearly three fourth of the total project affected persons have received compensation below Rs 30,000/-.

As far as the utilisation of compensation amount received by the PAPs is concerned, it is found that 55.25% of them have utilised the total amount for some or other purpose. 21% of them have spent 76- 99% of the total compensation amount received. This entails that more than three fourth of the total PAPs have utilised maximum proportion of the compensation amount.

3.1% of them have utilised below 25% of the compensation amount received. It is also noteworthy to mention here that nearly 7.3% of the PAPs have not spent a single pie from the compensation amount and have made it savings for the future use. Savings of higher proportion of compensation amount is found to be prevalent in Kanchagum, Hatikhaman, Jogiparitunda and Peringini village. While the situation is just reverse in Paikakupakhal, Kendukhunti, Bilamal, Tikiri, Osapada and Makapadar village where maximum proportion of the compensation amount has been utilised by most of the PAPs. It is important to note that among the PAPs who 100% deposit of the compensation money 52% are tribal, 38% are schedule caste and only 10% are OBC. The details range wise compensation is presented in Table 12.

The purpose of utilisation of compensation amount is proved and depicted in Table 13. Only 4.5% of PAPs have utilised their compensation amount for purchase of agricultural land in and around project villages. But in most of the cases the PAPs have utilised the compensation amount on account of their day to day expenses. Utilisation of compensation amount for the purpose of repair of house, education of children, agricultural work, purchase of movable assets is also found in some of the cases.

Involvement of PAPs in Resettlement Work by Project Authorities

Other benefits provided through UAIL for development of socio-economic standard of the project affected persons (PAPs) have been described below. UAIL has designed several income generation programme for the Project Affected Persons (PAPs) in general and the women in particular. Necessary support in form of training raw materials and marketing has been provided to the project affected women on pilot basis. Processing of spices like Turmeric and Tamarind and Dal were initiated. Women are also self employed in preparing hand pounding rice, making broom sticks, running small business groups. The tailoring unit is also from with an eye to develop few women PAPs. A support activities was also undertaken for improvement of agriculture and horticulture in the project affected villages by the way making the PAPs economically self sufficient. Through this programme, seed for crops like Maize, Ragi, Rice, Sunflower, Niger, Mustard etc. are provided for better yield. Seeds of vegetable and fruit bearing trees are provided. There are also provision made for supply of chemical fertilizer and pesticides. Agriculture allied activities like pisciculture, mushroom cultivation and bee keeping etc. are practiced by the PAPs through the help of the project authorities.

Social development activities by the project authorities have benefited a lot to the project affected persons. Intervention in health and sanitation sector has proved to be very useful. Preventive measures like mother and child care, immunisation and chlorination of drinking water in the project affected villages have been resulted reducing IMR, CMR and MMR. Morbidity in the area has also reduced considerably. Project authorities have also intervene for betterment of the sanitation facilities in the project affected villages. They have constructed village drains, tube-well, platforms and introduced smokeless chullahs, as a measure of up gradation of environment. A detail of the development activities undertaken by the project authorities and URDS is given in Table 14.

Although there is no scope in the resettlement and rehabilitation package of UAIL for the involvement of women but considerable efforts has been made to involve the women during recent past. The rehabilitation and resettlement work of UAIL is in existence for the last eight years. Let alone women the male outees have not been fully taken into confidence by the project authorities in their resettlement and rehabilitation program, although it is these displaced families who are the most concerned about their livelihood.

Thus the involvement of women was a far cry. During the study we have recorded the reaction the women on the project.

- 40% express no knowledge about the type of the project coming up.
- 20% feels despair.
- 10% improvement in the economic situation.
- 30% fear of losing house and land.

But on the data the women are considered and understand the need and rehabilitation process. This is because of the intervention among women initiated few months back in organizing Self Help Groups at villages. We have undertaken a sample study from 550 women about the preparation of women and their scope of involvement in the rehabilitation and resettlement work on the followings:

- Perception about standard of living after project.
- Scope of involvement in rehabilitation and resettlement work.
- Sharing leadership.

The outcome is as follows:

(i) Standard of living after the project

S. No.	*Variables*	*Category of Respondents*			
		SC	*ST*	*OBC*	*Total*
(a)	Increase in the income and so standard of living	52	06	28	86
(b)	Development in common facilities like health, education, drinking water, road and market etc.	36	21	36	93
(c)	Check the exploitation	32	17	18	67

Cond...

(d)	Development in the leadership status of women	47	07	19	73
(e)	Lost of land leading to poor economic standard	06	74	02	82
(f)	Both (a) and (b)	53	11	19	83
(g)	(a), (b) and (c)	22	06	24	52
(h)	(a), (b), (c) and (d)	13	-	01	14
	Total	**261**	**142**	**147**	**550**

(ii) Scope of involvement for women in rehabilitation resettlement work

(a)	Undertake village infrastructure work like road, drain, community shed, repair of school	78
(b)	Undertake plantation	82
(c)	Organise health, child welfare and festivals	62
(d)	Organise micro enterprise activities	67
(e)	Both (a) and (b)	114
(f)	All the activities (a), (b), (c) and (d)	147

All the respondents expressed their openion that these activities will be possible the SHGs only. Out of the 214 respondents those who are in favour of micro entrepreneurship activities the choice is:

- 42% production of building materials
- 40% Group based activities on processing and marketing of agriculture and forest produces including cultivation of fruits, vegetables and cash crop.
- 18% Petty business

Impact Assessment on Project Affected Person vis-a-vis Displaced Persons

Exploit the benefit of employment

Displace here we mean displacement from the habitat, from the land on which the target people depend for their livelihood from the socio-cultural value system which form their tradition. In the context of aboriginals, displacement can no way be consider as development as under the circumstances of illiteracy, ignorance and exploitation the poor PAPs will not be in a position to exploit the benefit of employment and entrepreneurship from the industrialisation. Once again it is outside business agents and Govt. servants who will enjoy the benefits.

Impact of Women and Children

In a developing country India large numbers of people are displaced every year to accommodate the distorted process of development. Development as conceived by the third world countries is industrialisation and allied sectors which are so fast that the poor people find it difficult to understand and managing the process is a big question. To some economists represents this progress of the nation. Unfortunately however, the obligation to make such sacrifice is imposed on the most vulnerable section of our society viz. poor and marginal farmers, daily labourers, tribal people and other unprivileged communities. The plight of the women and children is always sidelined. The resettlement and habilitation policies adopted by various project authorities, women and children who are most adversely affected by the displacement are never given any attention. Incase of unmarried women of 30 years it is and exception.

In view of the serious repercussions of displacement on women the following factors adversely affects the status of women in the society. (a) In the tribal society the women have a share and say on the agricultural produces as they work in the field along with the male folk. Loss of land will decrease their economic control over the family. (b) Loss of earning from forest, *podu land* and other common property resources and from non-farm activities. (c) Lost of vast agricultural land will reduce the scope for getting wages from agricultural labour. (d) Since the compensation payments are made usually to the male heads, it will convert the collective assets of the family which the women members also partly owned. (e) Women are neglected both by the project as well as by their family as there is no scope for direct or indirect employment in the resettlement and rehabilitation packages.

Changes in Socio-cultural Life

It is expected that there will be changes in the economic sphere of the outees through job opportunities. But women will be adversely affected as they will be neither benefited through job nor through any social and cultural exchange. The only compulsion after losing employment in land will be to work as daily labourers in transport, quarry and other low profile sectors.

Free Sexual Activity leading to Sexually Transmitted Diseases and Destituteness

A experienced from the major mega projects and industries in the district, in the absence of educated and skilled persons in the locality will lead to large flow of outsiders for skilled and semi-skilled jobs, including quarry, transport and business. Herewith give the example of the villages around the industries like J.K.Paper and IMFA, Therubali where such situation has taken place.

Most of the young girls and destitute works for daily labour with the local transport supplies of the industries, stone quarries, stone crushers, brick units. Where the labour consumption is 20% male and 80% in female. The tribal male folk being attracted to liquor does not concentrate in work. Hence the employees prefer to engage female workers in daily labour. Most of the male workers are in the category of semi-skilled and skilled workers like team leaders, work sarkar, driver, operator and supervisors etc., those who mostly outsiders with uncertain service conditions, low income and poor facilities. The skilled and semi-skilled workers leave their families in their respective native place which is always at a distance place. In the absence of attention from parents and guardians the women labourers used to come in sexual contact of these outsiders leading to illegal pregnancy etc. In many cases the outsiders use these ladies as kept with false promise of marriage and leave them alone while changing place of jobs. In this way the numbers of destitute are increasing in the area.

Unlike other areas there is no restriction of business in this area. Every day petty business people in large number comes to the area those include the seasonal cloth business men from Tamilnadu, Uttar Pradesh and West Bengal, the dry fish and fish vendors of Andhra Pradesh. Most of the fish, vegetable and fruit vendors are women those who takes the help of man folk in business. These people stay away from the families for months together and fall in prey of commercial sex workers.

Every third women in the area is a destitute mostly in the productive young age. As stated earlier the cause of destituteness is the out side workers engaged in extra marital life and the second being acceptability of the polygamy in tribal society. While in case of marriages within the community the women is again accepted for remarriage by relatives. But in case of marriages and extra marital affairs with outsiders and other caste the women are not accepted in the community and they don't have any other way except to go for illegal sex. Illegal sex no doubt lead to STD/HIV/AIDS and the rate of prostitution also expected to go up.

Increasing Difficulties in arranged marriages for Daughters

The women outees will face grater difficulties in getting married because of the demand for more dowry. The cash compensation received by the PAPs families will be center of attraction for bridegrooms and their parents looking for hefty dowry. As a result daughters marriage by the PAPs is an expensive affair and westage of compensation money. The process has already had an impact.

Impact on Quality of Life

Development induced displacement has resulted in wide spread traumatic psychological and socio-cultural consequences. These includes dismantling of production system dissertation of ancestral sacred zones or graves and temples, scattering of kinship group and family systems, disorganisation of informal social network that other mutual support, disruption of trade and market links etc. There is also a loss of social relationship which provide avenues of representation, mediation and conflict resolution. The very cultural identity of the community as well as the individual within it, is disrupted causing immense psychological and physiological stress. Thus it is clear that displacement brings in its trend certain adverse effects and risks which have economic, social and communal implications.

According to the World Bank, the rehabilitation policy should be such as to avoid or minimize displacement and in case when displacement unavoidable to provide. People displaced by a project with the means to improve on at least restore their former living standards earning capacity and production level through a process in which they participate through their own social and cultural institutions. The stress on these minimum requirements assumes importance because in all most all cases the displaced persons face risk of impoverishments.

Similarly, the rehabilitation policies adopted by project authorities have laid emphasis on improvement of the quality of life of the outees after their displacement. It is thus evident that impoverishment is the key issue which UAIL has given importance. In case of UAIL maximum effort has been made to minimize the displacement.

The impoverishment risk model captures not only the economic but also the social and cultural dimensions of impoverishment. It shows that during displacement the people lose i) natural capital ii) man made (physical) capital iii) human capital and iv) social capital. The model is able to accurately predict future outcomes, if the warnings are ignored.

Landlessness

Expropriation of land removes the main foundation upon which peoples productive systems, commercial activities and livelihood are constructed. This is the principal form of de-capitalisation and pauperisation of displaced people, as they lose both physical and man-made capital.

Unless these foundations is reconstructed elsewhere or replaced with steady income generating employment, landlessness sets in and the affected families are impoverished. Land for the poor is more than a resource bag and it has more than market value. It has emotional association for those who inherit it from their ancestors, it enables to grew food for subsistence and cash crops with which to obtain money to buy essentials it is often considered to be sacred, a status symbols that provides guarantee for easy access to loan and helps in getting better marriage alliance in the family and represents self-sufficiency and independence in a society bound by feudal norms. Besides, local religious belief and ritual customs are closely associated with land.

Landless also implies to loss of access to green vegetables, religious trees and gifts of nature. The economic values of medicinal herbs and plants with multiple wages which are accessible to the landed people cannot really be estimated.

Further landlessness has very serious social and economic implications not only for the owners of the land but also his family, children as well as for future generations as it provides hidden employment for every member of the family.

In view of the rise in the incidence of landlessness among the project affected outees, certain measures should be taken by the project authorities to overcome and counter the impoverishment risk of the landlessness. The following are being suggested: (a) "Land for Land" is considered to be the most viable options in any rehabilitation policy to pre-empt the emergence of the problems of landlessness. Hence the project authorities should take measures to rehabilitate the oustees on a "Land for Land" basis. (b) The land provided and the balance land of the oustees should be properly reclaimed and labeled also, so as it make it operationally productive. (c) Land allotted to the oustees shall be in one lot so that the operation on it is easy. (d) Care must be taken to provide land to the oustees near the resettlement site. (e) Replacement value should be paid for land so as to enable those who had lost land to purchase the same amount of land near their place of habitation, which UAIL has given importance in the R & R package and need to be practiced.

Marginalisation

Marginalisation occurs when families lose economic power and slide downwards. Unlike the case of these reduced to total landlessness due to displacement, middle income farms household do not become landless, but decline to the status of small land holders when displaced. But it is not only the middle farmers but also the other segments of the oustees population which get marginalised by displacement.

Marginalisation is caused by the deprivation of land, employment and home and indicates that loss of land, productive assets and livelihood will result a downward mobility among the oustees. Resettled families very often may not fully restore the economic capacities that they possessed in their habitat prior to their displacement. For instance, if those who own fertile land in the past are purchased unproductive and unleveled land, they invariably become marginalised among the landed people. Marginalisation will also occurs through the loss of income from extra agricultural sources in the locality which again were disrupted by the acquisition of the entire area (I.e. the village on the neighborhood) by the project authorities.

As mention earlier, the marginalisation of women, particularly tribal women due to displacement will reduce their status in the family and community. Women used to play an important role in the subsistence economy of their community by participating in both shifting and settled cultivation, collecting minor forest produces, growing vegetables in their kitchen garden before their displacement. Displacement will disrupt these traditional means of livelihood, such as occupations will be no longer possible in the new resettlement sites.

Food Insecurity

Forced uprooting increase the risk of chronic food insecurity defined as a caloric protein intake levels below the minimums necessary for normal growth and work. Sudden drops in the food crops availability and/ or income one inevitable during physical relocation and hunger on under nourishment tend to linger as long term effects.

In our agrarian society, crops are grown that provides food to the family for the entire year. In kitchen gardens, vegetables are grown almost throughout the year. One surplus food crops or vegetables are sold in the market. Hence, in years of good harvest the cultivators are usually self-sufficient as far food is concerned and do not depend on the market. But land acquisition in the project area has destroyed that self sufficiency. After, displacement, they need to spend money to procure food grain and vegetables. They also have to cope with high price of essential commodities.

Loss of Access to Common Property

For poor people, particularly for the landless and otherwise asset less peoples, loss of access to non-individual, common property assets belonging to communities that are relocated (forest land, water bodies, grazing land etc.) leads to a major deterioration in their income and livelihood levels. Such lost resources may be compensated.

Perception about the Socio-economic Life after Displacement (DPs)

The reaction of the displaced persons (DPs) in the wave of land acquisition and displacement is a mixed one, While majority of the DPs expect more gain and improvement in their standard of living. During the study, enquiry was made about the perceptions of the DPs in the post resettlement period. Nearly one third of them perceived that there would be an improvement in their socio- economic and living condition after resettlement. One third of the DPs feared that the quality of their life would deteriorate. Only few of the DPs from the second category thinks that life would not change much and remain more or less the same.

Coming to the caste wise distribution of the perception, in most cases the scheduled tribes people those who consists around 26% of the DPs perceives their future as one of the deterioration, once they are evacuated from their original habitat. The reason for this as identified during the field study are (i) Loss of their livelihood from land, (ii) Changes in their socio-cultural life by exposure to semi urban environment at resettlement colony (iii) decling economy (iv) different out look and expectation of relatives (v) decling status of female and (vi) change in social relations.

In case of the schedule caste community, although they realize the same situation, but they are hopeful of better standard of living under the perception of getting self employment and development in the standard of leaving. The SCs perceives a better income generation environment and scope of developing social status.

It is understood from the people that some of the local NGOs are behind the anti-project movement. While NGO action has been playing a major role in the socio-economic life of the affected area since decades, the absence of involvement of NGOs since land acquisition has resulted in the strong anti-project movement backed by local NGOs.

During the time of land acquisition the cost of land in the area was low and in the expectation of installation of more number of alumina refineries in Kashipur block, the cost of land has increased by four fold. Although, the compensation has been paid to the land losers, due to lack of administrative will and due to sympathetic attitude of the company. The land is still under the possession of the PAPs. The PAPs expects more amount of compensation to look for alternate land livelihood before loosing the possession.

The R & R is a complex game involving several stakeholders such as Government, promoters, DPs/ PAPs, NGOs elected representatives, affected community/ villagers and hosts. All these plays endeavour to gain maximum from the system. In the process, confrontation is encountered in each stage. Hence there is still resentment prevails amongst 30 to 40 percent of the PAPs. About 5% of the PAPs are yet to receive compensation those who are strongly opposing the process and sometime making all the activities stand still. This resentment has resulted in anti-project movement. Although the movement lacks support from 90% of the DPs/ PAPs, but it is still active with the support from third party sources.

Recommendation

(1) Policy

The project authorities have so far taken many discussions for rehabilitation of the affected people. But most of them have not been effective. Many of the discussion are found to be arbitrary and without any focus. Those are seems to be varying from village depending on the conveniences and capability of the project. In the past measures on rehabilitation varied depending on the organisation and strength of the affected people. As a result, many vested interest are associated with development projects and many PAPs, in the process, are deprived of the due rights and benefits of the projects.

In several cases apathy towards effective rehabilitation have crossed all tolerable limits of villagers and have caused social tensions as well as economic losses at project sites. While projects, if located and designed on the basis of rational, which should not suffer economic issues. On the other hand they must be rehabilitated properly and on the other, the project unit must function without any interruption or damages. This demands formulation of set of policies, which provides guidance to both projects and affected people forwards peaceful transformation of modernisation and progressive developments of the countryside.

Various sets of policies thus can be drawn up and they are linked with pre-rehabilitation measures, site selection and resettlement measures and related issues, measures of employment opportunities, infrastructure development, literacy and educational facilities, health facilities, employment measures, hinterland development, environmental protection etc. These policy sets are mainly derived from the analysis of rehabilitation policies taken up by UAIL. However, openions and experiences of PAPs are also considered and the views as well as expertise of the project official and others functionaries are given due weight age in this regard.

2. Literacy and Educational Facilities

Literacy and education are important pre-requisites for social rehabilitation. Age old beliefs must be removed and traditions must be broken through in order to make them realize the advantages of being educated. The following are some of the steps in this direction. (i) Parents must be convinced of the benefits of education. Interesting and attractive programmes like library, cultural and sports be introduced in all the schools. (ii) Selection of the rights type of teacher's with proper qualification is another essential requisite for the spread of education. Teachers should be devoted and sympathetic to tribal and should have the knowledge of the local tribal languages. (iii) The mother tongue is very important. An prescribed by the Dhebar commission it is essential to impart education to the tribal children in preparatory classes in their own dialects. However, they should also be encouraged to learn other languages as they move to higher classes. (iv) The environment in schools should be of the model type. Gardens and playgrounds would attract children. There must be some sort of audiovisual teaching arrangement. Discussions with the local teacher about the best method of imparting education would also beneficial. (v) Tribal culture should be respected and preserved. Agriculture, dancing and hunting and parts of tribal life and children should be given opportunities to display their own culture in a creative atmosphere. (vi) To overcome difficulties in education, UAIL should give greater importance to such voluntary organisation, which is working among the tribal with missionary spirit and zeal. (vii) A large number of adult education centers should be organised in order to eradicate illiteracy. Working women should be taught the means of maintaining sanitation and healthy and hygienic conditions. All these will lead to certain of awareness on education and rural health.

2. Health Facilities

Some amenities and facilities should be ensured in the resettlement areas. In this regard due attention has to be given to health care and drinking water facilities: (i) The main aim of the rural health centers should be to provide both curative and preventive medical care. For this purpose it is essential that arrangements should be made for regular visits of medical and auxiliary staff to all the affected villages. (ii) The health facilities initiated by URDS should be extended to all the affected villages on a regular basis. (iii) As per the R & R package of UAIL immediate step may be taken to establish a full fledge referral hospital.

3. Environmental Protection

(i) The development projects are associated with India's most controversial environmental issues. Problems such as water logging and drainage, health hazards like water born diseases, pollution of air, water, soil should be thoroughly examined before implementation of the projects. (ii) The resettlement plan should be drawn with a specific orientation towards preserving and improving the existing environment. There should be necessary provision for massive aforestation programmes around the plant and colony. (iii) Appropriate steps have to be taken to maintain the environment. In this regard, it is suggested that social forestry schemes should be implemented and first growing species of trees should be planted to provide fuel, fodder and fruit to the people. For plantation involvement of the people from raising seedling to follow up care should be ensured.

4. Hinterland Development

(i) Incentive should be mobilised from Government, banks, URDS in addition to the company's to the farmers in the surrounding villages for commercial crops cultivation and market gardening. These should be arrangements for price protection through cooperative marketing, minimum price fixation etc. to safeguard them from exploitation by middlemen, large traders, rack renters and others. The steps undertaken by the company to organize Self Help Groups among women is in line with this. (ii) Model agricultural farmers should be estimated to train the people on modern methods of production and marketing. UAIL should promote agro services and extension wings for adequate and timely supply of plants, seeds, fertilizers, implements and other inputs. (iii) The local farmers should be encouraged to adopt consumer preference based crops depending on the anticipated needs of the people. The District Agriculture Department should through its extension machinery, take the responsibility of motivating the people in this direction and guiding them. (iv) The principal of allotting land to the affected people be followed and if necessary, small irrigation projects to be executed in the new sites earmarked for the oustees entitled for agricultural rehabilitation. Development of micro-watershed should be the priority. *(v)* The integrated development of the region should be planned in such a way so as to attain balance between agricultural and industrial economy and between the rural and urban industrial way of life. Changes should be brought in cautiously and slowly so that the local people can adjust to the changed situations.

5. Autonomous Agency of Rehabilitation

Coordination between various state Government departments and other organisations including project authorities is essential for planned rehabilitation. Pretty long time is spent on solving unforeseen problems and this result in unnecessary delay. There is also the possibility, if the rehabilitation work is carried out by the same organisation, to relegate it to the state of a low priority task. In order to achieve better results details plan of resettlement, backed by financial allocation should be prepared as a part of the project design. If this is entrusted to an autonomous agency, possibly resettlement gets higher priority.

6. Involvement of Voluntary Agencies

Rehabilitation of people affected by development projects is a long drawn process. It involves an understanding of people and requires advance planning. It needs the coordinated efforts of specialists from diverse disciplines including those from voluntary and association, social workers, project officials and affected people themselves. The displace people confront problems for which they do not find the right officials to redress their grievances. In this regard, the involvement of voluntary agencies is most ideal. These agencies can act as pressure groups to extract desired benefits for the oustees. They could also act as liaisons between the displaced persons and the Government. Therefore, it is suggested that voluntary agencies should be involved in the process of rehabilitation. They can play a vital supportive role in implementation of rehabilitation programme.

Special Programmes for Women

It is suggested that there should be provision for designing special programme for women, particularly for those who are uprooted from traditional jobs, as an integral part of rehabilitation plan. This should include creation of opportunities for improving their education, health, family welfare, employment etc. in an organised way.

Involvement of Tribal Welfare Department

In most cases the tribal constitute overwhelming majority among the displaced population. Therefore, the involvement of tribal welfare department is essential in preparing the rehabilitation plans, arranging training programmes, developing business entrepreneurship, assisting in procuring loans etc. The department should keep a strict vigilance so that the innocent tribal who are receipt of compensation are not exploited by the private land dealers, middlemen and money lenders. Representative of tribal welfare department should be there in the rehabilitation and grievances committees.

The above recommendation, if followed, will certainly obviate many complications related to social and economic rehabilitation of people affected by the projects. Rehabilitation programmes should be formulated in consonance with the needs of the affected people in general and tribal in particular. Any further neglect will cause larger costs so society and defeat the very purpose of implementation of development projects in the region.

Conclusion

In the study area, the panorama of rehabilitation will be better, as the project authorities had drawn up programmes backed by efficient planning. It is expected that the conditions of evicted people will improve if the problems identified in this study are attended to and accepted for practice.

The simple people are exposed to unsympathetic by those who always attempted their subjugation. In contrast with their irreparable losses what the evicted people will gain are a few non-traditional jobs. But considering the status of jobs, most of them are no better than the manual unskilled labourers. Of course, industrialisation shall raise the improved health, education and housing facilities for a limited numbers of affected people and contributed to a growing consciousness of materialism.

Openion of the affected people, functionaries, representative of voluntary organisations, project and Government officials, social scientists and any other vary on the question of success and failure of the rehabilitation programmes. When taken together however, their replies are enough to say that rehabilitation programmes receive a low priority in project planning and execution. Even if the problems are known to them, the remedial measures are not prescribed, because they think that their responsibility ends with the payment of compensation and transferring the displaced families from one location to another. As a sequence, the failures are always overlooked without postmortem analysis and creating scopes for rectification if the mistakes which lead to failure again and again. But in case of UAIL a clear and efficient Corporate Social Responsibility (CRS) action has been initiated prior to the displacement which is exemplary. The R & R Package of UAIL aims at making the people capable enough to observe the process of industrialisation.

References

Asthana, Roli	1996	Involuntary resettlement: Survey of International experience, Economic and Political Weekly, Vol.31, No. 24.
Cernea, Michael M.	1988	Involuntary Resettlement in Development Projects: Policy Guidelines in World Bank Financed Projects, World Bank Technical Paper No. 80.
Cernea, Michael M.	1996	Public Policy Responses to development induced population displacements, Economic and Political Weekly, Vol. 31, No. 24.
Reddy, I.U.B.	1992	Displacement and Rehabilitation, Mittal Publications, Delhi.
Swain, M. & G. Khadanga	2001	Rehabilitation Measures and Pitfalls: A Case of Gohira, Orissa, The Eastern Anthropologist, Lucknow, Vol. 54, No. 3&4.
Thukral, E.G. et al	1992	Big Dams, Displaced People: River of Sorrow, River of Change, Sage Publications, New Delhi.
Frank, A.G.	1998	Reorient: Global Economy in the Asian Age, U. C. Barkley Press.
Pratheep, P.S.	2010	Proceeding LSCAC, Catholicate College, Mahatma Gandhi University

Acknowledgement: I should thanks to Dr. L. Nayak, Corporate Social Responsibility Manager, Utkal Alumina International Limited and Mr. P.K.Satpaty, Universial Service Organisation, Rayagada, Orissa for stimulating and assisting me for this article.

Table 2: Number of PAPs as Per The Land Acquisition

S. No.	Address Villages	*Tikri*	*Gokulmunda*	*Osapada*	*Bilamal*	*Mukapadar*	*Bagirijhola*	*Dwimundi*	*D. Koral*	*B. Muchkuni*	*Ramibeda*	*Tikarpada*	*R.M.Purnapadar*	*Kodipari*	*Jogiparitunda*	*Naringjodi*	*Ratachuan*	*Ambiliugudatunda*	*Hatikaman*	*Piringini*	*Lundurukona*	*Paikupakhal*	*Andirakonch*	*Konchguma*	*Gaimundatunda*	*Kucheipadar**	*Others**	*Total*
1.	Tikri	27																									7	**34**
2.	Gokulmunda	8	72	1																							28	**109**
3.	Osapada	10		96			7																				5	**118**
4.	Bilamal				91																							**91**
5.	Mukapadar					52																						**52**
6.	Bagirijhola						52			28		3													9		3	**95**
7.	Dwimundi					12	3	158	25		29															1	20	**248**
8.	D. Koral							3	331																	7		**341**
9.	B. Muchkuni									119																		**119**
10.	Ramibeda										52															155	5	**212**
11.	Tikarpada						3			58		81				2									98		5	**247**
12.	R.M.Purnapadar											45																**45**
13.	Kodipari													38														**38**
14.	Jogiparitunda														35													**35**
15.	Naringjodi															26												**26**
16.	Ratachuan																26											**26**
17.	Ambiliugudatunda																	36							25		5	**66**
18.	Hatikaman														5		1		35									**41**
19.	Piringini													16		5												**21**
20.	Lundurukona																				12	1						**13**
21.	Paikupakhal																					32						**32**
22.	Andirakonch													2									21				1	**24**
23.	Konchaguma																							10				**10**
24.	Gaimundatunda																								27			**27**
	Total	**45**	**72**	**97**	**91**	**64**	**65**	**161**	**356**	**205**	**81**	**129**	**Nil**	**56**	**40**	**33**	**27**	**36**	**35**	**Nil**	**12**	**33**	**21**	**10**	**159**	**163**	**79**	**2070**

*** = Villages are not affected by the Project**

Figures is verticle shows the no. of PAPs as per residential status

Figures is Horizontal shows the no. of PAPs as per record of rights

Table 3: PAPs Inhabitation Status by Land Lost

S. No.	*Name of the Residential Village*	*PAPs Land Lost*			
		Only in Same Village	*Only in Other Village*	*Same Village & Other Village*	*PAPs Total No. of*
1.	Tikri	27	17	1	45
2.	Gokulmunda	72	-	-	72
3.	Osapada	96	1	-	97
4.	Bilamal	91	-	-	91
5.	Mukapadar	44	4	8	56
6.	Bagirijhola	52	13	-	65
7.	Dwimundi	155	-	3	158
8.	D. Koral	317	11	14	342
9.	B. Muchkuni	102	69	17	188
10.	Ramibeda	28	5	24	57
11.	Tikarpada	76	43	5	124
12.	Kodipari	38	18	-	56
13.	Jogiparitunda	35	5	-	40
14.	Naringjodi	23	4	3	30
15.	Ratachuan	26	1	-	27
16.	Ambiliugudatunda	36	-	-	36
17.	Hatikaman	35	-	-	35
18.	Lundurukona	12	-	-	12
19.	Paikupakhal	32	1	-	33
20.	Andirakonch	21	-	-	21
21.	Konchaguma	10	-	-	10
22.	Gaimundatunda	11	116	16	143
23.	Others	-	190	26	216
	Total	**1339**	**498**	**117**	**1954**

Table 4: Number of PAPs by Ethnic Group

S. No	Village	SC			ST			OBC			OC			Total		
		M	F	T	M	F	T	M	F	T	M	F	T	M	F	T
1.	Tikri	8	9	17	1	3	4	9	4	13	4	6	10	22	22	44
2.	Gokulmunda	2	-	2	34	13	47	4	-	4	12	7	19	52	20	72
3.	Osapada	13	2	15	50	22	72	5	2	7	2	1	3	70	27	97
4.	Bilamal	2	-	2	70	19	89	-	-	-	-	-	-	72	19	91
5.	Mukapadar	3	-	3	39	13	52	1	-	1	-	-	-	43	13	56
6.	Bagirijhola	12	2	14	26	14	40	7	4	11	-	-	-	45	20	65
7.	Dwimundi	51	32	83	47	24	71	4	-	4	-	-	-	102	56	158
8.	D. Koral	196	100	296	32	10	42	1	-	1	2	1	3	231	111	342
9.	B. Muchkuni	16	1	17	93	34	127	24	11	35	5	4	9	138	50	188
10.	Ramibeda	-	-	-	30	20	50	3	4	7	-	-	-	33	24	57
11.	Tikarpada	11	10	21	14	10	24	47	32	79	-	-	-	72	52	124
12.	Kodipari	-	-	-	15	23	38	13	5	18	-	-	-	28	28	56
13.	Jogiparitunda	1	-	1	-	-	-	17	22	39	-	-	-	18	22	40
14.	Naringjodi	7	5	12	14	2	16	2	-	2	-	-	-	23	7	30
15.	Ratachuan	-	-	-	20	7	27	-	-	-	-	-	-	20	7	27
16.	Ambiliugudatunda	4	1	5	20	8	28	3	-	3	-	-	-	27	9	36
17.	Hatikaman	1	-	1	1	-	1	17	16	33	-	-	-	19	16	35
18.	Lundurukona	1	-	1	3	8	11	-	-	-	-	-	-	4	8	12
19.	Paikupakhal	16	13	29	1	3	4	-	-	-	-	-	-	17	16	33
20.	Andirakonch	3	1	4	9	6	15	2	-	2	-	-	-	14	7	21
21.	Konchaguma	8	1	9	-	-	-	1	-	1	-	-	-	9	1	10
22.	Gaimundatunda	5	3	8	22	6	28	69	34	103	2	2	4	98	45	143
23.	Others	29	8	37	131	30	161	7		7	7	4	11	174	42	216
Total		**389**	**188**	**577**	**672**	**275**	**947**	**236**	**134**	**370**	**34**	**25**	**59**	**1331**	**622**	**1953**

Table 5: PAPs by their Occupational Status

S. No	*Village*	*Agriculture & Agri-cultural Labour*	*Agl. Allied activities*	*Tinny business*	*Service*	*Artisans*	*Other*
1.	Tikri	43.2	2.3	-	4.6	-	44.9
2.	Gokulmunda	54.2	4.2	-	-	1.3	40.3
3.	Osapada	65.9	4.1	-	-	1.1	28.9
4.	Bilamal	70.3	1.1	-	-	-	28.6
5.	Mukapadar	75	-	2.0	-	-	23
6.	Bagirijhola	56.9	-	-	-	-	43.1
7.	Dwimundi	60.8	1.9	1.2	-	-	36.1
8.	D. Koral	59.1	2.9	0.6	-	-	-
9.	B. Muchkuni	68.7	2.6	-	1.0	-	27.7
10.	Ramibeda	50.9	-	-	-	-	49.1
11.	Tikarpada	55.7	1.6	-	-	-	42.7
12.	Kodipari	32.1	-	-	-	3.6	64.3
13.	Jogiparitunda	22.5	-	-	-	-	77.6
14.	Naringjodi	56.7	3.4	-	-	-	39.9
15.	Ratachuan	59.2	7.4	-	-	-	33.4
16.	Ambiliugudatunda	66.7	-	-	-	-	33.3
17.	Hatikaman	45.7	2.9	-	-	2.9	48.5
18.	Lundurukona	33.3	-	-	-	-	66.7
19.	Paikupakhal	30.3	-	6.1	-	-	63.6
20.	Andirakonch	19.0	-	-	-	-	81
21.	Konchaguma	100.0	-	-	-	-	-
22.	Gaimundatunda	54.6	2.8	-	1.3	2.1	39.2
23.	Kucheipadar	74.6	2.8	0.6	-	3.3	8.7
24.	Others	35.1	-	-	-	**2.8**	62.1
	Total	**58.4**	**2.1**	**0.5**	**0.4**	**0.7**	**37.9**

Table 6: PAPs by House Type (In Percentage)

S. No	*Village*	*Thatched Roof with Mud Wall*	*RCC with Pucca Wall*	*Tile with Mud Wall*
1.	Tikri	36.30	9.10	54.60
2.	Gokulmunda	30.60	2.80	66.60
3.	Osapada	61.90	- .	38.10
4.	Bilamal	57.10	-	42.90
5.	Mukapadar	21.40	-	78.60
6.	Bagirijhola	64.70	3.00	32.30
7.	Dwimundi	70.20	-	29.80
8.	D. Koral	64.10	1.40	34.50

Cond...

9.	B. Muchkuni	67.50	0.60	31.90
10.	Ramibeda	98.20	1.80	-
11.	Tikarpada	62.90	3.30	33.80
12.	Kodipari	96.40	-	3.60
13.	Jogiparitunda	90.00	2.50	7.50
14.	Naringjodi	100.00	-	-
15.	Ratachuan	100.00	-	-
16.	Ambiliugudatunda	77.80	-	22.20
17.	Hatikaman	54.20	-	45.80
18.	Lundurukona	100.00	-	-
19.	Paikupakhal	87.90	3.00	9.10
20.	Andirakonch	100.00	-	-
21.	Konchaguma	100.00	-	-
22.	Gaimundatunda	57.30	3.50	39.20
23.	Kucheipadar	56.50	9.00	34.50
24.	Others	67.65	5.40	27.00
	Total	**64.90**	**2.30**	**32.80**

Table 7: PAPs by Extend of Land Loss (in Acre)

S. No.	*Village*	*Below 25%*	*26-50%*	*51-75%*	*76-99%*	*100%*	*Total*
1.	Tikri	2	-	8	20	4	34
2.	Gokulmunda	20	12	13	58	6	109
3.	Osapada	25	15	20	50	8	118
4.	Bilamal	6	12	53	20	-	91
5.	Mukapadar	-	4	25	19	4	52
6.	Bagirijhola	23	19	11	24	18	95
7.	Dwimundi	-	48	100	55	45	248
8.	D. Koral	48	104	76	52	61	341
9.	B. Muchkuni	12	21	32	43	11	119
10.	Ramibeda	6	31	76	38	61	212
11.	Tikarpada	2	6	20	56	163	247
12.	R.M.Purnapadar	7	13	16	9	-	45
13.	Kodipari	22	16	-	-	-	38
14.	Jogiparitunda	19	14	2	-	-	35
15.	Naringjodi	10	5	6	2	3	26
16.	Ratachuan	19	7	-	-	-	26
17.	Ambiliugudatunda	28	17	18	-	3	66
18.	Hatikaman	21	13	7	-	-	41
19.	Piringini	10	-	5	-	6	21
20.	Lundurukona	6	7	-	-	-	13
21.	Paikupakhal	16	10	6	-	-	32
22.	Andirakonch	15	9	-	-	-	24
23.	Konchaguma	8	2	-	-	-	10
24.	Gaimundatunda	2	3	11	-	11	27
	Total	**327**	**388**	**505**	**446**	**404**	**2070**
	Percentage	**15.80**	**18.70**	**24.50**	**21.50**	**19.50**	**100**

Table 8: Particulars of Private Land in Kissam Wise (in Acres)

S. No.	Village	Bhalapani	Berna Pani	Bahal	Berna	Mala	Ata	Patit	Bagayat	Gharabari	Gochar	Rasta	Total
		1	2	3	4	5	6	7	8	9	10	11	12
1	Tikri	-	-	13.98	4.60	-	6.81	-	-	-	-	-	25.39
2	Gokulmunda	-	-	2.32	7.76	2.02	96.87	-	-	-	-	-	108.97
3	Osapada	-	-	3.38	4.00	-	60.25	-	-	-	-	-	67.63
4	Bilamal	-	-	-	-	-	45.13	-	-	-	-	-	45.13
5	Mukapadar	-	-	-	-	-	51.71	0.66	-	-	-	-	52.37
6	Bagirijhola	7.38	6.08	14.12	5.85	6.36	46.62	0.22	-	0.26	-	-	86.89
7	Dwimundi	-	-		2.04	22.89	455.16	-	-	2.90	1.82		484.91
8	D. Koral	-	-		9.00		428.66	-	1.46	9.50	-	-	448.62
9	B. Muchkuni	-	-	0.20	11.43	4.57	128.40	0.28	-	-	-	-	144.88
10	Ramibeda	-	-	31.38	21.07	18.13	96.78	0.18	-	9.86	-	-	177.40
11	Tikarpada	-	20.32	24.18	95.29	112.34	128.48	2.11	0.30	-	-	-	386.02
12	R.M.Purnapadar	-	-	-	-	-	13.00	-	-	-	-	-	13.00
13	Kodipari	-	-	1.04	8.05	1.10		-	4.61	-	-	-	14.80
14	Jogiparitunda	-	-	-	-	-	7.00	-	-	-	-	-	7.00
15	Naringjodi	-	-	-	-	-	8.30	-	-	-	-	-	8.30
16	Ratachuan	-	-		0.31	2.73	1.95	-	-	-	-	-	4.99
17	Ambiliugudatunda	-	-	1.98	7.22	4.95	17.02	-	-	-	-	-	31.17
18	Hatikaman	-	-			0.19	11.84	-	-	0.02	-	-	12.05
19	Piringini	-	-	1.03	4.84	-	3.92	-	0.38	-	-	-	10.17
20	Lundurukona	-	-	-	-	-	5.05	-	-	-	-		5.05
21	Paikupakhal	-	-	0.95	0.82	-	4.78	-	-	-	-	0.11	6.66
22	Andirakonch	-	-	0.52	0.25	4.22	3.96	-	-	-	-	-	8.95
23	Konchaguma	-	-	-	-	-	4.54	-	-	-	-	-	4.54
24	Gaimundatunda	-	-	-	-	-	3.66	-	-	-	-	-	3.66
	Total	**7.38**	**26.40**	**95.08**	**182.53**	**179.50**	**1629.89**	**3.45**	**6.75**	**22.54**	**1.92**	**0.11**	**2155.55**

Note: 1. Paddy- Rainfed -2, 2. Paddy I - Irrigated, 3. Paddy II - Rainfed, 4. Paddy II - Irrifated, 5. Paddy III - Rainfed, 6. Paddy III - Irrigated, 7. Dry- I, Paddy- I- Uncultivated, 8. Dry- I with fruit cultivation/ graves, 9. House/ Residential Sites, 10. Grazing Land, 11. Road (Villages)

Table 9: Shifting of Farming Category

S. No.	Village	Marginal Farmer		Farmer Small		Medium Farmer		Large Farmer		Land Less
		B.A.	A.A.	B.A.	A.A.	B.A.	A.A.	B.A.	A.A.	A.A.
1.	Tikri	12	20	8	2	10	6	4	2	4
2.	Gokulmunda	35	55	38	21	24	19	12	8	6
3.	Osapada	42	63	32	14	26	21	18	12	8
4.	Bilamal	-	1	22	63	48	23	21	4	-
5.	Mukapadar	16	28	20	12	8	6	8	2	4
6.	Bagirijhola	3	5	18	25	58	43	16	4	18
7.	Dwimundi	-	15	82	102	145	81	21	5	45
8.	D. Koral	-	30	123	121	156	89	62	40	61
9.	B. Muchkuni	18	33	21	35	58	28	22	12	11
10.	Ramibeda	-	15	103	43	112	18	32	8	163
11.	Tikarpada	10	22	97	59	84	61	21	9	61
12.	R.M.Purnapadar	14	16	11	14	16	12	4	3	-
13.	Kodipari	36	34	2	4	-	-	-	-	-
14.	Jogiparitunda	9	13	10	12	16	10	-	-	-
15.	Naringjodi	3	-	14	14	4	4	5	5	3
16.	Ratachuan	12	18	8	4	6	4	-	-	-
17.	Ambiliugudatunda	25	22	18	18	17	17	6	6	3
18.	Hatikaman	10	18	18	14	9	6	4	3	-
19.	Piringini	6	4	12	8	3	3	-	-	6
20.	Lundurukona	4	4	9	9	-	-	-	-	-
21.	Paikupakhal	30	30	-	-	-	2	2	-	-
22.	Andirakonch	10	12	8	8	6	4		-	-
23.	Konchaguma	-	3	6	7	4	-	-	-	-
24	Gaimundatunda	-	12	12		8	1	7	3	11
	Total	**295**	**473**	**692**	**609**	**818**	**458**	**265**	**126**	**404**
	Percentage	**14.2**	**22.8**	**53.5**	**29.5**	**39.5**	**22.2**	**12.8**	**6.0**	**19.5**

Note: B.A. = Before Acquisition, A.A. = After Acquisition Marginal Farmers = Below 2.5 acres, Small Farmers = 2.5 to 5 acres, Medium Farmers = 5.2 to 10 acres, Large Farmers = Above 10 acres

Table 10: Requirement of Government Land

S. No.	Village	A.J.A. in Acres	A.A.A. in Acres	Common Porperty Resource			Gochar	Village Forest	Other Kissam	Total area in acre
				Smasan	Dhama Pitha	Others				
		1	2	3	4	5	6	7	8	9
1.	Tikri	-	0.36	-	-	-	-	0.2	-	**0.56**
2.	Gokulmunda	-	-	-	-	-	0.14	-	-	**0.14**
3.	Osapada	-	0.32	0.08	-	0.24	-	-	-	**0.64**
4.	Bilamal	-	-	-	-	0.50	-	17.42	-	**17.92**
5.	Mukapadar	-	1.65	-	-	1.48	-		-	**3.13**
6.	Bagirijhola	5.13	59.82	-	-	0.72	0.3	4.77	0.74	**71.48**
7.	Dwimundi	0.18	17.62	1.92	-	3.07	10.52	2.64	30.86	**66.81**
8.	D. Koral	1.01	40.17	0.27	-	5.73	12.05	6.05	0.26	**65.54**
9.	B. Muchkuni	5.86	75.39		-	3.27		4.73	0.45	**89.70**
10.	Ramibeda	-	5.26	0.49	0.17	1.83	9.49	20.13	2.68	**40.05**
11.	Tikarpada	-	15.67	-	0.19	7.05	7.83	62.87	5.45	**99.06**
12.	R.M.Purnapadar	7.03		-	-	-	7.78	81.75		**96.56**
13.	Kodipari	-	0.50	-	-	-	-	-	-	**0.50**
14.	Jogiparitunda	0.51	0.14	-	-	1.48	-	-	-	**2.13**
15.	Naringjodi	-	6.84	-	-	-	-	-	-	**6.84**
16.	Ratachuan	-		-	-	-	-	0.16	-	**0.16**
17.	Ambiliugudatunda	1.56	2.11	-	-	-	2.28	0.47	0.45	**6.87**
18.	Hatikaman	2.87	0.23	-	-	0.03	1.26	3.62	-	**8.01**
19.	Piringini	-	0.95	-	-	-			-	**0.95**
20.	Lundurukona	-	5.76	-	-	-	0.40	0.32	-	**6.48**
21.	Paikupakhal	3.71	62.77	-	-	-		0.37	-	**66.85**
22	Andirakonch	-	21.54	-	-	0.12	0.74	0.58	-	**22.98**
23	Konchaguma	-	0.59	-	-	-	-	-	-	**0.59**
24	Gaimundatunda	0.54	1.56	-	-	0.52	-	-	1.94	**4.56**
25	Karanja Kupakhal	-	23.28	-	-	-	-	-	-	**23.28**
26	Dhudurapas	-	4.2	-	-	-	-	-	-	**4.20**
27	Kadalighati	-	6.81	-	-	-	-	-	-	**6.81**
	Total	28.4	354	2.76	0.36	26.04	52.8	206.1	42.83	712.80

Note: (i) Cultivable Waste, (ii) Uncultivable Waste, (iii) Burial Ground, (iv) Religion, (v) Common Land, (vi) Grazing Land, (vii) Village Forest, (viii) Unclassified Revenue Forest

Table 11: PAPs Compensation Range

S. No.	Village	Amount (in Rs) Below 5000	5001-10,000	10,001-30.000	30,001-50,000	50,001-1,00, 000	Above 1,00,000
1.	Tikri	16	4	6	4	2	2
2.	Gokulmunda	18	13	29	11	-	1
3.	Osapada	52	13	29	1	-	2
4.	Bilamal	50	11	25	5	-	-
5.	Mukapadar	10	9	18	9	10	-
6.	Bagirijhola	22	16	13	3	11	3
7.	Dwimundi	24	8	32	31	31	32
8.	D. Koral	75	39	109	50	39	22
9.	B. Muchkuni	2	34	69	31	18	16
10.	Ramibeda	5	4	27	9	9	3
11.	Tikarpada	51	9	21	14	19	9
12.	Kodipari	34	8	8	2	4	-
13.	Jogiparitunda	25	1	13	1	-	-
14.	Naringjodi	15	4	6	1	2	2
15.	Ratachuan	6	18	3	-	-	-
16.	Ambiliugudatunda	6	28	2	-	-	-
17.	Hatikaman	19	13	3	-	-	-
18.	Lundurukona	5	5	2	-	-	-
19.	Paikupakhal	18	3	10	1	1	-
20.	Andirakonch	9	5	4	3	-	-
21.	Konchaguma	1	6	3	-	-	-
22.	Gaimundatunda	20	16	34	19	24	16
23.	Others	38	25	37	33	21	8
	Total	**521**	**283**	**503**	**228**	**191**	**116**
	By Percentage	**28.2**	**15.4**	**27.4**	**12.4**	**10.4**	**6.2**

Table 12: Utilisation of Compensation by Percentage of Amount Received

S. No.	Village	100% Deposit	Below 25%	26- 50%	51- 75%	76- 99%	100%
1.	Tikri	-	-	-	-	25.00	75.00
2.	Gokulmunda	1.29	-	-	7.80	27.27	63.64
3.	Osapada	2.71			5.40	35.13	56.76
4.	Bilamal	1.16	3.48	4.66	4.66	11.63	74.41
5.	Mukapadar	-	-	-	7.85	35.29	56.86
6.	Bagirijhola	5.94	25.74	-	19.76	23.02	25.54
7.	Dwimundi	-	10.87	26.08	30.44	21.74	10.87
8.	D. Koral	2.85	2.27	5.68	7.94	31.25	50.00
9.	B. Muchkuni	10.08	20.16	-	-	31.09	38.66
10.	Ramibeda	5.72	8.58	8.58	11.42	11.42	54.28
11.	Tikarpada	-	10.53	5.26	15.79	42.10	26.32
12.	Kodipari	10.52	5.26	-	5.26	31.58	47.37
13.	Jogiparitunda	70.84	-	-	-	-	29.16

Cond...

14.	Naringjodi	-	-	-	25.94	18.51	55.55
15.	Ratachuan	-	-	-	-	53.84	46.15
16.	Ambiliugudatunda	-	14.87	-	21.62	28.38	35.13
17.	Hatikaman	55.56	-	-	-	-	44.44
18.	Lundurukona	-	-	-	-	-	100.00
19.	Paikupakhal	15.15	-	-	-	-	84.85
20.	Andirakonch	-	-	-	-	8.33	91.67
21.	Konchaguma	60.00	-	-	-	-	40.00
22.	Gaimundatunda	-	2.86	11.42	5.72	2.86	77.14
23.	Others	48.00	12.26	-	13.34	6.82	19.58
	Total	**7.27**	**3.12**	**5.04**	**8.26**	**21.06**	**55.25**

Table 13: Purpose of Utilisation of Compensation

S. No.	*Village*	*Purchase of Land*	*Purchase of Movable assets*	*Education of Children*	*Household expenses*	*Construction & Repair of house*	*Agriculture*	*Marriage of Spouse*	*Repayment of Loan*
1	Tikri	-	-	-	28	2	6	4	4
2	Gokulmunda	-	-	-	56	-	14	4	6
3	Osapada	-	-	-	62	6	38	4	8
4	Bilamal	-	-	-	76	4	22	6	12
5	Mukapadar	-	-	-	52	12	6	4	8
6	Bagirijhola	-	-	-	53	-	21	3	8
7	Dwimundi	16	19	35	109	6	-	12	21
8	D. Koral	14	8	14	267	23	62	36	42
9	B. Muchkuni	2	-	-	153	-	32	13	21
10	Ramibeda	2	12	2	42	-	2	6	13
11	Tikarpada	10	10	2	101	4	16	12	28
12	Kodipari	6	2	1	38	2	11	7	13
13	Jogiparitunda	-	-	-	6	2	8	2	4
14	Naringjodi	4	2	-	18	3	11	3	4
15	Ratachuan	-	2	1	17	-	6	4	11
16	Ambiliugudatunda	2	-	-	21	3	12	8	13
17	Hatikaman	-	-	-	4	-	12	3	6
18	Lundurukona	1	-	-	10	-	6	-	4
19	Paikupakhal	4	2	-	22	9	5	3	8
20	Andirakonch	-	-	1	17	5	3	-	6
21	Konchaguma	2	-	-	-	-	2	-	-
22	Gaimundatunda	4	-	-	111	12	32	13	33
23	Others	22	8	10	46	12	22	12	12
	Total	**89**	**65**	**66**	**1309**	**30**	**349**	**159**	**289**
	Percentage	**4.5**	**3.3**	**3.4**	**67.00**	**1.5**	**17.86**	**8.1**	**14.8**

Table 14: Developmental Activities by UAIL and URDS

S. No.	*Village*	*Road*	*Drinking Water*	*Sanitation*	*Health*	*Agriculture*	*Pisciculture*	*Literacy*	*Cultural & Sports*	*Promotion of SHGs*
1.	Tikri	-	*	*	*	-	-	-	-	-
2.	Gokulmunda	-	*	*	*	-	-	-	-	-
3.	Osapada	-	*	*	*	*	*	-	-	-
4.	Bilamal	-	*	*	*	-	-	-	-	-
5.	Mukapadar	*	*	*	*	*	-	-	-	-
6.	Bagirijhola	-	*	*	*		-	-	-	-
7.	Dwimundi	*	*	*	*	*	-	-	-	-
8.	D. Koral	*	*	*	*	*	-	*	*	*
9.	B. Muchkuni	-	*	*	*	-	-	-	-	*
10.	Ramibeda	-	*	*	*	-	-	-	-	
11.	Tikarpada	*	*	*	*	-	-	-	-	*
12.	Kodipari	-	-	-	-	-	-	-	-	*
13.	Jogiparitunda	-	-	-	*	-	-	-	-	*
14.	Naringjodi	-	-	-	-	-	-	-	-	*
15.	Ratachuan	-	-	-	-	-	-	-	-	*
16.	Ambiliugudatunda	-	-	-	-	-	-	-	-	*
17.	Hatikaman	-	-	-	-	-	-	-	-	*
18.	Piringini	-	-	-	-	-	-	-	-	*
19.	Lundurukona	-	-	-	-	*	-	-	-	*
20.	Paikupakhal	*	-	-	*	-	-	-	-	*
21.	Andirakonch	*	*		*	-	-	-	-	*
22.	Konchaguma	-	-	-	-	-	-	-	-	*
23.	Gaimundatunda	-	-	-	-	-	-	-	-	*

**** = Denotes activities undertaken***

10

Impact of Globalisation on Tribal Education in India: Challenges and Opportunities

Milan Kr. Shee and Dr. B. Sarkar

Introduction

The tribal people of India is the second largest group of the backward classes of the under privileged section. These tribal peoples inhabit as isolated group from the rest of the population. They are also isolated in terms of their rituals, social norms, values and cultural practices. As a consequence, they remain the most backward section from the main stream of Indian formal educational system. The census figure of 1931 discloses that only 0.7% of the tribal people were literate. After independence the Govt. of India has taken many initiatives for mainstreaming and increasing literacy rate, but unfortunately it never reaches to its goals.

Globalisation is a much known & much discussed phenomenon in the world's socio-economic system. The term has been widely used in the last twenty years. It is a complex process and which does not only refer to its basic economic sense but also it has several dimensions like technological, political, environmental, socio-cultural, educational, as well as, it includes all the aspect of modern human life. M. Waters define globalisation as "A social process in which the constraints of geography on social and cultural arrangements recede and in which people become increasingly aware that they are receding." (Waters, 1995). In this state the process of globalisation which brings a worldwide revolution in 1990, also influenced each nook and corner of human life i.e. economical, environmental, technological, socio-cultural, political and educational.

In India, during the early 1990's, the Government of India accepted the condition set by the World Bank, World Trade Organisation (WTO) and its affiliated and adopted a set of economic and other reforms. Policies of liberalisation and privatisation were adopted as part of their reforms. These reforms and changing policies have made Indian market open for the foreign trade and investment, privatisation of public sectors and rapid economic growth which have impact on Indian education system and as well as the indigenous community of India.

The process of globalisation along with liberalisation and privatisation create education, a service under the umbrella of general agreement on trade in service (GATS) which open a wide scope of privatisation. The Objectives of GATS is to establish a multilateral framework for services similar to trade in goods involving reduction in tariff and non-tariff barriers to trade. Trade in services has been defined under GATS in terms of four modes of delivery. Such as –

- **Cross – border supply :** delivery of education service via internet (e.g., international telephony, distance education, on-line courses)
- **Consumption abroad:** movement of students from one country to another for higher education (Indian students in UK Universities).
- **Commercial presence :** establishment of local branch campuses on subsidiaries by foreign universities in other countries, courses offered by domestic private colleges (Foreign universities may start establishment in India and offer their degrees)
- **Movement of Natural Persons:** temporary movement of teachers, lecturers and education personnel to provide education services overseas. (Indian teacher going to teach in foreign high schools, colleges, universities to some extent).

However, education, as a service industry, is part of globalisation process under the umbrella of GATS. The main subsector under the GATS in the area of education are primary, secondary, higher education, post secondary technical and vocational, universities degrees or equivalent, adult education and other education services. These aspects play a vital role on tribal socio-cultural condition and livelihood. Along with this, it also brings privatisation of different stages of education which effects tribal educational progress.

Objectives

1. To assess the impact of Globalisation on the Elementary stage of Tribal Education.
2. To examine, how Globalisation along with privatisation and GATS left impact on Tribal School Education.
3. To assess the Higher Education of STs and role of Globalisation.
4. To examine, how different aspect of Higher Education of STs influenced by the GATS.
5. To discuss some major challenges and opportunities regarding the tribal education.

Methodology

The methodology for this study is used as 'Existing Statistics Analysis'. Data have been collected from the different reliable sources like MHRD, DISE, AISHE, WENR etc. which help to make the conclusion. Due to the limitations of available data, this study is used as review of published literature sources related to Indian tribal education and Globalisation, and also consults various books and website sources.

Tribal Education of India and Globalisation

The tribal population of India has some distinctive features, among them one of the most important features is that they belong to the most backward classes in respect of education. The indigenous communities of India are more isolated from every aspect of Indian mainstream, they also stands far from the formal educational system of India, that is why the tribal education's profile has been very poor than other categories.

- ***Tribal School Education And Globalisation:***

The Elementary Education: The Gross Enrolment Ratio (GER) for STs in the elementary stage of education has improved considerably from 1986 – 87 to 2010-11. In the year 1986-87 the GER was 69.6% which increased to 88.0% in 2000-01 and in 2005-06 the ratio has been reached to 106.7% which is comparatively sound. Finally the ratio has reached to 119.7% in 2010-11 (Educational statistics at a Glance, MHRD, Bureau of Planning, Monitoring & Statistics, New Delhi, 2013.). Here in this context it is important that the Sarva Shikhsha Abhiyan (Education for All) was launched for achieving the Universal enrolment at the elementary stage. The SSA (EFA) is the sound result of 'Global Learning' which is influenced by Globalisation & Liberalisation.

The Secondary Education: The status of Gross Enrolment Ratio (GER) for secondary stage (IX-XII, 14-17 years) of ST's is much less than Elementary Stage. In the years of 2001-02 the total percentage was 25.7 in the secondary stage, where the GER in the elementary level was 88.0% and in the year 2005-06 it reached to 106.7% where in the secondary stage it was only 28.7% which was very poor than the elementary enrolment ratio. The growth secondary education of ST is not satisfactory like other categories. Here 'Drop-out' is the vital reason. From the table – 1, in the year 2000-01 the enrolment of primary level (I-V) was 101.1% but at the Upper Primary stage it was 60.2% and at the secondary stages it was only 25.7 % (**Source:** Educational statistics At a Glance, MHRD, Bureau of Planning, Monitoring & Statistics, New Delhi, 2013) these differences above near between 35-45%.

In this context the Drop-Out Rate in School Education of ST student is very high, specifically at the secondary stage. After elementary level the Drop-

Out rate has been increased highly towards secondary to higher, this is significantly high than SC (In the year 2010-11 56.0% (I-X Class) where ST's is 70.9%) and others. In the matter of drop-out or decreasing enrolment after elementary to secondary and higher stages some factors are inter related like poverty, lack of awareness towards education, isolated cultures livelihood, different dialects, uneven competition etc. besides this the common curriculum and the common vocational courses in secondary stage are not also oriented to tribal life and livelihood. This is the reason they felt hardly any interest in secondary and higher education. There the globalisation has left little bit impact. In this connection the process of liberalisation, privatisation and Globalisation (LPG) have left big impact on school education simultaneously ST's school education. During the early 1990's, the Govt. of India accepted conditions set by the WTO (World Trade Organisation) and well under the provision of GATS (General Agreement on Trade in Services) its consequence was liberal approach towards Indian educational field which results privatisation of Indian school education which has been growing rapidly.

How Globalisation along with Liberalisation and privatisation has been effected the Indian School education is clear, where in the year of 2000-01, central Govt. State Govt., Private Aided and Private Unaided Schools were accordingly 117, 5609, 3362, 6937 but after five years, in the year of 2005-06 there are 116, 7141, 3534, 15089 and in the year of 2011-12 strangely they are 114, 7716, 3335, 22763. Here except the Private Unaided School others categories of school do not create much impression, the private unaided school in between 2000-01 to 2011-12 it have been grown numerously to 15826 **(DISE data from 2000 - 01 to 2011 -12).** This is really strong & this is the effect of globalisation. In the matter of STs Student's school education, there private unaided qualitative school are very poor than other's categories as like their own situation. In this growing storm privatisation of school education in India has been created huge differences between ST's other categories in respect of private schooling. In the year of 2008 for the Lower Secondary stage to private aided & unaided school the ST's was 4.3 & 3.5% where ward 15.9%, 11.8% and OBC was 43.2 and 42.1%. At the Higher Secondary stage in private aided and unaided school the ST's enrolment percentage was 4.4 and 2.9 where the SC was 14.3% and 10.7% and OBC's enrolment percentage was 39.5 and 44.2 (Toby Linden's calculation from NSS data, 64 rounds. 'Secondary Education'). In this regard the tribal communities are stand far from the other categories. Maximum private schools are running by self finance that is why the admission and tuition fees are too high, relevantly it is mention worthy, some of the famous schools of Kolkata namely G.B. Birla, La' Martinious, Modern High School etc. where admission and monthly tuition fees are likely 50,000 – 1, 00,025 and 3200-6500 rupees at the lower infant level (Ei-Samay, Bengali News Paper, 19.11.2014). These private schools are mostly English Medium, highly expensive they have their own rules and regulation therefore, ST's participation & to get the qualitative advance education from the private schools are much low than other categories. This desperation and inability of STs make some questions about the quality and equality of school education in India.

- **Tribal Higher Education and Globalisation**

India is the third largest country for higher education system, in the world, next only to China and United states. After independence the progress of higher education and the growth of enrolment in higher education in India have been very impressive. For the ST's students it has also little bit increased, the GER of higher education of ST students (age group of 18-23 years) have been increased over the years i.e. in the year 2001-02 it may 4.2% where all categories were 8.1% which was increased to 11.2% & 19.4% in the year 2010-11. In respect of all categories students GER of higher education in the age group of 18-23 years the ST's GER is average but this is the entry level of higher education, it is not the total picture of higher education. In the stage-wise Enrolment of higher education of ST's enrolment in some important courses like Ph.D / D.Sc / D. Phil was 1.5, M.A. -250, M.Sc – 4.5, B.E / B.Sc. Engg. / B. Arch – 57.2, Medicine, Dentistry, Nursing, Pharmacy, Ayurvedic and Unini – 19.3 and B.Ed / B.T. is 9.4 thousand where in the same courses the total enrolment is respectively 36.0, 481.5, 230.2, 1668.2, 305.6 & 244.8 thousands (Educational statistics at a Glance, 2005-06 MHRD, Department of Higher Education-2008). In respect of total enrolments and SC's enrolment the ST's enrolment of higher education it is much weak. Since 1990's the higher educational scenario has been changed significantly due to globalisation along with huge introduction of ICT (Information, Communication, and Technology) & privatisation. This change has created so many specialised courses as per the demand of Global market and structure where the ST's student's enrolment is very poor.

Gats and Different Aspect of Tribal Higher Education: After 1990's the higher education sector has been changed in its nature and structure where the Division of Labour, use of ICT and Management approach left significant impact. The global demand towards higher education and the application of higher education has been changed day by day, in this changing scenario the most backward class like ST's students are left behind form the mainstream and competition of higher education. That is why the ST's students enrolment in different demanding courses i.e. computer application, management, technology, administration, trade etc. it's very low and some where nil.

At the same time, the GATS's effect on higher education in India is high, the management wise higher education institutes have been changed and it results rapid growth of private institution. In the year of 2000-01 the private-aided universities and colleges were 10 & 4997 total 5507 and the private unaided were 21 and 3202 total 3223 these numbers has increased for the private aided university and college were 10 and5750 total 5760 where the private unaided strangely 70 and 7650 total 7720 in the year 2005-06 (Source – ICRIER W.P. BY P. AGARWAL) relatively the enrolment of higher education in private institutions is too high in the year 2012 that is 58.9% (Source: Higher Education in India : Twelfth five year plan and beyond.) A matter of concern is that unlike the past. The large growth of these institutions, it is argued, represents commercialisation of higher education. (Tilak 2006: 114). It is rightly observed, "higher education is far too expensive to be made privately profitable unless it is reserved for the rich or is of very poor quality" [Patel 2003: 151]. Higher education under private institution is much expensive which the ST's student cannot afford. On the another hand, the two third of rich public institutions are below standard, in this situation the rapid growth of the private institution may have made the opportunities for enrolment in higher education but equally it has created the discrimination between rich and poor, elite and deprived section in higher education which has affected the ST's higher education.

Another Very Significant impact of globalisation along with GATS on Indian higher education is **'Consumption Abroad"**. In the last two decades the Indian student's enrolment in foreign universities colleges has been increased cumulatively. In the year of 2004-05 the Indian student's enrolment in abroad like USA, UK and Australia was respectively 80466, 15000, and 22279. [WENR (World Education News and Reviews), IDP, IIE]. Presently this trend is highly appreciated as a mechanism of globalisation but in the same situation the ST's students stand far from this because most of the ST's students belong to most the backward section where they never think about such enrolment in abroad along with this their economical, social, psychological and other circumstances also does not support them to get foreign higher education. Relevantly it is mention worthy that; the Indian Govt. had taken some initiative to provide higher education to ST's students in abroad. "In the year 2007-2008 the scheme of National Overseas Scholarship was converted to a Central Sector Plan scheme whereby financial assistance is provided to meritorious ST students for pursuing higher education abroad at the level of Masters and Ph.D The scheme envisages awarding 30 overseas scholarships every year, of these, 30 percent are earmarked for ST finalists. Grants are given to the selected candidates on 100 percent basis directly by the Ministry through the Indian Missions. The Eleventh Plan target was to award 50 overseas scholarships ST students. In the first four years of the Eleventh Plan, only 8 scholarships could be awarded (2 per year). 15 scholarships were envisaged in the year 2011-12. Specified field of study under the scheme have been revised for the selected year 2010-2011 in order to broaden the scope and benefit more students, the disciplines like Medicine,

Pure Sciences, Engineering, Agricultural Science and Management have been covered under the scheme."(12th Five Year Plan on Scheduled Tribes 2012-17)

The National Overseas Scholarships of Indian Govt. was no doubt a noble initiative in respect of present scenario of ST's and resents trends of higher education in spite of this the number of Scholarships per year for ST's students under the scheme is nothing in view of total picture of Indian higher education abroad where in the year 2004-2005 the enrolment of Indian students in abroad numeral 117745 this is the enrolment detail of only three counters (USA, UK, Australia) there are so many others. The opportunity of higher education in abroad or the National Overseas Scheme are not executed properly as the ST's student themselves are unable to grab these options because their educational and others background are not supportive. Therefore the ST's students enrolment in higher education may have increased (it is in entry level and their share in enrolment is still less than their share in the table population.) but as per the global market and modern trend in higher education they are left far behind. The process of globalisation has introduced broadly information, communication and technology the facilities of which the ST's students can not avail. This has made large difference between the ST's students and globalised higher education.

Major Challenges of Tribal Education:

Education as a phenomenon is very interrelated with other social phenomenon like economical, political, cultural, religious, geographical and so on. Globalisation is also such a process which influenced all these. So there are some major challenges regarding tribal education-

- The process of globalisation along with liberalisation, privatisation, commercialisation, FDI (Foreign Direct Investment) and the entry of MNC (Multi National Company) creates the mechanised farming, new agricultural policies and commercialisation of forest products which are likely to increase inequalities of income and consumption between regions and peoples and these have been also influenced highly on their education.
- The huge exploration of ICT requires more skill in all work and basically globalisation is biased against unskilled workers, mostly Schedule Tribe people are unskilled and that is why they are left behind from the competition of engagement in various job and they are distracted from the main flow of economic life.
- Globalisation is reduction in cultural diversity and promotes the cultural dominating values of consumerism, so that tribal life and livelihood is affected and the youth become restless, or disconnected from their educational achievement.

- The common curriculum could not attach the tribal cultural feelings and sentiment. Therefore, they feel apathy towards the conventional education.
- Another challenge towards education of ST's is language problem, maximum private schools and various higher educations were accepted by ST's students.
- ST's teacher participation in teaching profession is rare which does not inspire the ST's students.

Recommendation:

Indian Govt. has already taken so many initiatives, schemes and programmes for developing the schedule tribe community including the field of education but in spite of this there are no significant development of ST's, so from the above discussion there are some recommendation for educational development of ST and how to meet the further challenges.

- The Government needs to establish some policies which will protect the tribal community form the devil side of globalisation, and ensure their livelihood.
- The Non-Govt. and Govt. initiative should be needed to promote mass awareness programme among tribal community about the importance of education and about the various facilities allotted by the government and non-government sector because maximum of them have no idea regarding these.
- The Government needs to introduced different training programmes interrelated with the tribal culture, life and livelihood for improving their skill which will make them capable in the global market.
- It is needed to develop the public school in term of infrastructure, teachers and quality as per the global standard and ICT stand be needed to introduce for preparing ST's students for further education and making capabilities to face private's modern education.
- There are needed to develop an integrated and liberal curriculum development approach which will include the tribal cultural scene and some part of their life and livelihood.
- There is a great need for providing some vocational and technical educational courses at secondary level which will be mostly related to the tribal life and livelihood i.e. agricultural, forest management, art and hand craft etc.
- It is necessary to give importance to English language along with mother language from the primary level and for this reason the specialised teachers, balanced syllabus and encouragement towards ST's students should be demanded.

- Private sector in education should be controlled by Govt. and the private institutions, universities should not run for profit only but rather than run through charitable trusts / societies as a part of a corporate social responsibility (CSR).
- Open schools and universities should be established to after quality education at the least cost.
- The additional initiative and encouragement may be introduced for enrolment of ST's students in versatile higher education programme and abroad higher education in spite of this there may be needed to broad scopes for job in Govt. and non-Govt. sector in different section including teaching.

Conclusion:

The tribal people of India are the major weakest section from each nook and corner of social life and the lack of education is the root cause of this. Globalisation and its sub process like liberalisation, privatisation, commercialisation etc have an important role regarding the education system and these have an impact on tribal education. The impact of globalisation on tribal education not only have negative but there are some positive impacts too. Globalisation has introduced 'the global learning' and a liberal approach towards equality of education, the consequence of which EFA(Education For All) in India, SSA, Right To Education Act, 2009, Mead Day Mill Programme etc. have played a vital role for increasing enrolment of ST students in different stages of education.

Again the influence of globalisation has affected the education of ST student's through privatisation, commercialisation of different level of education and 'Consumption Abroad'. This changing scenario of modern education has made the gap between ST's and others, this gap may be called **'Educational Gap'**. In this paper all aspects of ST's education under the process of globalisation has been defined. Here it is essential to rethink, revitalize and reconstruct ST's education for ensuring the equal opportunities and balanced development in the era of globalisation.

References

12th Five Year Plan on Scheduled Tribes 2012-17 http://planning commission.gov.in as retrieved on 22.08.2014.

Agarwal. P (2006): 'Higher Education in India : The Need for Change'. working paper No 180, Indian Council for Research on International Economic Relation.

Ahuja, Ram (2001): 'Social Problem in India', Rawat Publication, Jaipur and New Delhi.

All India Survey on Higher Education (2010-2011): Government of India, MHRD, Department of Higher Education, New Delhi 2013.

Educational Statistics (2011-2012), Commissioner & Director of School Education, State Project Director RVM (SSA) Andhrapradesh, Hydrabad.

Educational Statistics At A Glance (2005-06), GOI, MHRD, Development of Higher Education 2008.

Educational Statistics At a Glance (2010-11). GOI, MHRD, Bureau of Planning, Monitoring and Statistics, New Delhi – 2013.

Hasnain, Nadeem (2004): ' Indian Society and Culture, Continuty and Change', Jawahar Publishers and Distributors, DDA Mkt, Ber Sarai, New Delhi.

Linden, Toby (2012) : 'Secondary Education' IDFC, India Infrastructure Report 2012, htt://www.idfc.comasretrieved on 22.08.14

N.R. Nithya (2014): 'Globalisation and the Plight of Tribals: the case of Kerala, India, The Dawan Journal, Vol. 3 No. 1, January-June 2014.

Newspaper: 'Ei Samay' (Bengali Edition) – 19.11.2014.

Patel, I.G. (2003): 'Higher Education and Economic Development' in J.B.G. Tilak (ed), Education, Society and Development: National and International Perspectives, APH for UNIEPA, New Delhi.

Rao C.N. Shankar (2012): 'Sociology'- Principles of Sociology with an Introduction to Social Thought', S. Chand and Company Ltd., Ramnagar, New Delhi – 110055.

Statistical Profile of Schedule Tribes in India 2010, Ministry of Tribal Affairs, Statistics Division, GOI. http://www.tribal.nic as retrieved on 25.08.2014.

Tilak, J.B.G. -(2006): 'Private Higher Education: Philanthropy to Profits' in Higher Education in the World 2006: The Financing of Universities, GUNI Series on the Social Commitment of Universities 1, Palgrave, New York and GUNI,

Trade In Education Services Ministry of Commerce and Industry, A Consultation Paper on 'Higher Education In India and GATS: An Opportunity', Trade Policy Division, Development of Commerce, GOI, http://commerce.nic.in as retrieved on 27.08.2014

University News (2004) Special Issue – Private Participation in Indian Higher Education: Contemporary Issues and challenges. New Delhi: Association of Indian Universities 42 (07), February 15-22, 2004.s

11

Welcome to the Unknown Destination

(Impact of westernisation and consequent globalisation on the Limbus of Kalimpong subdivision of Darjeeling District in West Bengal)

Biva Samadder

Introduction

The end of twentieth century witnesses the appearance of globalisation: a progression that moving towards a global culture, and confrontations to globalisation. After rapid industrialisation and urbanisation on the Globe, the Capitalistic world initiated the globalisation process for free market economy and removing the boundary of trade by selling branded products. The developed industrialised countries became beneficial by exporting their manufacturing goods with quality package, developing Research & Development (R & D), establishing democratic policy, building capacity of man power, advancing high –tech market. In due course of time the international market penetrated everywhere, even the indigenous land like 1056.5 sq.k.m largest sub-division Kalimpong of Darjeeling District. This change of globalisation has had both positive and negative impact on the tribal groups. The common allege against the globalisation is that, it is an extension of westernisation, modernisation empowered by free market economy, it perpetuates neo-colonialism. Beyond the economic and political debates, it is assumed that globalisation is a challenge to cultures, particular in marginalised communities and their identities.

Towards Global Village:

By globalisation we basically mean that the world has become more and more simply accessible and open to anyone of us. This process has made the modern nations and communities progressively more interdependent, accountable to the market forces and flexible to the changing currents. Almost every one of us is aware that there is no escape however strong our resistance might be, from the all too powerful grip of globalisation. For some people it has become a craze: for others it is just fashion, but, for the unaware Indian masses it is just a secluded dream or rather just a magic word. Any way, it enhances the levels and volumes of global interaction (Lewis:2002:334)· While the attempt of Globalisation has been to create a "global village", ensuring a "mainstream presenting" of the "marginalised" groups, this process in the recent years, has however, resulted in making the silence of the "other" more noisy than ever. The globalisation encompasses a series of processes, including diffusion and acculturation, working to promote change in a world in which nations and people are interlinked and mutually dependent. Promoting such linkages are economic and political forces, along with modern systems of transportation and communication.

Objectives of the paper:

This paper will discuss on the impact of Globalisation on the Limbus of Darjeeling District of West Bengal take their stand on the Globalised world.

The Limbu and the Darjeeling:

Darjeeling District has the most complicated boundaries from the past. The Northern part of West Bengal, popularly known as North Bengal, consists of six districts, namely Malda, South Dinajpur, North Dinajpur, Jalpaiguri, Cooch Bihar and Darjeeling. There are about 40 Scheduled Tribes in North Bengal, which is the habitation of 14,54,330 members (as per Census 2001) of indigenous or tribal people having the cultural diversities, whereas West Bengal's total tribal members are 44, 06.794 (2001 Census). The northern Bengal tribal group is in grouped with the North-eastern Tribal groups. The tribal population of North Bengal could be classified into three groups based on their location in three distinct socio-economic set-ups : (1) the Nepali-speaking tribes in the Darjeeling Hills, both tea gardens and outside, (2) the Central Indian tribes in the agricultural setup of Malda, South Dinajpur, Darjeeling, Jalpaiguri and Cooch Behar districts (in Cooch Behar and Jalpaiguri districts there are tribes of Monogoloid racial stock that have migrated from the North East and Nepali) and (3) the Central Indian tribes which constitute the labour force in the tea gardens in the Terai of Darjeeling district and Dooars of Jalpaiguri district.

The Limbu is one such tribal group in North Bengal,, who are the inhabitants of the Darjeeling District in the three block of Kalimpong hilly areas, Ghosal (2003) in his article on 'Limbu' in 'People of India' stated, the word 'Limbu' is derived from 'Li' (meaning 'bow') and 'Abu' (meaning 'Shooter'). Hence 'Limbu' means 'bow shooter' or archer. In Darjeeling District (W.B.) they are addressed by the honorific title 'Subha' meaning 'Chief', which is the offshoot of the "Kiranti" or "Kiranti" (Dalton 1872, and Risley 1891), which has a wider connotation, which covers Rai, Limbu,

Sunwar, Gurung, Manges and Tamang. They are supposed to be originated from the Tibet, from where they had migrated to Eastern Nepal before they finally settled to Sikkim and Kalimpong.. At the home they speak in their own 'Limbu' language. Now, they are more closely linked with tribal communities like the Lepchas, Gurungs, Bhutias rather than other Nepali speaking community in Darjeeling and Sikkim.

The researcher has not yet been found the Census Report particularly on Limbus of Kalimpong Subdivision of Darjeeling District. But it is mentionable that 'Limbus' and 'Tamangs' are already got the status of 'Scheduled Tribe' in Sikkim in the year of 2003 and in Darjeeling in the year of 2003.Presently, according to an unpublished report (2005) of 'YAKTHOONG SHONG CHOOMVO" (Association of Limbu Community) of Kalimpong Subdivision in Darjeeling District, the total Limbu population of Kalimpong Block-I, Block-II and Block-III, is, 9,303. In which Kalimpong Block-I constituted 5,843 Limbu people along with 1,035 families. These villages of Kalimpong-I where Limbus are sufficient in number, are Dungra Busty, Tanek Busty, Bong Busty, Pudung, Seokbibkhani, Yok Busty, Jarayo Taar Sindepong Busty, and a few in Kalimpong town.

On the hilly side of the Himalayan belt as the Eastern Himalayas a group is living from the ancient historical period. The group is Kirat by name, which is composed of four ethnic tribes : Limbu, Lepcha, Dhimal and Raj. The Kirat is a community which is composed of four ethnic tribes: Limbu, Lepcha Dhimal, and Rai. Among these, the Limbu is the dominant indigenous tribe and one of the oldest communities in the Panchthar and Ilam districts of eastern Nepal.

Topographically the Darjeeling district can be divided into two distinct tracts : the hilly areas in the north and the plain areas at the foot-hills of the Himalayas. In 2011 Census Darjeeling District has a total population of 1,84,034. The greater bulk of the people in the hills today are the Gorkhas, Sherpas, Nepalese, Bhutias and Tibetians. The Limbu is one of the indigenous tribes and is one of the ancient inhabitants of this district.

Kalimpong was growing as urban centre by virtue of its being the headquarter of the respective Darjeeling and Kurseong subdivision as also important entrecote markets served by a communication network with Tibet, Sikkim and Bhutan. Urbanisation through the establishment of a sanatorium at the nuclease town also led to growth of employment opportunities and hence to population increase. The declining of trade between India and Tibet has affected Kalimpong unfavorably. Like most other area of India Kalimpong has impact of globalisation in large scale by trading garments, handicrafts and emerging trends of establishment of worldwide information technology and communication network, but the new identity has also led to ethnic conflicts. When a whole community like Limbu adopts a habit, it becomes a custom. This imitation plays an important role in the conversion from habits to law that also specify the values of a society which become fundamental to their heritage. Although globalisation cannot erase an identity totally except creating hybrid identities.

Economy and Occupational Pattern

It is true as the dominant perception of India, that almost everywhere the tribes are conceived as people with symbiotic relationship with nature. This indication relates to the management of natural resources by various communities living in the regions on the basis of their traditional knowledge. Such knowledge actually depends on the level of engagement a culture has with natural resources. Limbus' traditions, values, beliefs and customs are also supported by the natural resources as an old Limbu saying, "ghar odar ho, vana vandhar ho" which means "the house is a shelter whereas the forest is a treature". But with a change in social and political perspectives, obvious changes were observed in resource management, conservation patterns and the process of decision-making and policy. The Limbus had communal land ownership called "Kipat" until the middle of twentieth century (Caplon 1970).

On this alleviation of hill station of Kalimpong, living on the middle hills at altitude varying from 3000 to 4000 ft. above sea level, similar to other communities of Eastern Himalaya, Limbus also failed to protect their forest. Although land is the main resource of Limbus but there are indications to prove that due to deforestation in Kalimpong subdivision the streams and wells became dry during winter and soil has suffered erosion. In such fragile eco system the Limbus are struggling. The hidden treasure of this ethnic community- their social ideas, lifestyles, religion and age-old belief system - are unfortunately are seems to be in great threat.

Only few small - scale industries have been run by the majority Nepalese which is indicated by the fact that Limbus present occupation is terrace cultivation and they also work as daily labourers in agricultural fields. A sizeable number of Limbu youths are enlisted in Indian Gorkha regiments. At present it is observed that some of them are engaged in various white collar jobs like teaching at schools and government and private sectors. Knowing and speaking Nepali language helps them in procuring economic and occupational facilities. Ironically, present day younger generation do not feel comfortable speaking in their own Limbu tongue. Modern forcess of changes are sweeping them fast. Because the issue of identity which has been oscillating continuously mainly through diverse migration modes and differential cultural contact situations in varied eco-cultural-territorial zones like Kalimpong. Because local of Kalimpong is sandwiched between the neighboring countries of Nepal, Bhutan and the state of Sikkim.

This paper is a part of the bigger study on the "Changing ways of life of the Limbus in the Kalimpong Block I of the Darjeling district "in the Bong (which have 10 villages) Gram Panchyat, Dungra (which have 8 villages) and Tashiding (which have 5 villages) Gram Panchyat. In those GPs the following table giving a representative and purposive sample of the changing economic system and occupational pattern in three villages, considering the limitation and objectives of the paper:

Table-1 : Percentage of households according to main employment type

	Bong Busty	*Chibo Busty*	*Pudung*
Agriculture	39 (73.5%)	53 (88.33%)	47 (78.33%)
Daily wage	8 (15.09%)	12 (20.0%)	7 (11.66%)
Private Company	23 (43.39%)	17 (28.33%)	2 (3.33%)
Government	12 (22.6%)	11 (18.33%)	5 (8.33%)
No. of households surveyed	53	60	60

Source: GFF village surveys (2011).

Note: Survey did not differentiate agricultural employment from own production. Also, each household was ascribed only one activity, so for example, rock-breaking as a source of income does not appear at all.

The above table shows that LImbus are largely involved in cultivation and eke out their existence by growing either maize, black lentil or millet. Inter-cropping with beans, chillies, pumpkin, sweet potatoes, arrowroots, turmeric, tapioca etc on their meagre lands.. Simultaneously they are getting involved in services in Govt. and private companies.

Impact of globalisation and identity of culture:

According to Lehman, Globalisation has two-fold ways of relations with local culture: i) Homogenisation and ii) Cosmopolitanism. We need to look at globalisation from the point of view of its impact on local indigenous cultures of Kalimpong. Modernisation has already made an inroad into the life and culture of its people. The globalised market economy as well as the **entertainment industry** has already encroached upon the traditional culture and the life style of the people of the region.

Like their most other counterpart of this region Limbu tribes combine the **macro-religious** practices with their traditional customs and beliefs. Because religion is emancipated from dogmatic belief and practices. To join the westernised modern world with hope of a improved future Christianity and Hinduism, the religions to which they have been converted in recent decades. Not only that but due to modern influence, exposer to mass media contact with urban, the Limbus have come into the fold of Hinduism and some of them have accepted *Saibaba, Ramdev* as **Godman**. But traditionally all the Limbus is followers of "Yuma Samyo Religion". According to the religion they believe that the Limbu's lives are guided by the philosophy of "Yuma Samyu" or "Yumaism". They believe that the life of each and every individual is the creation of the Almighty God "Tagera Ningwaphuma".

Hence some people have expressed the fear that large scale comodification of their cultures would erase their unique identifies. Authors like Appadurai (1990) and Featherstone (1996) however contend that globalisation cannot be simply measured from the set binaries of globalism and localism. There is a view that it is a force that will erase unique identities and traditions that it is the opportunity for unhindered trade and commerce, and economic empowerment.

The major impact of modernisation that expose the Limbu to processes are transport facilities, education, administrative and financial systems, change of religion, the commercial forces and others. The change in social conditions and pattern of living, as well as the emerging role of media towards women empowerment, responsible for women going out for jobs and this is responsible for the shift towards their "outdoorness". All these forces have affected their social and marriage customs, cultures and cultural heritage. Under this globalised cultural space, the larger question is, can unique identities remain pure and uncontaminated? To speak the truth, that is not possible because each community keeps on learning from other communities and thus the process of acculturation continues. The following table shows the impression of the development in three gram panchyats under study:

Table 2 : Basic information of the Local governance

Name of Gram Panchatyats	*Population (in percentage)*			*Literate*	*No of Schools*	*No of Roads*	*No of Health Centers*	*Electrification*	*Drinking Water Facility*
	Total	*SC*	*ST*						
1. Tashiding	3490	252 (7.22)	1259 (36.07)	2760 (79.08)	2	2	1	Yes	Tap Water
2. Dungra	6794	825 (12.1)	2021 (29.74)	5465 (80.44)	5	2	2	Yes	Spring Water
3. Bong	4609	411 (8.91)	803 (17.42)	3634 (78.85)	7	3	2	Partially	Partially

[*Note: Date report of the Gram Panchyat under Kalimpong – I Development Block. (2011)]

Keeping in mind the utilisation value, a community adopts new ideas and practices. It is now being a very common scenario like any other part of India that Kalimpong adopts the emerging trends of establishment of worldwide information technology and communication network.The researcher observed even in the remotest part of the Limbu villages like Dungra Bustee, Tanek Busty, Bong Busty, Pudung Busty and others in Kalimpong, Limbus are very much habituated with **mobile phone and Television.** Laptop, computer and other electronic equipments are not unfamiliar to the Limbus now.

While a culture makes some readjustment in adopting the new, similarly the new is reshaped to be appropriated by a host culture. It is also true identities already, always hybridized. Once any community opens its door to the forces of globalisation, its cultural assets and products are bound to be pushed for large scale commoditisation and loss of their unique identities. Not only the traditional **dress** or household but also the customs of **marriage enormously changed** due to influence of modern education in both male and female. Love marriage and inter-community marriages are not uncommon nowadays. Thus the tradition-modernity interface is a crucial component both in their identity re-affirmation and conflicts.

So it can be said that the major impact of westernisation followed by modernisation as well as globalisation that has been affected the Limbus of Kalimpong are as follows:

(i) **Westernisation :** Patterned behavior and Inter-personal relationship, western education, adoption of Christianity, changes in traditional identity of house pattern, dress and language

(ii) **Modernisation:** the impact of Hinduism and combine macro-religious practices affected their traditional religious believes. Popularizing the science and technology;

(iii) Globalisation :

(a) the ***media & communication*** as well as ***entertainment industry*** has encroached upon the traditional culture and the life style of the people of Darjeeling district.

(b) the new ***transport facilities***, ***educational development***, ***developed modern administrative and financial systems***, **the** ***commercial forces*** are affecting and changing their social condition.

(c) the Limbu women are going out for jobs nowadays. The emerging role of media towards ***women empowerment*** is responsible for the shift towards their ***"outdoorness"***.

(d) As a very result of westernisation the Limbus are very much habituated with ***mobile phone and television*** nowadays. The recent trend of information & technological development has been observed in modern Limbu society.

(e) the customs of ***marriage enormously changed*** due to influence of modern education in both male and female.

(f) from a very beginning of modern society Limbu has mislaid there. Today when westernisation acutely embedded in

Kalimpong, young Limbu generation are immensely accepted the global culture and unaware about preserving their own traditional treasure.

(g) The natural resources have been collected, processed and marketed in International markets, giving benefits to the large scale companies and primary stakeholder i.e. the tribals remain in their own traditional economy and in poverty. Kalimpong is a scorching spot of horticulture. There are Forty Six Nurseries which are owned by the non-Limbus. Kalimpong, which is the ecological hotspot of India has over forty six Nurseries which income for eighty percent of India's production of orchids that export all over the world.

Table-3 : Rates of return from flower production in Kalimpong

Activity	*Rate of return & means of payment*	*Weekly equivalent (Rupees)*	*Weekly equivalent ($US)*
Flower production (tulips)	5,000-6,000 Rs /- season (1 household in Pudung)	If selling season = 1 month, 1250-1500	$30-$35 (seasonal)

Source: Interviews during field work (data should be treated as estimates).

The following table shows the flori-culture and market has been developed under the influence of globalisation :

Table 4: Top Five Flori- cultural Products of Darjeeling District

BLOCK	*1ST*	*2ND*	*3RD*	*4TH*	*5TH*
KURSEONG	Gladioli 54,190	Begonia 51,475	Cymbidium 18,639	Gloxinia 6,465	Other ornamental flowering/ Bonsai etc5,121
MIRIK	Eucharis 34,375	Other Ornamental Flowers/ DGnbaj 10,325	Gerbera 8,850	Other Bulbous Plants 8,668	Clamelia 5,060
SUKHIA POKHRI	Other Ornamental Plants 36,122	Cymbidium 14,399	Eucharis 13,100	Gladioli 7.705	Begonia 7,650
BIJANBARI	Gloxinia 27,700	Gladioli 26,475	Gloriosa Spp 19,350	Begonia 17,550	Cyclamen 14,350
RANGOLI-RANGLIOT (TAKDAH)	Gladioli 82,375	Gerbera 13,809	Cyclamen 14,300	Begonia 10,505	Gloxinia 8,715

Cond...

KALIMPONG BLOCK - I	GLADIOLI 9,77,00	Other Ornamental plants Bulbs 84,540	Lilium Longifolium 56,500	Chinchirin-chee 43,500	Anthurium Andreanum 25,750
ALGARH (KPG-II)	Gladioli 7,61,800	Eucharis 83,600	Freeezia 32,800	Gloriosa Spp20,000	Easter Lily 18,500
GORUAHTHAN (KPG-III	Zepheranthes spp4,49,802	Haemanthus 3,42, 520	Eucharis 1,76,060	Caladium 1,22,000	Gladioli 1,122,220

Three hundred species of orchid are found around the subdivision, and Poinsettia and sunflower are some of the wild species that line the roads of Kalimpong. But most of these Nurseries are owned by non-Limbus. As such no big industry has been developed in this area of Darjeeling district. As mentioned earlier that only few small – scale industries have been run by the majority Nepalese which is indicated by the fact that Limbus present occupation is terrace cultivation and they also work as daily labourers in agricultural fields. The Limbus is not getting opportunities to be a part of this globalised market. This economical backwardness of Limbu reminds us that any kind of development should be synchronised with the environmental resource.

While we find the educated local inhabitants of the state are spacing themselves with their more advanced counterparts in other parts of the globe, their educationally challenged and financially strained brethren, who are religiously tied to their rationally behold traditions, for whom it is too late to clinch the newer challenges and lucrative opportunities. In the case of Limbus, they are educationally very much backward. Thus, globalisation is turning out to be a force. In Kalimpong area "Nepali" is the lingua-franca, which helps Limbu to procure economic and occupational facilities. But due to lack of advanced and formal education this Kiranti tribe is gradually losing their battle for survival. Though agriculture is the main occupation, but nowadays daily wages labourer is being their primary occupation. At present it is observed that some of them are engaged in various white collar jobs like teaching at schools and government and private sectors.

Limbus is very much inclined with their natural habitat. As regards to their socio-political administration, the traditional caste council 'Tumyanghang' or 'Jatisamaj' is still a trend among them. Within the tribe a Limbu's identity is deeply rooted in the village of his birth and residence. For a Limbu the identity affiliated to a village draws attention to clan affinity, possession of ancestral and other properties in the form of land holdings, participating in community rituals, celebrations, and in the governance of the village polity.

Conclusion:

It is true that in today's world, change is the only permanent. But at the same time, we must ensure that the changes are proportional to the needs of the society, rather than acceptance something blindly and aping others without caring for tradition, cultural values and society specific needs. A "new-born epidemic" of westernisation is knocking on the doorstep of the indigenous land. The changing value system and the dilution of the traditional lifestyle have removed the taboo against sex. The exposure to the outside world and lack of employment opportunities has changed the behavior pattern of the youth in Darjeeling District. As a result in Darjeeling hills one of the major health issues is HIV/AIDS as the number of people infected and affected gradually increased. Till November 2007, the total number of HIV/AIDS cases had reached 141 in Darjeeling hills on which 93 were men, 43 female and 5 were children. Experts say that casual sex, migration, alcoholism, drug addiction are the major reasons that are responsible for the spread of this infection. This is not just a problem of a region but the whole country.

We know that this great threat of modern society may cure on due course, we believe that by globalisation the world has become more and more easily accessible and open to anyone of us, but what we don't know is, can unique identities remain pure and uncontaminated ?

To be an effective player in the global market under an industrial and technological command the smaller communities like Limbu need to put their acts together and should have adequate resources and safeguards. The ethnic handicrafts of Limbu do have an opportunity to be globally marketed along with other products such as floriculture or nursery, food items, indigenous herbal products, beverages, dance and music. Otherwise a big question will remain unanswered, whether the Limbus will reach to their desired destination.

Suggested readings and references

Beteille, A. (1977). *Definition of a Tribe : Caste and Religion* (Ed.), Ramesh Tahapar, Delhi.

Biswas, P.C. (2009). Indian Culture, *Journal of Indian Research Institute,* vol.1, Part-2, University of Virginia, United States.

Call for Gorkhaland Renewed, *Darjeeling Times,* 13.01.2009.

Campbell and Hodgson (1872). 'Limbu' in E.T. Dalton's *Tribal History of Eastern India,* vol.32, Cosmo Publications, Calcutta.

Cemjonga Imana Simha (2003). *History and Culture of Kirat People,* Part 1-2, Kirat Yakthung Chumlung, Sikkim, Original from the University of Michigan.

Clearmountain (TB Subba).pdf-DSpace@NEHU

Community Based Survey of Village Development in Kalimpong Area, West Bengal, India (2010). Working Paper No. 3/2012, The University of Auckland, New Zealand, Centre for Development Studies.

Dash, A.J. (2011). *Bengal District Gazetteer : Darjeeling*, National Printing House, Delhi.

Encyclopedia Britannica (2012).' *Limbu Tribe* 'in www.britannica.com/ EBchecked/ topic /319023/Kiranti.

Ghosal, S. (1993). 'Limbu' in K.S. Singh (Ed.), *People of India (Sikkim)*, vol. XXXIX, Seagul Books, Calcutta.

Lewis, B. 2002. *What went wrong? Western Impact and Middle Eastern response* : Oxford University press.

Mercer, Kobena. 1994. *Welcome to Jungle*. London

Mitra, A. (1995). 'Limbu' in *People of India*, vol.XXXXIII, Part-2, Seagul Books, Calcutta.

P.Lama Mahendra (2012). *Globalisation and cultural practices in mountain areas, dynamic dimensions and implications*, Sikkim University Press, Gangtok.

Ramakant, Ramesh Chandra Misra (1996). *Bhutan : Society and Polity*, Indus Publishing, p.89.

Redfield, R. (1941). *Folk Culture of Yukatam*, Chicago University Press, Chicago.

Risley, H.H. (1891). *The Tribes and Castes of Bengal*, vol.II, Bengal Secretariat Press, Reprinted in 1981, Firma Mukhopadhyay, Calcutta.

Rivers, W.H.R. (1914). *Kinship and Social Organisation*, Constable Press, London.

Samadder, S. (2006). *The Hidden Treasure of Limbus*. Central Institute of Indian Languages, Bhasha Mandakini : Bangla: Language Bureau, Department of Secondary and Higher Secondary Education, Govt of India.

Sengupta, Soumen (2006). Next Weekend you can be at Kalimpong, *The Telegraph* [Retrieved on 12.09.2008].

Subba, J.R. (1999). *The Limboos of Eastern Himalayas*, Sikkim Yakhung Mundhum Saplopa, Sikkim, India.

Subba, J.R. (2005). *The philosophy and concepts of Yuma Samyo (Yumaism): the religion of Limboos of the Eastern Himalayan Region*, Sikkim Yakhung Mundhum Saplopa, Sikkim, India.

Subba, T.B. (1999). *Politics of Culture : A study of three Kirata communities in the Eastern Himalayas*, Orient Longman, Hyderabad, India.

Yakthoong Shong Choomvo (2005). *An Unpublished Report of Limbu Association*, Darjeeling (Regd. No. S/84521/96).

West Bengal Forest Development, report on Kalimpong area, West Bengal, India (2013) (www.wbfdc.com/major_activities.htm)

12

Microfinance to Livelihood Finance: Women as Agents of Change in Tribal Scenario

Dr. Barnali Maity

Introduction

Microfinance is the small scale "Financial Revolution" for the poor, who lack access to formal banking and related services, emerged as an innovation the world over. Microfinance refers to small-scale financial services for both credit and deposits. It is the provision of a broad range of services such as deposits, loans, payment services, money transfers, and insurance to poor and low income households and their microenterprises. Microfinance is a fascinating and empowering innovation in finance, especially provides low cost financing on a small scale to empower people to lift themselves and their families out of poverty. The two main mechanisms for the delivery of financial services to such clients are (1) relationship-based banking for individual entrepreneurs and small businesses; and (2) group-based models, where several entrepreneurs come together to apply for loans and other services as a group.

Microfinance is a range of financial services provided to low income populations who typically lack access to more traditional financial institutions. With insufficient collateral, a poor or no credit history, and often irregular income patterns, those living below the poverty line are considered too high a risk for traditional banks. With no other options, people commonly turn to informal collectors and money lenders who typically charge extremely high interest rates. Under such conditions, escaping the poverty trap can by near impossible. Microfinance institutions (MFI) attempt to fill the gap, providing some combination of savings, credit, insurance, and capacity building services, with the goal of facilitating the asset growth necessary to escape the cycle of poverty. It was evolving into an effective system for provision of financial services to micro enterprises.

Microfinance started off as a grassroots movement in the 1970s and over the last 40 years has grown in size, magnitude and geographical reach. As of December, 2010, over 3600 MFIs reported more than 200 million clients worldwide, of which over 135 million were living on less than US$ 1.25/ a day (Maes and Reed, 2012). The first example of an organised microfinance institution is generally accepted as being the Grameen Bank in Bangladesh in 1976. As an action research project, it was founded by Muhammad Yunus who started by making small loans from his own money at low interest rates to the rural poor around the village of Jobra, Chittagong University. Here, Yunus discovered that very small loans could make a disproportionate difference to a poor person. Jobra women who made bamboo furniture had to take out usurious loans for buying bamboo, to pay their profits to the moneylenders. In this context, the bank had lent small sums to such clients, filling the gap that traditional banks had left and cutting out local loan sharks. The model of small sums lent mainly to women, often organised into mutually supporting groups, was extremely successful, with very few loans left un-repaid and a wide range of social benefits. The award of the 2006 Nobel Peace Prize to Prof. Muhammad Yunus proved that his Grameen Bank experiment in Bangladesh has got the achieved success.

The term "Micro" literally means "small". But the task force has not defined any amount. However as per Micro Credit Special Cell of the Reserve Bank Of India, the borrowal amounts upto the limit of Rs 25000/- could be considered as micro credit products and this amount could be gradually increased up to Rs 40000/- over a period of time which roughly equals to $500 – a standard for South Asia as per international perceptions. The mantra "Microfinance" is banking through groups. The essential features of the approach are to provide financial services through the groups of individuals, formed either in joint liability or co-obligation mode.

Microfinance in India

The SHG-bank linkage programme has expanded at a fast pace in India to evolve into the largest microfinance programme in the world. The essential features of the approach are to provide financial services through the groups of individuals, formed either in joint liability or co-obligation mode. The group in this case does financial intermediation on behalf of the formal institution. This is the predominant model followed in India. In India, the National Bank for Agriculture and Rural Development (NABARD) is the pioneering agency of the SHG bank linkage model. NABARD was initiated in 1986-87 for its formation and promotion. But the real efforts were taken after 1991-92 from the linkage of SHG with different commercial banks through these schemes i.e. Rashtriya Mahila Kosh, 1993, Indira Mahila Yojana, 1995-96, Swa-Shakti Project (earlier known as Rural Women's Development and Empowerment Project), 16 October 1998, Swarna Jayanthi Gram Swarozgar Yojana, April 1999.

NABARD (2005) explains that the Self Help Group is a group with "an average size of about 15 people from a homogenous class. They come together for addressing their common problems. They are encouraged to make voluntary thrift on a regular basis. They use this pooled resource to make small interest bearing loans to their members. The process helps them imbibe the essentials of financial intermediation including prioritisation of needs, setting terms and conditions and accounts keeping. This gradually builds financial discipline in all of them. They also learn to handle resources of a size that is much beyond the individual capacities of any of them. The SHG members begin to appreciate that resources are limited and have a cost. Once the groups show this mature financial behaviour, banks are encouraged to make loans to the SHG in certain multiples of the accumulated savings of the SHG. The bank loans are given without any collateral and at market interest rates. The groups continue to decide the terms of loans to their own members. Since the groups' own accumulated savings are part and parcel of the aggregate loans made by the groups to their members, peer pressure ensures timely repayments."

Women in microfinance

Microfinance programmes targeting women have been a welcome corrective to previous neglect of women's productive and economic role. The Grameen Bank primarily lends to women who have, as the Grameen Bank (Grameen Bank, http://www.grameen-info.org/bank/bcycle.html) argues, "Proved not only reliable borrowers but astute entrepreneurs. As a result, they have raised their status, lessened their dependency on their husbands and improved their homes and the nutritional standards of their children." More than 96% of the Grameen Bank members are women ("Grameen monthly update in USD: December, 2013). In microfinance, internationally more than 80% of the poorest clients i.e., those who live on less than US$ 1.25/ per day, are women (Maes and Reed, 2012). In India, nearly 90% of the groups are women only groups. Prof. Yunus have justified for women borrowers in microfinance movement. Here two popular remarks from his book, "Banker to the Poor" are being quoted. First one is highlighting the impact of microfinance among women that is "UN studies conducted in more than forty developing countries show that the birth rate falls as women gain equality... I believe income-earning opportunities that empower poor women. .. will have more impact on curbing population growth that the current system of "encouraging" family planning practices through intimidation tactics. Family planning should be left to the family." Another one is why Grammen Bank targeting women i.e., "When a destitute mother starts earning an income, her dreams of success invariably center around her children. A woman's second priority is the household. She wants to buy utensils, build a stronger roof, or find a bed for herself and her family. A man has an entirely different set of priorities. When a destitute father earns extra income, he focuses more attention on himself. Thus money entering a household through a woman brings more benefits to the family as a whole."

Livelihood finance

Literally, "Making a living", is a livelihood. Livelihood comprises the capabilities, assets (including both material and social resources) and activities required for a means of living. A livelihood is sustainable when it can cope with and recover from stress and shocks and maintain or enhance its capabilities and assets both now and in the future, while not undermining the natural resource base (Chambers & Conway, 1991). In present day cash economy, without cash or finance, livelihood is impractical. Therefore, a livelihood is any set of economic activities through which a household meets its basic needs and earns some cash income. When carried out on a repetitive basis, or in the long run, these tend to become a "way of life".

Ideal livelihood finance is a set of development based interventions that involve improving the resilience of household livelihoods so that basic survival needs can be met on a sustainable basis. Therefore, Interventions need for diversifying livelihoods strategies, such as creating alternative income-generating activities; providing financial services, such as credit, savings and insurance; and strengthening markets. The first step towards a sustainable livelihood requires the necessary assets to generate income. Without an income, individuals and households are obliged to resort to adverse coping mechanisms, such as cutting down on basic needs or selling off any remaining productive assets. Without assets, earning opportunities decrease and many are forced to take on overwhelming debt. To prevent this spiralling cycle of vulnerability, it is imperative to act swiftly to make and protect the assets people have salvaged and replace or rebuild those that have been lost through active livelihood intervention and its proper promotion.

The dream of a healthy and educated society with no discrimination can be achieved through availability and accessibility of livelihood finance. The hope of a life that no one will sleep hungry, no one will die due to lack of medication, and all children without discrimination can read and write on their own then everyone will be the pillar of the society. If these are done then one shall conveniently conclude that there is livelihood improvement.

Microfinance and Livelihood Finance (a brief review)

Johnson and Rogaly (1997) state that the provision of microfinance can give poor people "the means to protect their livelihoods against shocks as well as to build up and diversify their livelihood activities". They also refer to examples whereby savings and credit schemes were able to meet the needs of the very poor. They stated that microfinance specialists are beginning to view improvements in economic security, rather than income promotion, as the first step in poverty reduction as this reduces beneficiaries overall vulnerability.

The impact of MF on livelihoods is focused in terms of the changes to livelihoods assets and the use of livelihood assets to cope with vulnerability. The provision of MF can assist the poor find the means to protect their livelihoods against shocks and to build up and diversify their livelihood activities. It helps to empower women by supporting women's economic participation and so promotes gender equity. Based on various case studies, they show how MF has played a role in reducing poverty, promoting education, improving health and empowering women. Concerning financial assets, MF contributes to enhance financial capital of livelihoods assets, which can be converted into other types of capital and be used for direct achievement of livelihoods outcomes (DFID, 1999). A study of 16 different MFIs from all over the world pointed out that having access to MF services have led to an enhancement in the quality of life of clients, had increased their self confidence, and had helped them diversify their livelihood security strategies and thereby increase their income (Robinson, 2001). Mayoux (2002) states that while microfinance have much potential the main effects on poverty have been: credit making a significant contribution to increasing incomes of the better-off poor, including women and microfinance services contributing to the smoothing out of peaks and troughs in income and expenditure thereby enabling the poor to cope with unpredictable shocks and emergencies. Impact of microfinance is being reflected significant increases in ownership of livelihood assets such as livestock, equipment and land. They stated that this should not be surprising as poorer clients are more risk averse and less likely to invest in fixed capital and so are more vulnerable to having to sell productive assets in the event of a shock (Marconi & Mosley, 2004). United Nations Capital Development Fund (2004) states that microfinance plays three key roles in development; it helps very poor households meet basic needs and protects against risks, is associated with improvements in household economic welfare, and helps to empower women by supporting women's economic participation and so promotes gender equity. Microfinance has come to play a very important role in the field of development, as illustrated by the launch of the Microcredit Summit in 1997. The Summit aims to reach 175 million of the world's poorest families, especially the women of those families, with credit for the self-employed and other financial and business services, by the end of 2015 (Microcredit Summit, 2005). 2005 was declared as the UN's International Year of Microcredit.

Research methodology

Sample Status

This study was conducted on tribal dominated Jhargram block of Paschim Medinipore district, West Bengal in India and the data were collected as the doctoral research programme. In this study, the women's collectives means the homogeneous group working as microfinance institution by its credit and savings functions is popularly named, SHG. Here, 142 women have been taken as the respondents from 13 women oriented groups. Among these women, 35.24% are Santhal, 39.05% are Mundas and 25.71% are Lodhas. Before sampling was started a list of women of micro-credit programmes was collected from the Block Development offices. The study is based on intensive and in depth study of women's collectives, which were initially formed by self help and later initiated by panchayat around 10-20 members with the deposited amount of Rs 30 per month.

Data Collection Instruments

The instruments used in data collection were Interview, Questionnaire and Observation. Data for the research was collected mainly through the administration of pre-structured well formed questionnaire to respondents. Two types of questionnaire were administered. All sets of questionnaire contained open and closed-ended questions.

Objectives

The study is to find out the impact of women's role in handling of microfinance on the livelihood of their household in engaging business entrepreneurships in tribal scenario. In terms of context, the study covers: deposits and access to credit; the effects of credit on household's income and savings promoting their overall education and health, their ability to participate in household decision making through women's employment. It is imperative to understand the ways in which women's active role contributes to transform microfinance into livelihood finance accelerating the economic growth through poverty reduction and overall the livelihood changes. Also the study has focused to design effective policies focusing limitations and difficulties faced the women in pragmatic application of microfinance that can make the contribution a reality.

Findings –

The data collection shows that women play a positive and praiseworthy role in handling of microfinance so that it may put a positive impact on their lives in tribal communities as much as possible. In this context, the study has compared changes in impact variables such as income, expenditure, asset making, education, decision making and overall capability. This is based on the enquiry of the type of change and improvement in the conditions of women's household before and after women's joining the MFI. Factors considered in this regard were; improvement in business, acquisitions of assets, increase in income, general health status of women and their family, educational status of women and their involvement in household decision making. It particularly focuses on the women members of the household who manage the cash flows of immediate and emergency concern for their basic survival.

It is important because it helps to change their status, confidence and position through their active handling of credit in the household and local community.

A livelihoods framework, based on that developed by DFID, was used to measure the impact of the performances microfinance women, by focusing on the making of capital assets of women's household. An important way of understanding the assets, or capitals, that people need to make a living is to categorize them into the following five groups. Impact of microfinance on the financial capital (e.g. household income), physical capital (e.g. household assets), human capital (e.g. health and education), natural capital (e.g. access to land and to water) and social capital (e.g. networking, support base) of household was assessed so that the overall impact their livelihoods could be ascertained. The findings of the study are based upon this analysis of making or building of the five livelihood capital assets through women's active efforts in MFIs.

Making of financial capital –

Financial resources include credit, income and savings from employment and marketing. Women are now earning a greater income than they did prior to joining the projects and they are now saving for the future.

Credit –

In these two blocks, the SHGs have been formed around 10 members. These SHGs are formed by the deposited amount of each member of Rs 30 per month and loan is given from the group at 2% rate of interest. After 6 months group opens an account in the bank in the name of self and then time-to-time credit process through bank is going on by proper evaluation of group members' entrepreneurial economic performances. They opened their accounts in various nationalised banks such as United Bank of India (85.21%), State Bank of India (7.75%), and Mallabhum Grameen Bank (7.04%); here, the choice of banks depends on nearest banking services and also the banking interest to attach these women.

Members of SHGs are getting loans under the security of SHG. Each SHG get loan of Rs 25, 000 as first dose/instalment. All of the groups which have been taken for the study, have also achieved 2nd dose loan from the bank. This is an indication of not only their ability to repay (and manage) loans but also shows a kind of commitment that women make towards repayment schedules since regular repayment and ability to pay back are important pre-requisite for repeat loans.

26.06% women have received money of Rs 7,500, 7.04% women have received money of Rs 8,500; 35.91% women have received money of Rs 10,500; 9.86% women have received money of Rs 13,700; 21.13% women have received money of Rs 15,000,

Here, amount of credit varies from minimum Rs 60, 000 to maximum Rs 1, 50,000 and the gap between the two installments of lending the credit is becoming one, two, three or four years. In receiving credit, 26.06% women have received money of Rs 7,500/; 7.04% women have received money of Rs 8,500/; 35.91% women have received money of Rs 10,500/; 9.86% women have received money of Rs 13,700/; 21.13% women have received money of Rs 15,000/ respectively. Here, individual loan sizes have been showing.

District Rural Development Cell (DRDC) from the state fund provides the groups Rs 5,000/ in achieving 1st gradation and Rs 10,000 in achieving 2nd gradation as revolving fund (R/F). This amount is non-refundable. Regarding their loan repayment status, results are appreciative by their regular interest payment.

Employment:

The impact of microfinance is to find out the specific economic activities which women were involved in and whether there have been any changes since they joined the microfinance. Participation in the economic activities helped them to change their status to self-employed. They are involved with different types of activities according to their preferences and availability. Actually, their preferences of activities depend on their expertness in own socio-cultural circumstances where they can make their products market oriented. They are involved in productive business, arts and crafts, shopping business, animal husbandry and other types of activities either through group process or through individual process. Most of their entrepreneurships based on home level, depending on market availability.

In this tribal scenario, 38.03% are involved in leaf plate making; 11.97% are in business like milking, puffed rice and firewood selling; 48.59% are in animal husbandry like goatery, piggery and 1.41% are at agriculture and fertilizer.

Income –

Women members independently involve in the economic activities either individually or with other group members. Therefore, they are now economically independent and contribute to increase their household income. In the collectives, 51.41% women earn monthly Rs 500, 35.91% earn Rs 1000, and 12.68% women earn above 1000.

Savings –

Due to independent source of income, they are attaching with the regular savings. Before, only 4.93% women personally had saved money regularly, after it has been increased to 90.84%.

Physical capital –

Microfinance has had a positive impact on the physical capital. Now women have more household assets than they had prior to joining the project. After joining the project, their family consumption pattern has been stable. They attributed this to the increase in their income. Their purchasing capacity has been increased.

Increasing Monthly Family Expenditure pattern -

STATUS OF CREDIT	LESS THAN 1000	1001-2000	2001-3000	3001-4000	TOTAL
BEFORE CREDIT	87 61.27%	34 23.94%	21 14.79%		142
AFTER CREDIT	31 21.83%	67 47.18%	30 21.13%	14 9.86%	142

The family expenditure has been increased due to increase income of microfinance women for engaging of self employment. Their economic contributions to their family expenditure raise their self confidence, own status and dignity in the eyes' of self and also family.

Acquisition of assets

Women's access to utilize the money is mediated by their relationship to men, either husband or father or brother. When, women buy assets by their own income, it contributes to an immense strengthening of women's position in the household. In microfinance, women have started to acknowledge the need for family assets by utilizing their credit.

Collected data reveals that all women invested the loan amount for own business and repayment of own credit, 25% women for family cultivation, 32% for medical expenditure of the family members, 55% for education of the child, 19%for house electrification, 35% for house construction, 39% for house repairing, 85% for own savings, 77% for other familial emergency needs. Regarding the purpose-wise credit utilised by the microfinance women, it is observed that all of the members have demanded credit for investment in own business purposes and have utilised for repayment of own credit. They use the credit for fulfillment of multipurpose needs and demands. It is observed that a larger share of credit by women is being utilised for repayment of credit, investment in own business and fulfillment of family familial needs, demands and own desires.

Consumption pattern –

Women members of the groups are independent to meet their personal expenditures, and they contribute their income at their household budgets. Before, only 52.44% women told that they had the stability in their regular family consumption, but after all women have received this opportunity through credit functioning.

Human capital –

Human Capital is Skills, knowledge, education, health, decision making and awareness. The training provided has had a major impact on the human capital of clients. The training has helped them to manage their businesses better and that they feel more confident as a result of the training. All were very enthusiastic about this impact on their lives. They are more comfortable running a business and managing money now, than they were prior to receiving their training. As a result of this training, loans are used more effectively, and clients have been able to increase their income and improve their livelihood security.

Education

Members in these groups are almost literate but not well educated. Among these women, 9.16% women are illiterate, 60.56% women just literate, 5.63% women are primary standard, 16.90% women VIII passed, 4.93% women Madhyamik passed, and remaining 2.82% H.S. passed. Women who were just literate in this article are striking. Through the initiation of women's collectivities, 60.56% women get literacy and basic education. The members had taken initiation the literacy and education among illiterate women due to smooth functioning, successful promotion, maintaining democracy, understanding the group's rules and regulations, fair calculation of savings and credit, to make co-members dynamism and prompt and proper utilisation of credit for economic enterprises individually or collectively.

Health –

Health of women is an important indicator in determining the over-all health of the society. One of the most important indicators of women's empowerment is control over their own fertility. Now, 91.55% have taken regularly the birth control technique. For making healthy child, the baby should intake certain immunisation followed by medical practitioners. They have to take BCG, DPT, and Booster respectively as per their child's age concerned. In women's collectives, 74.65% have followed the entire immunisation schedule for children.

Training Courses –

Financial skill and knowledge is achieved through a series of training programmes such as maintenance of registers, personality development, communication skills and entrepreneur development programmes. A group contributes a certain amount and members can turn to the joint savings for loans. After six months of being monitored, the group becomes eligible for a bank loan.

Ground based reality shows that all the microfinance women participated the training on orientation on group formation, dynamics and sensitisation at concerned block office in the group formative stage. Different training programmes are organised to create profitable economic entrepreneurship among tribal women. In the group's formative stage, each members of the group must be trained regarding group's dynamics, its mode of orientation and its maintenance by the initiation of block office. Different govt. organisations make arrangement of trainings for these group members. Here women mainly are involved in making traditional domestic products. Before, they made these products only for the fulfillment of requirement of households' consumption. The trainings help them for the transformation of domestic production to profitable, market oriented production. Here, 2.82% women get training on tailoring, 2.81% on wool knitting, 36.62% on leaf plate making, 19.72% on art and crafts and 38.03% on animal husbandry and all women get training through the initiation of B.D.O., DRDC and concerned Gram Panchayat.

Decisions in Household budget –

Now, part of the household budget is fulfilled by or through women, so the voice of women in the household economic transaction has been increased. Intra-household decision-making is a key indicator of women empowerment. Household's economic transaction involve with the expenditure on consumptions and other household requirements, child education, medical treatments etc. Before, 6.34% women had the voice in economic transaction, but after 69.72% women have made the voice in this regard.

Socio-political decisions –

The study has found a drastic change in the development of personality of women after joining the initiation. They make sound to establish their decisions in village oriented activities due to group cohesiveness. They have also been given a greater role in the community and village level for development as well as welfare programmes with their prior decisions. They are now becoming a part and parcel of village administration (Gram Sansad). Regarding voting behaviour, 49% women told that in this aspect they depend on men's decision due to either their own decisive lacuna or husbands' domination. Here it is crucial that due to low level of literacy they are being confused. Other external areas like protest against any violation, joining any association and other job involvement outside home 70% women take and control own decisions.

Awareness of women –

The movement towards economic independence and capacity to earn has strengthened the women's confidence and capacity. They have become more vociferous and have been able to express their needs, opinions and give shape to their dreams; even if it is in a small circle. Women have become aware and careful about their rights and circumstances. Microfinance has helped to build their awareness. Our constitution guaranteed the rights and duties for their every citizen. Deprivation of rights is punishable. Therefore, to claim rights, they have to aware about that. In this study, it is being noticed that 72.83% women were about their constitution and its related rights.

Natural capital –

Natural resources are such as land, soil, water, forests and fisheries. Livelihoods are also shaped by the available natural resources. Livelihoods depend, both directly and indirectly on use of natural resources. Therefore, the development of sustainable livelihoods requires balancing human needs for survival and the capacity of the environment to provide natural resources consistently over time. The quality of soil, air and water; the climatic and geographic conditions; the availability of fauna and flora; and the frequency and intensity of natural hazards all influence livelihood decisions. Microcredit is the vehicle, which creates self-employment through the proper use of available natural resources. Women use the loans and invest them in income generating activities. Mostly, it is a continuation of activities that they were already carrying out for household consumption. They now produce commercially for sell by utilizing the credit.

The role of women's self-employment is to be considered in a different angle. Their involvement in employment depends on the activities such as opportunities, communication, vocational training and skill development, too to be considered in accordance with the gender requirement. Hence, for women at grass root level development activities should be followed with correct approaches to meet the needs and appropriate time allocations and management at home level; link with easy to handle low cost appropriate technology application, utilisation of low cost natural resources and raw materials available in their environment. Most of their employment based on home level, depend on individual and neighboring market. Their home base industries and micro level employment meet the neighboring consumers' demands and requirements. They are involved with different types of activities according to their preferences and availability of raw materials which depend on circumstantial natural resources. Actually, their preferences of activities depend on their expertness in own socio-cultural circumstances where they can make their products according to market demand. They are involved in productive business, arts and crafts, shopping business, animal husbandry and other types of activities either through group process or through individual process.

In this study, women have been involved with productive entrepreneurship availability of natural resources, like leaf plate making; different business like milking, puffed rice and firewood selling; animal husbandry like goatery, piggery; agriculture and fertilizer.

Rearing animals at domestic level was mainly women's responsibility. Most women at tribal scenario rear animals for household consumption as eating milk, meat, egg and using fuel. In addition, sometimes these are used to meet emergency needs of the household. These activities were a part of household care and services. All these tasks undertaken by women are uniformly regarded as being within the realm of domestic services. After getting credit, theses activities have been carried out at larger scale for sell. At one level, this is a continuation of activities that women were already performed. The nature of animal rearing depends on habit of food and need based according to their own circumstances.

Social capital –

The vast majority of clients were very positive about the social impacts they experienced. From a social perspective, the close relationships and networks built within village banks has also been a very positive impact.

Linkage with the Markets

Markets were mostly taboo area of women. Now their engagements in business activities have made themselves of targeting their business more profitable, so they have able to establish the link with the markets to gain knowledge about recent products and price. Women are now producing for the market; their economic roles provide them the links to the market as buyers and as sellers both. In market linkage, women either collectively handle or individually handle all economic affairs with or without other family members. This linkage improves their bargaining power in transaction of price and exchanging of products. It also provides more exposure and mobility by communicating with persons of different nature, character and opinions, sharing their ideas, opinions, constraints and problems. This interaction in turn diminishes poverty of knowledge among women.

Increasing Bargaining power

Achievement of microcredit is the provision of effective marketing outlets to buy and sell their products. Their market linkages have made them more prompt in bargaining to achieve their demands. Besides, they now are more mobile in communicating with the officials to gain benefit from them. They have made sound in receiving maximum advantage by motivating the bank officials, panchayat members and other district officials etc. They now have associated with advertising their products to get more credit and advantages from the office. Besides, their increased awareness makes them vociferous to achieve their rights. All these activities enhaunce their bargaining power.

Socio-economic networks –

The socio-economic networking is vital for women to aware about surroundings and knowledge of rights and privileges. Before 62.68% women had the network, but after it have been increased to 77.46%.

Interaction with the Officials

The women have started to think of themselves more prestigious that officials were directly contacting them and various technical issues were discussed with them, and not with their in-laws. Because of women's involvement in enterprises activities and in the field of investment, extension officers now visit and discuss technical issues with the women.

Participation at different village and community services

Women members in the group have participated actively in different village and community services escaping from the private domain of the home. They directly have participated at literacy campaign, distribution of sanitary in the rural families and giving a lesson about the maintenance of health and hygiene, creating awareness among women in order to receive proper rights and privileges from the society, different community and village level meetings etc. They have given the company to provide the adequate health services for pregnant mother and newborn child by govt. health centers. They have showed the courage at standing against violence faced by any women in the family, solving households' internal conflict and clash among members in family, forming Mahila Samiti for their open discussion on any matters, standing at Panchayat election,

Protesting violence in the family and community –

Women are now vociferous to gain their rights from the society. They now get the platform to protest against any type of violence faced by women. The collectives make themselves more bold, prompt and active. They now protest against any type of discrimination, male superiority and domination faced by women traditionally. Before 31.69% women had the capability to protest against violence, but after 92.25% women have showed this courage of protesting.

Transaction with Banks –

They make all transactions to the bank collectively in the name of the group. Later individual women have started to open an account in self-name in the goal of saving money. Before, 48.59% women had kept transaction with the banks, after it have been increased to 82.39%.

Reduction of Vulnerability

A lack of collateral and an ability to borrow only small amounts at a time render women ineligible for loans from major national and private banks. In desperation to get out of poverty and to get little opportunity, they turn to village "Mahajans" (unofficial moneylenders), who offer loans at exorbitant interest rates. Before 90.85% women had taken loan from moneylenders. After, all women are free from the trap of moneylenders. So, one of the most important benefits of microcredit strategy is its ability to reduce vulnerability among the poor women. The credit strategy has helped borrowers to insure themselves against crises by building up household assets. Such assets can be sold if needed. They have used the assets as security or proof of credit worthiness when dealing with businesspersons or more traditional lending agencies. These reductions in vulnerability are important because they allow women to hold their own position in society. This is really a vital benefit for the great numbers of marginal women to overcome emergency crises and the arrested cycle of poverty. Further, the group-based approach has been recognised as having the capacity to empower the most vulnerable and marginalised, especially women, by creating a community-based structure that builds mutual support and trust. Such an approach allows for greater economic and social integration for the marginalised section of society, thereby directly addressing issues of vulnerability.

Conclusion

In the microfinance approach, women have proved their ability to solve livelihood needs. Field voice shows that in building their capability the tribal poor women have able to earn their own livelihood finance, though in a very slow pace. Through microfinance strategies of women's collective savings, they meet the urgent and emergency family needs instead of going to any informal sources, which had made them dependent and exploited their dependency. In providing sufficient space and support in microfinance, women have taken effective steps to control their lives. Women have made a platform for dialogue and cooperation, which gives support to overcome all the barriers in surviving the livelihood. In making cooperation, they are becoming self-reliant and enjoy life with full freedom and dignity because, the microfinance women group supplies slowly all the resources required for their livelihood. They all think that they have improved livelihoods to the extent of providing leveraging needed to start an enterprise. By linking with the market and different officials related with the rural development, they are becoming aware about the resources and actual path of gaining resources of livelihood.

Women now can manage to start new livelihood activities using the resources available through capacity building going through training courses. Engaging in income generating activity through microfinance, they are able to decrease their economic and social vulnerability. In microfinance interventions they can strengthen the livelihood strategies by empowering them and may take advantage of a broader range of economic opportunities. The roles of women are changing from subordinate household workers to income earners. Improved economic performance can lead to improve their livelihood status as well. As a result of their activities, livelihood status and security has been strengthened and increased.

In microfinance, increasing financial literacy of women is empowering them as it makes them to understand financial service requirements better and to improve their ability in savings. Women have able to make a savings culture among women. Accessing bigger loans in the future women will potentially lead to greater impact on their livelihood security, but equally important, the savings can be used to cushion women from threats they may face in the future and so can be used to protect their livelihoods. Savings play an important role in poverty reduction, in that savings in the absence of proper insurance serves as insurance for household. Savings improve future consumption for household. It is recommended that women have to be encouraged to convert much resource into savings mobilisation in the goal to improve the livelihood finance.

Women as active agents are working on to convert microfinance focus into livelihood security, it should encourage and supporting agencies have to analyse and assess the wider impacts of the projects they are involved in. The training provision is having a major impact on the skills and confidence of women and this should continue and be expanded according to their need based.

Through the use of microfinance as a tool for livelihood finance, where women can achieve much, it is important for the government and other related welfare agencies to focus on developing efficient legal institutions and the necessary infrastructure. Moreover, they should improve macro-economic policies and the regulatory framework which would make the financial system function more effective and efficient. Finally, availability and accessibility of Microfinance for women is a positive way of bringing a revolution not only in their livelihoods but also in the society.

References

1. Chambers, R., & Conway, G. (1991). Sustainable Rural Livelihoods: Practical Concepts for the 21st Century. Retrieved February 3, 2010, from http://www.smallstock.info/reference/IDS/dp296.pdf
2. DFID, 1999 - Eldis - Livelihoods Connect, Retrieved from http://www.eldis.org/go/topics/dossiers/livelihoods-connect/what-are-livelihoods approaches/policies-institutions-and-processes.
3. Jaen P. Maes and Larry R. Reed (2012) – "State of the Microcredit Summit Campaign report, 2012" Microcredit Summit Campaign,Washington D.C. www.microcreditsummit.org

4. Johnson, S. and Rogaly, B (1997) Microfinance and Poverty Reduction. Oxfam UK and Ireland, Oxfam Publications.
5. Marconi, R. and Mosley, P. (2004) The FINRURAL impact evaluation service – a cost-effectiveness analysis. Small Enterprise Development, Vol. 15, No.3, 18-28.
6. Mayoux, L. (2002) "Women's Empowerment versus Sustainability? Towards a New Paradigm in Microfinance Programs": In Lemire, Beverly, Pearson, Ruth, & Campbell, Gail. (eds.), *Women and Credit: Researching the Past, Refiguring the Future*. New York: Berg, 245-269.
7. Robinson, M. (2001) "The Microfinance Revolution: Sustainable Finance for the Poor", World Bank, Washington.
8. UNCDF (2004) Basic Facts about Microfinance, [Online]. Available from <www.uncdf.org/english/microinance/facts.php> [23rd August 2004].
9. Yunus, Muhammad, (2000) - Banker to the Poor. The University Press Limited, Dhaka.

13

Tradition and Transition: A Study of Jaunsari Tribe of Uttrakhand

Vandana Kumari

Introduction

The tribal India forms a distinct picture of the country. The tribal people are in fact, the original inhabitants of the soil. The tribal people are the part and parcel of Indian population. Tribal people are the backbone of our cultural heritage. The tribal people of the India lend a distinct hue to the multi-colored cultural fabrics of the country. Tribal groups can be divided on the basis of their ethnic characteristics, geographical distribution and linguistic affiliation. The tribes in India live in the forest and hilly region of the country with poor administrative and infrastructure backup. They are known as 'Vanyajati', Vanwasi, Pahari, Adivasi, and Janjati. Constitutionally they are scheduled as scheduled tribe (Anusuchit janjati). Tribes till today have retain their traditions, customs and regulations, since there is little difference between their social and economic life due to nearby rural area and external interference. It is due to the introduction of the development programmes in the area.

Development is an elusive concept and involves mobilisation of natural resources, augmentation of trained manpower, capital and technical know-how and their utilisation for attainment of constantly rising national goals, higher living standards and the change over from a traditional to a modern society. The essence of development is generally perceived as industrialisation and modernisation. Development is a multi-dimensional and multilinear process, calling for several "Complex interdependencies". The management and implementation of development programmes require an interdisciplinary approach.

Tribal development, over the year, has been a major concern of the government, voluntary organisation, social reformer, social scientist. Though majority of the tribes live under heart-breaking poverty, illiteracy, disease, exploitation etc. the only practical solution of the Tribal people lies in their integration in the national democratic set up of India. The words of article 46 of Indian constitution give right to ST people of better education, economic stability, social justice and protect them from all forms of exploitation.

As it is clear that government is making continuous effort to up lift of ST, but it is also true that all the efforts are not effective as it should be. Government programmes and planes should be re-oriented for the welfare of tribal communities. Economic and social development among tribal communities should be greatly accelerated. Rising level of well being, growing economic opportunities and greater integration with the rest of the population are essential both for the welfare of tribal community and the progress of the country as a whole.

The term development is often used in the sense of growth indicating a quantitative increase or progress in production, income, consumption of food etc. thus giving emphasis on quantitative aspect ignoring qualitative part of man. In the light of past experience it has become essential that schemes formulated should enable the tribal communities to secure an adequate share in the benefits of general developments and speed up their economic and social advance with the object of giving practical effect to these recommendations and assisting state and central government in evolving concrete schemes of development which are specially adopted to the needs and condition of tribal areas.

India has a large tribal population spread over the length and breadth of the country. Any developmental programmes without keeping tribal in mind will be meaningless. In the pre-independence India, the British followed a policy of segregation of the tribals, which besides serving their colonial interests, exposed the tribal to exploitation by non-tribals. The approach to tribal after independence, has somewhat changed and government has initiated a number of measures directed at the development of the tribal area.

Belshaw, however, gave equal emphasis on social, cultural, economic and other aspect of life. He observed, "Sociologically specking, development should be looked upon as an organised activity with the aim of satisfying certain basic needs and to psychologically orient the tribals to the inner strength, and appropriate social and cultural infrastructure to stand the pressure of the new situation and accrue benefits from the new programme and maintain higher level (1972). Development as has been observed by Beals and Heijer, may be consider as those changes which are required but have minimum disruptive effects on the concerned population.

Vidyarthi (1981), observed that development means growth any change which includes both the material and human- the socio-cultural factors which are an integral part of the dynamics of growth. He felt," while striving from the development of a group or an area, due emphasis has to be given to their traditional values and historical experiences". In fact, economist like Schumacher has also observed, "development, does not start with goods", it starts with people and their education, organisation and discipline. (1977:157).

With reference to development, Mahapatra has also observed that real development should consider the needs, values, and aspiration of the concerned population and local development are not likely to be in conflict with national objectives, but at the same time, the local people's aspiration and potentialities should be honored respected and accommodated (1980). Roy suggested that anywhere development would lead to the reduction of regional disparity and help in the creation of self reliant economy. Besides, it would lead to redistribution of income, equalisation of distribution of development benefits, reduction of social stratification and resource mobilisation without affecting quality of life and physical environment.

Unfortunately the progress or development of the tribals is not up to expectation for a number of reasons. As the programmes are plane-based and more emphasis is often given on the disbursement without considering the local felt needs, they often do not serve the real purpose for making the development programmes really successful; one must be aware of cultural traditions, eco-system, economy, history and ethnic. Their social structure, their cultural and their language are quite different from the general people of India. In course of time, in the post-independent age a lot of changes have taken place in the tribal areas due to immense endeavours of the Government their soocio-economic development. But, inspite of all endeavours, they are still poor as well as illiterate and are far from the mainstream of Indian society. The necessity of having education and better economic status is now felt by them.

Area of the study

Uttrakhand was constituted as a separate state in 2000 by bifurcation of Uttar Pradesh. It is often referred to us the 'Land of god'. The state is divided into two divisions, Garhwal and Kumaon with a total of 14 Districts. The study area is selected a tribal area in the hilly region administratively known as Jaunsar-Bawar of Chakrata tehsil of Dehradun district in Uttrakhand. The Jaunsari community is distributed in Chakrata tahsil of Dehradun district. It lies between latitude 30^0 31' 33 north and longitudes 77 45` and 78 72` east. The area is roughly oval in shape. Jaunsar and Bawar form the two constituted parts of Jaunsar-Bawar. Jaunsar consists of the lower half of this region, from Chakrata southwards, whereas Bawar includes the northern parts. Yamuna River forms its eastern boundary and separated it from Dehradun pargana. Tons river forms its northern-western boundary before it confluences with river Yamuna near kalsi. Jaunsar-Bawar pargana is surrounded by Tehri

Garhwal and Uttar Kashi districts in the east and north; basar, Raiengarh, Taroach, Jubbal and sirmaur in the west and the doon valley in the south. Precisely, this region is the north-western most area of the state of Uttrakhand, covering an area of 343.5 sq. miles. The southern of lower portion of the region is called as Jaunsar while the northern portion is called Bawar. Jaunsar is larger and triangular in shape bounded on the north by Lokhandi, on its east River Yamuna and on the west River Tones. The area spreads over 18 miles in length from north to south.

General social Character of the Jaunsari Tribe

The Jaunsari, a polyandrous tribe, derived their name after the region Jaunsar Bawar which constituted their original abode. Thus the 'Jaunsari' is a blanket territorial reference-term which embraces various unequal status-holding ethnic caste/ groups, viz., the so-called high caste comprising Brahman and Rajput or Khasa, the intermediate caste comprising Lohar, Sunar, Jogra, badi, bajgi etc. Jaunsari community people speaks 'Jaunsari' language, write in Devnagri script, and many among them can speak Hindi as well.

The society is primarily divided along castes lines and is stratified. The Brahman and the Rajput enjoy the highest position in the local socio-religious hierarchy and the Kolta occupy the lowest. Of these, the Brahman and the Rajput together constitute the ritually pure high caste while the lower caste Kolta are regarded as impure, Untouchables. Inter-marriage between the Brahman and the Rajput are possible and hypergamous unions are more in occurrence than the hypogamous unions. After caste, the most important social unit which regulates marriage is lineage. The Jaunsri allow divorce. Polyandrous joint family is the traditional pattern. Nuclear family also exists. The rule for inheritance are based on the principal collateral inheritance i.e. all brothers inherit property. However, in the customary practice of *Jetbang* the eldest brother is entitled bigger share while under the *Kanchbang* the youngest brother has similar right. Woman has no share in the family. They are non vegetarian in their food habit and their staple food comprises wheat, rice, *madua* and maize. They drink milk and many are fond of liquor.

Traditionally, the Jaunsari have been more or less self-sufficient in their economy. Most of the people earn their livelihood by agriculture in the form of owner cultivator (land owner cultivating the land with his own family member, with or without additional labourers), owner-cultivator cum tenant (those who cultivate partly their own land and partly on tenant land), tenant & landless labour.

Traditionally the Bajgi and Jagdi do not take agriculture as their main occupation. The Bajgi are traditionally drummers, but now they work as agricultural labour. The Jagdis are by tradition religious servicemen; usually Jagdis families serve the pilgrim's route to Yammunotri. A Jagdis may sometimes beat drums at the temple during the absence of a Bajgi in the village. But they are now also making their living by tilling the land. On the other hand, Rajputs are neither the traditional goldsmith nor the Badis the distillers. Badis are the carpenters. Agriculture is the most important economic pursuit of the people and occupational specialisation and cooperation in the village have been built up around agriculture. In fact Jajmani system, in which low caste people serve to high caste landowner, is still here to some extent. Among the agriculturists, there are four sub groups which define economic as well as social status. The traditional landowner belongs to the higher caste, the Brahmin next which have partial land and got partial from other villagers: this includes Brahmin Rajput & Jagdis. Third group: the tenants include Bajgi & Kolta. Last is the landless labourer i.e. Kolta.

The Brahmins and Rajput families are agriculturist. The Bajgi and Jgdis are artesian. The Kolta are agricultural labour in past they were mocha or shoe maker. The Bajgi and the Kolta are following their traditional Profession as Drummer and Serfs respectively.

In short, the characteristic features of hill economy make the families depend upon land wholly or partly, for their livelihood. In the village terrace cultivation is found. Field have been prepared by labelling the hard rocks, stones and boulders, the terraces beings supported by a stone wall called 'pusta' of height varying from 4 to 10 feet.

Tradition and transition

As Change is the continuous process in every society, Jaunsari too are not exception in this case. Villages has changed a lot in all spheres of life, visible and invisible both. From their traditional social organisation to modern institutions and from indigenous methods to advanced technologies are in transition stage and can be seen in present style of living. Older generation still try to maintain their age old traditional culture, important societal and village norms and values but its function has been changed now. Horizons has expanded for villagers, people of the village are coming in the contact with the external world for better education and employment, consequently social and economic life of the villagers are changing. People also have desire to find the better facilities for improving their life style and livelihood. The *Jaunsar* community was well known for its polyandrous character but in this changing scenario, it has been the matter of past only. New generation in the village is adopting monogamy and feel shy even talking about it. This change in marriage institution is occurring due to the interaction of the community from other external urban areas.

Problems in Planning for development

The basic problem with development plans for Uttrakhand is not the lack of awareness and development programmes, but the absence of an integrated and region specific approach to thinking about planning for, and implementing these programmes and schemes. For instance, environmental protection issue were approached without due regard being given to the needs of the people; infrastructure was developed without much attention being paid to its effective use for the local development.

Alternative option for the development considering the past experiences of unsatisfactory impact of development programme, it is necessary to modify the planning, strategies and approaches on the basis of different socio-cultural character and inhabitants.

Thakur Devendra and Thakur D.N. (2000), discussed economic planning since first five year planes and recommended that a positive policy of assisting the tribal should be formulated in order to develop their natural resources and evolve a productive life, which can prevent exploitation by more organised economic forces.

Majumdar D.N. (1962), the most famous study of his is Himalayan polyandry. In this he tried to paint a general picture of the culture of Jaunsar-Bawar in terms of the socio-economic structure as well as the ways of life and concept of values. He has also described certain significant changes taken place within the community due to, increased contacts of the local people with the outsiders. Mehta G.S. (1999), he has given an account of the development of Uttrakhand. He focused on hilly region of Uttrakhand and reveal that the basic problem for the development in this region is the absence of integration and region specific approach to think about planning for, and implementing these development programmes.

Vidyarthi (1981), observed that development means growth not only material but also human i.e. the socio-cultural factors which are an integral part of human life. He stated that the development of a group or an area, due emphasis has to be given to their traditional values and historical experiences".

Mahapatra L.K. (1980), described factors which are a barrier in the development of isolated tribal areas. He has also observed that real development should consider the needs, values, and aspiration of the concerned population and local development are not likely to be in conflict with national objectives, but at the same time, the local people's aspiration and potentialities should be honored respected and accommodated. Chaudhry Buddadeb (1981), he discussed on what needs to be done to persuade the tribals into joining the national mainstream without setting off any major upheavals. The main focus was on tribal economy, political system and unrest in the tribal areas and welfare measures to improve their lot.

Unemployment is a very fretful problem in this area. When we look at the economic pattern of the area then maximum numbers of people are involved in agriculture and doing the work of daily wage labour at construction sites (Wall making) in the neighbouring areas

Conclusion

State, central government and local agencies have been putting several efforts from decades for adequate development in this area for education, infrastructure, health and employment. Literacy rate is increasing. For better education there are schools, which are providing primary to intermediate level education. For girls there is ATS (Ashram type school).Due to Lack of institutions for higher educational facilities in the village area younger generation migrate in nearby towns and cities as they now understand the value and its importance. There is proper water and electricity facility in the villages but Sanitation facilities are poor. Toilet facilities which have been provided by the central and state government under different developmental plans have not been properly utilised by the community in the village.

As described the modes of livelihood are agriculture, labour work, to some extent business and services for the present generation of the village. Brahmins and Rajput have major portion of agriculture land, while low caste people and artisans are landless or posses little portion of land. Economic condition of the lower caste people is not good. Governmental schemes and plans related to employment have not worked effectively to raise the economic status of the poor villagers. MNREG is also not providing minimum 100 days work as told by the villagers.

Various plans and schemes implemented by the state and centre government being in the category of ST, villagers are not fully enjoying and privileged. Various programmes and schemes related to awareness towards better production and high yield and technologically advanced agriculture practices are not in use being a hilly region. Government plans keeping in mind their limitations being hilly terrain, certain schemes, actions and implementations of very specialised nature needs to be introduced in the area and particularly in the village.

References

Basu R. Ashok, (1985), *Tribal development programmes and Administration in india.* NBO Publisher, New Delhi.

Chaudhri Buddhadeb, etd (1982), *Tribal development in India.* Inter india publication, New Deldi.

FosterG.M. (1962), *Traditional culture and the impact of technological change. University of California*, Berkeley.

Joshi, P.C. (1978), *Ethnomedicine; Exploration of some folk concept in Jaunsar-Bawar.* Deptt. Of anthropology, university of Delhi.

Kumar Arvind (2004), *Trival development and planning.* Vol-2, Anmole publication Pvt Ltd, New Delhi.

Kumar Arvind (2004), *Trival development and planning.* Vol-1, Anmole publication Pvt Ltd, New Delhi.

Majumdar D.N. (1954), *Demographic structure in a polyandrous village.* The eastern anthropologist.

Majumdar D.N. (1956), *The functioning of school system in a polyandrous society-in Jaunsar-Bawar, Dehradun District U.P.*, The eastern anthropologist, 10(3).

Majumdar D.N. (1954), *family and marriage in a Polyandrous society.* The eastern anthropologist, 8 (2).

Majumdar D.N. (1962), *Himalayan Polyandr-structure, Functioning and culture change- A fiel study of jaunsar-bawar.* Bombay: Asia publishing house.

Rizvi S.N.H. (1980), *Jaunsariyon me parivar akar evam prajana pratiroop*, manav, 8 (1).

Rizvi S.N.H. (1980), *Family size, fertility and child mortality among jaunsaris.* Himalaya Man and nature, 5(8).

Rizvi S.N.H. (1991), *Medical anthropology of the Jaunsaris.* Northern book centre, New Delhi.

Sharma K. Suresh, etd (2010), *Tribes through the ages.* Vol-4, Vista international publishing house, delhi.

Singh J.P., Vyas N.N. (1986), *Tribal development: Past efforts and new challenges*, Himanshu publication, india.

Singh K.S., etd (2005), *People of india, Uttar Pradesh*, Vol-xlii, Part -2, Anthropological survey of India, Lordson publisher, New Delhi.

Thakur devendra, Thakur D.N. (2000), *Trival development and planning:tribal life in India*-9, Deep and Deep publication PVT Ltd, New Delhi.

Thakur devendra, Thakur D.N. (2000), *Trival development and planning:tribal life in India*-1, Deep and Deep publication PVT Ltd, New Delhi.

14

Tribal's Resistance in India: Perspective of Globalisation

Amlan Kumar Guha Thakurta

Introduction

The present paper attempts to discuss the tribal's resistance in India in the perspective of Globalisation. India has a rich tribal heritage. Population wise, globally, tribals in India are next only to Africa. As many as 422 tribals and sub-tribes inhabit different parts of the Indian sub-continent and constitute about 8.2 %(Census– 2001) of its total population. As many as four hundred fifty tribal groups live in isolated regions of the country. The Dhebar Commission (1960-1961) stated that within Scheduled Tribes there existed an inequality in the rate of development. During the fourth Five Year Plan a sub-category was formed within Scheduled Tribes to identify groups that considered being at a lower level of development. This was created based on the Dhebar Commission report and other studies. This sub-category was named "Primitive tribal group". The features of such a group include a pre-agricultural system of existence that is practice of hunting and gathering, zero or negative population growth, extremely low level of literacy in comparison with other tribal groups. Groups that satisfied any one of the criterion were considered as PTG. At the conclusion of the Fifth Five year plan, 52 communities were recognised as being a "primitive tribal group"; these communities were identified on the basis of recommendations made by the respective state governments. At the conclusion of the Sixth Five year plan 20 groups were added and 2 more in the Seventh Five year plan, one more cluster was added in the eighth five-year plan, making a total 75 groups were identified as PTG. No new group was stated as PTG on the basis of the 2001 census. Tribal do place love and they have excessive love for their land and forest. Every attempt should be made to restore the land and forest right of the tribal cultural types and ecological balance should be kept in mind.

Tribals' economy mainly based an agriculture. Occupations such as hunting, fishing, cattle and handicrafts are subsidiary to agriculture. The agriculture is the most predominant form of economy amongst the tribal. Over 96% of the population directly or indirectly depends on agriculture. Next to agriculture, Exploitation of forest resources is the most important source of economy of the tribal. Over 24% area of our country is still covered by the forests.

There was symbiotic relation between tribals and forests. Forests met the social, cultural, economic, political, religious and all other kinds of need of tribals. Tribals were so closely related of forests that they never through to maintain their existence without forests. That's why they used to project their forests; they even today have totemic relation with the plants, tree, animals etc. available in the forests. During the British period, tribal right over land and forest suffered a lot Rich cultural heritage of tribal were badly affected due to injustice and apathy shown by British Government. When India became free, our Government tried best of provide justice to tribal societies living in different hilly and forested areas of our country.

Tribals are still lagging far behind in the development areas. Like education, per capita income, per capita expenditure, health etc. Various evaluation reports related to tribal development reveal that benefits of those schemes have not gone in the hands of tribals.

A number of legislative, prohibitive and protective measures were taken to check the exploitation and oppression of the tribals and to bring them in the main stream of national development. Right from the first five years plan, a number of development programmes have been implemented following the various concepts, approaches and models of development. Now a number of poverty alleviation programmes are being run in which tribal beneficiaries have been selected. But in spite of all such efforts, tribals still need social justice.

Tribal do place love and they have excessive love for their land and forest. Every attempt should be made to restore the land and forest right of the tribal cultural types and ecological balance should be kept in mind. They are proud of their of their social culture heritage. But they have lagged far behind in development in comparison to other counterparts.

Jawaharlal Nehru accepted the western model of development, and the Second Five-Year Plan of his government emphasized rapid industrialisation. Big developmental projects in the forms of factories, dams and mines, which Nehru envisaged as the temples of modern India, sprouted up all over the country, mostly on tribal lands. Making the tribal people victims and refugees of development (Singh and Jabbi, 1995).

Various property alleviation programmes have been launched recently for the development of tribal. But the tribals are still poor and majority of them are below poverty line. They are still economically and educationally backward.

About six decades of independence and implementation of development schemes for the tribals have created developed and undeveloped groups with in the tribals. There is a need to rethink about social justice for the tribal. Tribal women as labourers are discriminated in paternal property, work and payment of wages. They are sexually harassed and abused by contractors, money lenders and others. There is urgent need to protect tribal women from exploitation. Unless awareness and consciousness is created, it is very difficult to provide social justice to tribals.

Under the circumstances they (tribal) have to depend directly or indirectly upon the agriculture. Tribals lived in and around forest happily with whatever little natural resources they had. They maintained. Place and harmony in the society through the institutions like council of elders, village head, village Panchayat, inter village Panchayat and tribal chiefs. Through there economy was subsistence oriented but they had rich culture and social heritage. But due to the effect of globalisation they are pushed to various other occupations instead of conventional occupations like agriculture and hunting, fishing etc. Though at heart they are very much fond of agriculture and/or its related jobs. But because of the gradual deforestation and increase in population area of forests decreasing day by day, hence scarcity of agricultural land becomes a burning problem to them. Moreover, due to escalating of media and information technology the change in lifestyle and enhancement of income attracting them also. Modern development of electronic communication like mobile phone, e-mail, and fax, computer, laptop, tab. etc and easy conveyance like car, bus, train and airplane brought man of this world closer to one another. Thus now a day's whole world has become like a small village, where a man interacts with any other man of the village as per his wish.

With the globalisation i.e. changing of many families from agriculture to service based economy brought drastic change in the status of women in the Hindu society especially among the upper castes, who were more conscious to get services in industrial or urban set up. Due to globalisation many type of posts with different economic and social status were created. Many became engineers of different ranks or general workers at lower ranks in the industries. Similarly in town or cities many became doctors, advocates, professors, school teachers, magistrates, clerks or lower rank staff in different offices. This brought much difference in the economic and social status of such boys.

Traditional occupation pattern has become conventional with the progress of agriculture and cultivation pattern. Now they are mainly agricultural workers, day labourers and settled agriculturists. Though many of them still practice the occupational patterns of hunting and food gathering in the days of insufficient food supply.

Diverse occupations of tractor driving, bus driver, labourer work, household labourer work, part-time agricultural work, brick-kiln industries labourer work etc., were cropping side by side. There few families whose main source of livelihood is from agriculture whereas there are others who assisted themselves by the subsidiary occupations discussed above. This diversity in occupation obliterated the possibility of globalisation. Due to irrigation facilities the vegetables production spread beyond the kitchen gardens, wherever irrigation was possible, viz. –on the banks of rivers and tanks. Thus vegetables appear in bulk in the market. The markets are influenced by urban factors. Thus globalisation changed the agriculture process of tribal. Thus the requirement of the agriculture could remain no more local in nature.

15

Status of Sanitation Among the Saber in Jwalkata Village Of Gurabanda Block, (Jharkhand)

Abhishek Chauhan

Introduction

Jharkhand, with an area of 79,714 sq. km, 24 districts and 32,620 revenue villages, accounts for 2.4 per cent of the total geographical area of the country. With a population of 2.69 crore, the state accounts for 2.6 per cent of the total population of the country. The rural and urban population of the state accounts for 77.7 per cent and 22.3 per cent, respectively of the total population, as per 2001 census. The rural population is more than 1/3rd of state's population and usage of proper sanitation facilities in these areas is nominal. This is one of the major reasons for health problems in rural areas.This Study focuses to understand the Problems of Sanitation facilities among the tribals of Jwalkata Village" which is situated in Singpura Panchayat. This panchayat is in Gurabandha Block which has recently come into existence in the year 2011.

World Health Organisation states "Sanitation generally refers to the provision of facilities and services for the safe disposal of human urine and feces. Inadequate sanitation is a major cause of disease world-wide and improving sanitation is known to have a significant beneficial impact on health both in households and across communities. The word 'sanitation' also refers to the maintenance of hygienic conditions, through services such as garbage collection and wastewater disposal.

This block is situated in East Singhbhum district of Jharkhand state. This study mainly focuses to understand the problems related to Sanitation being faced by the Saber tribe of Jwalkata village. Sanitation is the hygienic means of promoting health through prevention of human contact with the hazards of wastes. Hazards can be physical, microbiological, biological or chemical agents of disease. Wastes that can cause health problems are human and animal faeces, solid wastes, domestic wastewater (sewage, sullage, grey water), industrial wastes and agricultural wastes. Hygienic means of prevention can be by using engineering solutions (e.g. sewerage and wastewater treatment), simple technologies (e.g. latrines, septic tanks), or even by personal hygiene practices (e.g. simple hand washing with soap).

Objectives-

(1) To study the status of sanitation facilities in the village.

(2) To study the health practices done by Saber school going children, adolescent girls and mothers.

(3) To study the reason behind lack of sanitation facilities in the village.

(4) To Study the problems Of Sanitation.

(5) To Study the Governmental intervention in Saber village through TSC.

Research Methodology:

The study was conducted using both primary and secondary data. The data's are also collected from various books, articles, journals and blogs on Sanitation. The research paper is an attempt of exploratory research, based on the secondary data sourced from journals, magazines, articles and media reports. The annual reports published by various Governmental and Non Governmental Organisations of Jharkhand regarding Sanitation related activities are also taken into account.

Above all the interactions have been established with the persons who are engaged in implementing the Sanitation related programmes and plans among the Saber of Jwalkata village. As this provided authentic dimension to our research work.

Availability of Sanitation Facilities in the village

Proper sanitation facility and hygienic surrounding is the need of present time. There is an old behavior which is being followed by generation to generation (i.e.) defecation in the open. There is no proper sanitation facility.

Necessity of Sanitation Facility

- Proper sanitation facility helps us in leading a healthy and hygienic life.
- It helps in preventing chronic diseases like cholera, jaundice, typhoid, diarrhea and malaria.
- It is also necessary because small children are more vulnerable to diseases like brain fever, malaria, diarrhea, pneumonia and other deadly diseases.

- Due to unhygienic conditions people die out of above mentioned diseases.
- Due to improper sanitation facility females of the family do not feel clean and hygienic and have to face many difficulties.
- There is an increase in number of dropouts of girl child when they reach their puberty age.
- To bring self respect and dignity in girls and women.

Reasons for lack of Sanitation Facility

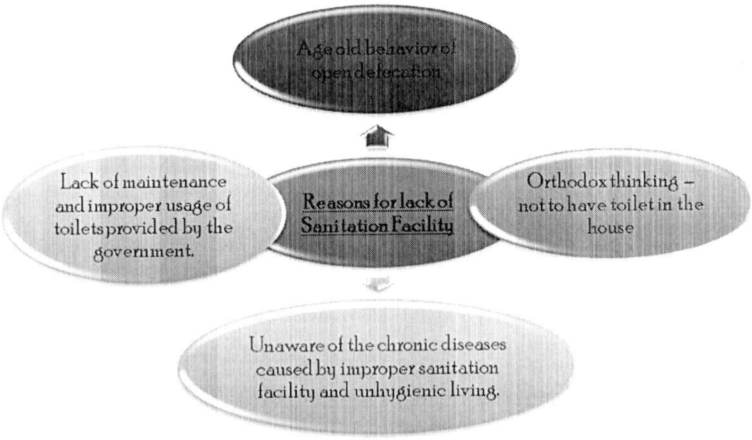

In our survey of the village households we found out that among the 46 households surveyed only 2 households had toilet facility in their house. Rest 44 household members went outside in the open to defecate. There is an old behavior which is being followed by generation to generation (i.e.) defecation in the open. There is no proper sanitation facility. Proper sanitation facility and hygienic surrounding is the need of present time. In this study our survey of the village households indicates that among the 76 households surveyed only 2 households had toilet facility in their house. Rest 94 household members went outside in the open to defecate.

The two households which have the toilet facility are also not up to the mark. It is used by the members who have gone outside settle and come occasionally to visit their family here. The hygienic level of a person or a family was measured from one more criteria that is Hand Wash Medium among the Saber of Jwalakata village. The personel hygiene level was tested through hand wash being done by the Saber individuals after coming from toilet. In this study there are three mediums of hand wash in this village—Soap, Ash and Others (Mud).It was observed that the Ash and Soap users are less in number compared to mud.It is not that Government has not taken any steps to improve Sanitation and Hygiene conditions of the Saber people in Jwalkata village but the changes taking place among them is slow which has been also made the major part of this study.

In village of Jwalkata, TSC (Total Sanitation Campaign) programme was initiative in the year 2009 but for some reasons it got abandoned. People of this village were unable to get the benefit of the programme. Money was collected from the villagers and material was dropped by them. But there was no proper construction which led to not in use of the single pit toilets. During this study of the village it was observed that many single pit toilets which were there but not in use. There was no maintenance of toilets as the villagers did not feel the need of it. In this study it was observed that among the total number of households only two of them had toilet facility in their houses. This shows the low standards of sanitation in this village. People used ash, mud and soap as the medium of hand wash. Soap was used less than ash. To improve the status of sanitation government had run its one of the flagship programmes that is TSC programme. The main problem regarding adoption sanitation facility is the age old practice of defecating in the open and the orthodox thinking of not have toilet in the house premises.

Problems of Sanitation

There are many problems related to sanitation. They are mentioned below:

Behavior of open defecation

From the ancient time people have done open defecation. Nature provides natural hideouts where people do it. People in the early morning go outside of their house in the open to defecate when no one sees them in the darkness. People may or may not carry with themselves a source of water to wash the dirt. If they are not carrying the water with themselves they go to any nearby source of water to wash. Women go little earlier than others to escape the embarrassments or shame of being seen by others. This practice is being followed till now. This age old practice is the biggest hurdles in the adoption of better sanitation facilities. People have to leave this practice and adopt the more hygienic way of sanitation.

Orthodox Thinking

There is an old thinking that toilet should not be in the house. It is an impure place it should be outside the house. The house has the Puja griha inside so the impure things and places should be kept far away. Some say it should be outside the homestead land so in most of the houses we will find the toilets in a corner of the Bari land. It increases the difficulties, one has cross the courtyard (or angan) and the Bari land to reach the toilet. It is a pain for children and old age people.

In this age of modernity and fast changing society, one should leave behind the traditional and orthodox thinking and adopt the new and modern techniques of way of living. The new thought is gaining pace by awareness spread by different

Unhygienic living condition

Improper sanitation and unhygienic living conditions are the main reasons for different diseases in the rural and urban masses both. Some people are unaware of the fact that unhygienic living conditions are destroying their life slowly and day by day. People take it lightly and get engraved with chronic, deadly and irreversible diseases like cholera, jaundice, diarrhea, typhoid, polio, malaria, etc. Jaundice, diarrhea & malaria are chronic and deadly diseases. Children are more vulnerable to these diseases. Children get polio disease due to unhygienic living condition and lack of awareness of the fact that there is a cure to it. TB or Tuberculosis is the most common communicable diseases which spreads due to unhygienic living condition and if not taken care properly. Children also get diarrhea which is very much common among them who live in unhygienic environment.

Practice of Healthy Habits

Children in the school learn healthy habits like

In our survey we found that children were taught healthy habits in the school but they did not get place to practice in the home and incorporate in their daily life as it is not practiced in his/her home. Like the children went to toilets in the school but had no toilet facilities in their homes. In such a situation a child will not adopt the change. For this the parents have to be taught and made aware of facts and needs of proper sanita.

Lack of Maintenance

"It is not our matter or thing why to bother". This saying fits accurately in the situation where government has provided toilet to the poor without their concern and interest. Poor people are unable to earn twice a day's meal, how will they maintain the toilets provided to them by the government.

They do not feel its need and are least bother to use it. There is lack of maintenance of toilets as their money and land is not engaged in it. The government should engage the beneficiaries in it for the better results.

Abandoned Programme

TSC Programme was started in this village and in whole Singpura Panchayat. But for unknown reasons it was abandoned. This decreased the interest of the villagers in the usage of toilets. In the beginning it was boosted up but later on it lost its pace and stopped. Money was taken from the villagers for the construction of toilets and in some place we found the sanitary material also but there was no proper construction and maintenance was nil. This is a very disheartening fact that people are not getting the benefit out of it and the money and effort of programmers went on a failure and waste. This programmers needs to be evaluated and restarted.

Summary & Conclusion

This Study indicates that Status of Sanitation Facilities and its Problems in the village of Jwalkata in Singpura Panchayat of Gurabandha Block which is in East Singhbhum District. The main aim was to study the status of sanitation facilities in select study area among the Saber tribe of Jwalkata village Jharkhand.The village is internally located amidst the forest. The terrain here is rough. There are very less means of transportation available here. People of this village use bullock carts and bicycles for transportation. Due to interior location mobile tower signal is also weak. The nearest town is around 10 km away.

The education level is also low. Students go to school but during the agricultural season go to work in the fields. The health status is poor of the village as there inadequate health facility. In this study of the village we found out that among the total number of households only two of them had toilet facility in their houses. This shows the low standards of sanitation in this village. People used ash, mud and soap as the medium of hand wash. Soap was used less than ash. To improve the status of sanitation government had run its one of the flagship programmes that is TSC programme. But due to unknown reasons it got stopped. Money was taken from the villagers saying that material will be provided and construction will be done. But the scenario is little different the material is left lose construction is incomplete.

This is visible in the village as there are many incomplete and abandoned toilets which are of no use. The main problem regarding adoption sanitation facility is the age old practice of defecating in the open and the orthodox thinking of not have toilet in the house premises. There are solutions to these problems, one should live a healthy and hygienic life, keep their surrounding clean. Awareness should be spread regarding ill effects of improper sanitation and unhygienic living. Parents should also be educated. TSC programme needs to be evaluated and restarted.

References

Bruijne, G. *et. al.*, 2007. Sanitation for All? Thematic Overview Paper 20. Netherlands: International Water and Sanitation Centre.

Government of India, 2004. *Guidelines on Central Rural Sanitation Programme: Total Sanitation Campaign. New Delhi:* Department of Drinking Water Supply. Ministry of Rural Development.

Government of India, 2007. *Guidelines on Central Rural Sanitation Programme:* Total Sanitation Campaign. New Delhi: Department of Drinking Water Supply. Ministry of Rural Development

Government of India, 2008. *Sustaining the Sanitation Revolution.* New Delhi: Department of Drinking Water Supply, Ministry of Rural Development.

Guerrant, R.L., Schorling, J.B., McAuliffe, J.F., and de Souza, M.A., 1992. Diarrhoea as a cause and an effect of malnutrition: diarrhoea prevents catch-up growth and malnutrition increases diarrhea frequency and duration. *American Journal of Tropical Medicine and Hygiene,* 47: pp 28–35.

Hutton, G., Haller, L. and Bartram, J., 2007. Global cost-benefit analysis of water supply and sanitation interventions. *Journal of Water and Health,* 5 (4): pp 481–502.

Murray, C.J. and Lopez, A.D., 1997. Global mortality, disability, and the contribution of risk factors: Global burden of disease study. *Lancet,* 349 (9063): pp 1436-42.

Office of the Registrar General and Census Commissioner, 2001. *Census of India.* New Delhi: Ministry of Home Affairs, Government of India.

16

Approaches for Tribal Development in the process of Globalisation

Dr. Debashis Debnath

Introduction

Globalisation, a new term of social change coined in the 1980s that derives a process that cuts across the boundaries of nations or in other words the process of expansion of economy from a developed to a developing nation and the opening up of the markets of hitherto insular economies of the world, consequentially cultures and societies prevailing a move towards a larger integration of the world and facilitating interdependence moving towards a global culture. In the Globalisation process the "free market" economy, "outsourcing and off-shoring economy based on labour skills for human capital", "global cities" have attracted MNCs to establish factories and offices in India, resulting into positive impacts such as development of services including information and communication technologies and increase in the share of world trade, foreign currency reserves, average growth rate of exports and so on. Globalisation has led increasing "interconnectedness of the world through new systems of communication" (Sacks, 2003, p. 26), and affects all areas of life. So, the driving process in the process of globalisation is incentives and integration. The most visible outcomes in the process are the development of transnational corporations and international banks having principal control over growing world trade and services rather than governments. This ever increasing capacity to communicate worldwide has resulted in the increasing domination of western cultures, whose economics and political institutions are most affluent and powerful. This process has had profound influence on less economically powerful and sovereign cultures. Development planners seem uncomfortable with ethnic diversity because it challenges the homogenizing tendency of economists to reduce populations to quantifiable groups. The most disturbing element in the process of Globalisation is its relentless drive towards cultural universalism of American or European culture and associated ideological frameworks, and its implied disregard and disrespect for cultural and language diversity. Under Globalisation there has been a great expansion of western culture. Beyond the economics and political debates, it is presumed that globalisation is a challenge to cultures, in particular, to marginalised communities and their identities. It is also feared that it may bring co-modification of their cultures and would erase their unique identities. In the sense of inclusive growth and sustainability of development, the development is much more than the economic growth. Globalisation is more than just about economics. It is not only about the ratio of exports to Gross Domestic Product (GDP) but also about culture, society, politics and people (Rangarajan, 2007, January 15). Accusations of cultural imposition and domination have been widely heard.

Indigenous people are on the cusp of the crisis in sustainable development. Their communities are concrete examples of sustainable societies, historically evolved in diverse ecosystems. Participatory development is possible only in smaller units that share a need structure and social facilities. The recognition of ethnic identities is essential to this. There are some 350 million indigenous people in more than 70 countries around the globe, speaking autochthonous languages, and who are marginalised and frequently denied basic human rights, including their cultural rights. In the social change perspective with the universal forces of changes like urbanisation, westernisation, modernisation and the Indian force of sanskritisation, the tribal identities are not in the crystallised phase of historical and political developments. Thus, tribals in India present a significant degree of cultural and ethnic diversity. They differ in their socio-cultural levels as well as in their behaviour patterns. Tribal situation in the country poses peculiar problems of development, not encountered in other areas. The peculiarities can be broadly summed up as geographical, demographic, socio-cultural and exploitative. Tribal development indicates serious challenges to the policy makers, administrators and development activists. The socio-economic forces of modernisation and development have no doubt brought some benefits to the people of respective areas, but the benefits accrued to them have been largely out weighted by the harm more to them. Development induced displacement, involuntary migration and resettlement has cause marginalisation of tribals and presented enormous problems to them. The new economic regime has led to privatisation and marketisation of economy and thus it has been treated as powerful threat to the survival of tribal communities (Singh, 2008). According to one estimate, irrigation projects, mines, thermal power plants, wildlife sanctuaries, industries, etc., between 1950 and 1990 in India, displaced 213 lakh persons. 85 percent of them are tribals (Fernandes & Paranjpe, 1997). The government is aware of (a) the eroding resources base and socio-cultural heritage of tribal population through a combination of development interventions, commercial interest, and lack of effective legal protection of tribal and (b) the disruption of life and environment of tribal population owing to unimaginative, insensitive package of relief. So, on one side the globalisation has been over-exploiting the natural wealth, without living anything for the indigenous population who are lacking social or economic choices to make profits in the investment in the market economy. On the other hand, to bring these large sections of the populations into the process of globalisation it's a great hurdle. The Government of India has attempted these by implementing various policies and programmes in tribal development in innovative and popular democratic way with support of NREGS, RTI act, Forest Rights Act and PESA 1996.

Although globalisation dehistorizes identities. It cannot certainly erase identity totally except crating hybrid identities. Today, identities are under a period of rapid evolution in matters of rights, articulation and solidarity movements and so on in our country. So it is the vital question as to whether it is feasible to make a pure, uncontaminated identity with a romantic notion of uniqueness.

Today, they face the challenges of extinction or survival and renewal in a globalised world. The impact of globalisation is strongest on these populations and they have no voice, therefore, easily swept aside by the invisible hand of the market and its proponents. Globalisation is not merely a question of marginalisation for indigenous peoples it is a multipronged attack on the very foundation of their existence and livelihoods (Pratheep, 2010).

There is much evidence that globalisation has, in aggregate, improved the human conditions. Bur it has different impacts on different people (Greig et al 2007). It becomes the rich very rich or mega rich. On the contrary for a large group – sometimes called the 'bottom billion' it has not made life better and may have made things worse, sometimes much worse. How we might reshape the globalisation, rather than hinders, the lives of the bottom billion- the losers from globalisation in both relative and absolute terms. So we intend to find out the possibility of more inclusive globalisation that reaches down to the bottom of the pyramid recognizing that globalisation has both positive and negative impacts.

Objectives of the paper

This paper will discuss the various approaches for the tribal development in the present day imagining inclusive Globalisation for tackling poverty and the effects of climate change with the enhancement of the capacities of the marginalised tribal poor to cope up with globalisation effects for livelihood securities

Indian Tribals and their development

Indigenous peoples, known as tribal peoples, have been living from seven pocket zones of the country, which have plentiful natural resources. The tribal groups inhabit in widely varying ecological and geo-climatic conditions viz. hilly, forests, tarai desert, coastal regions etc. Thus, the economy is based on natural resources with their own indigenous technology. Their habitats in the micro-environments show the distinctive cultural pattern with numerous ethnic varieties on the basis of the social norms, rules, traditional institutions and livelihoods. Their inseparable values of nature and culture are reflected in the world views, belief system and people's actions. Each community has consolidated their identities by several to myths of original, tribal endogamy identified customary practices.

In the history of environment, the colonialism and the feudal lords made the forest refugees, who have been surviving on collection of the forest products for their daily requirement, such as fuel (energy), fodder (livestock), food (health), fruit (nutrition), fiber (crafts), fertilizer (productivity), fishes (water). The history of oppression, exploitation and exclusion developed prevalent poverty amongst them as their surplus after self-consumption selling in the market provided them meager income. Due to the forestry activities under the State management regime the tribals became marginalised, providing only the labours only in the silvicultural operations. But as revealed in the Indigenous Knowledge System still they maintain the interactions with the biological diversities in the adaptive and co-evolutionary processes which suggest the socio-ecological system with the integrated system of human and nature.

The tribes have the civilisational and political definition. At the political level they are known as scheduled tribes to provide them constitutional provisions and benefits as 'protective discrimination notified by article No.342 of Indian constitution by their traditional occupation, cultural distinctiveness, language, backwardness and low techno-economic level. As per 2011 census the 596 communities are having 104,281,034 populations, constituting 8.6 % of the total Indian population, they account for a fourth of the population living in the poorest wealth docile. The starkest marker of tribal deprivation is child mortality. Under-five mortality rates among tribal children in rural areas remain startlingly high (at about 100 deaths per 1,000 live births in 2005 compared with 82 among all children).

The Tribal development in India is social and economic development of tribal peoples through phased manner and time bound integrated area development and other programmes suiting progressive elimination of all forms of exploitation and ensuring a move towards the goal of equity and social justice. Since 1950s from our Five year plan till 12th Five year plan the paternalistic development of the tribals initially focussed on education, roads, agriculture, which later transformed into area and community based development in sixth five year plan (1975-79) in the Tribal sub-plan and

Particularly Vulnerable Tribal Groups (PVTG) and finally participatory development in integrated and holistic manner with the approach of sustainable livelihood under Millennium Development Goals (MDGs). The later phase initiated the alternative strategies of development for workable sustainable development strategies and more equitable distribution of development opportunities.

Most of the tribal communities inhabit the placid forest environment. From Primeval times they have been depending on forests as a perennial source of natural resources, Till, 1955 when the Charter of Indian Forests declared by Lord Dalhousie, the tribal people enjoyed the freedom to use the forest and this has given them a feeling that the forest belongs to them as common property resource system based on social arrangement. Then, even after the 1894 forest policy of the colonial government did not affect the tribal people much because forest cover was vast and population was less. After independence the forest policy was redefined in 1952 and as per this traditional rights of the forest dwelling tribes were connected into certain concessions. The policy of 1952 withdraw several concessions which the old policy had scope for releasing forest land for cultivation by tribal people, (ii) provision for meeting the need of the villagers from the outlying areas in the reserved forests, (iii) no state control over the private forests of tribal people, and (iv) no restriction on free grazing in forests. The new policy turned the Lords of forests to subjects with certain concessions. The new policy restricted the rights of the tribal people in the reserved forests. Forest Departments induced contractors into the forests to realize maximum revenue and contractors became a source of uncontrolled exploitation of the tribal people. In many places tribesmen were at the mercy of the forest contractors and forest officials. There is a constant propaganda that tribal people are destroying the forests. The National Forest Policy in 1988 is pro-tribal policy. In the Act 4.6 of the that policy it has given clear guidelines for involvement of tribals in protection, management and development of forests, recognizing the symbiotic relationship of tribals with forest. Following up on 1st June, 1990, the government resolution for Joint Forest Management opened up new avenues of collaborative forest management with people. Till date 28 states have adopted the JFM policy so that over 1 lakh forest protection committees have been formed which has concerned above 14 million hectare of forest land of which above 90% are situated in predominant tribal areas. The new village institution has not taken only the responsibility of protection of the forest, but many developmental measures like increase of agricultural productivity, increase generation through non-timber forest product management alternative economic source through skill development, community initiative for increase of literacy or educational advancement, self-help group for credit of money to protect the tribal people from exploitation by money-lenders, availability of irrigation and safe drinking water to reduce the contaminated disease, village asset development and soon.

In the wake of the participatory forestry their decision-making rights and responsibilities from planning, implementation to evaluation have been prioritized. Development at grass roots two more institutions like civil societies or NGOs and market have been added to catalyze the developmental activities. In India, the tribals are chronically poor. To explore the tackling poverty in India the three fronts must be opened to combat:

- Opportunity (economic growth and employment)
- Empowerment (rights and democracy) and
- Security (Social support, social protection, law and order

Indian Tribals and Global poverty

Poverty remains an enormous problem worldwide, despite major reductions in the past 50 years. Reducing poverty, in all forms is the greatest challenge for the developing countries and to the international community. Of the world's 7 billion people, 1.32 billion people live on less than one dollar a day and 2.8 billion live on less than two dollars day. In our indigenous lands large sections of the tribals are found poor in the fringe forest areas due to their comparative less opportunities for their economic and social choices. The MDGs call for the integration of the principles of sustainable development into environmental policies. Environmental sustainability is being mainstreamed in forest policies around the world, particularly since UNCED, while the integration of the goals of poverty and hunger reduction in forest policies and plans is less widespread.

Community-based forestry, or participatory forestry, is particularly well placed to address poverty reduction. Community-based forestry is now well accepted and established in various countries in all regions, and programmes are beginning to generate financial and other benefits. Improving local peoples' rights and access to forest resources is a tool to the success of community-based forestry programmes. However, much still remains to be done to clarify and secure access rights. Many countries are working to strengthen forest governance, some through decentralisation processes that allow the poor to derive more benefits from forests and be more involved in decision-making and forest management itself

Under this socio-economic condition and the burden of rural poor on the natural resources and in pursuance of Govt. of India resolution in 1990 on Participatory forest management and its subsequent modification in 2000, giving an importance of people's involvement in protection, management and development of forest. The amended resolution in 2000 was passed to give more opportunity to the women and weaker sections along with NGOs involvement. Since the inception of World Bank aided and other International donor aided forestry project people's participation has been increased due to income generating activities and resource development work carried out in the villages, with subsequent betterment in the socio-economic condition of the people and poverty reduction (Shukla 2004). In the forest area the micro watershed treatment for soil conservation and ground water recharging as a part of Assisted Natural Regeneration in the nearby forest areas under FPC and Rehabilitation of degraded forest under VFC provided employment to the poor sections. Simultaneously, the plantations of NTFP yielding species viz. Neem (Azadirachta india), Mango (Magnifera indica), Aonla (Emblica officinalis), Mahua (Magnifera indica), etc. on the treatment sites. In total, 20006 ha. of forest was planted during this time. Thus employment generation, enhancement of crop productivity and various NTFPs yielding generate livelihoods (Debnath 1991). Thus, the programme has benefited the landless and poorest tribals through wage employee.

Forest Livelihoods

In the JFM program in the attempt was made to achieve the sustainable forest management with the livelihood improvement in the decentralised process. Thus, the benefits were derived in the two major ways; forest endowments (i.e. rights to forest) and forest entitlement (i.e. economic benefits from forest). Thus forest in the state can play an important role as a source of income and a basis for the livelihoods of forest dependent people. The principle service and products from forest include Non-Timber Forest Products by collection, processing, marketing, watershed projects for the enhancement of agricultural livelihood and environmental services i.e. ecotourism and other nature based entertainmental programs. The following table shows the types of livelihoods generated in the forest management programs.

Table 1: Types of Livelihoods generated from Forest Management

Sl. No.	Livelihoods Pattern		Types of Livelihoods
01	Natural Resource Based	a.	Collection of NTFPs: Collection of Nationalised NTFPs.
		b.	Processing of NTFPs, including medicinal and aromatic plants,
		c.	Value addition on Processed NTFPs, viz. pickles, morabba, Plate making, Bidi making
		d.	Marketing of NTFPs, including medicinal and aromatic plants
		e.	Cultivation of Mushrooms and medicinal and aromatic plants
		f.	Collection and cultivation of fuel wood, fodder, fruits

		g.	Production of Vermi compost and organic fertlizer
		h.	Preparation of bamboo 'thali' and bamboo works
		i.	Production of wood works: Toys, wooden utensils, neck-ties, decorative works, wooden idols, human figures, busket-making
		j.	Fishery works
		k.	piggery, duckery, goatery,
		l.	Afforestation and plantation
		m.	Nursery
		n.	Agricultural and horticulture, specially vegetables
		o.	Seri-culture
		p.	Watershed related like contour trenches, stop-dam construction, rafter construction, check-dam construction, tank construction, leveling of land, nullah bandhan (stream living embankments), and percolation tank.
		q.	Micro-enterprises e.g. Dalia preaparation, incense sticks, broom making etc
02	Non-natural resource based	a.	Tailoring
		b.	Driving
		c.	Grinding Flour
		d.	Watershed related
		e.	Infra-structure development e.g. road construction, school building, livestock shed etc.
		f.	Paper bag
		g.	Doll-making, mat-making,
03	Environmental Services	a.	Ecotourism related

Forest devolution and equity

In the decentralised process local forest management institutions viz. forest protection committee, village forest committees and ecodevelopment committee were created to bring the marginalised and poor rural people into the decision making forums, providing opportunities further empowerment and skilled development. In the each JFM committee in each village, all the adult members have the power of voting in the general body and executive body. Each executive body is constituted by 11 members, selected or nominated among women and landless labours. The involvement of women in decision making process has always been emphasized with regard to equal membership, resort representation, PRA based planning. In many locations women were consulted at the outset. In many divisions staff has introduced women's Self Help Groups to provide more livelihoods especially on the non-natural resource based as alternative economic sources. The collaboration with NGOs also was brought into policy for promoting leadership at the local level. The formal involvement of NGOs in assisting forestry project both at the field level and central level was also constrained by the perception of the 'tedious nature' of the process of contracting NGOs in the State were not accustomed to professional contractual relationships with Government agencies that bound them to specific tasks and responsibilities.

Within these constraints, there have been some remarkable initiatives of individual DFOs in several divisions of enlisting the involvement of NGOs and even developing their district / division level networks to provide 'value added' services in the areas such as

- Training of forest staff and VFC members in JFM related activities.
- Training for other income generating activities
- Communication for VFC/FPC/EDC extension and motivation.
- Communication to a wider audience about the transformation taking place through JFM.
- Marketing of forest products for income generating activity.

Since 1992, when the 73rd Amendment of India's constitution empower Panchayat Raj Institutions (local self-government) to perform a role in the management local natural resources (including forests) at the village level, Madhya Pradesh has been one of the leading states in the country in implementing the constitutional mandate. However, the linkages between the Panchayats and JFM committees have been strengthened when the state resolution was amended in 2001. The new resolution states that the Gram Sabha or village assembly under the Panchayati Raj system also constitutes the general body of the JFM committee. This allows for a more explicit linkage between these two decentralisation initiatives. The forest committees have formal links with the panchayats, where the *sarpanch* (the leader of the local government) is an ex-officio member of the committee. In addition the Memorandum of Understanding (MOU) is signed by the panchayat as well as the committee and Forest Department. It is expected that linkage between forest committees and Gram Sabha takes place through one of the eight committees of the Gram Sabha, the Estate Committee, which is expected to act as a Nodal Committee for the JFM committee and will further develop as a result of the change in legal ownership and of NTFPs, due to enactment of 'The provision of the Panchayats (Extension to the Scheduled Areas) Act', 1996. The introduction of Act means that net income from trade of MFP will be transferred to the primary societies, thus making the gatherers its owners.

Globalisation and environmental change

Economic globalisation offers opportunities for sustainable development but also brings important co-benefits, such as poverty reduction, access to energy efficient lighting and cooking, improvement of air quality and living conditions, and sustainable use of forest resources. Countries like India, the scope of clean development mechanism is vast. Global investment in climate change mitigation projects has increased in present time, which directly improves the livelihood of local communities through creation of employment or increased economic activities.

Forests play an important role in the climate system. The role of forest is well known in terms of many assets. It provides habitat to a wide range of living and non living things and also affects the human life by its important functions like biogeochemical cycle. The multiple benefits of forests include use values and non-use values. Forests are generally undervalued since a large share of forest contributions to the state and country revenue. It encompasses the economic uses of forests, including the management of forest resources for production, the role of forest development in poverty alleviation and the impacts of forest research and development. The importance of forest-based emissions as a driver of climate change is one of the most indirect and hard-to-prove causal pathways linking forests and livelihood security; most linkages between forests and livelihood security are more direct and more easily grounded in empirical research.

In recent years, role of forest dependent communities to environmental change has received increasing attentions among the scholars, globally. Global environmental change presents the considerable socio-economic challenges to the poor tribal communities. But at the same time, REDD+ and carbon markets provide direct financial incentives to the tribal. Tribal communities have long history in managing the forest resources. In fact, it is a tradition to protect and manage their forest for domestic and livelihood needs. Community-based forestry activities address the poverty alleviation and forest conservation. Several forest products including NTFPs, timber, fuelwood are being traded in markets and also being used for subsistence. In addition, several other benefits in the kind of ecotourism, biodiversity conservation and carbon sequestration present immense potential to the tribals in present day.

Due to the impact of biotic and abiotic pressure on our forests, many forest areas has been depleted and degraded due to policy failure in colonial & post-colonial phase until they were not recognised under 1988 forest policy. At the same time change in climatic conditions have also played a significant role on their regeneration rate and their growth. In this context, global carbon market meets the twin objectives: livelihood development and relieving the pressure on forests to aid conservation of wildlife and biodiversity and thereby contribute to sustainable development. The overarching benefit to the environment will be in the form of carbon sequestration to combat climate change.

Forest-based developmental activities recognize the influences and potential that the forests and other natural ecosystems have on climate adaptation/mitigation, and food, water, environmental, and livelihood security of tribals and forest dwellers specifically, and the nation at large, in the context of climate change. For instance, over the past decades, national policies of conservation and sustainable management have transformed the country's forests into a net sink of CO_2.

The National Mission for a Green India, known as the Green India Mission, is a part of India's plan to fight climate change. The aim of the mission:

Respond to climate change by a combination of adaptation and mitigation measures, which would help :

- Enhancing carbon sinks in sustainably managed forests and other ecosystems;
- Adaptation of vulnerable species/ecosystems to the changing climate; and
- Adaptation of forest-dependent communities.

The objectives of the Mission:

1. Increased forest/tree cover on 5 m ha of forest/non-forest lands and improved quality of forest cover on another 5 m ha (a total of 10 m ha);
2. Improved ecosystem services including biodiversity, hydrological services and carbon sequestration as a result of treatment of 10 m ha.;
3. Increased forest-based livelihood income for 3 million forest dependent households;
4. Enhanced annual CO2 sequestration of 50-60 million tonnes by the year 2020.

Thus, the Green India Mission is proposed to double the area being taken up for afforestation and eco-restoration over the next decade, which can raise fresh natural capital that is so vital for the tens of millions of people who depend on degraded forests. It can meet the twin objectives of assigning forest land to tribal and other forest-dwelling communities to enable livelihoods development, and relieving extractive pressures on core dense forests to aid conservation of wildlife and biodiversity. The overarching benefit to the environment will be in the form of carbon sequestration to combat climate change. The experience gained from the Joint Forest Management (JFM) programmes of the past will be invaluable. The JFM measures did not live up to their promise in most States and, in some cases, existed only on paper. In the main, they left forest communities feeling alienated. That, nearly 40 per cent of open forest remains degraded today reinforces the need for a vastly improved management system.

The Green India Mission recognizes the influences and potential that the forests and other natural ecosystems have on climate adaptation/mitigation, and food, water, environmental, and livelihood security of tribals and forest dwellers specifically, and the nation at large, in the context of climate change. For instance, over the past decades, national policies of conservation and sustainable management have transformed the country's forests into a net sink of CO2. From 1995 to 2005, carbon stocks stored in our forests are estimated to have increased from 6245 m tons to 6622 m tons, thereby registering an annual increment of 37.68 million tons of carbon or 138.15 million tons of CO2 equivalent. This annual removal by forests is enough to neutralize 9.31% of total GHG emission in year 2000.

The Mission acknowledges challenges on account of demand supply gap of various provisioning services from forests, particularly fuel wood, fodder/ grass/grazing; timber, cane/bamboo, NTFPs etc. creating unsustainable pressure, and contributing to degradation of forests and ecosystems. The productivity of Indian forests is low as compared to world standards, worsening the gap between demand and supply of various forest products. Through the scientific modeling done using RCM (Regional Climate Model) and BIOME model (BIOME 4), it was observed that more than 50% of the vegetation in India would find it less than optimally adapted to its existing location by 2085, making it more vulnerable to the adverse climatic conditions as well as to the increased biotic stresses of already challenged forest ecosystems. The forests would be vulnerable on account of the altitudinal and latitudinal shift of the species of the forest ecosystems and also on account of increased occurrences of fire, pest /diseases, invasive species, it is quite interesting to mention here that the extent to which NTFPs and community livelihoods are vulnerable change in species assemblage/forest type, forest die-back and loss of biodiversity. Forest dependant livelihoods may get severely affected, enhancing vulnerability of local communities.

However, to the changing climate including the coping strategies is not well established as of now. Therefore, the proposed project seeks to develop, enhance and provide an understanding of the ability of forest dependent communities to respond to the changing climate with a view of reducing livelihood threats and forest degradation through vulnerability and adaptation assessments within the NTFPs context.

Conclusion

In the end of 20th Century and in the beginning of 21st Century, the Ministry of Environment and Forests and the state Forest Department has taken a number of attempts of sustainable development of the forest on the basis triple-bottom line approach viz. ecology, economy and social & institution. The combinations of the ecological sustainability, economic stability and social acceptability &

institutional sustainability lead the achievements of the sustainable livelihoods in the shorter phase and sustainable development in the longer phase.

The conservation ethos of the indigenous peoples have been taken up into consideration by providing the due values to the indigenous knowledge of species diversity with multiple utility, sacredness of the areas, trees and water-bodies, cultural practices of beliefs and rituals, knowledge and religious affiliation of the medicinal men and its promotion of employment generation. In this manner, the protection of the traditional livelihoods became inextricably mixed up with the promotional livelihoods and alternative livelihoods in alternative strategies of development in workable sustainable development models. Thus the employment generations and the enhancement of income source focused approaches for poverty reduction and achieving sustainable livelihoods. In this context, the decentralised governance has been brought into action through the village institutions, viz. FPC, VFC, EDC, Panchayat and gram sabha, Non-governmental Organisations or Voluntary Institutions as Civil societies, Self-help Groups or women groups as Dwarka groups. In the process various issues have been emerged.

Climate change has created additional pressure on NTFPs availability in natural forest areas, threatening the local people's livelihood opportunities and making them more vulnerable. The average surface daily maximum temperature, by 2080 is projected to rise between 3.40C to 4.40C and the minimum temperatures are likely to rise by more than 4.40C all over Madhya Pradesh. During the same period, the eastern half of the state will experience more warming than the western half. Projections of rainfall for the period 2021 to 2050 indicates that there is likely to be decrease in winter rainfall from eastern part of MP to western part of MP. In pre-monsoon period, the rainfall is increasing only in the Southern part of MP, with decrease in rain fall in all other parts. During post monsoon period, slowly again the western end of MP is likely to face decrease in rain fall, with no change or little increase in rainfall in most other parts of the state.

It has been well recognised at global level that consequences of climate change has already started and would create severe impacts in near future. But, climate change impacts can be delayed or reduced to a certain extent. This can only be possible when existing atmospheric CO2 will be restored in terrestrial natural ecosystems like forests and in its soil. Forests can contribute to climate change mitigation in four ways:

(i) increase in forest area through afforestation/reforestation;

(ii) increase in carbon density of existing forests at both stand and landscape scales;

(iii) sustainably managing forests for harvesting forest products and

(iv) reducing emissions from deforestation and degradation.

The potential of these activities have already been recognised in global climate negotiations. These activities can fulfill dual responsibilities of Government. Forests' based livelihood opportunities would remain in sustainable manner for local people and quality and quantity of forests would also be enhanced in coming years as NAPCC' mission states.

References

Fernandes, W., & Paranjpe, V. (Eds.). (1997). Rehabilitation policy and law in India: A right to

Livelihood, New Delhi: Indian Social Institute.

Greig A, Hulme, D. and Turner M. 2007. Challenging Global Inequality : Development Theory and Practice in the 21st Century. London : Palgave

Pratheep, P.S. 2010. Globalisation, Identity and Culture: Tribal Issues in India. LSCAC 2010 Proceedings, pp 149-159.

Rangarajan, C. (2007, January 15). Who's afraid of gobalisaton? The Economic Times.

Sacks, J. (2003). The dignity of difference. New York: Continuum.

17

Anthropology, The Tribe and the Nation – State: The Indian Expereince (Professor P.K. Bhomick Memorial Lecture)

Dr. H.K. Bhat

Mr. President, scholars and friends,

I feel greatly honoured by the Institute for Social Research and Applied Anthropology (ISRAA), Bidisha, for the invitation to deliver this lecture in commemoration of Late Prof. P.K. Bhowmick, a great teacher and researcher of anthropology and also the founder of ISRAA. I am touched also at delivering it in this *karmabhoomi* of Prof. Bhowmick.

I shall endeavour in this lecture to give an account of the relationship of anthropology to the concept of tribe (or the concept of 'primitive' as it was known in the 19th century). Then, I shall proceed to look at the relevance of the term tribe in the present century in relation to the concept of nation-state with special reference to India. Nation-state is considered now all over the world as the highest form of societal development and it is also considered as the pinnacle of civilisational culture. The focus of the discussion will be India as the present author feels that the concept of tribe is the most abused term of anthropology by Indian social scientists, politicians and the general public. The contradictions of the tribe and the nation-state is more apparent in India than anywhere in the world.

To begin with let me briefly state why I chose this topic about the concept of tribe. I know that this was one of the important concepts of anthropology till recently. It is no more relevant to the anthropologists in other parts of the world whereas in India it still evokes interest not only among the public but also among the politicians and the social scientists, especially anthropologists. But, I feel very uncomfortable when a fellow Indian boasts that India has more than 700 tribes with a population of over 84 million people, constituting over 8.6% of the total population.

On the other hand, another fellow Indian takes pride about the antiquity of India's civilisation which is more than 5000 years old. The fact of the matter is that our tribal ancestors in India had more than 5000 years to transform themselves from the tribal stage to the civilisational stage. Should we believe that socio-cultural transformation in India is so slow. I really feel ashamed when someone who is well-educated, well-placed in society, well-travelled in the globe, and professes one of the great religions of the world introduces himself as a tribe ! It is very difficult for me to comprehend such a statement. (see Misra, 1986).

I have done some ethnographic studies among the Scheduled Tribes in Meghalaya and Karnataka and lived with them as a participant observer. In my entire career in anthropology since 1972 I have not come across any Scheduled Tribe who wanted to get out of this categorisation.

Many people in India, including Scheduled Tribes and some social scientists, think that the label of tribe is granted to certain communities for ever. They think that it is like some racial features. Some people including some scholars and common people, eulogise the virtues of tribal life that it should be preserved for ever. They fail to understand that the process of cultural transformation involves shedding some of the cultural elements and acquiring some new elements. Of course culture is cumulative. But all elements of culture are not carried forward during cultural evolution. It is the job of the anthropologist to educate the public about man and his cultural heritage. In this respect, atleast Indian anthropologists have not reached to the public. Part of the blame goes to the anthropologists for their failure as responsible citizens of the country.

Another reason for choosing this topic is my role as an anthropologist to study or evaluate reports about the communities of Karnataka who demand their inclusion in the ST list. I am also in the Advisory Board of Karnataka State Tribal Research Institute since last year. At present there are 50 communities listed as ST out of a total of 299 communities in Karnataka. About 100 more communities aspire for the status of ST. Hence, anthropologists are requested to conduct ethnographic studies on such communities. When a report comes to me for evaluation, several members of the concerned communities who are well placed in society (like civil servants, doctors, lawyers, teachers and IT professionals) contact me with a request to recommend their communities for inclusion in ST list. It is an embarrassing situation. I also question myself, why people want to go back to the earlier stages of human development.

Anthropology and the 'Primitive' Community

The so-called primitive communities in the form of bands or tribes which were small and self-contained human settlements were the subject matter of anthropological studies in the later half of the 19th century. All the leading anthropologists of the day wrote in general about the 'primitive' societies. Some of them like L.H. Morgan, H.S. Maine, J.F. McLenna, J.G. Frazer, and F. Boas wrote on specific social institutions or primitive societies. Early pioneers of anthropology were not anthropologists by training but they became anthropologists in the course of doing anthropology. A.C. Haddon who organised Torres Straights field expeditions to Melanesia and F.Boas who organised the Jesu expedition to Baffinland in the arctic region of North America laid the scientific foundation to anthropology by the turn of 19th century. However, social-cultural anthropology became a full-fledged science in the first two decades of 20th century by the efforts of A.R. Radcliffe-Brown and B. Malinowas, who described Andamanese and Trobriand cultures, respectively. They were described as 'primitive' cultures without reference to anything outside of them. These cultures could be understood by one man working on them. They were isolated, self-contained, history-less little communities. The anthropologist became the jack of all social science trades learning about economy, politics, religion, kinship, family, marriage, law etc. Thus, the 'primitive' cultures were described as unique designs of life and compared them as if they were natural wholes around the world.

The reality changed after these communities came in contact with the civilisational cultures, mainly through the colonialists, missionaries, traders and anthropologists. Since then the 'primitive' isolates began to decline. The world has truly become one great society in the 20th century with the birth of a large numbers of nation-states. Almost all societies are now connected to cities and civilisations. Many anthropologists declared in the 1930's that anthropology studies all human societies, 'primitive' or civilised, single or complex. Study of urbanisation and industrialisation is as important to the anthropologist today as the study of villages or rural communities. Today anthropology studies everything about man and his works. As the number of 'primitive' societies were declining, anthropologists first focused on peasant studies and then on civilisational studies. Peasants and *urbans* constitute one society as stated by Krocber (1948). Further, he said that anthropologists in the past were studying 'organisms' (i.e. societies by themselves) but now they study organs (i.e. different parts of larger societies).

Constitution of India and the Tribes

The constitution of India intends to constitute the country into a secular, democratic republic providing its citizens justice, liberty, equality and fraternity. As a follow-up it included affirmative action for the promotion of the interests of certain communities notified as Scheduled Tribes (ST), Scheduled Castes (SC) and Religions, Minorities, following partly the policy of the British rule. Reservation in legislature, government service and educational institutions were provided to SC's and ST's in the name of social justice. The constitution of India thus considered the collective rights of certain communities and not the individual rights of all its citizens irrespective of caste and creed. Later, more communities were added to this list in the name of Other Backward Communities (OBC). Special protective provisions were given to the ST's under Firth and Sixth Schedules of the constitution.

The Scheduled Tribes in India: Current situation and issues

The population of scheduled Tribes in India was .... in 1951 and in 2011 it was 8,43,26,240. The number of ST's also rose from .... to about 700 during this period. The population of Bhil, the largest ST, is above five million people spread over in several states whereas the smallest ST, the Onge of Andaman and Nicobar islands numbers around 100. The percentage of ST's in India's population in 1951, 1961, 1971, 1981 and 1991 and 2011 was 6.25, 6.87, 6.94, 7.76 and 8.08, 8.6 respectively.

Article 342 of the constitution of India provides for the Scheduled Tribe status to certain communities in India based on the recommendation of the state and central governments which is finally approved by the parliament of India. Neither the constitution nor the government orders mention the criteria to declare certain communities as ST's. However, the first Backward class commission set up in 1953 under article 240 of the constitution while making recommendations for the revision of ST list laid down the criteria as follows: 'They live apart in the hills and even where they live in the plains, they lead a separate excluded existence and are not assimilated in the main body of the people. Scheduled Tribes may belong to any religion. They are listed as Scheduled Tribes because of the kind of life led by them" (quoted by Roy Bruman, 1999).

Scheduled Areas and Tribal Areas

Article 244 of the constitution allows special administrative arrangements for certain states under scheduled areas and tribal areas. Scheduled areas come under Article 244 (1) which is also called V Schedule Area, whereas Tribal areas come under Article 244(2) which is also called VI Schedule Area.

The so-called tribal communities in India have been called by different names in the censuses of India since 1891 as follows: forest tribes (1891), animists (1901), tribal animists (1911), hill and forest tribes (1921), primitive tribes (1931), backward tribes (1935) and tribes (1941). Finally, they were named as the scheduled tribe in the constitution of India in 1950.

The essential characteristics laid down by the Chanda Committee (1967) and the Lokur committee (1965) for a community to be identified as a Scheduled Tribe needs to be elaborated and specified as follows:

a. Indications of primitive traits : These traits should be specified in terms of all the major aspects of culture like Economy, Political organisation, Religion, Kinship, Literacy, etc. The primitive tribes in respect of these aspects should be perceived from the evolutionary perspective. All the human societies are supposed to have undergone evolutionary changes from the socio-cultural perspective as follows: Band > tribe > chiefdom > civilisations. (consisting of peasantry and urbanity). The primitive traits were given up by majority of the human societies during the last five thousand years or so. However, a few human societies could not undergo changes due to certain circumstances. The anthropologists have to indentify such communities who were stuck up at a particular state in the evolutionary ladder. The socio-cultural criteria for the different stages may be summarized as follows:

b. Distinctive culture;- Is the community having distinctive features in terms of kinship, religion, economy and political organisation, etc., which are not found in other communities? If they share most of the socio- cultural features with other communities, it means that they are a part of a larger society, i.e., part of the civilisation culture in which there are two major segments known as great and little traditions.

c. Shyness of contact with the community at large: Man used to live in isolation during the precivilisation stage. Sometimes he had contacts with other tribal communities for taking/ giving the women as wives (friendly situation) or during feud or war (hostile situations). After the emergence of civilisation about five thousand years ago, the band, tribe, chiefdom, societies faced mainly two situations: retraction or absorption. The retracted communities become isolated and other communities are absorbed into the larger civilisational societies leading to loss of most of their cultural features. Shyness has to be understood from the above perspective taking the community as a whole vis-a-vis other communities.

d. Geographical Isolation: This is hardly possible in the contemporary world. Almost all the religions of India are now connected by roads, railway lines and water ways. Radio, telephone, internet services are also available. However, the habitat of particular communities have to be studied from this perspective, also to know the extent of isolation.

e. Backwardness: Backwardness of the community in the modern world should be measured on the basis of human development index consisting of nutritional, health, educational and economic statuses. A standardized scale should be designed to measure it.

Evolutionary Perspectives on Human Society

After the birth of anthropology in late 19th century, the leading anthropologists of the day like L.H. Morgan, E.B. Tylor, Henry Maine, MacLennan and J.G. Frazer posited the unilinear evolution of human society considering the so-called 'primitive' society at on end and the Victorian society of the West at the other end. To demonstrate the unilinear evolutionary process they selected each one of the major social institutions of human society such as family, marriage, religion, kindship, political system, etc, to trace the volutionary development from pre-civilised (i.e., primitive stage to the civilised stage. Systematic studies were conducted on social institutions of the 'primitive' societies in different parts of the world and the data were presented in a unilinear scheme. For example, the institution of marriage was shown to evolve as follows: promiscuity to group marriage to polygamy to monogamy. The evolutionary theory of 19th century is also known as classical evolutionism. It was attacked in the early part of 20th century first by the diffusionists and then by the functionalists. The functional anthropologists besides giving the functional theory of culture, perfected the method of anthropological field studies under the leadership of B. Malinowski.

More scientific theories were required to demonstrate the evolution of human societies. Some American anthropologists, popularly known as neo-evolutionists, like Leslie White, Julian Steward and Marshall Sahlins proposed the new theory of evolutionism known as neo-evolutionism. Archaeologist Gordon childe also contributed to the development of this theory. By using the improved method of field work the neo-evolutionary anthropologists proposed different theories to explain the course of development of human society. The ecological method developed by Steward was also combined to other method to explain the evolutionary process. The neo evolutionists emphasized the notion of cumulative development in culture. This approach emphasizes the quantitative difference between cultures. They showed that cultures can be arranged along some scale ranging from small to large members, less to more amount of harnessed energy per capita per year. etc. According to another group of American anthropologists, culture evolves as the ability to use different natural resources expands or as culture is able to control more and different environments (Marvin Harris). According to the archaeologist Gordon Childe another index of evolutionary cumulation in culture is the increase of population since the Paleolithic age. In this approach each ethnic unit has to be compared with others in terms of occupational specialisations and organisational types in the population.

M.H. Fried, an American anthropologist, studied the evolution of social stratification in human societies as an index of evolutionary change. He used two measures in determining the stage of evolution, namely, (a) a ratio between positions of prestige available for any given age sex grade and the number of persons capable of filling them and (b) a ratio between strategic resources and persons possessing access to them. In order to measure the evolutionary changes in human society both quantitative and qualitative variables have to be taken into account (Wolf, 1968: 94-95). Variables related to environment, energy conversion, division of labour, population, access to resources, access to prestige positions, intensity of communication within and without the community and cognitive complexity of the members of the society can be measured quantitatively. Qualitative variables related to world-view, values, etc., should also be noted.

The neoevolutionary-ecological model of the American anthropologists identified the following major stages in the development of human society (Lenkeit, 2001):

(a) **Foraging societies:** subsisted on hunting and food collection.

(b) **Horticultural and pastoral societies:** Subsisted on crops raised by using primitive technology and dairy products of domesticated animals.

(c) **Agricultural societies:** raised crops by using advanced technology and irrigation, and

(d) **Industrial societies:** produced non-agricultural products by using machines.

The societal groups identified at foraging economy are generally known as bands and tribes. These groups were known in the 19th century as the 'primitives', the subject matter of anthropological studies. Bands lived in groups based on two types of kinship, viz., family band which consists of a number of nuclear families. The second type of group is a patrilocal band which also consists of a member of nuclear families. The population of bands is around 50 individuals. The foragers have few material possessions. Reciprocity is the principle of economic distribution. Nomadic life-style was followed by all. During the entire palaeolithic period humans lived in bands.

Neolithic period saw the emergence of horticultural and pastoral ways of life, carried out separately or together. The common type of horticulture is known as slash-and-burn horticulture. Humans adopted sedentary life-style. They used primitive technology in raising crops. Food production through horticulture and animal husbandry increased the carrying capacity resulting in bigger kin groups. Lineage and clan based kinship (segmentary) structures became the basis of social organisation. Unlike foragers, horticulturalists and pastoralists owned property. Wherever pastoralism dominated, the society adopted partial or full nomadic life-style. All these changes happened during the Neolithic period just before the emergence of intensive agriculture and the civilisational culture. Tribal societies continued upto this time without any road block.

Emergence of urban centers, irrigation, central administration with bureaucratic structure and kingship transformed some of the tribal societies into peasantry. Agriculturalists and pastoralists who came under the control of the urban rulers are classified as peasants. Peasants are food producers largely for self consumption and partly for the consumption of urban dwellers. Hence, civilisational society has two components, i.e., the peasantry and the urbanites. In the course of development of civilisations, tribal societies around them were gradually absorbed into them and transformed as peasants. Until the emergence of nation-states, the tribal societies had the option to resist the absorption. But, emergence of modern nation-states since the 16th century did not leave any option to the tribal societies to remain independent, atleast from the economic and political points of view.

Bands and tribes, the first forms of human society, are also called stateless societies. According to Lucy Mair, such societies had only primitive forms of government and the governing was based on kinship relations (1972). Kinship is irrelevant as a principle in modern state society. In a stateless society there is no recognition to territorial authority, although the members of the society lived in a recognised territory. The idea of a ruler or government controlling a territory and claiming obedience from all people in it, marked an important stage in the evolution of state society. There is no independent place for a band or tribe in a state society. Their livelihood pattern has to be approved by the state authorities. In a modern state society, hunting is completely illegal.

Eric Wolf, an American anthropologist, has identified somewhat different levels of organisation in the growth of culture.

He has broadly classified cultures into two categories and places them in polar relationships (1968:95). At the lowest level are the totipotent or unspecialised cultures. Foraging societies which subsist on hunting and gathering to eke out their living represent the earliest life-way of humans. In this way of life each group has at its command all the cultural components necessary to relate man to environment, man to man and man to universe. Such groups are capable of replicating the entire gamut of components while fissioning into two or more separate units. The population is capable of doubling from one generation to the next. Only such groups underwent transformation during the Neolithic and civilisational periods, few continued even upto the modern period by resisting transformation to the next levels. Evans-Pritchard has termed such societies as segmentary in his monograph on the Nuer society (1940).

Kin groups (lineages and clans) were the bearers of totipotent culture. An ideal unspecialised unit consists of a number of nuclear families capable of providing all services to members and also absorbing all tensions. Such units proliferated throughout the world until the emergence of industrial revolution, the next major qualitative level of human society. All social relations were of symmetrical type. The carrying capacity of a territory varied in foraging and slash-and-burn cultivation societies.

With the rise of civilisational culture, we can see the beginning of irrigated agriculture which ultimately gave rise to industrial revolution around 16th century. Growth of differentiation, specialisation, increase of privileged positions, asymmetrical social relations, movement of goods and labour to the center and their redistribution to the commoners are some of the features of an industrial society. Increased energy conversion enabled the people to develop specialised machinery. This society necessiated the creation of state society to maintain law and order and for distributing the surpluses.

Modern nation-states emerged about three hundred years ago and the process is complete now. There is no territory in this world which is not claimed by one nation–state or the other. The nation-states have engulfed all the previous forms of human societies. Even if they exist they have to be subservient to the nation-states.

Wolf has analysed the different aspects of culture during the course of its evolutionary development (1968:98-101). He opines that all the aspects of culture are equally characterized by cumulative development towards a maximal value (Ibid, p.98). Cumulative character is mostly found in the technical order because it is capable of division of labour. It also involves in specialisation in skills and knowledge which results in growth. In contrast, there are other components in culture which are not cumulative in the above sense as their capacity cannot be measured in a unidimensional scale. But they exhibit a capacity for multiple combination. E.B. Tylor had suggested a statistical method to measure the frequency of a particular combinations. Aspects of culture such as forms of marriage, residence rules, types of marriage, kin terminologies, magical beliefs, forms of burial, etc., are not cumulative and progressive. We can measure only the multivalence of their character. For example, it will be absurd to show different types of descent (matriliny to patriliny to bilaterality) or different forms of marriage (promiscuity to groups marriage to polygamy to monogamy) as progressive cumulation. Wolf is of the opinion that this perspective of culture is the earlier perspective of culture suggested by diffusionists (culture as a mechanical model) and functionalists (culture as an organic model) (1968:101).

The term ‘primitive’ which was in use for nearly 300 years, was dropped by English language anthropology after the second world war for mainly two reasons, first due to the disappearance of isolated cultures and second, due to its negative connotations (Hsu, 1964). The term implied a sharp dichotomy between two kinds of societies, namely, Western and non-Western.

But, anthropologists continued to accept the differences between traditional and modern societies. The traditional societies were described as pre-capitalist, having communalistic economic system, small-scale having multiplex roles, exhibiting pronounced equality and fraterning in social relationships. On the other hand modern societies were characterized as capitalistic, large-scale, having segmented roles.

Anthropology began as an academic discipline with the study of the so-called 'primitive' societies in the 19th century. The term 'primitive' was used by the public in general, but the anthropologists made it one of the basic concepts of this science. Later, they had to abandon it as the term evoked resistance from the people to whom it was used.

Anthropologists started to substitute the term 'primitive' by other therms such as simple, small-scale, face-to-face, tribes etc.

Evans–Pritchard has defined tribe as an acephalous political system (e.g. Nuer). Political units are formed on the basis of the principle of kinship. All the units in the society are similar.

Robert Redfield opined that the predominant form of human living throughout the history of mankind was small community which he designated as the 'little community' (1960). About three quarters of humanity lives in villages even today. Redfield identified the following criteria to identify the little community.

1. Distinctiveness : having group consciousness and clearly marked boundaries.
2. Smallness : amenable for personal observation, some part of it is fully representative of the whole, that is, understanding one section is sufficient to understand the whole.
3. Homogeneous : activities and thinking of all members are much alike, with reference to age and sex. It also means slow – changing. Careers are repeated from generation to generation.
4. Self-sufficient : the needs of the members are met within the society.

Further, Redfield states that these qualities of distinctiveness, smallness, homogeneity and all providing self-sufficiency are present in them in different degrees.

Evolutionary Stages from Band to Civilisation

Socio cultural aspects	*Band*	*Tribe*	*Chiefdom*	*Peasantry*	*Urbanity*
Kinship	Basis of social organisation	Basis of social organisation	Basis of social organisation	Partly basis of social organisation	Not relevant for social organisation
Religion	Animism; great religions absent	Animism; great religions absent	Animism; great religions absent	Emergence of great religions	Recognition to only great religion

Political system	Egalitarian, no position of authority	Egalitarian, no position of authority	Partly egalitarian, no position of authority	Kingship & Nation states	Kingship & Nation states
Economic system	Non-monetary economy; absence of market economy	Non-monetary economy; absence of market economy	Non-monetary economy; absence of market economy	Monetary economy based on market	Monetary economy based on market
Educational system	Preliterate	Preliterate	Preliterate	Partly literate; large section of the society is illiterate	Partly literate; of the society is literate.

From Tribehood to statehood

Some anthropologists give emphasis to the political institution to distinguish the tribe from the state. In band society political institution is not clearly identifiable. In a tribal society it takes distinct identity. According to M. Fortes and E.E. Evans – Pritchard several tribal societies in Africa had primitive states. They classify societies on the basis of the nature of political institution into two types: stateless and state. They called the states of some tribal societies as 'primitive' because they lacked government. All the modern states have well established governments (Herskovits, 1969: 194).

D.G. Mandelbaum in his article 'From tribe to state' originally published in 1956 stated that the state is a larger grouping which has the means to control the behavior of its members by using force. The state is made of a member of local communities, certain members of which, have the power to act for all and they can make the people to do certain things and not to do other things (Hammond, 1968: 156). Regarding the formation of a primitive state, Mandelbaum remarked that in the early days confederations of many tribes emerged to fight a common enemy. The League of the Iroquois is cited by him as an example. New states were also formed though conquest (Ibid, p. 157).

A state can be called a nation-state when a group of people who not only are organised into a state, cut also have a common way of life (Ibid, p. 157).

A.L. Kwelber distinguishes between nation and state as follows: 'Politically nation and state are one; as we speak of the united Nations. But an essentially single nationality can comprise several states that in modern political terminology are called nations.... On the contrary, most large states, especially empires, have comprised of a variety of nationalities (1948: 226-227). Further, Kroeber states that in conventional language the word nation had two contrasting meanings : (a) first, it denotes a people organised under one government; (b) second, it denotes a people of common origin, tradition and language which can also be called a nationality (Ibid, p. 227). Nation-states such as Canada, South Africa, Switzerland, China, Russia etc. have different nationalities in this sense, but each one of them is a single body politic (i.e. a nation).

T.K. Oommen, an Indian sociologist, says that although nation and state are generally used by the public interchangeably the social scientists should distinguish between them. According to him state is 'a political entity, nation is a cultural entity' (1990-12). Further, he states that nation-state, which first originated in Western Europe a few centuries age used the principle of one-nation, one state. When more than one nation existed in a single state as in great Britain, then V.S.S.R. etc. they were recognised as nationalities. A nation is also a linguistic collectivity (Ibid, p.12). Oommen considers India as a multi-national state. (Ibid, p.13).

Etymologically, nation is derived from the Latin word natus meaning 'to be born'. Hence, it suggests common origin of the members of the nation. According to Fried its meaning is very close to the meaning of tribe (1975:106). B.N. Mukherji, an Indian Historian, the Indian word *jati* also indicates nation (2001). There are different definitions of the concept of nation. Political, ethnic and cultural. According Mukherji political unity under a central government is not an essential factor for the existence of a nation. He says that it is rather a geo-cultural personality and considers the Indian sub-continent a nation.

Nationhood in the Indian sub-continent dates back to the 6th millennium B.C. when urbanisation started on the banks of Indus river contributing to the emergence of Harappan also known as (Indus Valley) civilisation. It flourished during the 3rd and 2nd millennium B.C. when literary texts like Vedas, Brahmans, Upanishads etc. were produced by the literati section of the society. India, from which the contemporary term India is derived, was the territorial name since 6th century. B.C. to this sub-continent. The names Hindu and Hindustan were used much later by the Muslim invades from the North-west part of India. Maury, gupta and other empires and kingdoms also flourished during / after 1st millennium B.C. The entire sub-continent, known at present at South Asian region, was one nation until 1947. Some scholars are of the opinion that the 'geographical and cultural compulsions in the nation's history were ignored at the time of dividing India in 1947 (Ibid, p.10).

Etynologically, the word state is derived from the Latin word status which means condition. The present meaning of state originated in the writings of Machiavelli during the 16th century A.D. Government is an inseparable part of state as it is the term in India can be traced to 3rd millenium B.C. (Ibid, p.39). state is a specialised political system which emerged during the civilisation (scupin and DeCorse, 2009: 223).

The identity of a community as a tribe ceases, the moment it becomes a part of a nation-state. This process of absorption may be due to the decision of a tribal community, the state society or both. Hence, there is no place for the tribe in the nation-state society.

Tribe in Indian History

The ancient scriptures of India like the Vedas, Brahmanas puranas and Ithihasas have mentioned the names of different communities of India. Some of them like Kirata, Jana, Vis, gandharva, Pisacha are considered to be the names of tribes. According to Roy Burman these tribal communities played the role of bridge and buffer among the politically organised kingdoms (1994). The Mughal rulers did not disturb the tribal population and the tribals remained in isolation. Arrival of the British in the 16th century brought some changes in the tribal life of India. The British and the 'tribals' were in conflict situations for about two centuries and finally the British adopted the policy of non-interference in the 'tribal' – dominated areas. Thus, in 1935 the British government declared Excluded Areas and Partially Excluded Areas. The British administration was kept to the minimum in these areas. The same British policy was followed by the Indian government treating the so-called 'tribal' communities as a separate category of 'Scheduled Tribe' in the constitution of India. The British classification of the Indian population into 'tribal' and 'non-tribal' was not critically examined by the makers of the constitution of India. The natural process of state formation in India for about 6000 years, since the beginning of Indus Valley civilisation, which was temporarily distorted by the Mughal and European invaders for about a thousand years, was completed ignored by the political leadership of India since independence. The politicians made to believe a section of Indian population, classified as Scheduled Tribe, that it is a permant gift from the makers of the constitution. Can our nation state get rid off this 'tribal' tag and move forward?

The scheduled tribe communities in India exhibit enormous amount of diversity in racial features, languages, occupations, habitat, religious beliefs and practices etc. it is not a homogenous group in any sense.

Transformation of tribes in India

Tribal societies were subjected for transformation with the emergence of civilisation centers all over the world. Indus Valley civilisation which emerged around 2300 B.C. to 2000 B.C. in an area of about two million square kilometers in North-western India triggered the transformation of tribal societies in India (Bhattacharya, 1998). Thus, we have a history of about 5000 years of civilisational culture. The transformation of the tribal societies during the historical period was natural process. Hence, it was gradual and we find the co-existence of both tribal societies and urban centers in the same civilisational culture.

The distinction between tribe and caste is questioned by some anthropologist (Misra, 1977) According to them tribes in India, since the emergence of civilisational culture, never remained in isolation. They had interactions with other communities either in uni caste or multi-caste villages for various socio-economic purposes.

The models of tribe-caste continuum and tribe peasant continuum made by S.C. Sinha is not applicable in most of the places in India (1965). It has only limited application.

The Question of Indigenous People

Some scholars and authorities find a link between the categories of indigenous people and tribal people. It is estimated that there are about 5000 indigenous and tribal people in the world according to the report of ILO published in 1994. (quoted in Roy Burman, 2003). The term indigenous is used in three different senses. Chronological, relational and normative (Roy Burman, 2003) ILO uses the term in the chronological sense, that is, membership claiming on the basis of autochthonous descent and it is equated with tribe. Use of the term in relational sense is common, especially with reference to the recent past to show that certain people came first and the others came later. According to the normative sense all those people who feel that they are rooted in the surroundings and belonging to a particular territory are indigenous. They reject the chronological and relational meanings.

Conclusions

1. Anthropologists cannot study any community at present without reference to the outside world. There are no self-contained, self-sufficient committees i.e. tribal committees.
2. All communities in the world are members of larger wholes known as nation-statess. There is no place for tribe in a nation-state.
3. The leaders of various reservation categories (including that of scheduled tribe) have become 'vote banks' for the politicians and during the elections they are approached for votes.
4. Using the term indigenous to certain communities is highly dangerous for the unity of a nation-state. A nation-state treats all its citizens as equal. Who came first and who came later is not an issue here. All citizens are treated equally. Hence the term indigenous has no relevance in a modern nation-state.
5. Some of the scheduled tribes of Andaman islands are in a unique position since they are forcibly kept in isolation by the policy of the govt. of India and the Supreme Court of India. All the fruits of civilisation should be made available to them. Modern healthcare,

education, communication facilities etc should be made available to them in a controlled manner.

6. Declare India as free from tribal population immediately, excepting certain communities in Andaman islands for a limited time frame.
7. Calling some communities as Adivasi or indigenous is very dangerous as it is against the very spirit of a nation-state. Such terms should be dropped immediately from public discourse.
8. Some anthropologists consider scheduled tribes as economically and geographically marginalised populations with respect to a mainstream Indian population. (Channa, 2008: 469). It is a flawed argument, as mainstream is not constituted on the basis of community, but on the basis of individual achievement. Individuals of almost all the communities in India belong to this group.
9. The communities included under the list of Scheduled Tribes should be made to understand that this is not a permanent status accorded to them. It is only a changing phase. No community should remain in that state for a long a time. In the era of planned development and change the period taken by a community to transform itself from band to tribe to chiefdom should not be more than ten years or so. Therefore, the concerned authorities should deschedule ST communities from time to time after proper evaluation of their socio-cultural status. Any nation state- having a large portion of its population in the tribal stage, cannot boast as a developed state.

References

Atal, Y 2008, A Note on the Concept of Tribe, The Eastern Anthropologist. Vol. 61(4): 440-450.

Barnard, A. and J. Spencer (eds) (1996) 2003, Encyclopedia of social and cultural Anthropology London: Routledge.

Beteille, A, 1977, The definition of tribe, In Tribe, Caste and Religion in India, Ed. By Ramesh Thapar, Delhi: MacMillan India Ltd.

Beteille, A. 1974, Six Essays in comparative sociology, Delhi : Oxford University Press.

Bhat, H.K, 1991, Hinduisation of tribes : critique and perspective. In Tribal thought and culture. Ed. By B.N. Saraswati New Delhi, Concept Publishing Co. pp. 217-224.

Bhattacharya, D.K. (1987)1998, An Outline of Indian Prehistory, Delhi: Palaka Prakashan

Bose.N.K, 1953, The Hindu Method of Tribal Absorption. In Cultural Anthropology and Other Essay. By N.K. Bose, pp. 156-170.

Channa, S.M, 2008, "Tribe" The Concept and its Relevance in Post-Modern world. The Eastern Anthropologist, Vol. 61(4), 461-472.

Chaudhari, Mamata (1976), 2012, Ancient Indian tribes and their integration into the Hindu society. Journal of Indian Anthropological society, Vol II (2). Reprinted in The Science of Man, ed. By S.B. Chakravarti and A. Basu. Kolkata : The Indian Anthropological Society, 2012.

Chopra, P.N. (Ed), 2003, The gazetteer of India, Vol-II: History and Culture New Delhi: Publications Divisions, Ministry of Information and Broadcasting.

Dube, S.C. (ed) 1977, Tribal Heritage of India, New Delhi: Vikas publishing House Pvt. Ltd.

Evans-pritchard, E.E 1962, Essays in Social Anthropology, London, Faber and Fabre.

Evans-Pritchard, E.E. (1951) 1996, Social Anthropology, New Delhi: Universal Book Stall.

Fallers, L. (1963) 1971, Equality, Modernity and Democracy in the New states. In Old Societies and New States. Ed. By Clifford geertz, New Delhi : Amerind Pub. Co. Pvt. Ltd., pp. 158-219.

Fried, M.H, 1975, The Notion of Tribe Menho Park, California : Cummings Publishing Co.

Ghosh, A. 2008, Recreating the tribe ever a new. The Eastern Anthropologist, Vol. 61(4): 485-506.

Herskovits, M.J (1947) 1969, Cultural Anthropology, New Delhi : Oxford and IBH Publishing Co.

Honigmon, J.J. The Development of Anthropological Ideas.

Izard, M 1984, State, Origin of In The Social Science Encyclopedia. Ed. By A. Kuper and J. Kuper, London : Routeledge and Kegan Paul, pp. 821-22.

Izard, M, 1984, Stateless societies : In The Social Science Encyclopedia, Ed. By A. Kuper and J. Kuper London : Routledlgle and Kegan Paul, pp. 820-21.

Kluckhonu, C. (1949) 1963, The Missors for Man, Newyork, Mcgraw Hill.

Kroeber, A.L. (1948) 1967, Anthropology, New Delhi : Oxford and IBH Publishing Co.

Leach, E.R. 1982, Social Anthropology Glasgow : Fontana Paper back.

Lenkeit, R.E. 2001, Introducing Cultural Anthropology, New York : Mcgraw-Hill Mayfield.

Mair, L (1965) 1972, An Introduction to Social Anthropology, London, Clarendon Press.

Mandebaum, D.G. (1956) 1968, Social Gumpings. In Cultural and Social Anthropology, Ed. By P.B. Hammond, New York : MacMillan Co. pp 146-163.

Minogue, K. 1984, State, In The Social Science Encyclopaedia, Ed. By A. Kuper and J. Kuper, London: Routledge and Kegan Paul, pp 818-20.

Misra, K.K. 2008, On 'tribe' and 'tribalism', The Eastern Anthropologist, Vol. 61(4): 429-440.

Misra.P.K. 1986, The tribal world and its transportation. The David McAlpin and Sally Sage McAlpin lecture for 1986, Mysore : A Dhvanyaloka Publication, 1888.

Misra.P.K, 1977, Tribe-caste: A non-issue Journal of Indian Anthropological Society, Vol 12, (2) : 137-150.

Mukherjee, B.N, 2001, Nationhood and statehood in India : A Historical survey. New Delhi: Regency Publications.

Nash, M 1966, Primitive and Peasant, Economic systems, San Francisco, California: Chandler Publishing Co.

Oommen, T.K. 1990, State and Society in India : Studies in Nation Building. New Delhi, Sage Publications.

Pocock, D 1975, Understanding social Anthropology, London, Hodder and Stoughton.

Prince, G 1984, Tribe, In The Social Science Encyclopedia. Ed. By A. Kuper and J. Kuper, London, Routledge and Kegal Paul, pp. 869-70.

Redfield, R. 1960, The Little Community and Peasant Society and Culture Chicago : The University of Chicago Press.

Roy Burman, B.K. 2003, Indigenous and Tribal Peoples in world system Perspective. Studies on Tribes and Tribals, vol 1(1): 7-27.

Roy Busman, B.K. 1994, Tribes in Perspective, Delhi: Mittal Publications.

Scupin, R. and C.R. Decorse (2008) 2009, Anthropology, New Delhi: PHI Learning Pvt. Ltd.

Singh, B and D. Tyagi 1984 : Tribe: definition and concept, an analysis. Journal of Social Research, 27(2): 42-64.

Sinha, S.C. 1965, Tribe-caste and Tribe-peasant Continue in Central India. Man in India, Vol. 45, pp 57-83.

Sinha, S.C. and B.D. Sharma (eds), 1977, Primitive Tribes : The First step. New Delhi : Ministry of Home Affairs, Govt. of India.

Siva Prasad, R. 2008, I Tribe a Fiction? The Eastern Anthropologist. Vol. 61(4). 451-460.

Srinivas, M.N, 2002, Collected Essays, New Delhi: Oxford University Press.

Vidyarthi, L.P. and B.K. Rai, 1976, The Tribal Culture of India, New Delhi : Concept Publishers.

Wolf, E.R. 1966, Peasants, New Jersey, Englewood Cliffs : Prentice – Hall.

Wolf, E.R. 1968, The study of Evolution In Anthropology, Ed. By Sol Tax. Chennai: Higginlothans Pvt. Ltd.

18

Cultural configuration and change: a study on the Ho tribe of Jharkhand (Sarita Bhowmick Memorial Lecture)

Dr. Subhrendu Maiti

The Ho, one of the scheduled tribes, in the state of Jharkhand, and are predominantly concentrated in the Kolhan i.e. present East and West Singhbhum districts of the state. According to their tradition, they belong to the same family of Munda and they came in Kolhan from Chotonagpur. It is said that when the Ho came to settle in the Kolhan area, the entire jurisdiction was occupied by Bhuinyas and the Jains. They were driven away by the Ho and the Kolhan was ultimately inhabited by them. They belong to Proto-australoid racial stock.

Jharkhand meaning "the forest area" is geographically known as the Chotonagpur Plateau of India. It is a region of great unevenness consisting of a succession of plateau, hills and valleys drained by several large rivers. It is one of the areas rich in minerals with huge reserve of coal, iron ore, mica, bauxite and limestone, along with considerable reserve of copper, chromite, asbestos, kyanite etc. On 2nd. August 2000, the Parliament passed the Bihar reorganisation Bill to create the state of Jharkhand. The genesis of demand can be traced when Jaipal Sing, the Oxford educated hockey captain of 1928 Olympics, rooted the idea os a separate state from the consisting southern part of Bihar. After a prolonged agitation sparring over fifty years by the people of tribal dominated areas of Southern Bihar, Jharkhand, the 28th.State of the Indian Union came into existence on 15th. November 2000, the birth day of legendary tribal freedom fighter Birsa Munda. The Jharkhand is the homeland of aboriginal races such as Santals, Mundas, Oraons, Hos, Bhumij, Birhor and the like.These indigenous people of the area are known as *adivasis* literary meaning 'original settlers' or the earliest inhabitants. The tribal people of Jharkhand grouped into thirty two in distinct communities, but all are not at the same level of socio-cultural and economic development. On the one hand there are major tribes –the Santal, Oraon, Munda and Ho- who are numerically and politically dominant tribes, on the other there are number of minor tribes who are only able to live out a bare existence. All the communities possess their distinct cultural identity which they are determined to preserve. The majority of them live in a state of semi-starvation throughout the year. Most tribes speak different languages, pursue different occupations and have different cultures. This inequality in the life and culture of the tribal communities often stay unnoticed, and the life and culture of the dominant tribal communities reflect the life and culture of the tribes in general where the changes are noticed in all spheres of life, in socio-cultural and economic milieu.

Structure, theme and mythical origin:

The main focus of this study is the Ho adivasi with special reference to their socio-cultural life, their deprivation and marginalisation due to development (the situation of the rural Hos can be generalised to other tribal pockets in Jharkhand) programme. Tribal communities in Jharkhand have been affected by the development approach that basically feeds on the over exploitation of natural resources in the tribal territory. It not only displaces tribals from their traditional homeland but also invites large numbers of non-tribals in to tribal region.

With regard to the origin, history and culture of the so called tribal communities of our country, we are to believe the names attributed to them by the dominant neighbouring communities. Almost all the tribes have their own names by which they recognize themselves. The Ho have synonyms like Kol, Larka Kol, Kolh etc. The etymology seems to be merely a concentrated from '*horo*' i.e. man which is used by the cognate tribes of the Munda, and the Santal, are not called by the outsiders as '*horo*'. In case of the Ho the tribal name of the original stock whence "Hos, Mundas and Santals are sprung, has obtained popular recognition in the slightly altered from, as the distinctive name of the branch which inhabits Singbhum and which may now be regarded as a separate tribe". In west Singbhum they form the largest group among the different tribal communities residing in the district. Living in the jungle areas of southern part, the Ho resisted contact with the outsiders with considerable success till the British finally subjugated them in 1836.

The Ho or the Larka Kol (fighting Kol) a non-Aryan tribe, have been classed linguistic purposes as Kolarians, but the term 'Kol' for scientific purposes embraces the three cognate Kolarian tribes of Munda, Ho and Bhumij. Dalton describes them as Kolarians, distinguishing among them, the 'Munda Kols' in Chotonagpur proper and the Larka Kols in Purulia and Dhalbhum. The Ho have a tradition regarding the creation of the world and the origin of human race which have much national and international significance for Anthropological study. One of the myths regarding origin it is said that '*Oteboram and Singbonga* were self created. They made the earth with grass and trees. Next they created animals, first those that man domesticated and afterwards the wild ones. A boy and girl were then created and put together in a cave to people the world. Finding them to innocent to give any hope of progeny, *Singbonga* thought them in preparation of '*illi*' or rice bear which excites the passion, and in course of time, they brought forth twelve sons and twelve daughters. When the first parents had produced those children, *Singbonga* prepared a feast of flesh of buffaloes, bullocks, goats, sheep, pigs, fowls and vegetables, and making the brothers and sisters pair off, asked them to chose the kind of food they wanted for their sustenance before starting out into the world. The first and second pair took bullock and buffaloes flesh, and they originated the Hos and the Bhumij, next took the vegetables only and became the progenitors of Brahmins and Kshatriyas. Other took goat and fish and from them are Sudras, one pair took *sal* fish and became Bhuiyas, two pair took pigs and were the ancestors of the Santals. One pair got nothing and seeing this the Hos gave them of their surplus, and descendants of these became the Ghasis, who were menials in Kol villages, and are supported even today the Hos of Kolhan."

Glimpses of Cultural Life

The tribal society is a simple society and homogeneity, absence of hierarchy are the common phenomena. It has been argued that the tribal are not separate group, rather they represent a layer of Hindu culture. Social as well as cultural organisation is the way in which relationship among the members of a cultural system are organised to facilitate the carrying out of the characteristic activities. It is the functional aspect of the social structures, including units and institutions.

The Ho society is divided into a good number of subgroups or *killis* (clans, septs etc.). The Ho village may be inhabited by members of one *killi*, or it may contain two or more *killis* though one of the latter happens to be dominant over the rest. They serve these *killis* as surnames which can strengthen their clan identity. All most all the *killis* take their name from some animals, plants or material objects. These are described totemistic and many of their beliefs have been related to many taboos and superstitions which are alleged to possess about their totem. Exogamy is the general rule. The totemistic names that are found among the Ho, do not mean that the animal or plant denoted by a *killi* was worshipped, propitiated or venerated by them, or that there were any dietary or other restrictions connected with these animals or plants.

Many Ho *killis* are identical with Munda *killis* which are be expected since the Ho and the Munda are brought part of what was once one tribe.

Some *killis* are common to both Hos and Mundas. *Killis* like Bodra, Soy, Purty, Jojo, Samed, Barla, etc. are noticed both the Ho and the Munda respectively. All most 133 *killis* are noticed among the Ho of Jharkhand. It is interesting to note that the *killis* take the names of the villages rather than the opposite e.g. the names of Deogam, Ichagutu (a hillock where there is an *icha* i.e. bush), and Kudada(water near a Jamun tree), are clearly village names. It is true that the Ho obviously moved into South Singbhum through this area. This also conforms to their tradition. The *killi* is observed very carefully during marriage alliances. They are very much aware of *haga* (brother in a broad sense) relationship and they did not or do not maintain marriage relationship. The Ho consider clan as a unlineal group having common mythical ancestors. All the clan members take part in each family ceremonies in connection with birth, marriage, death etc. Besides, great economic co-operation is expected between the members of the same clan and it acts as a unit of co-operate activity.

Family is the basic social unit among the Ho and it influences the individual in every phase of life. From the nature of their composition, the Ho family may be grouped into several categories, according to the members of families and their residential, social and economic relations. It is common among the Ho to establish separate families after marriage or sometimes after having a child. A nuclear family is predominant feature of the Ho social system. A good number of factors play an important role for the establishment of nuclear family. The Ho live in small huts. Generally it consists of one or two rooms; hence it is very difficult to lead a private life in presence of the parents, Besides, most of the villages are situated close to the forest. All the materials received for construction of a hut are easily available at free of cost, from the forest. The Ho are economically poor and they mainly subsist on agriculture or agricultural labourer. It is very difficult to a man to shoulder the responsibility of the entire family and it is also difficult to collect sufficient food to sustain a large family under such conditions. This economic pressure leads them to the fragmentation of the joint or extended family.

Interpersonal relation perpetrates between the members of the family, which is based on cordiality, mutual love, affection and sympathy. Even when the married sisters are divorced, they usually get back to the natal family and remain there either till the dispute is settled or they are remarried elsewhere. In the Ho family, father is the supreme authority. He manages the family affairs. He has final say in the family affairs and decisions. But he does not take any decision by his own will. He seeks the opinion of his wife and young children before arriving at a final decision. In order to run the family smoothly, the division of labour is followed based on age and sex. The children assist their parents in the performance of household chores. The aged members look after the kids, chicks, goats and house when young men and women go to perform work in the forest and the field. However, the division of labour is mainly for running the family smoothly. In the late childhood, the brothers and sisters start maintaining distance. The brothers play with the boys of their age group and the sisters play with the girls of their age group. The brothers assist their father in the agricultural works while the sisters assist their mother in the performance of domestic chores. The sisters do cooking and serve food to the brothers. They have strong we feeling.

The Ho are a patriarchal people having patrilineal descent in clan, patrilocal residence and patrilineal succession to village offices like headmanship and priesthood. Each family is affiliated to a particular clan and some families worship specific gods and goddesses as their family deities. All the members of the family worship these deities on the eve of festivals for securing family well being. At the time of family feuds or scandals spreading in the family or confrontation arising out of differences of opinion among the members of the family, elderly members generally settle the disputes amicably. In extreme case, when the disputes cross the family barrier and reach in public, the headman or the village council is informed for settling the disputes. Inter-family linkages are close knit and cordial. Economic assistance and making a group solidarity among different families are other aspects that forge inter family linkages.

With regards to marriage rules, endogamy in terms of community level is practised by the Ho. Marriage within the same clan is strictly prohibited. They avoid to marry within the lineage group and also within the close kin members. Adult marriage is in practice. Among the Manki-cum-Munda class it is noticed that a tendency to lower the age of marriage for the girls in imitation of their Hindu neighbours. Monogamy is the most prevalent form of marriage but in certain situation bigamy or polygyny is observed in case of barrenness, having no male child, illness or physically unable to lead the married life or the first wife practises witchcraft, sorcery, adultery etc. The Ho do not have any customary barrier for taking more wives. In such case the children of the first wife are generally entitled to a larger share of the family property than those of other wives. The usual way of acquiring mate among the Ho is by negotiation which is settled by bride price. Society also approves pre-marital sexual freedom. This is particularly observed during the Maghe festival held in winter. The bride price in kind includes dresses and ornaments of the bride, dress for the bride's parents, grand parents, brothers and sisters. The rice, pulse, goat, vegetables, etc. are also demanded to provide feast to the community members. Recently among the Manki-Munda class a changing form has came into vogue known as *diku-andi*. In this system of marriage, in addition to traditional custom, some local Hindu rites have also been added, such as participation of a Brahmin priest and the employment of the Hindu barber.

There is no bar to a Ho marrying his mother's brother's daughter or father's sister's daughter. If the wife proves barren, a man is entitled to get his wife's unmarried younger sister without payment of bride price. A widow is free to marry again even after the birth of children. In such cases children remain in the father's family. A man has right to marry his elder brother's widow. However, there is no rule that the widow should invariably marry her husband's younger brother. Marriage with younger brother's wife is strictly prohibited among them. The elder brother strictly avoids younger brother's wife, both by touch and commensality. A divorced woman can marry a person of her choice, but the information about her divorce should be announced and approved by the Panchayat. Similarly a divorced man can also marry again but the same (mentioned above)formalities may be fulfilled by himself. A married woman can be recognised by the use of *sindur*(vermilion), *noa* (iron bangle), and *sankha* (conch shell bangle)which are considered as symbols of marriage.

Divorce may be allowed in the Ho society either by the husband or the wife and the case is decided by the Panchayat or the village council. No particular ceremony is associated with the dissolution of marriage. When a wife wants to be separated, she goes to her parental house or elopes with a man of her choice and never comes back to her husband's house. However, in all cases of divorce, the tribal council tries to convince the parties of either side about the necessities of a peaceful conjugal life and prevent separation. The Ho society approves remarriage in both the sexes. Widow and widower remarriage is also approved by the members of the community. In case of remarriage no elaborate ritual ceremony is observed which generally performs in the usual marriage. In such cases only the permission of the village headman is sought and the consent of the bride is secured and at last a subscription or the royalty is paid to the village council. Both junior levirate and sororate are allowed in case of remarriage. But there is no hard and fast rules for arranging such marriage. It depends on the willingness of the concern party.

Right of inheritance among the women is somehow or rather restricted, i.e. under normal circumstances they do not get share of their parental property. Role of women in economic life is important. Despite their domestic chores they engage in many economic activities. In the economic field women engage in the collection of fuel, fodder, *mahua* fruits and selling them in the market or to neighbouring families. During agriculture and harvesting seasons they remain busy in hoeing, transplanting, weeding, harvesting, threshing and other related activities. The women play important role in the preparation of rice beer. Besides, in other pursuits, they engage in the road construction, digging well etc. as day labourer and also in activities as and when required. The Ho women have innumerable role in social life as sister, wife and mother. In the life cycle rituals they have their specific role associated with birth, marriage and death. In the religious life the women perform fasting on certain occasions and ceremonies for the welfare of family members as wife and mother. Women are not much aware of political activities. At the time several elections male members influence them and accordingly they perform their adult franchise in favour of personal likings of the members. Except economic activities in the field the women earn money by selling *hanria* (rice beer), fire woods, *sal* leaf plates, etc. in the market and the road sides in their inhabited areas. In fact, the Ho women are very much laborious in habit in habit and as a result they have intricate rights and obligations into day-to-day life of the family. Though there is no such prescribed right for women yet, their obligations as per social, ritual and religious norms are many and explicit.

Economic life

The economic basis of life is attached to agriculture supported by fuel, wood collection and wage earning. Besides, occasional hunting and fishing are their diversions from the monotomy of an uneventful occupation. The year is divided into three seasons and there are twelve months of the year with different activities distributed over them according to the needs of agriculture.

Land is their major economic resource which they have classified into three categories like *bari* land, *don* land and *tanr* land. The *bari* land is situated just by the side of the house where different vegetables are grown especially in the rainy and winter seasons. In *don* land, paddy is cultivated and in *tanr* land coarse variety of paddy, maize, millet, *kurthi* etc. are cultivated. Coarse variety of paddy, maize, *til*, *arhar*, *kurthi* and some vegetables are cultivated by dry cultivation method and the cultivation of paddy is done by the method of wet cultivation. Each family has their own agricultural implements and most of the families are owned with he-buffaloes and oxen for the purpose of cultivation. Most of the cases they do not hire labour for agriculture. They do agriculture by own family members and exchange of labour with other families of the village.

The economic activities of the year may broadly be classified into three seasons where the people remain engaged in different occupations. These seasons are summer where most of the trees remain out of green leaves and people sleep under the tree where they find shadow. Another is rainy season when roads remain muddy, the river becomes flowing and people do not try to move out except in urgent needs. Last one is winter where people have to sleep inside the hut and cover the doors with straw which makes a cracking sound. The most important crop among the Ho is paddy. It is the most suitable crop in their cultivable land as per climatic condition is concerned. The soil is usually fertile particularly in the *bari* land. They cultivate paddy mostly by way of transplantation, the most important method of cultivation. Both transplantation and broadcast sowing are known to them, the latter form is specially suited to uplands. They realise the use of replenishing the soil by using manure and use it except in low land. They also leave some land fallow, for a year or so and allow the cattle to graze and fertilize the land with their excreta. Transplantation and weeding are the traditional duty of women who work in groups and move from plot to plot till the fields are weeded.

Among the Ho, watching the crops becomes necessary when they begin to ripe and when harvested and deposited. Damage of crops is done by wild birds, squirrels, cattle and certain pests. They feel the necessity of scare crows, beasts, etc, Improved leafy sheds are also put up so that watch can be kept on the fields at night. Besides, after harvesting they store the crops in a particular place where they prepare a temporary conical shaped hut thatched with straw so that wild animals can not attack suddenly, villagers take turns in these, and as soon as any alarm is raised by beating of a tin can, the villagers run to assist the watchman. There is no rigid sexual division of labour among the Ho, excepting the use of the plough and the hunting by bow and arrow, and few other occupations are considered as taboo among the women folk. Many of the men's occupations are done today day by women, while the former sit as idle spectators. The gradual disappearance of economic taboos among them and the change of attitude of the men with regard to the household arrangements and the principal economic activities which made women economically more important to the family.

The entire Singbhum which includes both East and West districts is very much rich in its mineral wealth which has given rise to important mining and industrial centres, namely, the iron mines of Gua, Noamundi, the copper mines at Musabani, the great Tata Iron and Steel Factory at Jamshedpur and he cement factory at Jhikpani, Jadugora mines etc. These centres have attracted a substantial number of tribal people, who however, mostly occupy the unskilled ranks. They have not been able to adjust their habits to wage earning economy and are often unable to utilize the hard earned money beneficially. A large proportion of money is spent in liquor and the purchase of unessential fashionable imported goods.

Religious beliefs and community festivals

Belief in both animism and animatism are the principal form of religion among the Ho. The religion is entirely practical concerned with happiness in the world. Supernaturalism is divorced of any ethical context. Beliefs in spirits or *bongas* is the major root of religion. The spirits form a hierarchy, the presiding deity of the pantheon is the Sun God or *sing bonga*, who created the universe. He is always worshipped with offerings of liquor and meat. It is very curious that the animals offered are mainly white in colour. Only second to *sing bonga* in power is the great *harang bonga* who is in the way of presiding deity of the clan. The village has its sacred grove *jahira* where the village tutelary god *dissauli* resides with his consort *jarira buri*. *Nasera bonga* residing in water is the presiding deity of water and for such he has to be offered turmeric powder. The household deities or ancestral spirits, *oa bongas* are worshiped regularly on each festive occasion. The functions of the deities are generally beneficial for man unless unduly irritated, A good number of spirits like *dansi bonga, churin, mahali bonga, gora* etc. are considered as malevolent spirits who bring sorrows of mankind in the form of illness, death or failure of crops.

The sacred specialist among the Ho is called *deuri* who performs communal worships on behalf of the villagers. Almost in all the villages there is a *deuri* priest who's post is hereditary. He worships the *bongas* on the occasion of every important festival, this being generally performed in the sacred grove. He offers prayer along with offerings of *illi* (rice beer) and fowl.

Belief in witchcraft is very extensive among the community. The witches are supposed to move about the dead at night, completely nude and assemble under a tree and dance. A woman suspected of witchcraft is generally driven away from the village, after severe beating. Sometimes it gives rise to fatal results. There are professional witch finders, *khonses, sokhas* etc. who divine the name of the witch responsible for a particular case of disease or ill luck. On such belief Conl. Dalton stated that "All disease in men or animals is attributed to one or two causes, the worth of some evil spirit who has to be appeased, or spell of some witch or sorcerer, who should be destroyed or driven out of the land. In the latter cause, a *sokha* or witch finder is employed to divine who has cast the spell, and various modes of divination are restored to. One of the most common is the test by the stone and *paila*. The latter is a larger wooden cup, used as a measure for grain. It is placed under a flat stone as a pivot for the stone to turn on. A boy is then seated on the stone supporting himself by his hands; and the names of all the people in the neighbourhood are slowly pronounced and each name is uttered, a few grains of rice are thrown at the boy. When they come to the name of the witch or the wizard, the stone turns, the boy rolls off". In this way the victim person is identified, the person is denounced and in many cases all his family members are sentenced to death in the belief that witches breed witches and sorcerers whose taint is in the blood. There are still more than a dozens of murders every year due to the belief in witchcraft.

There is no place for idolatry in traditional Ho religion. They do not have any concept of good or evil and corresponding belief in heaven or hell associated with soul. They believe that the soul is ordinarily invisible but may appear at will in any form.

Community festival

The tribal religious worship is mainly communal or congregational at the occasion of festival. Personal worship is not well developed. On the occasion of each festival; the head of every family makes sacrifices, offerings and libation to their ancestor spirits in sacred tabernacle. In communal festival, the 'we' feeling is intensified and social solidarity is strengthened.

The Ho have to earn their living by sweat of their brow. But the drudgery of economic life is intermittently relieved by regular cycle of festivals. Each festival is marked by the following essential features: -i) The houses are repaired, cleaned painted the occasion, ii) Offerings are made in the sacred grove, iii) There is excessive drinking of *illi* (rice beer), and iv) There are common dances while sexual restrictions are relaxed.

The Ho observe seven important festivals which they regard as their community festivals though many of the festivals are observed by other tribal societies also. These festivals are: i) Maghe Parab, ii) Baha Parab, iii) Haro, iv) Damuair or Babamnuth, v) Jamnara vi) Kalam and vii) Batauli. In all festivals, the objective of worship is the village *dessauli*, through prayers offerings are offered to *singbonga* and other *bongas* of lesser distinction. Most of the festivals are associated with the agricultural activities and ceremonies are performed to increase the festivity of fields, to protect the crops from natural as well as supernatural calamities or as a part of thanks giving service to the village tutelary *bongas*. The motives of these festivals are the same as that manifested in the rites of all agricultural communities with whom they share the land, but the mode of worship and the manner of participation are somehow or rather interesting.

Besides, due to long contact with the Hinduism, many of the Hindu ceremonies are observed by the Ho where their own indigenous festivals have not been allowed to fall in disuse. Cultural contact with the outsider has resulted in adoption in many of the latter's festivals; but this adoption means only a participation in many fairs held during major Hindu festivals and occasional sacrifices to certain Hindu gods and goddesses. The worship of Mahadeva at the *Chait Parab* and of the goddess Laxmi during the autumn and goddess Kali during *dewali* and *phagu* is becoming popular among the Ho. Besides, impact of Christianity, the Christian Ho celebrate Christian festivals and visit the local church on every Sunday. They are also guided by the Church authority. The Ho have believe in *bhuta preta* (spirits) and witchcraft. They have strong belief in evil spirits which causes disease and death. They go to the *ojha* for the cure of attack of evil spirits.

There are a number of fairs in different part of Kolhan where the Ho visit during the slack season, and where they spend time in dancing, drinking and in other pastimes. Two important fairs of West Singbhum namely Jojohatu, twenty five miles from Chaibasa, held for a week on the occasion of Hindu festival Chait Parab, and the fair Lagia, ten miles from Chaibasa held for three days on the same occasion, are the popular centres for periodical congregations among the Ho.

General observation and factors responsible for change

Although the conflicting naming of the tribe in the census list posses a great difficulty in proper identification of a community, the present study contemplates on the Ho, which are also known as Larka Kol, Kol, Hara, Horo, etc. The 'Larka Kol' in the Singbhum district (undivided) of present Jharkhand are said to play a significant role against the British action during many millenarian movements in the area. The confusion in proper naming of the tribe is due to the use of multiple names to denote the same community. A few of the informants said that the word 'Kolha' is used by the other communities to address them, while the word Ho is used by the Ho themselves to identify their own community. It is said that the indigenous word Ho refers to man in general, and in that sense only human beings can be designated as Ho.

The cultural pattern of the Ho has been observed which revealed that there is considerable divergence in manners, customs as well as in economic activities also. These variations are due to different factors like changes in the historical or political conditions of the country pronounced in varied geo-ecological settings. Sometimes the clean caste communities influence the socio-economic and cultural life of the Ho by the immediate appeal of their superior culture. All these factors jointly brought about great changes in the life of the people. In a dynamic society, the change is a continuous process, in which shaping and reshaping of material, social and cultural life, with frequent adjustments and readjustments, are a natural phenomenon.

In the absence of sufficient relevant data it is not possible to build up a systematic past history of these people, yet it can be said that they were predominantly forest dwellers and had forest economy. Sometimes they had to exploit the forest produce for consumption as food and exchange these with others to secure the necessities of life. Thus, a slow but continuous contact with the so called progressive communities was maintained all along.

Change is inevitable for any society at any point of time and at any place, hence the human society is being rightly characterized by many as the changing units. But usually, while the internal or endogenous changes take a long span of time to get exposed, the external or exogenous changes become too soon apparent to draw the immediate attention of an observer. Besides, in many adaptive changes, the Ho society was exposed to the vagaries of modern forces of industrialisation long before independence unlike many other tribal communities and the marks of change in various aspects of their life and culture can easily be noticed.

Forces of industrialisation and subsequent urbanisation greatly affect the structure and function in all spheres of life related to socio-economic organisation among the Ho. For instance, in respect of family, more than 70 percent of the families among them are nuclear. This change in the structure of the family affects the interpersonal relations as well. The conventional functions of the family as the socializing and security agent are found to be gradually declining. The situation is still worse in the villages located either in the urban fringe or at the heart of an industrial-mining location. In respect of marriage, the excess of bride wealth and the eventual higher percentage of spinsterhood among the Ho had drawn the attention in their indigenous custom to bring about a compromise for a reasonable bride wealth and to remove this traditional bottleneck from the Ho social structure. Impact of the industrialisation and urbanisation by way of free mixing of the young members and co-workers has reduced the marriage hazards to a great extent. Marriage by love and elopement has become a common phenomenon under the prevailing state with post marital approval of the parents. The clan exogamy has also removed some of the prevailing social evils and rise in the flexibility of marital ties is also noticed. The rate of divorce has now gone up considerably, ending up with many broken families among the Ho. Changing family relations have often influenced the kinship ties and obligations. Kinship terms are found to be changed due to the influence of the neighbouring communities in an urban industrial setting.

Economy among the Ho has also been changed due to the impact of industrialisation and urbanisation. It is mentioned here that 51.5 percent of the total workers are engaged as daily labourers in different mines and industries. This has partially jeopardized the traditional economy. Wage earning has made them more self-centric and the bond of emotional attachment is gradually declining. Gradual increase in the use of modern sophisticated electronic gadgets, cosmetics, which thought to be needs rather than luxurious in urban industrial as well as rural areas have direct repercussion on the Ho economy. These developments are responsible for the high expenditure and growing indebtedness, despite a higher level of income.

Like all other aspects of social and cultural life, changes in religious beliefs and rituals among the Ho have been widely observed. Under the influence of modernisation, the Ho, once a communy of the staunch believer of spirits and *bongas* has started consulting local doctors and visiting near by government hospitals for common illness. In some cases, relief from the disease by the modern medical treatment has convinced them gradually abandon the belief in the malevolent spirits. But interestingly the deep rooted religious beliefs have not been completely swayed away, in spite of these gradual changes. Spirit and ancestor worship still continues in many cases till now and they are still believed to be the chief regulator of the life and destiny.

Most of the annual rituals are planned keeping in view the agricultural cycle. Important ceremonies like Magh Parab, Baha Parab, Hera Parab, etc. are however symbolically observed in many cases. The importance of life cycle rituals has been greatly declined due to modern forces of change. Social and religious superiority of the religious functionaries has been automatically reduced to minimum. A new order in the Ho society seems to have emerged, mostly based on rationality and judiciousness.

Considering the above factors, it can be said that the Ho society now passes through a transition between tradition and modernity. Although modern forces have changed their life style to a great extent, their adherence to tradition and maintenance of a Ho cultural identity still continues through these constrains. They have gradually adopted the modern changes, but their satisfaction seems to lie with the old convention of simple, co-ordinated living and belief in their sovereign *bongas*. As a tribe the Ho are self respecting and industrious. They are cheerful in disposition and greatly enjoy social fellowship. We found them open hearted and ready to answer questions when once their confidence had been gained. They have strong emotional feelings which can be seen from their music and songs. They enjoy nothing better than a long of song and drum. We find little evidence of their disobedience to the rules of the tribal codes of morality. Taken all in all the Ho are a lovable people and as one comes into intimate contact with them, he feels that much ought to be done to alleviate many of their difficulties and handicaps under which they bravely carry on.

References

Bhatt, S.C. 2002: The District Gazetteer of Jharkhand, New Delhi, Gyan Publications.

Dalton, E. T. 1960: Descriptive Ethnography of Bengal, Calcutta, Govt. Printing Press.

Griffiths, Walter G. 1993: The Kol Tribe of Central India, Calcutta, The Asiatic Society.

Lal, R. B. 1959: Glimpses of Tribal life in Bihar, Patna, Pub. Relation Deptt.

Majumder, D. N. 1950: The Affairs of a Tribe, A study in Tribal Dynamics; Lucknow.

Misra, K, K, 1987: Social Structure and Change among the Ho of Orissa. Delhi, Gyan Publishing House.

Oraon, P. C. 2003: Land and the People of Jharkhand. Ranchi, Tribal Welfare Research Institute

Risley, H. H. 1981:Tribes and Castes of Bengal. Vol. I & II, Calcutta, Firma K.L. Mukhopadhyay.

Ray Chowdhury, P.C. 1958: Bihar District Gazetteer of Singbhum District, Patna, Superintendent Sec. Press.

19

Impact of Western Culture on Santals: A Case Study on Cultural Adoption Among the Tribal Girls of Birbhum District, West Bengal

Debasis Mondal and Debotri Chakraborti,

Introduction

India is a secular country where the people have the freedom to practice any religion and also to convert into another religion of their choice. So, all the cultures are freely accepted and respected by the Indians. It's an environment to cultivate or build oneself ethically, socially and in all other aspects that lead an all over human development. Indian culture is richly known in other parts of the world since the ancient age. Its multi-diverse flavour has been consistently unique in its very own way. Manners, traditions, living and trading patterns etc. are one of the graceful components of Indian culture. The most important feature of Indian culture is its values. These values are deeply rooted within the heart, mind, body and soul of its dwellers. But, the influence of western culture started in India during the 19th century when the British established their colony in the country. Western culture, considered as the most advanced culture on globe, has started surmounting its flavour on Indian roots. Western culture has always shown its influence on Indian society. This could be for the multiple reasons like fascination, dreamy autonomy etc., which are somehow absent in Indian culture. Western culture conveys and promotes the ideas and values of advanced civilisation across people of India. The culture of India has been shaped not only by its long history, unique geography and diverse demography, but also by its ancient heritages. Regarded by some historians as the "oldest living civilisation of Earth", the Indian tradition dates back to 8,000 BC and has a continuous recorded history for over 2,500 years. Westernisation should not affect the core traditions of Indian society but may change the lifestyle and apparent characteristics of the society with the graceful add-ons like punctuality, trustworthiness, loyalty, professionalism should be welcomed and adored. Due to globalisation the rich culture of India is disappearing. The most impact is of western culture on India culture. Western culture is based more on materialistic factors where as our culture has a spiritual base. These changes are like the betraying our old way of life, which we obtained through our ancestors. Updating is necessary but getting washed-off in influence is wide of the mark. If this continues, days will not be far away when the famous Indian civilisation would be buried not by others but by the Indian themselves. The lack of morals, the lacking faith in God, having late night parties, the influence of drugs and alcohols, least interest in Indian languages like Sanskrit, Hindi, Celebrating mothers' day, fathers' day, valentine day, fools day etc rather than celebrating our Indian festivals and thus wasting their precious time of life, thinking to be independent at an early age. Indian Culture, which is one of the oldest & richest cultures, is now days posing a serious threat as western culture is establishing its strong base in India and slowly and gradually wiping the Indian culture. It had already made its presence in Metro's & now slowly heading towards other parts of India. There's no harm in taking good things from western but this does not mean that we should completely adopt it and pretend to be western and misrepresent our identity. It is understandable that India is growing in every field and there is necessity of knowing all the cultures and their traditions. To some extent it is fine but we should not pretend that we dislike the Indian values and likes only western culture. We have to preserve our identity. One thing should be always kept in mind that western world is looking India for its honesty and its rich Cultural heritage. It is very unfortunate that today's generation has very little knowledge about their culture, traditions & their roots. This is not their mistake but the mistake of their parents who does not enlighten their children about their roots about their rich cultural heritage. Contradictory to it Parents feel proud in giving the western Sanskaras to their children. Children are brought up in this atmosphere. They are thus kept miles away from Indian culture. There is no harm in giving the knowledge of other cultures and traditions as Indians have made their presence in every part of world and it is very necessary that we should have knowledge of their culture, traditions and their language. We should do but to the limit, which is really needed, and also take care that our new sprouts are well versed with Indian culture and its values. It is the responsibility of parents to inherit the same and for this it is very necessary that parents should also be well versed with Indian culture and traditions. No doubt in that, the western culture is versatile and has taught to be self-independent but this does not mean that we will forget our culture at all and blindly follow the western culture. Since India has the tradition to take good things from others but this does not mean that we will completely forget our values. We should feel proud that we are Indian s and we have such a rich cultural heritage which is very rare and should carry this forward and inherit the same to our new blooms that are going to be our future.

Cultural appropriation refers to the adoption of some specific elements of one culture by a different cultural group. It differs from acculturation or assimilation in that "appropriation" or "misappropriation" refers to the inclusion and absorption of cultural elements from minorities or immigrants into the predominant culture. Cultural appropriation is most commonly used to denote the use by cultural outsiders of a minority, oppressed culture's symbols or other cultural elements. Cultural appropriation is applied to introduction of forms of dress or personal adornment, music and art, religion, language, or social behaviour. In practice, cultural appropriation involves the 'appropriation' of ideas, symbols, artefacts, image, sound, objects, forms or styles from other cultures, from art history, from popular culture or other aspects of human made visual or non visual culture. Anthropologists have studied the process of cultural appropriation, or cultural borrowing (which includes art and urbanism), as part of cultural change and contact between different cultures.

Literature Review

- In his book on 'The Folk Literature of Bengal', Sen Dineshchandra (2006); analyzed the Euoropean folk culture, Bengal Renaissance, folk literature of Buddhists & Hindus & also about Mohamadans culture of Bengal. Mainly he focused on the influence of each culture on others, the adaptation.
- In his book on 'Tribal Heritage:A study of Santals', Culshaw.W.J (2004),he discussed about the making of a people, their life, daily lifestyles, about their culture, folk tradition like folk tales, myths, the clan organisation, about their festivals, their rituals etc. Even in the last part of this book, he also told us about the impact of Christian Missions & Missionaries on them. How Christianity bring them into a new community. The book is a mirror of Santals creed - culture & rituals.
- In the paper on 'Folk Media and Rural Development', Dr.Harish Kumar (analyzed that how folk media & rural development are interrelated with other. Specifically how folk media help in rural development, impact of folk media over rural development Therefore, for The Punch newspaper to fulfil the mission of being a veritable instrument of social change.
- Naskar Reshmi (2011), in her paper on 'The Role of Folk Media and Participatory Communication in Rural Development: An Exploratory

Case Study of Combating Child Marriage in Malda' stated that the Role of folk media plays a vital role in social change of women is very crucial in a country like India. She concluded that that child marriage is violation of child rights. Communication especially folk media can take a important key to social & cultural development of their society as well as whole nation.

- In their paper on 'Folk and Traditional Media: A Powerful Tool For Rural Development', Mohanty Manashi and Pritishri Parhi (2011) explored that the indigenous role of folk media which facilitates communication among the rural mass for socio- economic growth& development. They observed the vital role of message delivery & performance with full accuracy & precision. They concluded with that the age of electronic folk media is as well as important for rural development.

Research Questions

- How Santali girls are influenced through western culture?
- What is the impact of westernisation on tribal society with special reference to Santali girls?

Objectives of the Study

- To analyze the concept of western culture.
- To examine the using habits of media among the Santali girls of Birbhum district West Bengal.
- To analyze the impact of westernisation on tribal society, especially on the Santali girls.

Research Design and Methods

Research Approaches:-. Qualitative and Quantitative both research approaches were employed for picking up the empirical data from the field. Hence, the secondary data were picked up from various sources like books, journals, articles, conferences, published and unpublished research work etc.

Methods & Techniques:- A Case Study method has been applied by following observation participant and in-depth interview techniques for picking up the empirical data from the field. Structure questionnaire and some open ended questions had been used as a tool of data collection.

Universe & Population:-Here, the research universe is Scheduled Tribes and the population are a sub-caste of the Scheduled Tribes like Santal. The present study has been made in Durgapur Dhannyasora village under the Sian-Muluk Gram Panchayat of Birbhum district, West Bengal.

Sampling:- Non probability sampling like purposive sampling were utilised here as well.

Sample Size:- The total sample size is 52,. Hence, the total Schedule Tribes population here are, in which females and males respectively.

Results & Discussions

Now first we have to understand about culture. Culture is the characteristics of a particular group of people, defined by everything from language, religion, cuisine, social habits, music and arts. The term Western culture has come to define the culture of European countries as well as those such as the United States that have been heavily influenced by European immigration. Western culture has its roots in the Classical Period of the Greco-Roman era and the rise of Christianity in the 14th century. Western culture is a body of knowledge derived from reason. This foundation of reason has made possible a vast accumulation of understanding related to reality or nature, including human nature. This understanding is represented in several core ideals and values, which include individualism, happiness, rights, capitalism, science and technology. Western culture can also be referred to as advanced culture; this is because its ideas and values promote the development and sustainment of advanced civilisation. Western culture began in Ancient Greece. There and in the Roman civilisation it developed until the start of the middle Ages when it largely vanished from Europe. During the middle ages, Western culture resided, instead, in the Arab / Persian world to a modest degree. It has only a modest presence in most of the rest of Asia as well as Latin America and Eastern Europe. In much of both Africa and the Middle East, Western culture currently has little meaningful presence. Then the rediscovery of Western culture in Europe in the Late Middle Ages prompted the Renaissance. Western culture's continuing development then led to the Scientific Revolution, the Enlightenment, the American Revolution, the Industrial Revolution and to what is considered today as modern civilisation. Today, Western culture has at least some presence in nearly all nations of the world. It does not currently exist, however, anywhere in a perfect and complete form. Wherever Western culture exists, it is at least partially mixed—and often largely mixed—with non-Western culture. Eastern culture generally refers to the societal norms of countries in Far East Asia (including China, Japan, Vietnam, North Korea and South Korea) and the Indian subcontinent. Like the West, Eastern culture was heavily influenced by religion during its early development. In general, in Eastern culture there is less of a distinction between secular society and religious philosophy than there is in the West. Western culture currently dominates in many Western and Central European nations and several nations settled by Europeans and their descendants. Western culture also significantly exists in many Asian nations, such as Japan, South Korea, Taiwan and Singapore, and it is increasingly influential in India and China. There's no harm in taking good things from western but this does not mean that we should completely adopt it and pretend to be western and misrepresent our identity. It is understandable that India is growing in every field and there is necessity of knowing all the cultures and their traditions. To some extent it is fine but we should not pretend that we dislike the Indian values and likes only western culture. We have to preserve our identity. One thing should be always kept in mind that western world is looking India for its honesty and its rich Cultural heritage. It is very unfortunate that today's generation has very little knowledge about their culture, traditions & their roots. This is not their mistake but the mistake of their parents who does not enlighten their children about their roots about their rich cultural heritage.

'Durgapur Dhannyasora' is one of the most culturally enriched village of Birbhum District, West Bengal. This is mainly a Santali village, & round the year all the Santali festivals are celebrated here along with other hindu festivals. Hool Festival is the main attraction of this village which is not celebrated other Santali villages. "Durgapur Sidhu Kanhu Lokosanskriti Kenda" this folk cultural centre is the pillar of this village. Santali boys & girls are trained here for all the festivals performances & also for the football. There is a big playground for football practice & the main attraction is girls' football team. Girls' are too much addicted with football & it cannot be denied that this is one of the biggest impacts of Media & Westernisation. It cannot be thought that in far flung village of Bengal Santali girls are watching football world cup & also motivated through that. Even they celebrated the occasion with party among themselves. They are economically not belongs to very sound family. They are working, they are school going even above all the uncomfortable situation they loved to play football. 5P.M means, its' a time for playing football. No bindings are matter to them. This is one of greatest achievement of that folk cultural centre & overall the impact of westernisation. It can't be thought that in a remote village Santali girls are playing football & this is a positive impact of westernisation.

The importance of folk cultural centre and its potentialities are played a supportive role in development of the tribal communities in particular and other marginalised sections in general. The term 'Folk Culture refers to the unifying expressive components of everyday life as enacted by localised, tradition-bound groups those are existed in rural society. The concept of Folk culture is primarily focused on traditions practiced by small homogeneous rural groups living separately and keeping themselves isolated from other groups of the society. The tribal groups satisfy all their needs in the village. They have a sense of unity and a feeling of amiability towards each other. Folk cultural centre has its own principles, ideas and moral values. They try to create a noble society where tribal people can live in harmony with other human beings and collectively taking part in the process of nation building.

Folk cultural centre maintains communication within a community or group and also tries to identify areas of agreement and disagreement among those, who are actively participating in rural development. It is the job of folk cultural centre to keep communication with the tribal groups and find out the problems that create barriers on their pathways of social development. In India, the indigenous community communication modes and channels tend to have variations from one ethnic group to another. These communication modes and channels are based upon the communities, especially the tribal community, policy makers, planners and administrators as well. These communication modes and channels should be identified in bringing social and cultural change in tribal society and utilizing these communication channels to provide the maximum information to the disadvantage section of the society. Folk cultural centre is used as one of the most important tools of rural communication in tribal areas. It reaches at the grass root level and equipping tribal communities with new skills. In a transforming country like India, which is vast, over populated and having large resources, the skills, attitudes and knowledge of the tribal groups have to be developed and utilised such things to get optimum results for national development. So, it works as an agent of indigenous communication at grass root level as well as acts as an indicator of tribal development in rural areas.

Conclusion

The present paper depicted the real scenario of Santali girls in this particular tribal village & even if the role & impact of westernisation & media on their society. Tribal girls play very crucial role in their society. Indeed, it has revealed that media are not too much important in their day to day life. Media like news paper, television & radio are used by them, only for entertainment but in subconscious somehow media plays very important role for making of a developed society. The present study also shows that tribal girls contribute outstanding efforts for the advancement of their society. Their love for football can create a reference for all the tribal girls of rural Bengal. Hereafter, the fact is that we can't able to change the situation without improving the condition of the tribal girls, but they have to understand the importance of them for their betterment, which only can make a developed society as well as a nation. In fact, without help of the media, the changes take place in tribal society that is not possible. The present paper concludes that the influence of western culture has greater impact on tribal girls, more over in which motivate them to play football. So, we cannot deny the impact of folk cultural centre which motivates the tribal girls to practice even the football & make a love for it. Therefore, it is the effect of folk cultural centre, which will make this village much more culturally developed in respect to other 'Santal' villages of Birbhum district and finally for this only the village is culturally enriched and as well as developed.

References

- Audhary S.N.- 2009,Tribal Development Since Independence, *Concept Publishing Company,*New Delhi.
- Chiovoloni M. - 2004. 'The Interactive power of Local and Traditional Communication Systems', *Ileia Magazine,* April 28, 2004, pp:1-4.
- Culshaw. W. J - 2004, Tribal Heritage: A Study of Santals, *Gyan Publishing House,* New Delhi.
- Daudu S. 2009. Problems and prospects of folk media usage for agricultural extension service delivery in Benue State. Nigeria. J Hum Ecol, Volume -25(1), pp: 19-24.
- Ghosh, Biswajeet - 2006, 'Globalisation and Cultural Change', Indian *Journal of Development Research and Social Action*, Volume - 2, No. 1, Jan-June.
- Johnson, Kirk - 2005, 'Globalisation at the Crossroads of Traditions and Modernity in Rural India', *Sociological Bulletins*, Volume -54, No. 1.
- Kumar Harish – 2006 'Folk Media and Rural Development', *Indian Media Studies Journal,* Volume -1, No.1. July-Dec.
- Kamala R. – 2004, 'Forging a Link between Indigenous Communication. Effective Community social work Practice and National Development', *Stud Tribes Tribals, Volume* - 2(2), Pp: 89-95.
- Lent, John E. – 1978, 'Grassroots Renaissance: The Increasing Importance of Folk Media in Third World' Nations Paper presented at International Seminar on Folk Culture, *Institute of Oriental and Orissan Studies, Cuttack,* Orissa, India, December Pp: 19-23.
- Mohanty Manashi and Pritishri Parhi – 2011,'Folk and Traditional Media: A Powerful Tool for Rural Development', *Journal of Communication,* Volume - 2(1), pp: 41-47.
- Naidu P.R. - 2009, Tribal Development in India: A Curtain Raiser, *Adhyayan Publishers & Distributors*, New Delhi.
- Pani Niranjan & Jitendra Sahoo –2008, Tribal Development, *Mahamaya Publishing House,* New Delhi.
- Pati Jagannath.- 2004, Media And Tribal Development, *Concept Publishing Company,* New Delhi.
- Thakur Ashutosh - 2001, Tribal Development and Its Paradoxes, *Author Press Publication,* Delhi.
- Yadappanavar.A.V - 2003,Tribal Education In India, *Discovery Publishing House*, New Delhi.
- **rani.midatala - 2009, problems of tribal education in india: issues and prospects, *kanishka publishers,* new delhi.**
- Shailendra Kumar - 2012, 'Role of Folk Media in Nation Building', *Voice of Research,* Volume - 1, Issue – (June) 2.
- Sen Dineshchandra - 2006, The Folk Literature of Bengal, *Gyan Publishing,* New Delhi.
- Shah. Vimal P.& Tara Patel - 1985, Social Contexts of Tribal Education, *Concept Publishing Company,* New Delhi.

- **thakur.d.n &thakur.d - 2009, tribal education, *deep and deep publications*, new delhi.**

Web Sources

- www.ruralgov.nic.in
- www.birbhum.gov.in
- www.wikipedia.org
- www.google.co.in

20

The Kharia Identity: Study of Forest Ecology and Economy of Indian Tribe

Srikrishna Mondal

Introduction

The human groups are constantly interact with their habitat. The quality of human resources is intimately connected with available of the natural resources. Availability of natural resources depends on the ecological condition. The demography and human ecology closely inter-related. The tribal groups had adjusted themselves with their varied ecology since immemorial time. It can be said that Human ecology has been defined in Encylopedia of Social Sciences(1959); "Human ecology deals with spatial aspects of the symbiotic relations of human beings and human institution. It aims to discover the principles and factors involved in the changing pattern of spatial arrangement of population and institution resulting from the interplay of living beings in a continuously changing culture".The concept of nature man spirit complex has to be analysed in terms of cultural ecology (Vidyarthi, 1963), cultural ecology is an one of the theoretical stratige subscribed to the view point that an intimate relationship exists between cultural and its surrounding environment (Mnaa, 1981).

Honigman (1976), suggest that physical environment lead to changes in the natural features cultural milleu and necessities a new kind of adaptation. Steward(1969) feels that cultural ecological adaptation are responsible for distinctive cultural tradition. Ever the functioning of a culture according to him is considered by environment condition. In 1910, Coupland wrote, "the district is now singularly destitute of wild animals and game of all description. The cultivation and clearing of jungles for this purpose has widely extended during the last 20 years, and denudation of the jungles, even where the land is not required or suitable for cultivation, almost as if not more rapidly. After rapid industrialisation and urbanisation, the end of 20th century witnesses the appearance of globalisation: a progression for free market economy and removing the boundary of trade by selling branded product that moving towards a global culture; and confrontation to globalisation: in the from of intense expression of the local for preservation of indigenous culture and identities. In view of evolutionary sequences of progressive development, it is only likely that once proclaimed singularity of identity being exposed to the forces of transformation will undergo change in order to assume plural attributes. For a clarity of the phenomena as well as for due appreciation of the processes involved in the manifestations of singularity or plurality of identities, a close attention to the system of categorisation seems important. The natural resources have been collected, processed and marketed in international markets giving benefits to the large scale companies. Tribals are remain in their own traditional economy and poverty. There are about 608-scheduled tribe groups are living in India. there are many tribal group were primarily depended on the forest production as well as natural resources. The impact of strict forest policies, deforestation and industrialisation, globalisation have cumulative effect on their economy, social life, mythical believe and practices and identities.

The Hill Kharia is to be hunting and gathering tribe belonging to the proto australoid racial stock and mainly inhabit Bihar, Madhya Pradesh, Maharasta, Jharkhand, Orissa and West Bengal in India. In Purulia the Hill Kharia are found in 7 out of 16 police station situated at the eastern side of district they found in three police Bunkura, Paschim Medinipur districts contiguous with Purulia, in Murbhanj District of Orissa, in Singbhum and Dalbhum district Jharkhand and some isolated parts of West Medinipore. ROY S.C.(1937-56) who made an exhaustive ethenographic study sub divided the entire Kharia into three main section on the basis of Geographical location, economy identity and culture- The Dudh Kharia, Dhelki Kharias and Hill Kharias. The total population is about 957971. The Dudh Kharias are the most advanced and conscious section of tribe who mainly live at Ranchi to Gangpur sate. They live in settled villages away from the forest and hills. They have as their neighbors various hindu castes with whom they come into frequent contrct. They have taken to agriculture and other fruitful occupation. The Delkhi Kharias can be found in Gangpur, Jaspur and Raigarh District of the central Provinces. They live in settled village and come in close contact with neighboring communities. Agriculture is main source of them.

The ethenic identity of Hill kharia is very much conjectural Historically the term 'ethnos' has a prejor-ative connotation. Aristotle used this term to denote natural inferiority of slaves to the citigens (Roy1990, P,265) over the length of the time,the ancient connotation of the term has much waned off, but even then a faint shade of the past continues in the perceptions of many. There is however non general agreement as to what actually the term ethnic group means.

In America normally minority groups are catagorise as ethnic groups but in ethnic conflict the connotation of the minority is by and large absent (1990). Glazer and Moynihan (1976).describes ethnic group as a social group which consciously shares some common and is primarily be decent basing on both (1969) Hicks and leis (1969) and other,Pathy (1988p.18) observed that ethnic group is used in anthropological literature to designate a population which is part of a plural scociety and yet is largly biologically self perpetuating, shares a common cultural tradition and language, has an ascribed membership which identifies it self as being alile by nitue of a real or ficititious common ancestery, and identified by other as constituting a distinut in a plural scocity".

The Hill Kharia so called because they used to live in and around hilly tracts they are some time referred to as 'Pahari Kharia'. The peasants among whom they lived called as Khariya, the tribe now used the mythical term as their name Sabar.The Hill Kharia of Purulia say that, they do not have the social intercourse with Hill Kharia language, style of life are thought to be different those living in Purulia. The Purulia district the largest concentration of Hill Kharia is in Manbazar P.S., which also happen to be the largest police station of the district. Approximate population of Hill Kharia is 15000 (fifteen thousand) in Purulia District. The Kharia originally belong to a nomadic tribe wondering in search of food for occupying large territories. They were forest dwellers and traditionally hunter and food gatherers, who used to maintain their livelihood by collecting edible roots tubers herbs and fruits from the forest and killing the animals, they were totally dependent on the forest. Their life was intricately related with the forest eco – system. Their adaptation to the environment is direct and simple. Their previous mode of subsistence pattern receded due to the deforestation and ecological changes.The Kharia socio-economic activity and social identity have been changed.

Area of study : - I have studied three villages namely Kulabahal village under Hura Block, Babujore village under Puncha Block and Pargora village of Bundwan Block. The total population of Kharia tribe. Being a migrated community, the Kharia of Kulabahal able to preserve very little originality, because of the easy accessibility of the PuruliaTown, whereas Pargora being located as the fringe of the jungle, gives the Kharia residing here less exposure to the modern life. Pargora and Babuijore villages are located at the vicinity of forest. The total population of the studied villages is 504.

Block	*Village*	*Schedule Tribe*	*Schedule Caste*	*OBC/ General*	*Total Population*
Hura	Kulabahal (JL. No. - 47)	386	75	719	1180
Puncha	Babujore (JL No. –12)	154	0	899	1053
Bundwan	Pargora (JL No. – 88)	196	0	159	355

(as per census 2001)

Methodology :- The present study is based on the emperical study and literature review. The field work have been done among the Kharia of Kulabhal village under Hura Block, Babujore village of Puncha Block, Pargora village of Bundwan Block.. The data have been collected by using the standard tools and technique of social Anthopology which includes observation, structure interview, household schedules and case study were also used to trace the hunting gathering mode of living and agricultural process.

Objectives:-

i.. To understand the ethnic identity of the kharia ofPurulia and accross the India.

ii. To analyse the changing of subsistence pattern in the light of the ecological depletion of natural resource.

iii. To understand the forest dewlling ilmpact on the socio –economic life of the Kharias.

iv. To evaluate the status of present day dependency on the medicinal plants on the respect of their health condition.

v. To understand about the changes of social isolation and social identity.

vi. To understand about the participation in various development programme.

Ecology of Kharias:-The district Purulia (specifically identified as one of the most backward areas of the state) belonging to the Western border of West Bengal is virtually an extension of the Chotonagpur plateau and beaus a topographical feature which stand in quite contrast with the other plan areas of the state. The district is located in the humid sub tropical climate region or comes under plateau region characterized by arid and dry zone and is specified as chronic Drought Prone Area (DPA).

The basic economy of the district is agriculture. But is severely handicapped by drought condition. Because of erratic and scanty rainfall, there is frequent failure of crops leading some times to famine or near famine situation. The hilly undulated terrains put up a further constraints and substantial portion of land is a uncultivable waste. The situation worsened by poor communication system, it is not easy to reach its some what inferior parts, particularly during rainy season. The Rate of literacy is somewhat lower than else where in West Bengal. The topography of the district hilly and undulated. There are numerous hillocks in south, forming a continuity with the Dalma range. The district grifted with wide and scattered forests Sal, Palas, Mahua, Simul and some other forest animals. The constant erosion in the sloped area indiscreet cutting and grazing in the habitation, the forest resources now become scanty.

In Purulia the climate is generally much drier than eastern part of the state, though from early March till the beginning of June hot westerly winds prevail and the heat during the day is oppressive. The mean maximum temperature is between 24.44^{0}C and 21.11^{0}C during December and February respectively. The temperature rises to 31.66^{0}C in March and in April and in May to 39.44^{0}C. throughout the rainy season the temperature remains about 332.22^{0}C but sometimes drops to 31.11^{0}C in October and 28.88^{0}C in November

Literature review Concern with the Kharia Identity

According to E.T. Dalton (1872) entitled his book "Descriptive Ethnology of Bengal" describe about the mythical concept of Kharia origin. Their mythical beliefs that they are came into earth from peacock egg. They are lived at Rotasgarh in patna. Later on they have migrated to 'KoyalRiver'. The Kharia tribe have mainly devided into three groups Dhelki Kharia, Dudh Kharia & Pahari Babanya Kharia.Risley(1891) point out the pure Kharia identity of the settled agricultural Kharias of Lohardanga district of Bhiar. He writes "Even now there is little left to show that come from the same stock as the wild Kharias who inhabit the crests of the higfest ranges in Manbhum and Tributary states of Chotanagpur and Orissa" Two points are discussed, with special attention.Firstly,the Kharia everywhere are not engaged in the same type of economic activity and secondly,barring a few, they are economically marginalised.

Dr. D.Sinha(1984) studied entitle- The Hill Kharia of Purulia-'Impact of Proverty on a Hunting and Gathering Tribe'. He describes about the economic crisis of the tribe who suffered from economic deprivation severely.Sometimes Kharias are subject to criminal activities.As such they stigmatized as 'Criminality'. They had believed to be race of criminal and treated so by and large number of inhabitants.In 1989 Prof. Chandi Das Mukhopadhaya – Asian Studies Vol – 7, Page No. – 63: - "The crimes and criminals among the Kharia of Purulia" – According to Prof. Chandi Das Mukhopadhaya. These Kharia people with smaller and scattered population live in remote and isolated areas. They are still pre – agriculturist stage and mostly depended on outmoded forest economy. They are solely depended on the jungle produce. At present due to denudation of the forest areas these people have been ecologically and economically displaced. The interactional pattern between the Kharia and the village peasantry has not fully crystallised. The Kharia have engaged in commited crimes from petty thefts to bulglaries, robbers, large dacoits and even murder i.e. has tried to show that Kharia Sabar about 98% people engaged in anti social activities.A good number of Kharias have now been equated with the Lodhas and as such, the benefits earmarked for the PTG (Primitive Tribal Group) also accrue to them. Originally, the Kharia like almost West Bengal, Bihar and Orissa are supposed to comprise a single tribe, there and notable cultural differences between them. From the development point of view also each of these groups could be differentiated from their counterpart'. Banerjee H.N.(1962) wrote a short article on "socio-Ritual status of the Kharia in theethnic background of Manbhum" in Bulletin of the Cultural Research institute.It was an essay dealing mainly whith a comparative account of different significant social custom of the tree ethnic groups- the Kharia, the bhumij and the mahato of Southern Manbhum.He has pointed out that unlike their neighbours such as Bhumijs and mahatos, the Kharia are deprived of the ritual services of other castes and they have made no consolidated social movements to raise their status.

The Kharia are not only the primitive and backward. They also suffer from criminality. They are alleged to be notified as criminal Tribe under the criminal Tribe Act of 1924. Act was repealed in 1952 and Kharias are officially declared to "Vimukta Jati". Criminal propensity among the Kharia people deters easy and spontaneous interactive between Kharias and the villagers in general. In all villagers Kharia are migrated from in different period of history either in search of employment or selection of habitat due to some social reasons. Incomes of most of the members derived from selling of fuel, laborers for agricultural works, are low and uncertain. A few of them, occupy very negligible amount of land. Due to different ecological constraints and poor economic condition of farming population the growth of the villagers have been arrested

Now most of the Kharia people deal settled life. Their economic condition have been changed from nomadic hunting gathering to settled agricultural activities. The material culture and social relation have been changed in relation to change of subsistence patter

Table No. -2

Demographic Analysis:—

Sl No	*Age group*	*Male*	*Female*	*Total*
1.	Upto - 4	26 (9.96)	25 (10.28)	51 (10.05)
2.	5-9	31 (11.87)	26 (10.69)	57 (11.24)
3.	10-14	32 (12.26)	23 (9.46)	55 (10.89)
4.	15 -19	20 (7.66)	27 (11.11)	47 (9.27)
5.	20-24	18 (6.89)	18 (7.40)	36 (7.10)
6.	25-29	23 (8.81)	20 (8.23)	43 (8.48)
7.	30-34	20 (7.66)	28 (11.52)	48 (9.52)
8.	35-39	19 (7.27)	14 (5.76)	33 (6.50)
9.	40-44	20 (7.66)	15 (6.17)	35 (6.90)
10.	45-49	14 (5.36)	11 (4.52)	25 (4.93)
11.	50-54	12 (4.59)	7 (2.88)	19 (3.74)

Cond...

12	55-59	6 (2.29)	5 (2.05)	11 (2.16)
13	60-64	5 (1.91)	12 (4.93)	17 (3.35)
14	65+	15 (5.75)	12 (4.93)	27 (5.32)
15	Total	261 (51.78)	243 (48.21)	504 (99.98)

Analysis of Table No. – 2

From the above table, it is observed the total population of the studied villages are 504, out of them 261 (51.78%) are males and 243 (48.21%) are females. The total population has been categorized into various age groups on the basis of age and sex. The total male population is 261. Out of which 26(9.96%), 31 (11.87%), 32(12.26%), 20 (7.66%), 18(6.89%), 23(8.81%) 20 (7.66%), 19(7.27%), 20(7.66%), 14 (5.36%), 12 (4.59%) 6(2.29%), 5 (9.91%) and 15 (5.75%) are belongs to the age group of (0-4) year, (5-9) years, (10-14) years, (15-19) years, (20-24) years, (25-29) years, (30-34) years, (35-39)years, (40-44) years, (45-49) years, (50-54) years, (55-59) years and (60-64) years and 65 years and above age groups. Similarly the total female population has been categorized on the basis age and sexes and their total number is 243(48.21%) of its total population. Out of them the frequency of female is 25 (10.28%), 26(10.69%), 23(9.46%), 27(11.11%), 18(7.40%), 20(8.23%), 28(11.52%), 14(5.76%), 15(7.40%), 11(4.52%), 7(2.80%), 5(2.05%), 12(4.43%), are belongs to the age group of (0-4)years, (5-9) years, (10-14) years, (15-19) years, (20-24) years, (25-29) years, (30-34) years, (35-39)years, (40-44) years, (45-49) years, (50-54) years, (55-59) years and (60-64) years and 65 years and above respectively. It is significant to note that highest population is 57 belong to the age group of (5-9)yrs out of which 31 and 26 are males and females respectively. The highest age - group 65 yrs and above and their number total number 27. Out of them 15(5.75%) and 12 (4.78%) are males and females respectively.

Table No.– 3,

Family types among the Kharia

Types of Family/ Village	*Nuclear Family*	*Joint Family*	*Extended Family*	*Conjugal Family*	*Broken*	*Single*	*Total*
Kulabahal	22 (19.46)	9 (7.96)	5 (4.42)	7 (6.19)	2 (1.76)	1 (0.88)	46 (40.70)
Babuijore	12 (10.61)	11 (9.73)	2 (1.76)	4 (3.53)	5 (4.42)	1 (0.88)	35 (30.97)
Pargora	17 (15.04)	7 (6.19)	7 (3.53)	2 (1.76)	0 (0.00)	2 (1.76)	32 (28.32)
Total	**51 (45.13)**	**27 (23.89)**	**11 (9.73)**	**13 (11.50)**	**7 (6.19)**	**4 (3.53)**	**113 (100.00)**

From the above table, it is observed that the types of family among the Kharia in the above mention villages. In this table the types of family has been categorise into 6 – group viz; nuclear family joint family, extended family, conjugal family, broken family and single family respectively. The total number of the families are hundred thirteen out of which 51 (45.13%), 27(23.89%), 11(9.73%), 13(11.50%),07(6.19%), and 04(3.53%) are belong to the family of Nuclear, Joint Family, Extended Family, Conjugal Family, Broken Family and Single respectively. The total number of nuclear family is 51 out of which by 22 (19.46%), 12 (10.61%), 17(15.04%), are belongs to the villages of Kulabahal, Babuijore and Pargora respectively.

Similarly joint family of the villages are 27 out of them 09 (7.96%), 11(9.73%), and 07(6.91%) are belong to the Kulabahal, Babuijore and Pargora respectively. The total number of extended families are 11 out of them 05 (4.42%), 02(1.76%), are belong to the villages of Kulabahal, Babuijore and Pargora respectively. It is also found that there are several numbers of families are conjugal and their numbers are 13 out of them 07(6.19%), 04(3.53%), 02(1.76%) are belongs the villages of Kulabahal, Babuijore and Pargora respectively. Generally conjugal family comprises of husband and wife without children. The next category is broken family where the absent of husband and wife either deceased or divorce or separated from the nuclear family. The total number of broken is seven out of them (0-1.76%) and 05(0.42%) are belong to the villages of Kulabahal, Babuijore respectively. It is significant to note that there is no broken family in the village of Pargora. From the above study it is also highlights that there are also 04 households are comprises of only single member of each family. The single household is 01(0.88%) 01 (0.88%) and 02(1.76%), are belongs to villages Kulabahal, Babuijore and Pargora respectively.

The literacy status

The literacy status in the above mention villages. The level of literacy has been classified into 5 categories viz. illiterate, Can–Sign, Primary, Secondary, and higher secondary level of Education. The total population of the villages are 504, out of them 270 (53.57%) 104 (22.63%), 22(4.36%), and 02(0.39%) are belong to the level of category illiterate, can – sign, primary, secondary and higher secondary level of education respectively. From this table the literacy level of male members are 261. Out of them 118(23.41%), 55 (10.91), 68 (13.49%), 18 (3.57%), and 02 (0.39%), are belong to the category of illiterate, can- sign, primary, secondary and higher secondary level of education respectively. The female of literacy level is indicating that 243, out of them 152 (30.16%), 49(9.76%), 38(7.53%), and 04(0.79%), are belong to category of illiterate, can- sign, primary and secondary level of education respectively. It is significant to note that there is no female members belong to the higher secondary level of education. Nowadays due to modern impact of education through various agencies like as non formal education, adult education and Sarba Shiksha Abhijan. The people of the villages are less interested to being a literate member of the society. A few number of male student is going to the outside of the village and stay at Ashram Hostel for them education.

The Land Holding Pattern

It is found that the landless families are 43 (38.05), out of its total land holding household. Out of 43, 17(15.04), 16(14.15) and 10(8.84) are belong to the villages of Kulabahal, Babuijore and Pargora respectively. As landless families who have no agricultural land but they made their houses in the PattaLand which are provided by the Government. Rest of houses have some amount of land for agricultural purpose. This amount of lands are categories into five groups according to their landholding capacity.

These groups are firstly who lands upto 10 katha, secondly who have 11 - 20 katha, thirdly 21-30 katha, fourthly 31-40 katha and fifthly 41 and above kathas of lands. In the village Kulabahal 11(9.73), 03(2.60), 04(3.53), 6(5.30) and 5(4.42) are belong to the above mention categories. In the village Babuijore the land holding capacity of the families are 11(12.38), 02(1.76), 04(3.53) and 02(1.76) are belong to the said category respectively.

It is significant to note that the category of 31-40 kathas of landholding family are not found in the village Babuijore. In the Pargora village the landholding families are 04(3.53), 05(4.42), 04(3.53), 06(5.30) and 03(2.65) are belong to the above mention category. The highest amount of lands is 41 katha and above found in the above mention villages. The total number of households are 10 out of which 05(4.42), 02(1.76), and 03(2.67) are belong to the villages of Kulabahal, Babuijore and Pargora respectively. The total landholding households are indicating that they have more less agricultural land which are mainly mono cropped and depend on monsoon rain. As a result production of crops are various in relation seasonal variation. The production of food substances are not much adequate to fulfill their livelihood.

Table No. –4

Occupational status among the Kharia Tribe.

Occuptional category	*Agriculture & agricultural labour*	*Daily & Migratory Labour*	*Forest Collection*	*Sal leave processing Broom making*	*House wife and cattle raising*	*Students and unable*	*Total*
Male	40(7.93)	80(15.87)	20(3.96)	9(1.78)	15(2.97)	97(19.24)	261(51.70)
Female	16(3.17)	38(7.54)	26(5.16)	15(2.97)	63(12.50)	85(16.86)	243(48.21)
Total	56(11.11)	118(23.41)	46(9.12)	24(4.76)	78(15.47)	182(36.11)	504(99.99)

It depicts that the occupational pattern of the Kharia in the district of Purulia. The total members of the Kharia population are 504, out of them 261(51.78) and 243(48.21) are belongs to Males and Females respectively. Majority of the people are engaged in forest related activities. It is highlight that 46(9.12) person are depend on forest products to maintain their livelihood out of them 20(3.96) and 26(5.16) are male and females. At the same time some person are takes Sal- leave plate making as their profession. Out of the 09(1.78) and 15(2.97) are males and females respectively.

Some persons who have some amount of agricultural lands, they are engaged in agricultural activities to produced agricultural crops for maintain there livelihood. The number of these person are 56(11.11) of its total population. Out of them 40(7.93) and 16(3.17) are males and females respectively. The younger generation those who are physically stronger they have adopted as a migratory labour in various activities near by the town and other parts of the states. Their numbers 118(23.41) of its total population out of them 80(15.87) and 38(7.54) are males and females respectively. Besides some persons are also engaged in household activities and their numbers are 78(15.47) of its total population. Out of them 15(2.97) and 63(12.5) are males and females respectively. It is significant to note that the impact of modern system of education the Kharia boys and girls are going to school for their education. The total number of students are 182 (36.11) of its total population. Out of them 97(19.24) and 85(16.84) are males and females student respectively.

Social Aspect of the Kharia –

Health condition of Kharia and practice of ethno-medicine:-The Kharias people are suffering from various types of disease like parasite diseases epidemic and endemic disease. Children are suffering from cough and cold, Bronchopneumonia Meseals, Typhoid and parasite infected diseases. Adult male and female suffering from Filarial infected diseases Leprosy, Tuberculosis Malaria, Small Pox specially female are suffering from Anemia. The children are suffering from incidence of diphtheria, Tetanus and Whooping Cough. They are frequently suffering from small pox, Dysentery etc. owing to sheer ignorance on the part of the registering agents. The incidence of acute and Chromic diseases is greater. The adult male and female suffer from hypertension and paralysis. Female folk also suffer from Anemia.

Incidence of diseases with seasonal variation among all sex and age

Seasonal Diseases	*Children*	*Adult Male*	*Adult female*
1. Summer	Meseals, Fever	Fever, Small Pox	Small Pox, Headache, Migrane
2. Rainy	Bronchitis dysentery, Influenza	Dysentery, Gastritis, Amoeboid	Dysentery, Amoeboid, Gastritis

3. Autumn	Typhoid	Amoeboid Dysentery	Fever
4. Dew Season	Bronchitis, Fever	Rheumatism Malaria	Malaria
5. Winter	Cough and cold	Malaria, Asthma, Paralysis, Rheumatism, Tuberculosis	Asthma, Malaria, Paralysis
6. Spring	Para typhoid	Paralysis	Paralysis, Small Pox

N.B. Both acute and chronic diseases are aggravates in different season.

For health care service the villagers primarily depend on village medicines. At present dependence on modern medicine / Govt. Health Service is increasing. In case of complication villagers visit the BPHC at Hura, Bundwan and other community for their knowledge regarding medicinal plants admire Hill Kharias. Interestingly during the survey I was found that the consciousness about the family planning among the female members is quite high. They are very much aware about the good effects of limiting family size. They adopt various methods both indigenous and those supported by the Govt. Health Service.

They use different types of medicine plants for their ill health condition which are found nearby forest.

Table No – 5

Use of Medicinal Plants

Sl. No.	*Botanical identity*	*Medicine use as informed by the Kharia*	*Location*
1.	Achyranthes aspera Linn. Family :- Amaranthaceae	Root is used in asthma and in parasitic infection	Nearest forest V.N. Apang
2.	Andrographis Paniculata Nees. Family – Acanthaceae,	Crushed root is applied on wounds used to cure fever, worms, dysentery general weakness.	Nearest forest Kalmegh.
3.	Hemidesmus indicus(L) Schutt. Family :- Asclepiadaceace Anantamul Dudhi Lata (Indian Sarsaparilla)	Root are used in venerab diseases and in rheumatism. Leanss and roots are refreshing and stimulating. Died roots are useful in fever, skin diseases, loss of appetite, syphilis leucorrhoea	Nearest forest
4.	Adhatoda zeylanica A. – Vasica Basak	It is used as expectorant in Bronchitis recent information has confirmed the usefulness basak.	Nearest forest
5.	Curcuma domestica	Rhizome is used in skin diseases and in wounds. It acts as a blood prmifer.	Nearest forest

Contd...

6.	Ocimum sanctum Linn Family – Lamiaceae Kalo Tulsi	Science of rushed is given with honey in cough and cold.	Nearest forest
7.	Butca monosperma Family – Fabaceae (Palash)	Gum and seeds are medicinal. Gum used to treat diarrhoea. Seeds used as anthelmintic and used on wring worm.	Nearest forest

They use various types of medicinal plants, these are very few illustration. Beside they intake Allopathic medicine and Homeopathic Medicine. There Quak practisoner's who save health care role performance. There are sub health center within the village or outside of the village. They are gradually access to take the advantage of vaccination for their baby and family planning method. Previously antenatal care totally done at the home, Now Kharia expectant mother are hospitalised for antenatal care with the help of Panchayet or Village Anganwadi Worker. There are held Blind operation Sibir, Leprosy and Tuberculosis awareness camp organised by Panchayet and local NGOs.

Magico-Religious beliefs and practice:

The kharia belief in supernatural belief is manifested in all their activities. The Basuki is the prime date is of the kharia. There for they have worship Basuki(Earth goddess).They now sacrifice pigs and fowl instead of human beings.Previously they use to practice humane sacrifice.The kharia belief in ancestral spirit. The Kharia believe in the survival of the soul after death,those who die an unnatural death and woman,Who dies during pregnancy or in child birth, are not given funerary rites,They do not achieve full spiritual status and ghost to be continue covering around the village.They have performed two types of funeral ceremony both burning burial.The kharia Practice magic, to control some spirits to cause harm.They worship some gods and goddesses for prosperity and happiness and to be relearned from tention and anxiety. The main deties are propitiated by kharia are Manasa, Kali,Shiva dharma thakur, Garam thakur (village deity), Karam, Bura-Buri (ancestral spirits), Tusu, Chandi. The traditional deties were basulei Baram(Garam) Yugini. Most of deities are barrowed from the neighboring Hindu peasant community excepting a few of teir old tradition. They have two than i.e. Garam than and Thakur than. Most of the kharia household have Tulsi mancha.They have no definite temple or sacred spot is conspicuously absent. The same spot is used for several years of worships. Onlyundressed of stones are generally considered as the resting place of stones.

Some Kharia Gods and goddess are worshipped at the kharia hamlet level and few are the at village level.Subscription is raised and this mainly done for general welfare of the Kharia.Sometimes individual level of worship is meant for seeking protection or welfare of the individual or his family. It is common practice for the Kharia, to offer sacrifice of animal of various types which can procure.A large number of goats,fiwls and pigs are offered as sacrifices in which female do not take part in such activity.They simply express their gratitude, promise for the future worship and sacrifics and seeting protection,help and sacrifice in their own language.

Addiction pattern : - They are traditionally addicted on 'Hardia' and 'Muha alcohal. Beside they are habituated to take Biri made local Kendupata and Canabis. They drink alcohal at the time of ritual performances of Mahato community. It is take as their special opportunity. Now in the Babuijore and Pargora village both male and female are regularly drink alchohale. They are drinking alcohole in state of selling the rice which is given by Panchayet Office. Even if they sale their tile of own house to buy alchohal from local people or market.

Development by N.G.O. :- The most significant role in rehabiliting the Kharia Sabar community and restoring its lost dignity is now played by N.G.O. of Purulia District. There are some N.G.O., take a initiative for Kharia development in relation to their health and disease, household industry agriculture operation and so forth. Paschim Banga Kharia Sabar Samity has been able to make enduring contribution to the cause of the Kharia Sabar through the untiring effort and commitment of its core member including its guiding spirit. Smt. Mahasweta Devi admirably assisted by the Sabar Samity Rajnowagarch village. They also take initiative for their education. Presently they continuing one primary school. There are about 82 registered student, 30-40 students only attend the school regularly. One Kharia Sabar Hostel set up at Pargora village of Bandwan Block under State Tribal Welfare Department where 20 student are permanently stay for their education.

Development by Panchayet : - The Government of West Bengal has initiated several scheme for alleviating the living condition of Kharia, including employment generation and provision of land and credit. Panchayet have helped to setup a Kharia house from Indira Abash Yojana. They also give 30kg of rice per month to a Kharia family under Annapurna Yojana with free of cost. They give 40 kg of rice in the rate of Rs 2.00 per kilo under Antardaya Yajona. Self Help group is formed by the Panchayet member among the Kharia humlet. There are only one women group for invest Rs 30.00 per month. Self Help Group project is formed in the village Kulabhal and Pargora. Men folk is formed a self help group in the KulabhalVillage. This cash money utilised in the perpose to make a broom stick, salpata plate and rope.

JointForest Management : - It is the participation of local people or tribal people for forest development. It is help to engage as wage earner in various activity like tea plantation and preservation of sapling. They are engage as a Sal Pata collector, Mahua Seeds Collector and Kendupata, deposit at forest office and received Rs 30.00 per day. The Kharia people engage as a day labourer for harvesting timber. On the other hand the dacoit activities is control through the participation of the local Kharia people.

Conclusion : -The life of the Hill Kharia was almost connected with primitiveness with the gradual depletion of the forest cover and their subsistence pattern. The ecological degradation creates difficulties to their secondary primitvisation descending down from evolutionary scale shifting from hunting gathering economy. The hill Kharia gradually accustomed about the agriculture operation and agriculture labourer.

The problems are gradual depletion of natural flora and fauna and forest area. The hilly slopes and undulating topography are unfavorable situation for carriedout agricultural operation. The laterite soil have less potential for water retention. They have get 'Patta land' from land revenue dept, and patta land are maximum non fertile and high land. (Dahi land) Agriculture is not fruitfull occupation to the Kharia of Purulia district.

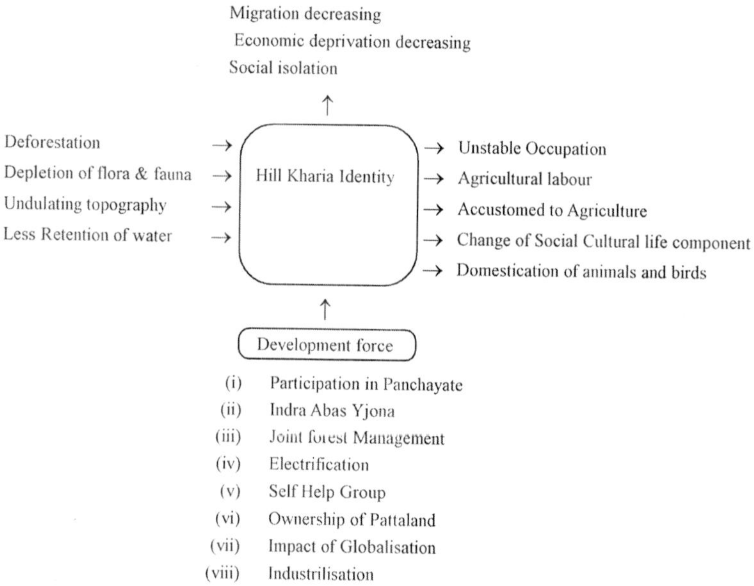

The Schematic diagram for interaction with Physical and social environment of Hill Kharia

The traditional subsistence pattern of economy i.e. hunting and gathering of the Kharia has been shifted to marginal cultivation. But the cultivation of main crop is not efficiently done due to small plot of land and undulating topography. Previously they had mainly dependent on food gathering economy and they partially earned their livelihood by collecting wild roots, medicinal herbs, hunting and selling of other forest produces. But deforestation of the areas has brought changes into economic life. They are trying to adjust to their activities like agriculture but it always not fruitful. They suffer from lack of money and insufficient diet. Sometimes they involve in crime to solve their economic problems. Economic crisis create the mental depression in socio cultural life. These criminal activities create social isolation from the peasants communities. There are two basic problems i.e. ecological condition of their habitat and small plot of cultivable land. On the other hand displacement and unsuccessful agriculture are two factors for marginal deprivation. Social isolation has been developed from the pleasantry way of life. Dr. D. Sinha wrote the economic displacement and consequent poverty as one of the causes seems to have validity. Poverty generates a sense of deprivation, which provoke the people to engage in other unsocial activities.

Historically, the root of Kharias being stigmatized as deviant lay in the colonial period. The Kharias belong nomadic tribe, wondering in search of food for occupying large territories. They were forest dwellers and traditionally hunter and food gatherers, who used to maintain their livelihood by collecting edible roots tubers, herbs and fruits from the forest and killing the animals. They were totally depend on forest.

When forest, the only sources of Kharia economy were declared as the protected areas. The incoming money lenders, Zamindars and Izzera class (lease) from Hindu peasant community brought wide transformation of region materially and culturally. The forests were to be first denuded by the merchant, Land holders and colonial Goverments during the first decades. Such devaluation and categorisation was a mode existing power the British Govt. Perhaps it was thus that the local administrative machinery brought Kharias under the perview of criminal Tribe Act – 1924. One done it was enforced by law and became a mode of social oppression. Thus during the first decade of the century. The Kharias being ousted from forest economy were forced to come in contact with the establishment village society for seeking shelter and occupation but in most village Kharias were given shelter not as moral functional caste group or as normal inhabitance. Village land lords established Kharias family in tract of the village area to exploit their labour. However a client patron relationship home developed the homeless Kharias and landlords. Kharias was employed by the landlords when the required to make a fight one another. As a whole the Kharia in many village were obliged to survey because they were dependent on landlords or the village peasants for their habitation and Socio – economic security in village society.

Their previous mode of subsistence pattern receded due to the forestation. They are tried to lead a sattle life in the village demography and adjust themselves in the pre agricultural stage of living. But agricultural obstacle for laterite stony soil forced to them alternative means of livilihood. Now they are partially depend on forest resource, and agriculture labour. The scope of waget earning opportunity within the village as well as in the neighboring village is not adequate as against the demand. Due to proverty lack of better income grown up boys of Kharias families. Taken to opportunity of 'Bangal' profession as alternative ocupation. Some of the Kharias engaged at the dacoits activity and criminality. They isolated from the village peasantry due to their stigma of 'criminality'.The social mobility with neighbouring community is increasing in consequence with particepation in panchyate system,education center, health program and some socio-religious festivals.

The Government of West Bengal and Government of India have initiated several scheme for alleviating the living condition of the Kharia in relation to their house type, agricultural land, domestic cattle and poultry, employment generation for day labourer. They are gradually trying to adjust themselves in the rural folk of Bengal.

SUGGESTION:

Keeping from above discation in view to the put forwards some ideas and problems for the development of the Kharias—

1. Extension services for agriculture are weak. At present small plot of land distributed among the Kharias but quality of land not good to carry out agriculture. Only 4.16% Kharias people have (31-40) Khatha of agricultural land and land less 15.47%.
2. Joint forest management programmed will be more strengthened to engage the Kharias people at various activities like tree plantation and preservation of sapling, collection of seeds and etc.
3. Free supply of high-yielding seeds and chemical fartiliser, pesticide will be attracting to the Kharias to do agriculture.
4. Training will be provide about cultivation at undulating topography and irrigation facilities will be provide if possible. Also training is required knowledge about cattle rising and Poultry. Subsidy loans and free distribution of lives stock.
5. Knowledge should be provide about preparation of agricultural land and prevention soil erosion.
6. School education of children up to Madhyamik and adults education programmed would be arranged.
7. Marketing facilities should be improved for supporting for supporting activities of co-operative marketing and purchase forest and agricultural produce.
8. Awareness camp will be arranged for community health and modern medicine. Developed about the knowledge of traditional ethenomedicine and schooling of children.

9. Academecion and action Anthropologist would be employed to uplift their socio-economic development.
10. Participatory approach will be more strength in the level of social foresty, joint forest management,and agro-economic activity.

Bibliography

1. Dalton, E.T., "The Kharias" Descriptive Ethnology of Bengal, Calcutta (1872), pp 158-161.
2. Das, T.C., The Wild Kharias of Manbhum, Calcutta, 1905.
3. Das, T.C., The Wild Kharias of Bhalbhum, Anthropological Paper No. 3 (1931), University of Calcutta, 1936.
4. Enthoven, R.E., "Kharia" – Tribes and Castes of Bombay, Bombay, (1922), 1992.
5. Majumder, B.C., The Aborigines of the Highland of Central India, The University of Calcutta, 1927.
6. Risley, H.H., "Kharia" Tribes and Castes of Bengal, Vol. 1, Calcutta, 1891, pp 466-472.
7. Sinha, Dikshit, The Hill Kharia of Purulia, Anthropological Survey of India, Government of India, 27,Jawaharlal Nehru Road, Calcutta – 6, 1984, pp. 4-5
8. Banerjee, H.N. 'The Kharia of Modhupur, Singhbum District and Neighbouring Regions'. Bulletin of the Department of Anthropology, vol. 8, No. 2,1959, pp. 91-202.
9. Banerjee, H.N. 'Socio – Ritual Status of the Kharia in the Ethnic Background of Manbhum'. Bulletin of the Cultural Research Institute, West Bengal. Vol. 1, No. 2, 1962, pp. 16-28.
10. Bharal, G.P. 'Denotified Communities and Their Problems of Rehabilitation. The India Journal of Social Work, Vol. XXVIII, No. 4. January, 1968.
11. Datta, B.N., 'Kharias Ethnological Notes on some of the Castes of West Bengal', Man in India, Vol. 15, 1935 pp. 196-224.
12. Mukhopadhyay, Chandidas, 'Crime and Criminals of Purulia' Asian Studies, Calcutta (7), April-June,1989.
    - 'Kharias', Socialist Perspective, Calcutta, (12), June – Sept., 1989.
    - 'Folklore a Vehicle of Ethnic Protest' Folklore, Calcutta, Dec., 1989.
13. Roy, S.C. 'Past Migration of the Kharia Tribe'. Journal of the Bihar and Orissa Research Society',1935.

14. Chandra Ramesh, Environment Forest and Tribes, (Anthropological Concomitance) Udaipur, New Delhi, 2000.
15. Das Rajat Kanti, Development From Tribal Perspective, (A study of Santal, Bhumij and Kharia – inhabited Villages of Midnapore, West Bengal). Kolkata- 12, 2005.
16. Sinha Dikshit, The Hill Kharia of Purulia, (A study of impact of poverty on a hunting and gathering tribe), Anthropological Survey of India, Kolkatta –16, 1984.
17. Biswal Debendra Kumar, Impact of Eco-Degradation on Food and Ethnomedicine of the shifting cultivator Primitive tribes in Orissa. 251-260, Man and Life – Vol. 28 Nos. 3-4 July – Dec, 2002.
18. Acharya P.K., Fund Allocation, Expenditure and development of Primitive Tribal Groups: A Case study in Orissa, 223 – 237. Man and Life – Vol. 28 Nos. 3-4 July – Dec, 2002.

21

Search for Theoretical Model to Measure Displacement: Anthropological Reflections

Ch. Syam Kumar

Introduction

This paper is divided in to three parts. In first part its tries to present an analysis of the roots of displacement in India during colonial rule and post-independence era and how it took strenuous step to accelerate its pace by building mammoth irrigation dam projects and other developmental projects. In second part, it narrows down to seek for the anthropological theoretical models which will be helpful to measure displacement and also to understand peoples' impoverishment risks being faced. In third part it tries to examine one of the theoretical model which was proposed by Michael Cernea i.e. Impoverishment Risks and Reconstruction model to measure displacement and rehabilitation of Banjaras (Lambadas) who were displaced due to construction of Nagarjuna Sagar Dam. On this basis it tries to find out the flaws and lacunae within the IRR model and suggests modifications to the theoretical models enabling them to measure the problems of Project Displaced Peoples (PDPs) and Project Displaced Families (PDFs).

Displacement during colonial rule

The colonial government perceived the tribes essentially as encroachers and enemies of the forest, who plunder the forest for their selfish ends. With the Indian Forest Act 1878, The Forest Act of 1927 and State enactments, the state gradually gained monopoly over forests. Forests were declared as reserve forests from where tribals were driven out. Tribals who occupied these forests earlier, lost their habitat, their land, livelihood and all else that they had. Over a period of time, the engagements of tribals and other poor peoples who have access to forest land and forest produce were severely curtailed. The tribals were removed from their familiar and settled livelihoods. Large forest areas were declared either as reserve forests, or as sanctuaries and national parks. Constructions of dams, reservoirs and hydro-electrical projects have further resulted in huge displacement of tribals on thousands of hectares of forestlands. Many tribal villages were washed out in the process. Compensation and rehabilitation have touched only the peripheral of the problem.

Post independent scenario

Since independence in 1947, a series of large dams were built on some of the major rivers in India. Large dams were expected to solve the problem of hunger and starvation by providing irrigation and boosting food production, controlling floods and providing much needed electricity for industrial development. It was this grand promise that prompted Pandit Nehru, our first Prime Minister, to call dams **"Secular temples"** of modern India. Environmental and social costs of such large dams were thought to be an inevitable price that one had to pay for such development. Such projects include dams, power, mining, industrial and allied infrastructures, transport network, urban development, commercial forestry and so on. Some of these projects have brought adverse effects due to displacement of people from their original place of habitation due to acquisition of lands in large-scale. Development-induced displacement in the country has brought severe economic, social and environmental problems to the displaced people. Magnitude of people displaced and severity of the problems due to multipurpose dam projects is too high as compared to other projects in the country. They also lead to submergence of high quality land, destruction of the watershed, disturbance to the delicate ecological balance and distortionof the surrounding environment, loss of wildlife and irreplaceable precious flora and fauna etc. By considering the above said losses Kothari (1995) says: "The experience of post-Independence period from projects across the country suggests that the long drawn out process of displacement has caused widespread traumatic psychological and socio-cultural consequences like the dismantling of traditional production systems, desecration of ancestral sacred zones, graves and places of worship, scattering of kinship groups, disruptions of family system and informal social network".

Impact on tribals

India has the second largest tribal concentration in the world after Africa. The Scheduled Tribes constitute around 8 percent of population in India. It is estimated that some 21 million to 42 million people have been displaced by dams and reservoirs (India Country Study 2000).According to the Census 2001 the Scheduled Tribe population in Andhra Pradesh, is 50.24 lakhs. A large part of its natural resources lay in the hilly areas, as well as the major rivers originate from the mountains; most of the development projects have been executed in those areas. Thus, a significant number among the displaced people are the tribals and other economically marginalised rural people, who dwell in the vicinity of rich natural resources for their livelihood. It has been pointed out that a large majority of those displaced belong to the poor, deprived classes. Almost 40% of those displaced by dams belong to the Scheduled Tribes (SC. ST Commissioner's report1990; Kothari, 1995) and another 20 % belong to the Scheduled Castes (Fernandes, 1995). The most serious consequence of development-induced displacement for the tribal people has been the dispossession of land, both; agricultural and homestead, along with the loss of their traditional occupation. Walter Fernandes has attempted to estimate the displaced persons during the period of 1950-1990. The table below shows the magnitude of displacement in India.

Table.1: A Conservative Estimate of Persons Displaced By Various Categories of Projects.

Sl. No.	*Type of project*	*No. of Displaced*	*No. of Rehabilitated*	*Backing*
1.	Coal and other mines	17,00,000	4,50,000	12,50,000
2.	Dam and Canals	1,10,00,000	27,50,000	82,50,000
3.	Industries	10,00,000	3,00,000	7,00,000
4.	Sanctuaries and Parks	6,00,000	1,50,000	4,50,000
5.	Others	12,00,000	3,00,000	9,00,000
	Total	**1,65,00,000**	**39,50,000 (25% approximately)**	**1,15,00,000 (75% approximately)**

Source: Walter Fernandes, J C Das and Sam Rao: Displacement and rehabilitation-an Estimation of Extent and Prospects. Indian Social Institute (1989).

Survey of Literature

Anthropological studies on displacement and rehabilitation started in India around the late 50's and early 60's. Two important studies of this period are worth mentioning. One is Roy Burman's (1962) study of displaced tribals of Sundergarh district of Orissa due to the construction of Rourkela Steel Plant highlighted various factors affecting the process of displacement. And the second one is Karve and Kimbker's (1969) study of Konya Dam Project dealt with the impact of displacement and rehabilitation on family and kinship system of the uprooted communities of Maharashtra (S.M. Patnaik, 2000).After the 1970's and the early 80's the primary concern of the anthropological studies was the issue of economic versus social cost, the antagonism towards big dam, the state policies on displacement and rehabilitation, and macro-level evaluation of large dams in India (Shatrugna1981, Joshi1987, Reddy 1988, Iyer 1989, Fernandes and Thukral 1989, Baboo 1991). One of the noticeable study of this time would be the work of Agarwal, Sudhakar Rao and

Gurivi Reddy (1985) who were engaged in understanding the Yanadi tribe which is to be displaced for the construction of ISRO (Institute of Space and Research Organisation), Sriharikota. They had developed a model which is of action oriented and people centric with its philosophy to introduction of change without loss of identity and increase self-reliance.

Towards the later part of the 80's and early 90's social anthropologists had given attention to this issue of displacement by coal mining, by NALCO Projects, Upper Indiravati Hydro Electric Power Project in Orissa, (Behura and Mishra 1988, Baboo 1992, Mahapatra 1992, Baviskar 1995). Behura's study of relocatees of Rengali dam in Orissa analyses the rehabilitation policy, highlights the economic problem and socio-cultural consequences. It provides an understanding of the dynamics of social change with special reference to sibling relationship, nature of cooperation, causes of conflict and the institution of kinship and marriage. Anthropological studies started to stress on people's participation and involvement of anthropologist or sociologist in the issues of displacement and rehabilitation apart from the socio-cultural and ritual disarticulation due to displacement and resettlement in new areas. There are studies which provide suggestions or recommendations to policy makers based on their empirical field level experiences (Maninder Gill and Jayantha Perara 2000, Arpan Sharma 2003, Roxamine Hakim 2003, Mamata Swain and Ganesh Khan danga 2001, Manish Kumar Verma 2004 Kunj Bihari Nayak 2004, Hari Mohan Mathur 2006, Rambabu Mallvarapu 2007, Misra K.K. 2007).

Theoretical models

From the above review, three anthropological models are identified. They can be used to explain the displacement and rehabilitation within anthropological framework. They would also be useful to estimate or to quantify the socio-cultural loss besides economic and educational loss. They are: Action oriented Model by Agarwal, Sudhakar Rao and Gurivi Reddy, Scudder and Colson Four Stage Model, Impoverishment Risks and Reconstruction Model by Michael Cernea.

Action oriented Model

This model was proposed by Agarwal, Sudhakar Rao and Gurivi Reddy while they are working with the Yanadi tribe in Sriharikota, Nellore District, of Andhra Pradesh, India. They thought of understanding the culture and give suggestions to the government of India before Yanadi's are displaced because of forthcoming ISRO building. Since they found no suitable model to understand the Indian tribes from Indian perspective, they had evolved their own model that is presented in next page.

They advocated that anthropologist has to play dual roles. One is researcher and the other is change agent. Former role is to take up the problems and needs of people for evaluation from the emic perspective, prioritizing them and give suggestions to tackle the problem that eventually lead to introduction of change. Later role insists that just by giving mere suggestions is not enough, being a change agent anthropologist must examine the suggested solutions in consultation with sponsoring agency and evolve strategy of introducing the change and monitor the direction of the change.

Reflection

Action oriented model proposed by Agarwal C. Binod, N. Sudhakar Rao and Gurivi Reddy is the Indian model suggested by Indian anthropologists who have the experience and exposure to the Indian tribes. This has lot of advantage if it is really implemented as it was in ISRO project. Involving the anthropologist or sociologist is the key to successful resettlement of Yanadi tribes.

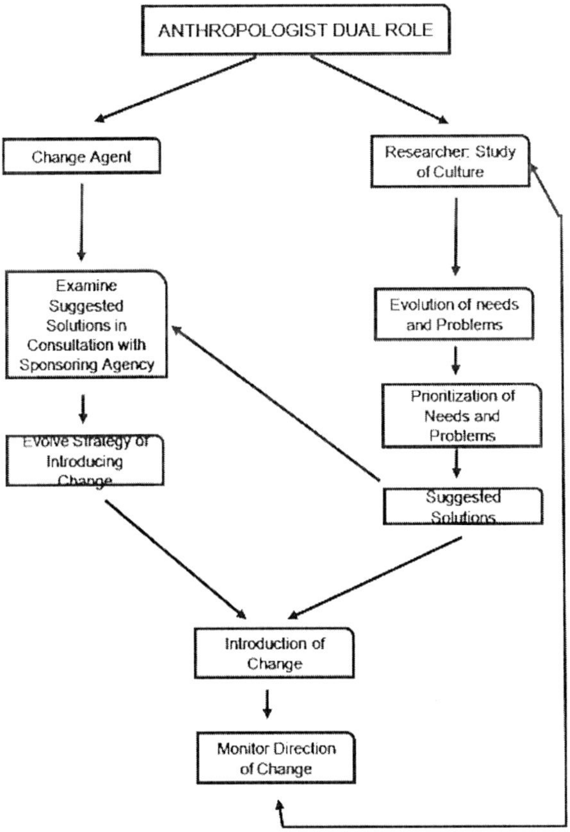

Source: Agarwal,Rao and Reddy 1985:4

Scudder and Colson Four Stage Model

In the early 1980s, building upon earlier approaches that dealt primarily with the processes of voluntary resettlement, Scudder and Colson proposed a four-stage model of, how people and socio-cultural systems respond to resettlement. The stages were labelled Recruitment, Transition, Potential Development, and Handing over or Incorporation. In the recruitment phase, policy-makers and/or developers formulate development and resettlement plans, often without informing those to be displaced. During transition phase, people learn about their future displacement, which heightens the level of stress experienced. Potential development occurs after physical relocation has occurred. Displacees begin the process of rebuilding their economy and social networks. Handing over or incorporation refers to the handing over of local production systems and community leadership to a second generation of residents that identifies with and feels at home in the community. Once this stage has been achieved, resettlement is deemed a success (Asthana 1996).

Reflection

This four-stage model proposed by Scudder and Colson is aimed to provide static picture of displacement and it does give suggestions neither to policy makers nor instructions in favour of Project Displaced Persons and Project Displaced Families to be implemented in the prescribed four stages. People's participation has not taken into consideration in this model, it has not thrown its light upon people's problems at these four stages and remedies for their problems, and it indirectly encourages displacement by neglecting the people's livelihood, environmental, educational, socio-politico-economic loss and cultural disturbances which is to give prime importance among all losses. It tries to provide description and diagnosis of the disease called displacement and resettlement but not the prescription and prognosis of the disease called displacement and resettlement. It has not considered the loss of flora and fauna in original villages which can't be replicable. It has not made any attempt to give suggestion/s to policy makers. It doesn't have any guiding principles not only to rebuild the economy of displaced people but also to build socio-cultural institutions in the resettlement colony.

IRR Model

Cernea's Impoverishment Risks and Reconstruction (IRR) model arose in the 1990s. In contrast to the Scudder and Colson model, the IRR model does not attempt to identify different stages of relocation, but rather aims to identify the impoverishment risks. Michael Cernea formulated this model to reconstruct the impoverished risks of the people by displacement. He points out the following 8 risks. 1. Landlessness, 2. Joblessness, 3. Homelessness, 4. Marginalisation, 5. Increased morbidity and mortality, 6. Food insecurity, 7. Loss of access to common property, 8. Social Disarticulation.

1. Landlessness: - The moment people were displaced from their village they become landless people. Their land, which is cradle of their culture, will be lost. 2. Joblessness: - When people are displaced, landless people will lose their wages. Even agriculturalists will lose their job i.e. cultivating land. Service workers (carpenters, pot maker), artisans or small businessmen will become jobless people. 3. Homelessness: - Loss of housing and shelter may be only temporary for many displacees but for some it remains a chronic condition. In a broader cultural sense, loss of family's individual home is linked with the loss of group's cultural space. 4. Marginalisation: - It occurs when families lose economic power. Middle class families will become small land holders, small shopkeepers will be slipped in to below poverty thresholds. Psychological marginalisation also occurs. Marginalisation enters into their social and behavioral veins. Economic marginalisation begins long before actual displacement. 5. Increased morbidity and mortality:-Serious decline in health will be caused social stress, insecurity, psychological trauma, diseases, particularly parasitic and vector borne diseases such as malaria. Unsafe water supply and poor sewerage system will lead to epidemics and chronic diarrhea, dysentery etc. The weaker people of the society, infants, children, pregnant women, and elderly people- are affected strongly due to unhygienic conditions. As a result the rate of morbidity goes up than the normal.

6. Food insecurity: -Forced displacement increases the risk and people will fall into chronic undernourishment, intake food level will be down seized because of food insecurity. 7. Loss of access to common property: -Typically, loss of common property assets is not compensated by government relocation schemes. Even in rehabilitation colonies, problems start with neighboring / host community with the common property (Forest lands, Water bodies, Grazing lands, Burial grounds, etc.). 8. Social Disarticulation:-Forced displacement tears the existing social fabric. It fragments communities, dismantles social organisation and interpersonal ties, kinship groups become scattered as well. They feel that they have lost their cultural identity. Community's spatial, temporal, and cultural determinants are gone.

Framework to reconstruct the risks

Michael Cernae also had given a Framework to reconstruct these eight risks that is being presented below. From Landlessness to land based resettlement, From Joblessness to reemployment, From Homelessness to house reconstruction, From Social disarticulation to community reconstruction, From Marginalisation to social inclusion, From Expropriation to restoration of community assets, From Food insecurity to adequate nutrition, From Increased morbidity and mortality to better health care

Michael Cernea's Impoverishment Risks Reconstruction Model has its own uniqueness as it has four functions. The first function is A diagnostic function: - Explanatory and cognitive function, the second one is A predictive function: - Warning and Planning function, third one is A problem-resolution function: - For guiding and measuring resettlers' reestablishment and the fourth one is A research function: for formulating hypotheses and conducting theory-led field investigations.

Additions to the IRR model

Apart from these eight risks, scholars like L.K. Mahapatra (1996), Robinson (2003), Sarbeswar Sahoo (2005) and Syam Kumar (2009) added four more impoverishment risks for the displaced people. They are as follows: Loss of Educational Opportunities (L.K. Mahapatra, 1996), Loss of Access to Community Service (Robinson, 2003), Violation of Human Rights (Sarbeswar Sahoo, 2005), Loss of Live Stock (Ch. Syam Kumar, 2009).

Displacement due to Nagarjuna Sagar Dam

Nagarjuna Sagar Dam is masonry Dam built on the Krishna River in Nagarjuna Sagar, Andhra Pradesh, India. It is the world's tallest masonry dam, at a height of 124 meters, and creates a reservoir holding up to 11, 472 million cubic meters. The hydroelectric plant has a power generation capacity of 815.6 MW with 8 units (1x110 MW+7x100.8 MW). Two canals were constructed to supply water from this reservoir to provide irrigation water for four districts i.e. Nalgonda, Prakasam, Khammam, and Guntur. The right canal (Jawahar canal) is 203 km long and irrigates 1.113 million acres (4,500 km^2) of land. The left canal (Lalbahadur Shastri canal) is 295 km long and irrigates 1.03 million acres (4,200 km^2) of land. Total Catchment Area is about 215000 sq. km (83012 sq. m).Approximately fifty two villages were submerged in this water reservoir and 24,000 people were affected. The issue of rehabilitation of the villagers from these submerged villages can be examined in order to understand the relevance and applicability of anthropological theoretical models to decipher social realities when a particular community is in a state of flux. Keeping this in view this paper tries to present the experiences of one of the resettled colonies i.e. Chinthala Thanda in which people from three different Banjara hamlets of Nalgonda district were resettled in Guntur District.

IRR Model in Anthropology

In a broader sense, IRR Model has its own unique and intricate relation with anthropology in all eight risks pointed out by Michael Cernea. Many anthropologists used this model to know the intricate tribal problems during displacement and resettlement, few anthropologists tried to give suggestions to the policy makers based on their empirical fieldwork experience.

Landlessness

Being anthropologists, we cannot isolate land from the natives' culture, as land is the cradle of their culture. For the purpose of this study, land has been divided in to three types based on the cultural importance. There may be other types of land that have immense cultural significance but study restricts to test the three types of land. They are: Agricultural Land, Cremation Land and Grazing Land. In these three types of land, socio-cultural factors can be observed. In agricultural land, before starting the agricultural work for that year, natives offer or perform some of the culturally driven religious activities like sacrifices or pooja and other religious performances to seek favors from gods or goddesses, for better yield. When they lost their original land, in which they have been practicing agriculture since time immemorial they not only lost the agricultural land but the cultural or religious activities, which were associated with their agricultural land.

As far as the cremation ground of their original village is concerned, during the burial of the dead, there will be many kinship obligations in cremation ground in disposing the dead, (The relatives are obliged to undertake various religious performances and prayers for dead person's soul to rest in peace in heaven). When they are displaced and resettled in alien places (Resettlement Colony) the government had no concern about this cremation ground and did not allot a place for village burial ground where plethora of their cultural and religious and kinship obligations were being performed in the original village.

As far as grazing land of their original village is concerned, in original village, traditional political leaders used to mark the grazing land boundaries to clan members in the Thanda. Accordingly, they must feed their livestock in the original village. Likewise, it has unique and intricate relation and association with socio-cultural institution. On contrary to their original village, in the resettled colony there was no grazing land provision for their livestock. When the oustees gone to the neighbouring villages to feed their livestock, there started rivalries between them and their neighbouring villagers, and it has created havoc in the resettlement colony.

Joblessness

Even in simple societies or preliterate societies, we can find occupational diversification and segmentation. For example, priest in the tribal habitation will not go to the field for cultivating the land as it is prescribed to him that he should be in the temple and perform religious rituals and ceremonies. He has to obey and perform the religious activities only. A carpenter will never adopt the washer men's job. Banjara's hamlet was simple and small in their number in original village; but still they had occupational diversification. They adopt their jobs according to their financial status and according to the instructions given by their elderly family members. They adopt agriculture and pastoralism. Although, they are in need of making agricultural implements, they don't produce these implements because it is inferior and can only be undertaken by carpenter who comes to their hamlet from the neighbouring village. But in resettled colony, in the early days of resettlement having no option they were forced to adopt new occupations.

Homelessness

For Banjaras home is the centre of their culture in original village as it has a place for their gods and goddesses and a place for their livestock which was considered worthy to worship. Structure and facing of the house used to be decided by the Priest. But in resettled colony there is no priest involvement in deciding about the entrance to the house. As a result, there is no place for livestock and fixed plans were given by NGO members called Village Reconstruction Organisation (VRO) who initiated the construction of their houses in the resettled colony. Home in original village and home in resettled colony which was constructed by VRO's initiation is different in structure and size.

Marginalisation

One of the bitterest outcomes of displacement is marginalisation. Michael Cernea talks about three types of marginalisation. 1. Psychological marginalisation; which actually starts when they were informed about their displacement from their original village and resettlement in alien places. 2. Economic marginalisation; which actually starts for them during resettlement itself. Nominal compensation paid to them was spent in no time as they have to construct the house and get each and every thing to live (food grains) from the market as they were resettled in alien land. 3. Social marginalisation; this was experienced by the Banjaras when rivalries were taken place with neighbouring villages with regard to grazing land.

Increased morbidity and mortality

In the original village, there used to be ethno-medical practitioner who was well versed with ethno-medicinal plants and preparation of ethno medicine with the leaves, tubers and plants, which are abundantly available in the forest. In the resettled colony, in initial years morbidity and mortality were high; as the government did not provide hospital facility. Ethno-medical practitioner was also in helpless position as they were away from the forest and their entire village was submerged in the reservoir. As a sequel, morbidity and mortality rate increased in the resettled colony.

Food insecurity

Banjaras experienced this loss also. In their original village, they were habituated to eat wheat bread. Rice was considered the sacred food as it was offered to the gods and goddesses. However, in resettled colony, especially in the early years of resettlement, they were forced to eat rice, which has religious importance and considered as sacred food as they have no grains to make wheat breads.

Loss of access to common property

The Banjaras also experienced this loss as they lost access to their common property like forest, grazing land, cremation land, and water channels of their original village. In resettlement colony there was neither common grazing land, nor cremation ground, nor forest and forest produces like fruits, which they collect and sell them in neighbouring villages and towns in their original village. Even water channels were not available in the resettlement colony for the purpose of drinking.

Social Disarticulation

Michael Cernea talks about social disarticulation that tears the existing social fabric. It fragments communities, dismantles social organisation and interpersonal ties, kinship groups become scattered. They feel that they have lost their cultural identity. Community's spatial, temporal, and cultural determinants have disappeared due to displacement.

Added loss by the researcher i.e. Loss of Livestock

Michael Cernea did not mention in IRR model about this loss. Based on the empirical data collected during the fieldwork and meticulous analysis of the data, it is proved that the Banjaras of Chinthala Thanda had experienced the loss of livestock as government officials did not allow the livestock for transportation by Lorries from the original village to the resettlement colony (Chinthala Thanda). The Banjaras are known for their pastoralism. This is true with the oustees of the Nagarjuna Sagar Dam also. In original village, they had both oxen and goats. However, during the displacement and resettlement government did not allow their livestock to be transported by Lorries. Nevertheless, for Banjaras livestock has tremendous importance in agriculture and in life cycle rituals too. This loss of livestock has affected their agricultural practice and life cycle rituals in the resettlement colony during the initial years. Although, their livestock is one of the source of their livelihood it has not taken in to consideration by the government officials. The Banjaras were informed in their original village that transportation facility will be provided from the original village to resettlement colony only for men and women but not for the livestock. As a sequel, all of them sold out their livestock in Devarakonda market of Nalgonda district at a low cost and came to the resettlement colony without livestock.

Oxen: A Constant Companion of the Banjaras

We the human beings have long history of our civilisation. The bio-socio cultural evolution was associated and accompanied by the animals like horse, donkey for our requirements. We are well aware of the fact that our fore fathers made use of elephants at the time of construction of historical monuments which are being considered as ornaments of India and international tourist spots. To support this statement Taj Mahal is the best example. We are well aware of the various facts that our forefathers made use of donkeys for transportation; but in Rajasthan camels are being used for transportation, in rural India live stock (goats, oxen, buffalos, chickens) are of not only economic assets, movable property but also they had cultural, ritual and ceremonial importance. Even in metropolitan cities also we can't restrict ourselves with our fellow human beings alone but we are deeply attached to domestic animals where by people dwelling in metropolitan city also yearn for pets. That is the kind of human-animal association we have been maintaining since time immemorial. Same is the case with that of Banjaras-Oxen association as Banjaras have long history of cattle rearing and pastoral life. The emotional attachment with oxen is seen than the loss of oxen is more than just loss. They feel that their family member is lost, if their oxen are lost, as it has not only supporting them and serving them but also stand as a symbol of religion.

They feed oxen as they feed and look after their children. Without oxen it is unimaginable be a Banjara. In ancient times, they used oxen for transportation from one place to another place as they were constantly wandering. They used to place their luggage on the oxen during their journeys from place to place. When they settled to live in hamlets or Thandas, then onwards they started to make use of the oxen in agriculture for ploughing the land for agriculture and for carrying the yielding on cart to the Thanda. In off-season the Banjaras, leave oxen freely so that they can graze in the open fields. They also go along with oxen to feed them and to herd them in the forest or in the field or in open grazing land. Banjaras care about the oxen and their health also.

During the festivals oxen are decorated beautifully by different colours. The oxen's tails are trimmed and decorated beautifully. Horns of the oxen were also cleansed with water and decorated with the flowers. Much care is taken during the Dipawali (Diwali) festival. A day before the festival the oxen are worshiped. They call it as *govardhana pooja* (worshipping the lord Krishna). The cow dung is used for plastering the floor of their houses.

Many people give several reasons for the importance given to the oxen. It is domesticated and mild animal; it is so powerful; it obeys and does not behave cruelly; it can walk long distances also; it eats grass and leaves which are plenty on the earth; it can bear hunger and thirst; it carries a lot of weight; it accompanies the other oxen; it will not forget the way in which it walks to return, it can withstand any weather conditions their back part is convenient to place luggage. The Banjara equate feeding oxen with fulfilling dharma (doing righteous acts). According to them, it is associated with their deity

Krishna. Although, oxen are part and parcel of the Banjaras' life, the government officials did not care about the livestock and announced that transportation facility is only for the people but not for the livestock. Therefore, having no option they sold in Devarakonda market at cheaper rate.

Conclusion

Among three anthropological theoretical models IRR model seems to be excellent and functional as it is well designed anthropologically. As the IRR model has four functions in which research function is also one. By utilizing this function based on the empirical data collected during intensive field work other risks can be added. Various scholars added risks to the ones identified by Cernea, still there is a space for others to adopt this model and to add few more risks or losses based on the empirical data. Cernea deserves appreciation as he provided space for research and further development of his IRR model unlike Scudder and Colson who proposed four stage model.

Acknowledgments

My heartfelt thanks to my M. Phil supervisor Prof: K.K. Misra and all faculty members at the department of anthropology, University of Hyderabad for their continuous guidance and lenient encouragement.

Bibliography

1. Agarwal C. Binod., N. Sudhakar Rao and P. C. Gurivi Reddy (1985), Yanadi Response to Change: An Attempt in Action Anthropology. New Delhi: Concept.
2. Asthana Roli. (1996). Involuntary Resettlement: International Experience. *EPW, 31 (24), 1468-1475.*
3. Baboo B. (1991). Big dam and tribals: the case of the Hirakud dam oustees in orissa. *Social Action, 41(3), 288-303.*
4. Baboo B. (1992). Development and Displacement: A Comparative study of rehabilitation of dam oustees in two Sub urban villages of Orissa. *Man in India, 72 (1), 1-14.*
5. Baviskar, A. (1995). In the Belly of River: Tribal conflicts over development in Narmada Valley. *Delhi: Oxford University Press.*
6. Behura, N.K., and P.K. Nayak. (1993). Involuntary displacement and the Changing Frontiers of Kinship: A Study of Resettlement of Orissa In M.M. Cernea and S.E. Guggnheim.eds., *Anthropological Approaches to Resettlement: Policy, Practice, Theory.* Boulder, Colo.: Westview Press.
7. Das, J.C. Fernandes Walter, Samrao. (1988).The extent and prospects of Displacement. *Social Action, 38(3), 264-281.*

8. Hakim, Roxanne. (2000). Agricultural Land: The Case of Hill Vasavas Displaced by the Sardar Sarovar Dam India. *Eastern Anthropologist, 53 (1-2), 73-94.*
9. Hakim, Roxanne. (2000). Changing Religion and Ritual in a Vasava Bhil community impacted by Involuntary Resettlement. *Eastern Anthropologist, 53 (1-2), 271-310.*
10. Iyer Rajani. (2005). Displacement and Resettlement: Bhima Irrigation Project in Mahatashtra. *Social Action, 55(2), 167-178.*
11. kothari Smitu. (1996). Whose nation? Displaced as victims of Development. *EPW, 31(24), 1476-1485.*
12. Mahapatra, L. K. (1991). Development for whom? Depriving the disposed tribals.*Social Action, 41(3), 271-287.*
13. Mahapatra, L. K. (1995), *The Orissa resettlement and rehabilitation of projects affected persons policy, 1994: A critique,* Social Action, 45, (3):318-326.
14. Mahapatra, L. K. (1995). The Orissa Resettlement and Rehabilitation of Projects Affected Person's Policy, 1994: A critique. *Social Action, 45 (3), 318-326.*
15. Mahapatra, L.K. (2000). Resettlement with participation: The Indian experience.*Eastern Anthropologist, 53 (1-2), 121-140.*
16. Mahapatra, L.K. and Sheela Mahapatra. (2000). Social Rearticulation, In M.Cernea and C. McDowell (eds), Risks and Reconstruction, *Washington,DC: The World Bank.*
17. Mallavarapu Rambabu. (2007). Development, Displacement and Rehabilitation: An Action Anthropological Study on Kovvada Reservoir in West Godavari Agency of Andhra Pradesh, India.*International Journal of Social Science, 1(1), 35-41.*
18. Mathur, Hari Mohan. (1999). The impoverishing Potential of Development Projects. Resettlement Requires Risk Analysis, Development and Cooperation, *No.6Frankfurt: Deutsche Stifrung fur International Enteicklung*
19. Mathur, Hari Mohan. (2000). Big Projects and Poverty: Displacement and Resettlement in Rajasthan, India. *Eastern Anthropologist, 53 (1-2), 193-200.*
20. Mathur, Hari Mohan. (2006). Making Resettlement Work: Issues in Planning and Management.*Eastern Anthropologist, 59(2), 157-177.*
21. Michael, M Cernea (1996), *Public policy responses to population displacements,* EPW, 31, (24):1515-1523.

22. Michael, M Cernea (1997), the *risks and reconstruction model for resettling displaced populations,* World Development, 25, (10): 1569-1588.
23. Michael, M. Cernea (1995), *Understanding the preventing Impoverishment from displacement: reflections on the state of knowledge,* Social Action, 45, (3):261-276.
24. Misra Kamal. K. and Narendra Bondla D.J. (2007). Resettlement and Rehabilitation in India The emic Tribal Perspective. *C.W.S: Hyderabad.*
25. Pandey, Balaji. (1998). Displaced development,Impact of Open Cast Mining on Women, New Delhi: *Friederich Ebert Stifung.*
26. Patnaik, S.M. (2000). Understanding Involuntary Resettlement: An Anthropological Perspective. *Eastern Anthropologist, 53 (1-2), 141-160.*
27. Perera, Jayantha. (2000). Compensation versus Rehabilitation in the Singrauli Resettlement Projects India. *Eastern Anthropologist, 53 (1-2), 53-72.*
28. Sahoo Sarbeswar. (2005). Tribal Displacement and Human rights violations in orissa. *Social Action, 55(2), 154-166.*
29. Sapkota, Nogendra. (2000). Using the Risks and Reconstruction Model in Resettlement Planning: KaliGandaki Dam, Nepal. *Eastern Anthropologist, 53 (1-2), 201-212.*
30. Sarbeswar, Sahoo (2005), *Tribal displacement and human rights violations in orissa,* Social Action, 55(2):154-166.
31. Swain Mamta, & Ganesh, Khadanga. (2000). Rehabilitation measures and pitfalls: A case of Gohira Colony, Orissa. *Eastern Anthropologist, 53 (1-2), 285-297.*
32. Walter, Fernandes (1991), *power and powerlessness: development projects and displacement of tribals,* Social Action, 41, (3):243-270.
33. Walter, Fernandes (1995), *an activist process around the draft national rehabilitation policy,* Social Action, 45, (3):277-298.
34. Walter, Fernandes (1995), *Displacement and rehabilitation,* EPW, 30, (39): 2460.
35. Walter, Fernandes (2005), *rehabilitation as a right: where is the policy,* Social Action, 55(2):123-137.

22

Significance of Traditional Community Festivals of the Santal in Maintenance of Ecological Balance to reduce effect of Global warming

Sudip Bhui and Pradip Kumar Mandal

Introduction

Global environmental education has a short history as its institutional and formal curriculum. Anthropogenic causes of environmental degradation after industrial civilisations breach the sustainable relationships between Earths and its creatures. The human get achieve a n enormous means by their inventions and discoveries capable to change effects of nature in course of safety and comfort living from the Neolithic cultural periods. Then they become regulators of nature and gradually in accordance of increasing population density bring forth a boost to breach the harmony of man-Nature-Earth relationship. People, from their pristine period keep a close proximity with nature which starts to decay as degree of technological advancement. Indigenous people remain at a less advanced phase of exploitation of existing natural resources. On same way the intermingled socio-cultural life of these people makes recurring effort to keep harmonious relation between man and nature. Cultural sanction of Tribal people (i.e. Indigenous in case of India) empowered through rituals, taboo and customs regulate the culturally affiliated regular and occasional behaviour. In majority of Tribal religions advocate nature as messiah, mother, protector or host for their people. Nature is the abodes of their ancestral spirits. Reminiscence of the bygone days reflects these ethical matters by their beliefs and worldview of the Tribal people.

Ancestors of the Tribal communities go through enumerable trial and error interaction with natural phenomenon in course of collection and cultivation of food and other commodities like medicine, house material safety etc. these invaluable experiences were included in realm of religious thinking and beliefs. Trial and error interactions some time get scientific base also, for these potentialities scientists, policy makers; academicians give importance this indigenous knowledge in searching the means for sustainable environment as well as advancement of human civilisation. Fair and festival s among the tribal people is enriched with a vast body of indigenous knowledge to serve their community in region specific and universal problems. The Santal community with an enriched cultural heritage are known to the literal by a series of research investigation from study of colonial administrators, native amateur and other. They are the most numerable tribal community in west Bengal and make domination throughout eastern India.

Literature review

There are several conventions and conferences in quest of sustainable environment. Article 8(j) of the Convention on Biological Diversity requires parties to "respect, preserve and maintain knowledge, innovations and practices of indigenous and local communities embodying traditional lifestyles relevant for the conservation and sustainable use of biological diversity."(Jones, 2012).Indigenous communities generally have a concepts of origin of their land and nature through god's creations and is as an integral part of many traditional indigenous religious belief systems (Ntiamoa-Baidu 1990). Indigenous knowledge is the local knowledge which is unique to a given culture or society (World Bank, 1997). Indigenous Knowledge is the information base for a society,and facilitate in communication and decision-making. Indigenous information systems are not static and are continually influenced by internal creativity and experimentation along with contact with external systems. The religious belief serves a UNGA report advocates frequencies of participation of indigenous women experts in mitigate climateChange throgh planning and decision making processes(UNGA,2009).Indigenous Protected Area under Australian Government understand great cultural significance to the people as a, traditional tribal territory which place patronize as mythologically important sites(CA,2007) as an active force in protection of rare forest species (Pandey 2003).Participatory mode of preservation utilised in want of rains, good health of livestock and for fendingoff possible natural hazards. In purpose of well being of domestic cattle, people from some parts of Karnataka,offer miniature images of cattles (Kalam 1996). The Bhils tribal of Ratanmal,offer food and liquor to their Sacred Groves on Deepawali (Nath 1960). In case of Tribal of West Bengal, social gathering takes place in the vicinityof Sacred Grovess on the eve of Salui and Karam festivals (Deb and Malhotra 1997). Similarly, Anthwal et al. (2006) found some people of Uttarakhand perform their religious rituals with Azadirachta indica (Sheela asthami, Nimb saptami), Ficus bengalensis(Vrat savitiri), Aegle marmelos (Bilvamengal sawanke somvaar), etc.

Objectives

The present research work is focused on following Objectives:-

(i) Find out the basic nature and purpose of fair and festival of the Santal community of southern West Bengal in purpose of sustainable environmentin mitigate Global Warming.

(ii) Analyse the concerned beliefs and worldview in searching of environmental protection.

(iii) Examine the relation of seasonal natural changes and occurrences of festivals in relation of regional climatic sustainability..

Methodology

The data for this research was gathered with a preliminary survey, among the elderly folks of the Santal community from villages under Manbazar and Balarampur block. Structured questionnaires are collected from the potential informants found from the preliminary survey. Queries emerge from the literature survey are helpful to frame these questionnaires. Some case studies are also taken in purpose of special rituals and procedures of festival.

The Santals has a number over two millions in India, have been enumerated in Bihar according to the 1941 census as 13, 92, 744as amended after the transfer of territories to West Bengal in 1956. This tribe habitation is mainly in the states of West Bengal, Jharkhand, Odisha, Jharkhand and Assam.

Santal follow the Sarna religion. Their God and Goddess are Marangburu, Jaheraera, and Manjhi. The most amazing fact about Santhal is that they pay respect to the ghosts and spirits like Kal Sing, Lakchera and Beudarang etc. Santals have village priests known as the Naiki and Shaman Ujha.

Santals mainly celebrate the Karam festival which falls in the month of September and October. They celebrate this festival to please the God to increase their wealths and free them from all the enemies. It is the tradition among the Santals to grow the Karam tree outside their house after the purification process. Other festivals of the Santals community include Maghe, Baba Bonga, Sahrai, Ero, Asaria and Namah. They also celebrate hunting festival called Disum sendra on the eve of Baishakhi Purnima. This study was undertaken in four villages of Balarampur and Manbazar blocks.

Festivals of the Santal

Round the year the 'Santals' engage themselves in the worship of nature in some way or other. They have been worshiping for generations the tree, stone, water, Sun, land, fire, or rather the so-called Panchabhutas' that constitute the cosmos.

Traditionally, the year for the 'Santals' begins from the Bengali month 'Magh' that corresponds to the month of February in English calendar. Of all the festivals they have, mention may be made of

[1] 'Maghmura'-a festival to occur at the end part of the Bengali month 'Magh'.

[2] 'Baha'-a festival of flower in the Bengali month Phalgun' and Chaitra.

[3] 'Maa-morre'-a religious festival to occur at the Bengali month 'Baisakh'.

[4] Eroy sim'-a festival of agriculture in the Bengali month 'Baisakh' & 'Jaistha'.

[5] 'Asari'-a festival of plantation in the Bengali month 'Asar'.

[6] 'Karam'-a festival of work and plantation related to the Bengali month 'Bhadra'.

[7] 'Hardier sim'-a festival for good harvest related to the month of `Bhadra'.

[8] 'Dasay'-a festival for expansion of the Santal community related to the Bengali month 'Aswin'.

[9] 'Jan thard' — a crop harvesting festival.

[10] Saharay- festival for pleasure in the Bengali month 'Kartick'.

[11] 'Akhian'-festival of hunting in the Bengali month Pous'.

However, 'Maa-morre', 'Saharay', 'Dasay' and 'Akhan' have no direct impact on environmental association for which they have not been discussed here.

We can go through major festivals of Santal community-

(1) 'Maghmura'- The Santal religious activity of a year really begins with the festival whichd they call 'Maghmura'. The word 'Maghmura' derives from two words 'Magh' [the Bengali month] and ['mura' the end part]. Therefore the festival is seen to occur at the end of the month 'Magh'. This religious performance was done generally by keeping a huge stone under the shade of a bunch of long 'sal' trees at the extreme corner of the village.

The adults of each house bound to be present there in the occasion. The place of puja is a platform to count and record the number of people of the said village; may be a type of annual census. Apart from this, the people engage themselves in performing the worship of the 'panchabhutas'- the five essential elements. Then special medical suggestions are given to the household adults to take necessary steps to get rid of many diseases. For examples people are denied to use oil and to take glossy meals etc.

They are administered with special concoctions made of several herbs and roots namely Nikantha, Anantamul, Shetmul, Ramdatan, Bonkul etc. It is peculiar enough that they are most democratic in their spirit as they take all these medical doses unhesitatingly sitting together in one fixed place. This is done to foster in them the power of immunisation in a natural way. The chapter never ends there; on this occasion medicines are given for each house to keep them safety measures against diseases for the entire year.

(2) Baha:- The santals observe this festival in the month of Phalgun and Chaitra the month following Magh. They worship in this month three gods represented respectively by Marang Bum (the big hill), Jaher Ayo (the soild that is tilled) and Morre Ko Turui Ko. (the Santa! Counter part of Panchabhuta).

The Word 'Baha' itself is flower, and therefore this festival religiously suggests that the people will be forbidden to enter the forest till the flowers beging to sprout in the 'sal' trees, This religious injunction has a motive which is explicit. These people want to see nature in her fullest from and the most spontaneous manifestation without any human intervention. In this time nobody is allowed to kill wild animals. Financilal punishments are rules. In this festival they sing many songs like this:-

" Hesa ma Chotere
Ja gosay tude doy rage kan.
Bare ma laobere
Ja gosay gutrut doy saheda."

As a fact, efforts are being made through these religious rights to preserve nature and the wild life. In spite of their abysmal darkness of ignorance, their environmental awareness is praiseworthy. It is not denying the fact that 'poverty and greeneryare one and the same thing; indeed they are synonymous.

(3) Eroy-Sim:- This festivalis observed in the month of 'Baisakh' & 'Jaistha', the period of early monsoon. The work[4] 'eroy' means seed and the word 'sim' means cock. Cocks are sacrified at the altar of the village deity for better yield. Agricultural activities in the agrarian santal community are not allowed in this period to enter the forest. This is done to avoid loss of the saplings.

(4) Asari:- The festival is observed in the shade of such huge plants and the area that surrounds it. With this festival the Santals go for planting after the seeds germinate and become standard shaplings.

During this festival, generally it is seen that plantation is a routine programme. Everybody participates in this plantation business. Trees are planted not only near the place of puja but also the area surrounding it. The present a forestation agenda owes much to them. It had already been a part of their religious activities.

(5) The festival related to the month of 'Bhadra' is 'Karam'. The word 'Karam' means work. The festival is observed in the shade of huge plants popularly known to them as 'Majhi than'. The 'Karam dal' i.e. a branch of specific tree is planted in 'Majhi than'. The 'Karam dal' is coverd by a new cloth. The head of every family gives a true account of his own family,touching the 'Karam dal'. One song of this festival is :-

Aokare dom Jaham Lena
Sili lekan karam.
Aokare dom Upel lena
Nao hori dour.
Bure re dom Janam lena
Sili lekan karam dow.
Harare dom Upel lena
Nao hori dour.

Seven days prior to the festival, 'Jawa brata' i.e. the festival of germination of seeds starts. This festival is rigorously observed. This germination is the symbol of production of corns. The santals vow to do away with evil deeds and to dedicate themselves to noble mission. They also vow to withhold famine, produce corn and worship tre as deity. These, no doubt, testify to the santals' consciousness of nature.

The second festival related to the month of Bhadra' is popularly known as 'Hiriar Sim'. This festival has special significance for them. As the name suggests, this goes with the sacrifice of the cocks at the after of deities for overwhelming joy for bumper harvest and green wood atmosphere. In this time, to protect the growing plants and the crops especially the paddy plant from insects. They spread leaves of various trees which act as insecticides.

Festivals and Caring Objectives among the Santal

	Important Months	*Festivals*	*Caring and worshipping objects*
1.	Magh	Magh mura,	Sal Tree, Pancha Bhut, medicinal herbs like Nilkantha, Anantamul, Shal mul, etc.
2.	Phalgun	Baha,	Big Hill, Sal and other trees, conservation of animals
3.	Baisakh and Jaishtha	Ma More, Eroy Sim,	Things responsible for better Agricultural production
4.	Asar	Asari,	Seedlings, plants of tree
5.	Bhadra	Karam, 'Harier sim'	Germinations of seeds of crops

The abovementioned table express the major festivals of the Santal tribe commence and celebrated with harmony of seasonal change. Their month starts with Magh (Jan-Feb) when flowers of Sal tree blossom their ancestors were hunters gatheres, so hunting festivals also present now. Productivity of animals ans plants of forest is also subject of their festive activities. Annual and bi-annually medicinal herbs die after winter season in this relation they preserve and discuss about these herbs. Now, their main occupation is agriculture and agricultural activities are endorsed with their religious and festive life.

Discussion

Natural specimens are surviving, contribute and maintain regional biodiversity to absorb excess heat of earth and environment. Plants have own mechanism to maintain the water cycle through their various rate of evaporation through total body area. Seasonal cycle maintain a good rhythm to perennial heat transmission in respect to soil and soil contents. Religious life oriented festivals and fair are closely attached to seasonal changes of surrounding flora and fauna, climatic conditions. The essential things in their day to day life especially in occupation, subsistence get importance as ingredients in the processes of these festivals. Seasonal rhythm and harmony extent their influence in socio-cultural life of the habitants and create an web in mind of these people. Performances strongly advocate preserving, nurturing and remaining un-interrupted in natural course of life support phenomenon. Traditional beliefs and ethics exist as latent to socio-cultural life. These factors regulate daily activities and thinking of the particular community. Through these concepts help them take care the elements of nature on the way to sustainable earth. Discussions, performances and hearing about glory of stewardship of their renowned ancestors. Interactions of ancestors with Devine objects and personalities also act as regulating guideline in religious performances. Folk story, lore, ballads, song are also gear up the devotion and pleasure of these festivals. People get motifs and cognitions to interact with these natural plants and animals over make contribution in their personalities.

Conclusion

The reflections from festival prove their mentality as equity among the natural members both flora and fauna. In this ground they respect these elements and remain interruptions in reproduction, propagation and survival of plants and animals. The Santal generally live in hilly and forest area and abstain from well communicable civilised area in proximity of nature generally less educated. Printed and communicable media to protection of environment are not available and intelligible to them. But traditional system of regulating environment protection is more effective to them. Government of Australia, Africa, and New Zealand take initiatives in policy, research and implementation level to utilise indigenous knowledge on way to sustainable Earth. In India, more than 8% of its inhabitants belong to the Indigenous group. Many committees are formed from indigenous people in cope of problems of Global warming. It is difficult and almost impossible to apply same method in different climatic zones in this connection expertise in regional traditional knowledge preserved from ritualistic life along with the festivals. Except participatory actions in preservation, there are very few initiatives present here. In coming days we have to make more and more unique research to live in sustainable mother Earth.

References

1 Anthwal A, et.al. 2010 Conserving biodiversitythrough traditional beliefs in sacred groves in Uttarakhand Himalaya, India.Resour Conserv Recy 54:962–997.

2 Bodding P O 2013(reprint) Traditions of Institutions of the Santal; Gian Publishing, Delhi.

3 3.Commonwealth of Australia 2007 Growing up Strong;*The first 10 years of Indigenous Protected Areas in Australia, Australia.*

4 Culsaw C J 1949(2013) Tribal Heritage; a study of the Santal, Gian Publishing, New Delhi.

5 Deb D, Malhotra KC 1997 Interface between biodiversity and tribal culturalheritage: an exploratory study. J Hum Ecol 8:157–163.

6 Jones, G 2012 Special Report, March 2012;The Importance of Indigenous Knowledge and Good Governance to; Ensuring Effective Public Participation in Environmental Impact; ISTF NEWS, Maryland 20814, USA

7 Kalam MA 1996 Sacred Groves in Kodagu District of Karnataka (South India): ASocio-Historical Study. Institute Francais de Pondicherry, Pondicherry, India

8 Mahapatra P M and P C Mahapatra 1997 Forest Management in Tribal Area; Concept Publishing,New Delhi

9 McNeely, J. and D. Pitt. 1985. *Culture and Conservation: The Human Dimension in Environmental* Planning.(eds.): Croom Helm Press, Dover, New Hampshire.

10 Menon V 2012 Envirinment and Tribes in Indian Context; concept (ed.), New Delhi

11 Murmu K C 2004 The Santal Customs of Usages ; murmur brothers, Jamshedpur

12 Nath YVS 1960 Bhils of Ratanmal, Maharaja Sayajirao University. Baroda. Oxfordand IBH Publishing Co., New Delhi, pp 289–300

13 Ntiamoa-Baidu, Y. 1990. "Coastal Wetlands Conservation: The Save the Seashore Birds Project." In *Living With Wildlife: Wildlife*

Resource Management with Local Participation in Africa. edited byA. Kiss. World Bank, Washington, D.C.

14. Pandey DN 2003 Sacred Forest: The Case of Rajasthan. India in Forest Service,India, pp 1–16
15. Paty C R 2007 Forest Government and Tribe; Concept Publishing, New Delhi
16. Rappaport. R. *1979. Ecology, Meaning and Religion.* Berkeley, North Atlantic Books; California.
17. Rappaport. R. 1968. *Pigs for the Ancestors.* Yale University Press: New Haven
18. Sumner,J 2006 protecting farmers' indigenous knowledge: organic agriculture and environmental adult education ; Adult Education and Community Development Program, University of Toronto, Toronto.
19. United Nations General Assembly 2009 Report of the Indigenous Peoples' Global Summit on Climate Change, 20 – 24 April 2009,Anchorage, Alaska
20. World Bank. 1987. *Ghana Forestry Sector Review.Report No. 6817-GH.* World Bank.,Washington, D.C.

23

Rites of Passage among the Totos of Bengal, India: Tradition and Transformation

Md. Intekhab Hossain and Syed Abul Hafiz Moinuddin

Introduction

A small isolated tribe known as the Totos comprising of 1268 people (NBU: 2004) including 671 males and 597 females have been residing at the foothills of the Himalaya closed to Bhutan in a small village named Totopara in Jalpaiguri district of West Bengal since time immemorial. It is said that Totopara is the only place in the world where this tiny group of tribes are concentrated. Totos are one of the most primitive tribal groups of the world and are considered as vanishing tribe. They have been retaining their many traditional customs, cultural traits, rites and rituals due to their confinement in complete isolation. Their various unique and strange customs and rituals related to their various stages of life are also enduring. These Indo-Bhutanese Mongoloid stock aborigines are not only one of the Primitive Tribal Group (PTG) of West Bengal but also one of the six underdeveloped tribes of the state. It is believed that these indigenous people have been living there for at least seven generations from today and according to the linguistic researches of Dr. Grierson and Prof. S. K. Chatterjee, they speak in Sinno-Tibetan language and do not have any script. Most of the youth can speak Bengali and Nepali which are the mediums of instruction in the local schools. As Mitra (1951) states, "Excluded from the President of India's list of seven Scheduled Tribes in West Bengal the Totos suffer an anonymity which is wholly underserved. He has the unique distinction of belonging to a very rare race; it lives in only one village in the wide world, has a spoken language of its own and numbers only about 325 souls". Anthropologists agree that the culture and language of the Totos are completely unique to the tribe distinguished noticeably from the neighbouring Rajbongshis, Koch, Mech or the Bhutanese Sharchop tribes of the region.

Discussion

Life cycle is a typically used metaphor denoting the passageway of a human being through the successive stages of life from birth to death through childhood, adolescence, adult life and old age. With regards to the rites of passage of Indian tribes, Vidyarthi and Rai (1977) have pointed out that the diverse *sanskars*, mostly on the event of bath, marriage and death, are also part of a tribal's life. The parents, elders and friends facilitate him in order to acquire a mate and a ritual of marriage is performed. The songs and dances of marriage enthuse him to the new wedded life. The coming and resent of relatives on the event connect him in a close kinship relation. When he is blessed with a child after a lapse of time, it is the good grace of the spirit and ritual of birth is crucial for propitiating the gods and the ancestors. This is also taken as the wish of spirit when his parents attain old age and depart this life and the ritual of death becomes a must to satisfy the deceased for the benefit of the living members of the family. Therefore, all these *sanskars* lead to the ritualistic socialisation of a tribal individual. The mythologies behind the diverse rituals, gods and deities give him a psychological sanction in order to lead his life and behave in the way of his community members. While talking about the life of the tribal, Vidyarthi and Rai (1977) state, "The tribals observe different *sanskars* mainly on three occasions, viz., at birth, marriage and death. A few other *sanskars* like the ceremony to approve socially a man as father of a child (without taking note of the biological factors), name given ceremony, etc., are also observed. Each of these tribal *sanskars* is preceded or followed by a sacrifice of an egg, fowl or animal. Like Hindus the tribals also worship and invoke their *kul* or *Gotra devata* (god of clan or lineage), Family deities, *sthan-devata* (god of the place) *and gram devata* (god of the village) during different ceremonies of the *sanskars*.......An individual proceeds from one experience to another in the course of his life, in order to that he may feel himself more and more at one with his people of which he is part. A tribal child (male or female) first experiences all love and affection in the lap of his mother. He is mostly near her or on her back. He learns a few modes of behavior from his elder brothers and sisters who take care of him in their mother's absence and in their leisure hours and in this way he comes in contact with friends, older boys and girls, neighbourhood and so on. He gradually comes of age and gathers new experiences and behaves accordingly. The different rituals or *sanskars* only signify that the individual is being entrusted with certain obligations and responsibilities for his own welfare as well as for the welfare of the community." Therefore, the study of life-cycle means the study of incidents happened in different stages of life of every individual.

Birth Rites of the Totos

The birth rituals of the Totos are very interesting and also strange. They consider children are the reborn of their grandfather or grandmother, or father or mother, or any other immediate kin who dies. With regard to the birth of a child among the tribe of India, Vidyarthi and Rai (1977) point out, "In every tribe of india, we find a certain degree of knowledge about the secret of birth of a child. Though the father and mother are held directly responsible for the birth still the supreme Bonga, Dharmesh or God is supposed to be the sole and ultimate authority. The birth of a child which satisfies the natural eagerness of parenthood is joyful occasion for them, whether the child is male or female. But as the girl in most of the tribal societies of India fetches a bride price for the parents, the father of a female child feels slightly exalted." Generally, there is no any proper care during pregnancy among them. The pregnant girl or woman is involved in household activities, agriculture, fetching water and also goes to the jungle to collect fuel. But before and after delivery about two months are taken for the care of the mother. During that time she does not go out even her parents' house. Delivery takes place in the groom's house and during that time relatives including one or two oldest and also experienced women from bride's house come and they are remain present at the house of the groom. One of these women cuts the umbilical cord by a typical knife called *'Lengtosey'* in Toto term. Then the umbilical cord is buried into a hole under the ground. After birth up to about one month the husband lives separately outside his wife's room. For the healing of wound, that particular knife is being rubbed on that injured area several times for few days. Sanyal (1972) states "After a child is born the mother spins out some thread (*Shang-de*) herself and colours it with turmeric and ties it round the hand of the child. It is usually done on the seventh day. Sometimes on the ninth, eleven or fifteen day this is done. In any of these days the village Chowkidar, a Government employee, or the headman (Mondal) or any priest comes to the house at dawn and gives the child a name……The Chowkidar, the headman, or the priest, whoever happens to come for the purpose at first, drinks a bowlful of liquor and then the members of the house-hold drink. The child must have a drop in its mouth. Then the child gets the blessings '*Janwalla*' (God be pleased with you). The Chowkidar or the headman or priest moves round the village to tell everyone he meets the name of the new born. In naming the child usually the name of the great grandfather is repeated." They keep a name given ceremony after seven or nine days when the umbilical cord is detached from the new born or birth and a name is given by the village priest and consecutively worship is organised on this day which they call *'Madingpapoua'*. For this occasion they clean the baby and wear the baby new cloths. On behalf of the new born family, their relatives from different neighboring villages or places are invited to join the ceremony. As per their financial status they perform feast period. The financially weak family is not capable to do so while the family who is financially sound performs the activity of feast period called *'Badilangpapua'* in their local terminology.

Marriage Rites of the Totos

Marriage is a societal union in which two adult persons of both sexes are bound together for an eternal relationship. "Marriage is generally considered a contract by the tribals. This gives rise to a certain pattern of selecting mates which is generally followed when both boys and girls are still adults. Due weight is given to the views of both the boys and the girls in the selection of a partner. The tribal marriage is generally regarded as a civil contract and not a religious sacrament and, therefore, religious solemnisation does not take place (Majumder and Madan, 1956)." Among the Totos the main conception behind marriage is that it is the way by which one can become esteemed in the society. These people are monogamous in nature and posses single spouse at a time throughout the life. In case of the death or divorce of the spouse the Toto can remarry and remain monogamous again. The cases of divorce are hardly found in their society. This endogamous tribe does not permit exogamy but in few cases exogamy is happened due to fall in love. Preferential cousin marriage is the most prevalent form of marriage practiced by this indigenous community. Basically cross-cousin marriage is formed among the Totos of Totopara. In such marriage, the bride is to be a daughter of groom's father's sister or groom's mother's brother's daughter and vice-versa. But in some cases, we also find marriages outside cross-cousin. There are two prevalent ways of acquiring companion found among them, Marriage by negotiation and Love marriage or marriage by elopement.

Marriage by negotiation is the traditional way of marriage practice among the Totos. In this case, the parents of the groom side come to the bride's house first and talk to her parents about their son's marriage with their daughter and if the bride's parents agree with the groom's parents, then marriage is fixed which is called betrothal. But the date of the ceremony is totally depended on the capability of both of their financial circumstances. The financially sound family organizes the ceremony immediately whereas the financially weak family or who is unable to do so at the same time due to some diseases or work pressure or some other sort of problems at that moment, they take some times. But the time-duration should not be more than one year or one and a half years and must be before the birth of a first child in order to organize the marriage ceremony. Ultimately, they must have to organize the ceremony and invite all the villagers along with their relatives for the social recognition of the married couple. As Sanyal (1972) points out, "In recent years marriage customs of the Totos have undergone some changes. The father of the son goes to the house of the girl with the proposal of marriage carrying with him some pan-gua. If the marriage is settled either the girl comes away with the father of the groom or she is allowed to stay on with her father till she grows sufficiently older. She then goes to the house of her father-in law and lives with the boy. During her stay in her father's house she may be married elsewhere provided due compensation in the shape of one pitcherful of liquor and rupees five only are paid to the father of the boy. But after the girl comes away to the house of the boy no question of marriage elsewhere arises."

Love marriage or marriage by elopement is occurred when two lovers are not allowed to get married by each or either of their parents, they run away and get married. In such case both of their parents' permission or consent does not perform any role. The circumstances of divorce, though very rare, when arise in the life of the Totos, the administrative committee comprising of the members of both the families and also the villagers who act as a medium in order to look after the matter in case of divorce is going to be formed. The committee, at first, give advice to both the groom and bride to compromise each other's fault or guilty. Next to this step when they come to realize one's guilty, they give punishment to the culprit but if the culprit denies his or her blame, the offender is assaulted and beaten by hand and sticks. After giving such punishment to the offender, ultimately divorce takes place between the couple.

Remarriage is permitted among the Totos in case of both the widower and widow respectively. But it takes at least one year after the death or separation of the previous spouse to get remarried. After the death of the wife, the husband usually marries his deceased wife's younger sister which is commonly known as sororate but in case of the death of the husband, the wife is not allowed to marry her husband's any sibling which marriage is known as levirate. Hence, sororate is permitted but levirate is prohibited among the Totos. But the widow or the widower is not compelled to remarry. It is up to their respective choice.

Totos are eligible to keep pre-marital relationship in case of only those who are unmarried and in the meantime are bound and determined to get married with the fixed or same individual. These two persons are socially permitted to keep pre-marital physical relationship and also are allowed to live together for a long or short time period. However, they cannot bring new born unless or until a marriage ceremony is organised inviting all the community members at the ceremony as per their norms. Incest marriages are firmly prohibited among the Totos. In their marriage applying turmeric and cosmetics or any other form of formalities are not maintained usually. Dowry is almost absent among these primitives.

Death Rites of the Totos

Death is the ultimate conclusion of the existence of an entity. It is one of the expected phenomenon happened with every individual at a certain phase of life due to some certain specific reason. As Vidyarthi and Rai (1977) observe, "Like other men of the world, the tribal people also have no definite knowledge about the nature of death, but they take it as a mystic terror. They have a conviction that death is an accidental event and the anger of the so-called gods and deities, the ancestral souls, sorcery, with-craft, etc., are responsible for the same. In the case of suspicious death, the sorcerer or witches are punished directly by beating them to death or indirectly by the magic with the help of special witch diviners.

As in other societies, the tribals also have a set of actions to deal with the death of their people. When a death occurs a series of customs are observed at different stages like before the funeral, after the funeral, etc. All the activities and rituals performed after the death of a person are called death-rites prevailing in a particular community to which the dead belonged. The tribes of India have a pattern of dealing with the dead and various rites are performed at different stages like:

(i) Observances in the house of the deceased; (ii) Mode and place of disposal of corpse, *viz*., (a) Cremation, (b) Burial, (c) Exposure, (d) Preservation, (e) Disposal in water; (iii) Mourning period and ceremonies, *i.e*., mourning rites and purification; (iv) Funeral Feast; (v) Annual death ceremony or Final death ceremony or Ancestor worship." However, the Totos believe that death occurs due to ill-treatment of diseases and malevolent spirit attack. Here are some universal conclusions regarding the concept of death among the aforesaid privatives. They believe that the death occurs mainly due to disease and attack of evil spirit. When anybody goes to the mountain or hill or jungle to collect fuel or anything else or goes outside the village where the individual sees any supernatural being in the journey and she or he becomes shocked and afraid dangerously owing to which the person may be died shortly and suddenly after coming back to home.

When the any of the family members first realize the death of the individual, the news is first informed to the head of the family and gradually others and afterward to the neighbors. At this time, an old man particularly belonging to *'Dantrodey'* clan who is called *'Leimy'* must have to come to utter the word *'Dineampura'* meaning the person is dead. The role of *'Leimy'* is very crucial. They cannot bury their dead body until the *'Leimy'* comes.

The neighbors and the *'Leimy'* make a *'Topa'* made of bamboo stick by which they bring the dead body which they call *'Limu'* at the burial ground. After placing the body on the *'Topa'* without removing his or her cloths or without departing any objects he or she had possessed with his or her at the time of death. The four persons either from the family members or from the neighbors and the *'Leimy'* bring the death body by the *'Topa'* carrying on their shoulder to the burial ground along with a small group of 12-15 persons who are the relatives or the neighbors of the deceased persons but at least 3-4 individuals must be *'Leimy'* who dig a hole about 2-3 feet depth for lying of the body comfortably by them. After digging the hole the dead body is placed along with a compulsory sum of Rs 20/- to Rs 21/- and a meal. In the former days, they had the tendency to burry all the deposited hard earning money, any expensive object or a big amount of money or ornaments of the deceased person along with the dead body. The four men give sand on the hole and after fulfilling the hole with sand, some medium to big sized stones of about 1-4 feet are technically placed around the buried place so that wild animals cannot easily take away the dead body from the hole.

Pollution period is observed by this tribal people. They purify themselves by washing their hands and legs with warm water after returning from the burial ground. This period is observed whole the day by the male members of the family and it lasts up to a week in case of the female members of the family. During these days they feel very sorrow and grief. The widow of a deceased person maintain pollution period for about a year obeying some taboos. It is same in case of male but some extra customs he is to maintain, such as he does not use wrist watch, bracelet, won't climb the trees and will carry a stick for one year. Husband or wife, as the case may be, is restricted to attend any ceremony, festival or occasion and also do not cross any cutting tree or rope and will carry umbrella. With regards to hair, the female can only apply oil but do not comb over it. The female is again not allowed to go out of her husband village. She has to refuse all kind of ornaments or any objects made of iron. Even she is also restrained from making up herself and wearing new cloths. The males use to avoid their hair cutting for one year from the death of his wife.

When one year is over, people belonged to the same community come and take the stick away and throw it in the name of the diseased person. Somebody from those people also cut hair of the male. These people again tell the female to accept the ornaments and break all the taboos. After completion of the pollution period of one year the widower or the widow is allowed to remarry and lead conjugal life again if the individual wishes to do so.

There is a myth prevailed in the Toto society pertaining to the death. They believe that the soul of the deceased person returns back to the house through the birth of a newborn and also comes in dream of its widow or widower or parents or any immediate relative of the deceased person. They would believe in the earlier days that if they fail to burry any objects or things that had been using regularly by the deceased when it was alive, the departed soul of the death enters into its house where it would live and taking the things it goes back.

Conclusion

The foregoing discussion reflects the life-cycle rites of the Totos marked by three distinct stages- birth, marriage and death. Different socio-religious functions are associated with these three phases of life. This is called rites of the passage or life-cycle rituals. With the influence of the outer world and various forces, their traditional way of thinking and perception as regards birth, marriage and death has now undergone a little modification and change. It is due to impact of different factors like urbanisation, modernisation and globalisation in the life of these aborigines.

Their conception with regard to the birth of a newborn is that the child is a gift of God. Though most of the families call mid-wife for the purpose of child delivery, but in complicated cases the pregnant woman is also admitted to the nearby health centre. They are also taking precaution before and after delivery.

Two types of marriages are practiced among them marriage by negotiation and love marriage. Child marriage is not seen among them. It is found that the average age at marriage is around 18 years in case of the girls and it is about 21 years for the boys. Preferential cousin marriage is prevalent among this endogamous tribal group but at the present time they are also getting married with their non-kin groups.

In course of time many traditional customs and rituals of this primitive tribal group have undergone change owing to various internal and external factors. Besides evil spirit attack is the sudden cause of the death, they believe today that the death occurs mainly due to ill-treatment of diseases. The Totos of Totopara also have no specific acquaintance about the nature of death like other men of the globe, but it is a mystic terror to those primitive people. They believe that the departed souls return to their houses through the birth of a new born and also come in dream of the widow or widower, or parents or any other immediate kin of the deceased. This notion is still prevalent among the people under study that death is an accidental incident which is caused due to the anger of the so-called gods and deities. They have a conviction that various ancestral souls, witch-craft, sorcery and so forth are held responsible for the same. They further believe that the sorcerer or the witches can be punished directly by the practice of magic with the help of special witch doctors or shamans.

References

Bhattacharya, B. and Bhattacharya, M. (1996), *Dynamics of Tribal Demography*, Calcutta: Aparna Book Distributer

Bhattacharya, M. (1998), *Toto at Cross Roads*, Calcutta: Aparna Book Distributer

Bhowmick, P. K. (1994), *Primitive Tribal Groups in Eastern India: Welfare and Evaluation*, New Delhi: Gyan Publishing House

Chaudhuri, S.K. (2004), *Constraints of Tribal Development*, New Delhi: Mittal Publications

Das, A. K. (1969), *The Totos*, Sp. Series No.11, Govt. of West Bengal, Kolkata: Cultural Research Institute

District Magistrate (2001), *Current Status Report on Totopara*, Jalpaiguri, Govt. of West Bengal

Hossain, M. I. (2012), "*The Totos and their Rites of Passage*", Man and Life, Vol. 38, Nos. 1-2, Jan-Jun, 2012 & pp. 129-138.

Majumder, B. (2001), *Jalpaiguri Jelar Janajati in Pachimbanga*, (Bengali), Govt. of West Bengal, Kolkata: Department of Information and Culture

Majumder, D. N. and Madan, T. N. (1956), *An Introduction to Social Anthropology*, Bombay: Asia Publishing House

Mitra, A. k. (1951), *District Census Hand Book-Jalpaiguri*, Appendix-VIII, Kolkata, West Bengal: Directorate of Census Operations

Sachidananda & Prasad, R.R. (Eds.), *Encyclopedic Profile of Indian Tribes*, Vol.-IV, 1998, Delhi: Discovery Publishing Pvt. Ltd.

Sanyal, C.C. (1972), *The Meches and the Totos of North Bengal-Two Sub-Himalayan Tribes*, West Bengal: North Bengal University Publication

Toto, D. (2001), *Totoder Samaj o Sanskriti in Paschimbanga* (Bengali), Govt. of West Bengal: Department of Information and culture

Vidyarthi, L. P. and B. K. Rai (1977),*The Tribal Culture of India*, Delhi: Concept Publishing Company

Wikipedia, the free encyclopedia, *Toto people*, accessed on: 27th Sept. 2014, available at: http://en.wikipedia.org/wiki/Toto_people

24

Socio-economic Transformation of Tribals: A Study on the Impact of Outside Intervention Among Santals

Dr Sujit Kumar Paul and Anindya Mitra

Introduction

The Tribal population is the aboriginal or indigenous inhabitants of India and is found in all parts of our country. For centuries tribals have been living a simple way of life based on the natural and forest resources and developed a unique cultural prototype congenial to their physical and the consequent social environment. This primitive community in fact originated from one of the oldest ethnological section of population, lives in isolated areas as distinct group – both culturally and ethnically, and is usually backward – socially, educationally and economically. The gamut of tribal life has a well-intentioned socio-cultural framework. It has definite dimensions ingrained in the value system and ideology of the respective tribe. The underlying philosophy of their actions is well defined within their traditional social structure. They cultivate their commonly accepted rationale regarding various explanations. And it provides for a pattern of living which is broadly understood by the members of respective tribes. Thus the whole gamut of tribal social structures represents a compact network which can scientifically and validly explored and understood only within the holistic background. But unfortunately the proper understanding could not be met by the agents of development and remained a gap in the exploration and understanding of totality of tribal socio-cultural structure.

The tribes are categorically recognised in constitution of India and even otherwise. Certain special provisions and privileges have given to the tribal people for helping them to develop socially and economically. However, the achievements of the planned effort are not satisfactory except in some specific areas. The efforts for developing tribal community some times created problems in native systems rather than helping the tribals live better and healthy life. Likewise, some transitions have caused due to unintended cultural contact over time. Some of these changes have culminated into disorganisation in tribal life and culture as the new ideas and innovations failed to fit in the normal ideological format. In recent past various impinging forces of change, both from within and outside bring some kind of transformation and deviation in the tribal socio-cultural framework of life. The continuous interaction with non-tribal community has caused some changes in the organic world of tribals and is reflected in tribal socio-cultural framework at both micro and macro level.

Objectives of the Study

The main objectives of the study are as follows:

- To identify the outside interventions and the transforming scenario of socio-economic structure in Santal villages of Santiniketan.
- To assess the impact of transformation in the Santal village life.
- To recommend some measures for development of Santal villages without influencing the actual identity of tribal-life.

Area and Methodology of the study

The present study has been conducted in five tribal villages surrounding Santiniketan of Birbhum District, West Bengal, viz. Balipara, Baganpara, Kaliganj, Piarsonpalli and Goalpara. The methodology adopted in this study keeping in view the broad objectives and scope of the study. The interview method and PRA exercise especially the Focused Group Discussion (FGD) has been used to gather the primary data. Total 100 households (20 households from each of five villages) were selected and surveyed by random sampling method for generating the primary information. The FGD was conduced for gathering perceptions and opinion of villagers about the changing scenario of their socio-cultural structure and also to cross check the information generated through the field survey. During the field study the characteristics of tribal socio-cultural structure and their way of interaction with society and surrounding environment have been studied cautiously. The transformation that took place in the surrounding physical, social and cultural resources and the impact on human environment has been studied using primary and secondary information.

Santals of Santiniketan

The Santals form one of the largest tribal groups in eastern India concentrated mainly in Bihar, West Bengal, Orissa and Tripura. In origin they belong to Austro-Asiatic kol group branched from the Austric family. Generally, the tribal people are identified primitive, illiterate and backward communities. But the Santals are more adaptive and their lifestyle is not so primitive like some other tribe. The Santals are the major tribal group in Birbhum district and locally known as 'Majhi'. In Birbhum district they comprise nearly 6.74 per cent of total population and 89 per cent of tribal population. The socio-economic and traditional life-styles of Santals bear the print of natural environment. Santals were the primitive inhabitants of Santiniketan a well known place of Birbhum district and till the date exists in small habitats or villages surrounding Santiniketan with its partial nature-oriented traditional identity. But in the last few decades Rabindranath Tagore's Santiniketan has became a global tourist hot spot and receives huge number of tourists, almost round the year and many of them come to visit in these tribal villages. Although, over the time outside intervention has become a matter of worry that the age-old traditional earthen cultures of tribals turned into gradual losses and lead to socio-cultural modification. The reason is particularly due to increasing influx of tourists as well as the changing taste of the people in this Santhal-community. So at present, the multi-culturalism is being gathered and gradually the event of the erosion of cultural resource has been accelerated. However, the global attention on Santiniketan has accelerated the process of development in the surrounding villages by both the government and private institutions with special focus. As a result the Santiniketan including tribal villages have experienced a rapid development in physical as well as social and financial resources of the area.

Results and Discussion

The law of dynamics is universally applied to every society and Santals of Santiniketan are no exception. The Santals of Santiniketan exposed to the continuous forces of change, both indigenous and exogenous, which have serious implications on their life-style and culture. It has been observed that Santals got exposed to the consumerist ideology and thereby move away from their traditional community value system. The Santals are experiencing a changeover from their community ethos to a totally new culture and system (without adequate preparation). However, slowly the Santal communities absorb the value system of this culture.

Transforming Factors and Agents

It has been found that both external and internal factors are responsible for the gradual change in socio-cultural structure of Santals of Santiniketan locality. The continuous and immeasurable number of tourists and their enquiring behavior i.e. interest to know about Santal community is one of the major factors responsible for changing the originality of the age-old traditional culture. This is because during the cross-cultural interaction both positive and negative ideas have transferred to the Santal community. It has been found that often Santals are more interested to copy and adopt all the bad and good things from the educated persons from outside than upgrading their quality as human being. The good and bad practices of local non-tribals and University students (Visva-Bharati is a Central University of National importance in Santiniketan) are also responsible for cultural change of Santal people especially of the Santal youth. However, rigorous attempts of various development agents have helped the Santal community to uplift their standard of living as well as bring socio-economic modifications. Likewise, the globalisation processes have serious implications for the socio-cultural change of the tribals. The electronic media and its promotional events have developed a homogeneous consumerist culture and value system on Santal society. The unawareness and backwardness of Santal community is also a factor for changing scenario of their socio-cultural transformation. The fast and bright image of outer world attracts the simple Santal people and exposed them into a world which is unknown to them. In the study area political pressure has also became a determining factor for socio-cultural transformation. The cooperativeness, intra-group and inter-group harmony have been an integral part of Santal social structure and deeply rooted into their value system. But the recent political scenario has resulted in the deterioration of the tribal lifestyles and cultural changes.

Transforming Scenario of the Santal Villages

The Santals of Santiniketan are mostly rural, illiterate and hard working. The socio-cultural status of Santals is also changing based on the development of infrastructural facilities. All the five studied villages are well interconnected by roads which result decrease in inter regional disparities in all sphere of life. Food habits and material culture is changing gradually. The percentage of literate person has increased. Various development initiatives along with cultural diffusion and acculturation through the interaction with other non-tribal people in each sphere also bring changes in long term process. It has been found that Santal traditional society is gradually transforming into a modern society. Due to inflow of outer people as temporal/daily tourists or as a permanent resident, affect the local people's socio-cultural behavior severely. The changes recognised in various spheres of Santal life are:

Change in traditional Social Structure: Social structure of a society is nothing but the institutions by which relationships between men and women of a society are determined. Thus, social structure is concerned with the principle forms of social organisation i.e. the type groups, associations and institutions and the complex of these, which constitutes societies. Family occupies a unique place in the society. The traditional joint family structure has been changed over time. Now, the Santals mostly prefer nuclear family than joint. In the study area 74 per cent sampled families are found nuclear in nature. Recent changes in Santal socio-cultural structure involve greater individualism and stronger patriarchy. However, a Santal society traditionally goes with equal opportunity and scope of men and women in all aspects. It has been revealed from the elder respondents that the Santals have respects for their elders, rituals and religious framework, their ancestor and nature. But recent changes have resulted in the deterioration of the tribal lifestyles. Especially the young generation has lack of respects to their traditional ethos. The Santal villages had their own law and traditional Panchayat which deal with social customs, traditions, mores, codes governing, family disputes, interpersonal relations, religious rites and festivals and political safeguards. But now the government Panchayats gives governance powers to the tribal community. In last two decades organised grouping concept by means of 'club' and 'SHG' is also become a part of their life which acts as a functional improvement of the society. Another interesting fact has been found that the average age at marriage has some how improved. The early marriage has been a general custom of the Santal society. The elder generation has opined that at their time almost cent per cent female were married at the age below 18 years. But in recent time the scenario has changed. The study also revealed that 35 per cent female got married at age below 18 years, 54 per cent female got married at age above 18 years and only 11 per cent female got married at the age above 21 years. There is not much change in the observance of other rituals like, funeral rites, birth and many such other ceremonies.

Changes in Human Status: The changing perceptions and tastes of the Santal people in these villages changed their surrounded environment. Now-a-days, a trend of modernisation is common in these villages. The educational level of these villages has changed remarkably. Around 38 per cent people of sampled household are found literate. The villages have primary school and ICDS centers. The children of these villages also go to the schools of Bolpur, Jambuni and Goalpara for secondary and higher secondary education. Even some children have admitted to Patha Bhavan and Siksha Satra – the schools of Visva -Bharati University. It has been found that most of the young people do not want to speak their own language. Many of them get used to speaking and being educated in Bengali medium. The Santal women also became very conscious about the education of their children. Some of them sent their children in English medium school for assessing modern education system. The Government, University Authority and other agencies also developed the skill and entrepreneurial thought among the Santal communities of Santiniketan and as a result the attitude of Santal people has improved. The Santal especially the youth has become complex and one kind of individualistic thought and approach has been found during the study.

Change in Economic status: The economic status also has changed drastically. Changing of occupational structure can be usually expected with the change of generation as well as cultural aspiration. It can be clearly seen from the result that only 20 per cent continues with the same occupation as their ancestors practiced and as much as 80 per cent has changed their job in this recent generation. They shifted from their traditional agriculture and forest based livelihood to service and trade based occupation. Most of the Santal people have shifted to labour oriented work like mason, house care taker, household servant, car driver etc. Due to higher demand of handicrafts, hand-made fashionable goods and commodities in local market as well as global market most of the villagers changed their occupational bases i.e. they try to devote their physical and mental labor to develop cottage goods. Again due to development of a tourism industry in this village some people also joined there to earn more money. The access to financial institutions like Bank, MFIs, and Insurance has increased. It has been found that 76 per cent people have Bank or Post office accounts. The Santals of this area are also using modern agricultural technologies for getting better production. With the development of economic status the pattern of expenditure also has changed. They have increased the percentage of expenditure in education and health aspects. However, most of the expenditure has made in purchasing of modern gadgets like mobile phone, iPod, TV, Motor Bike etc. It has been found that 92 per cent households have a mobile phone, 85 per cent have a TV and 11 per cent households have a motor bike. The access to health facilities also improved. For any kind of health emergencies Santals are now accessing both Government and Private health care centers instead of going to their traditional *Ojhas*, priest and local quack doctors. Some Santal villagers also play their own traditional song and dance for tourist entertainment on regular basis and took it as their livelihood. However, the tendency of excessive consumption of liquor, cigarette and other intoxicants and purchase lottery ticket has increased which indicates high level of income leakages.

Change in Traditional and material Cultural: With rapid urbanisation around the Santiniketan the Santal villages have been facing certain cultural degradation. Their traditional background has slightly changed from being 'deep rooted' due to adaptation of modernised behavior. For instance, some Santhal of this village do not wear their traditional dress during festivals and also do not follow the cultural behavior during special occasions in their life. An interesting fact came out from the direct interview that only 9 per cent of the people like to wear their traditional dress all the times, more than 52 per cent like to wear only during the festival and 39 per cent people (mostly the modern generation) do not like their traditional dress and have completely switched over to the modern dresses. Modern dresses like Jeans, top, maxi and etc are now became very common. The 'bala'/ wrist bangle of iron, Christ-locket on neck, cosmetics are used as the symbol of modern fashion among younger. The villagers' knowledge about their festivals and rituals is presented that 64 per cent people have knowledge about their festivals and 36 per cent (mostly the new generations) have only limited and outward idea about their festivals. The new generation people are more interested to spend the festival days in good restaurants, cinema halls and amusement parks instead of spending time in their villages with family. Pattern of celebration has also been changed. Now they prefer Hindi and Bengali film songs and dance rather than their own traditional song and dance. The Santals are now also take part in Bengali festival like Durga puja, Kalipuja, Sarswati puja and etc. Likewise, a trend of modernisation has come in these villages. For example - use of television, electric fan, pressure cooker, cycle, radio, mobile, dish TV are being found in these village. About 70 per cent of people use electric fans, radios, cycles. During field visit, modernised cemented sacred temple has been found in Santal villager rather than open aired nature based worship. Almost every households use modern utensils made of aluminum, glass and steel. A visible transition has been seen in the recreation practices. The Santals who were once entertaining themselves with folk traditions are now gradually shifting to modern means of entertainment such as watching TV, Cinema etc. The practice of group drinking has also been changed. The Santals who were once preferred their traditional drink rice beer or 'haria' and 'tari' are now taking foreign liquor.

Impact of the transformation

The outside intervention in the Santal villages of Santiniketan has mixed type of impact – on one side it has friendly and fruitful impacts and adverse-eroded on other side. As a result of this various aspects of modernisation and globalisation have intervened within these tribal villages which bring positive changes in their perception, knowledge, daily life style, food habit and health aspects. On the other hand, their festival and rule-rituals; the eco-specimen nature oriented culture is being deteriorated from its root. Through the interaction with globalisation, Santal of these villages have changed their knowledge and experiences and which are well observed in the villages like:

- Knowledge about the outer world, their dresses, languages, behaviors, food-habits, rule, rituals, religions, cultures, utensils, ornaments
- Formal school education
- Modern technologies of Agriculture
- Health and hygiene practices
- Political attention, participation and experiences
- Infrastructural improvement like tube-well, concrete well, club, Disc T.V.
- Access to modern medical services
- Entrepreneurial knowledge
- Tourism knowledge
- Knowledge on various Government programmes

However, modernisation and globalisation has slowly poisoning for tribal life because it will destroy the cultural resource of Santhal community. It has been clear that over time Santal's life has got into or adopted aspects of globalisation and deposited their traditional resource under the bank of *Bisshwayan* (globalisation) permanently and ultimately they will lose their own all specimen heritage: their racial identity, cultural knowledge, rituals, systems, festivals, life-style and environmental knowledge. So ultimately, a mixed up situation came fore-front in the present study.

Conclusion

The Santal called them "Hor Hopon' or the son of man. Santhal-life and their cultural panorama is a resource to our 'Cultural-Bank'. So it has become an important task to manage, preserve the traditional cultural life of Santhal's community. Cultural resource must be managed because they are threatened. It is also a true fact that ignorance to ideological framework of tribal cultures has been shown by the agents of change engaged in the planed programme of development. However, the close contact and interaction with visitors as well as with the neighbouring villagers and impact of schooling, the process of democracy and social justice had gradually led them to greater social awareness in general and in particular the awareness of their rights. In other words, the developmental interventions have led to a slow but steady process of social and economic empowerment of Santals of Santiniketan. This social process has led the Santals of Santiniketan to a social transition from folk society to the peasant society life practices.

References

Bhowmik, Pradip Kumar; 1993: *Dynamics of Tribal Development*, Inter-India Publications, New Delhi.

Chacko, Pariyaram M.; 2005: "*Tribal Communities and Social Change*": Sage Publications, New Delhi.

Chowdhury, S.N.; 2012: *In search of Sustainable development: Scenario in a Tribal Village of Madhya Pradesh,* Serials Publications, New Delhi.

Majhi, A.S.; 2010: *Tribal Culture Continuity and Change*, Mittal Publication, New Delhi.

Mann, R.S. and Mann, K.; 1989: *Tribal Culture and Change*, Mittal Publication, New Delhi.

Pachauri, S.K.; 1984: *Dynamics of Rural Development in Tribal Areas*, Concept Publishing Company, New Delhi.

Sen, P. 2003: *Changing Tribal Life: A Socio-Philosophical Perspective*, Concept Publishing Company, New Delhi.

25

Living of the Baiga in the forest villages of the Baiga Chak: An anthropological insight on Forest Policy and Baiga rights over the forest resources

Ashok Pandey

Introduction

The Forest Rights Act (2006) envisages a new hope of light for Scheduled Tribes and other Forest Dwellers by recognizing their traditional rights and valuing their contribution for generations in maintaining as well as sustaining forest ecology. However, the other side of the coin i.e. Forest Policy of the Indian Government changed with colonial period of British Government to Independence or free India but one thing was common and that was sophisticatedly marginalizing the most deprived sections of people who were true guardians of the forests from time immemorial. The Baiga is one of the Primitive Tribal Groups (PTG), now coined a new term by Ministry Of Tribal Affairs as Particularly Vulnerable Tribal Groups (PVTG). The research article focuses anthropological insight on the basis of the fieldwork conducted in forest villages of the Baiga Chak (comprising fifty –two villages).When we consider the Forest Policy we can trace its importance and manifestations from a low level of interference and good deal of co-operation to high level of interference and exploitative nature in course of time. For example, earlier scriptures found referring Ramayana and Mahabharata epics mention the Adivasis(Tribes) as performing good roles in sustaining and maintaining forest resources and its ecology. After the later Vedic period, Budha age, Mauryan rule, Gupta Age, sultanate period, Mughal rule up to the later Mughals even the forest ecology was not disturbed. But forest ecology was exploited and looted as it began the British era of administration. The valuable forest resources tempted greed for imperial government of British in India deliberately formulated Forest Policies that grossly exploited natural resources in general and forest resources in particular. British government thought to generate income from forest resources like costly woods, fruits, medicinal value herbs, etc.

The first Indian forest Act 1865 gave authority to British Government of rights over forests and waste lands Government Reserve Forest. On 19th October1894, the British government in India formulated Forest Policy that emphasized upon the need for proper administration of tribal and rural population residing in and around the forest. Through this forest policy had provision of employing forest officials and state control over forest rights was strongly established and legalised and at the same time tribal rights on forest resources curtailed to great limitations. The scenario of free India after independence more or less experimented in similar fashion by formulating National Forest Policy 1952 in national interest but curtailing rights of tribal communities and forest dwellers by classifying forests as protected forests, national forests and village forests thereby even prevented the grazing of cattle's in this new forest policy and tribes exploited in forests as labourers for forest officials and contractors in the name of forest development or national development. Again the National Forest Policy 1988 made little difference in formulations as it also only empowered the state over deprived tribes living in forests by providing major decisions in forest department officials and only adding few concessions for the benefit of officers who felt real need of help and co-operation from tribes residing in forests as readily available help and thus mooted for their own sake in this policy as Joint forest Management (herein after JFM). The JFM is a people's participation in forestry by involving local people that is tribes from the forest. This approach through JFM only helped forest officials and its department but exploited in another form the forest dwellers. (Upadhyay & Pandey; 2003).

Now the Forest Right Act(2006) tried to bring justice to the deprived tribal and other forest dwellers communities by providing them certain legal rights and privileges by promoting their rights in forest produce Precisely Minor Forest produce (herein after MFP) and certain piece of land allotted to the deprived lot living in the forest for generations.

Research Methodology

This research article is based on the data collected from the forest villages of Baiga Chak in the Dindori district of Madhya Pradesh (India). Though the Baiga Chak is dominated by the Baiga primitive tribe distributed in fifty-two forest villages but the data used in this article is limited to the following forest villages namely Jalda, Bona, Chanda, Kharidih and Sitalpani. Here the field work for the D.Phil. research work, "The Baiga: A Study in Nature-Man-Spirit Complex" was conducted during the year 2010 and 2011. The experiences and observations revealed in these forest villages are mentioned in this article in the light of forest policies and Forest Right Act 2006 of the Indian Government and its impact and manifestation in the lives of the Baiga. The research methodology involved was fieldwork using anthropological tools and techniques i.e. participant observation and non-participation observation, structured and unstructured interviews, case studies, genealogies of the Baiga living in such forest villages. The key informants were from the Baiga families of the forest villages and were both Baiga men and women. The rapport established with the natives revealed personal information and hardships faced by the natives in their daily life. The total number of Baiga households interviewed on issues relating to Forest Rights Act 2006 was sixty households randomly selected from the forest villages mentioned above during the fieldwork.

Analysis & Discussion

The Baiga now placed as Particularly Vulnerable Tribal Group (PVTG) really observed in the field as an exploited and weakest deprived tribe of the country. The shifting cultivation practiced long ago has been very limited more precisely hardly practiced now days. The Bewar cultivation as it was known is hardly remembered when it was interviewed among the Baiga families residing in these forest villages. The pain of the deprived lot revealed after observing over a month with them through participant observation it was found that subsistence economy prevails in most families (85 out of 105 Baiga people were hardly had proper dresses, food, proper education and children malnourished and women fragile and weak). The Baiga families residing in these forest villages visits the forest regularly to get MFP like Harra, Baherra, Chiraunji, Maidachaal, Chiruanta (a kind of vegetable) fruits like jamun or mango or imli, etc. according to their seasons of availability. But the fear of the forest officials and dominant contractors who snatch their produce in name of forest or government property and rights make them vulnerable and their voice is not heard in any court of justice.

A new feature was observed in Sitalpani, Jalda, Bona and adjoining forest villages where the Baiga are exploited by the greedy contractors and smugglers for cutting down the trees of harra and behrra for the produce at a time neglecting the future problem of disturbing ecology of the forest potential. This is not limited to anyone forest produce but to many forest resources including costly woods from the trees of Sal and other medicinal value shrubs and herbs in gross amounts. The disturbance of the forest ecology and limitations observed despite The Schedule Tribes and other Traditional Forest Dwellers (Recognition of Forest Rights) Act 2006 that was passed by Indian parliament on 18th December 2006 and its date of commencement 31st December 2007 seem failed in implementation. The training module and implementing agencies of the government and forest department is still insensitive to the poor tribes. The awareness about Forest Rights Act 2006 was very low during the 2010 and 2011 in most of the remote forest villages where during the fieldwork it was interviewed from the Baiga men and women. Only 17 persons out of 85 Baiga people expressed their awareness of such Forest Rights Act 2006 for them. Also many confused it with JFM and several case studies revealed that the dominant Baiga and Gond families will take away their share of MFP and on paper beneficiaries only inflated in government records.

The poor economic condition and low literacy is common feature observed and at the same time belief system ingrained in the mindsets of the Baiga prevent them any advancement or raise any voice against their exploitation to the sahukaars who at low cost purchase their forest collected MFP in times of their urgent need of money. The funds and scheme do not have furnished satisfactory results as there is no proper distribution of such fund are met to the larger targeted group of Baiga. Some politically aware and affluent members from the Baiga communities and some Gond tribe powerful familes dominate and usurp most of the rights and privileges meant for whole Baiga community. Thus, a kind of exploitation by the few dominant families, from the Baiga gets advantage of benefits provided by the government. So the Forest Policies framed is not meeting the needs of target group Baiga people residing in these forest villages.

Conclusion

A sort of creamy layer though not affluent too much but relatively also seems to emerge in the forest villages of the Baiga Chak in the families of the Baiga community. Equidistribution of forest rights and its resources were not observed during the fieldwork. The stratified and concentration of power in few hands were observed in the forest villages. Thus the exploiters are not only the dikus that is outsiders but also the powerful brethren of the Baiga themselves who share more profits and rights and exploit the labour of the larger members of the Baiga. Thus forest rights over resources is hardly distributed to the larger section of the Baiga and forest policies of the government is playing a foul play in the name of development, conservations of forest resources. The authoritative position of forest department and insensitive official with middleman and contractors all generally look down upon the poor Baiga and exploit them in various ways. To meet desired results for promoting Baiga rights government needs proper awareness campaign for their forest rights as well as make such evaluation and intervention to improve their economic political and educational standards by providing to larger number of the Baiga people and not the few dominant among them who snatch lion's share of the rights over forest resources.

References

1. Bose S. and Others, Changing Patterns of Land use Among the Baigas of Madhya Pradesh, 1987, Anthropological Survey of India, Calcutta.
2. Munshi Indra, The Adivasi Question Issues of Land, Forest and Livelihood. EPW, 2012, Orient Black swan, Hyderabad.
3. Upadhyay V.S. & Pandey Gaya, Tribal Development in India a Critical Appraisal 2003, Crown Publications, Ranchi.

26

Ethno- medical practices among the Lodhas of Keshiary block of Pachim Medinipur disctrict: Issues and Chalanges

Arup Bera

India is a country where 10,42,81,034 i.e. 8.6% of total population is recognised as tribe. Lodha is a Primitive Tribal Group (PTG) having 84966 i.e. 1.9% of the Schedule Tribe (ST) population. The Lodhas, traditionally Mundari speaking population, are presently found to occupy the forest covered tracts of Paschim Medinipur district of West Bengal, Mayurbhanj district of Orissa and East and West Singbhum district of Jharkhand, broadly known as Jangle Mohall.

They stay at the hut, covering the leaf-fringed wall. But now some of them reside in the house was made out by mud made tiles, C.I.sheets, asbestos. They eat kandumul (tuberous-root), collecting different food grains from the forest and edible snails from nearby ponds. They earn for their livelihood by selling of forest products like wood, maul, honey and Sal leaves. The male members of Lodhas use bows and arrows and axes for hunting. The female collect inferior food in the forest.

The term "Ethno-medicine" is gaining popularity over a period of time. Ethno–medicine generally gives emphasis on the study of beliefs and a practice related to the sickness of an individual. Till today most of them are dependent on nature, utilizing their environment and ecology with the help of their given technology. Ethno-Medicinal plants play a central role as traditional medicines used in many cultures and tribes. The use of plant-based medicines is as old as human history. Most cultures in the world have traditionally developed expertise on plant-based therapy.

The medicine men use some indigenous methods that have a support for their religious beliefs with a view to cure people suffering from various diseases. These medicine men are the carriers of the healing traditions, which have been orally transmitted from generation to generation. They are the knowledgeable persons who directly use the medicinal plants and herbs and other parts of the plants used for healing treatment. The Lodhas of Keshiary block in Paschim Medinipur district have a strong faith on ethno-medical practice along with modern medical system.

Relevance of the present study

The importance of present research and investigation of ethno-medical system of any tribal community is immense. Because it is an accomplished fact that the tribal and non tribal or aboriginal people of our country enjoy more ethno-medical security than the so called modern medical treatment. Most probably their ethno-medical system is more effective than other prevailed system of medicine.

The present study contemplates to understand the ethno-medical practices prevailing among the Lodhas of Keshary block in Paschim Medinipur.

Objectives

The main objectives of the study are:

1. To study the method of ***ethno-medical practices*** adopted by the traditional tribal medicine men for treatment and curing.
2. To suggest ***measures for further improvement*** of the initiatives.

Materials & Methods

For anthropological research most important is the field work on which depends the results of the research. The present research work has been conducted applying the participant observation method. However some other methods have also been applied for the purpose of collecting facts.

The following methods have been selected to fulfil the stated objectives.

(a) Selection criteria of the study area

Keshiary is located under ***semi forest area***, Secondly the studied block is Integrated Tribal Development Project (ITDP) block. Thirdly the concentration of Lodhas are more in this block in comparison to other ITDP blocks in the district.

(b) Sampling procedure and size

The unit of study is the household. Data were collected among the Lodhas of ***two*** villages namely ***Kukai*** and ***Saldanga*** under Keshiary block. A total number of 112 ***households*** were selected for present study. The distribution of sample size of the selected studied block along with selected villages is mentioned bellow in **Table–1.** Beside the households sample, altogether various types of health practitioners consist of tribal medicine men, homeopathy and allopathy practitioners were considered of in-depth interview. A total number of ***11 health practitioners*** were interviewed for the study. The distribution of various types of health practitioners from Keshiary block mentioned bellow in **Table-2.**

Table: 1 Distribution of Lodha sample households in the villages under Keshiary

Block

Block	Village	Sample size	Block wise total sample
Keshiary	Kukai	92 (82.14%)	112 (100.00%)
	Saldanga	20(17.86%)	

Source: Field level

Table-2 Distribution of various types of health practitioners from Keshiary

block

Types of health Keshiary (11)	**Name of the block** Practioners
Ethno medical	06(54.55%)
Homeopathic	
Registrar	1(9.09%)
Non registrar	1(9.09%)
Allopathic	
Registrar	——
Non registrar	3(27.27%)

Source: Field level

(c) Tools and techniques

All recognised anthropological methods of fieldwork have been applied to collect qualitative as well as quantitative data. Methodological consideration tried to cover general survey, participant and non-participant observation, personal and group interview for rigorous micro-level data collection. The researcher interviewed the respondents as per their conveniences accordingly the time was fixed.

Ethno-medical practices

The Lodhas of Keshiary block belief and practice ethno-medicine to cure different diseases and accidental cases as well as any physical problem faced in their daily life are given below:

Table-3 Ethno-medical treatment to cure general ailment in the studied blocks.

Sl. No.	*Name of disease*	*Way of treatment*
1.	Diabetes	Chirata (*Swertia chirata*) plant soaked in as well as blood purification water is consumed/the leaves of sada nayantara (Catharanthus alba) is consumed.
2.	Bronchitis	Basak (*Adhatoda vasica nee*) leaf extract is consumed.
3.	Heart Problem	Arjuna (*Terminalia Arjuna W & A*) bark is soaked in water and consumed.
4.	Jaundice	Kulekhara (*Asteracantha longifolia Nees*), kolmi plant, helencha and turmeric juice is taken in empty stomach.
5.	Rheumatism	Rasun (*Allium sativum*) boiled with Mustard oil massage in the affected area.
6.	Asthma	Smoking of kaladhutra (*Datura fastuosa*) Leaf/ after removing the feather and skin of the cock-roach are boiled in water and the Pulp is taken.
7.	Diarrhoea	Whole plant juice of chota dudhi(*Euphorbia hirta)* is consumed.
8.	Leprosy	Kalihaldi(*Curcuma ccaesia*) plant is applied
9.	Skin disease	Neem (*Asadirachla indica*) oil is extracted from the fruit and applied on the affected area.
10.	Tuberculosis	Roots of apang (*Achyranthes aspera Linn*) and vectomi are applied.
11.	Worm	Root juice of seem or bean/paste of uchha or karala is best medicine for worm.
12.	Itching	Apply the paste of shon leaf on the infected area.
13.	Filaria	Juice of bindhi roots is taken.
14.	Night blindness	Applies juice of basil leaves at the interval of two hours.
15.	Ear trouble	Little warm garlic oil is applied in the ear/warm juice of betel leaves is poured in the e ear.
16.	High blood pressure	Juice of sajna leaf is taken.
17.	Fever	Fried monasa (*Cactus*) leaves is taken with water.
18.	Anemia	Kulkha (*Asteracantha longifolia Nees*) leaf juice is taken.
19.	Cold & cough	Tulsi (*Ocimum sanctum*) leaf extract with honey is taken.

20.	Dental infection	Root juice of bajradanti (*Barleris cristata*) is applied on the affected area.
21.	Constipation	Paste of green ginger (*Zingiber officinale Rose*) and neem (*Azadirachta indica*) leaf is taken.
22.	Headache	Apply of paste of patharkuchi (*Bryophyllum pinnatum*) or jaba (*China Rose*) flower on the forehead.
23.	Menstruation	Paste of bud of jaba (*China Rose*) flower and problem jiggery is taken.
24.	Sexual disease	Root of gycira and ramdatan (*Smilax macrophylla Roxby*) are applied.
25.	Tumor	Root of gurum antia is applied.

Sources: Field level

Table-4 Frequency distribution of common type of disease found among the Lodhas in Keshiary block (n=112)

Variables	*Keshiary*
Types of disease	
Rheumatism	18.23
Cold and fever	11.29
Sexual disease	13.72
Tuberculosis	02.19
Digestion problem	13.78
Diabetes	02.39
Anemia	08.16
Boil or septic boil	06.72
Eye problem	08.93
Skin-disease	10.90
Hepatitis	02.12
Filaria	01.57

Sources: Field level

Table-4 shows the frequency distribution of common types of disease found among the Lodhas of Keshiary block. From this table, we also found most of the people in Keshiary block suffered by rheumatism. Except this highest percentage of people from Keshiary block are suffering by sexual disease, digestion problem and cold and fever. Skin-disease, eye problem, anemia, diabetes, boil or septic boil, eye problem, tuberculosis, hepatitis and filaria are some common type of disease found among the Lodhas in Keshiary block.

Table-5 Frequency distribution of types of treatment found among the Lodhas in Keshiary block (n=112)

Types of treatment	*Keshiary*
Ethno-medical	25.54
Magico-religious	04.46
Homeopathic	06.25
Allopathic	63.75

Sources: Field level

From the **Table- 5**, it is clear that most of the people (63.75%) in Keshiary block are treated by allopathy. After this, ethno-medical treatment is second highest (25.54%) treatment type practiced by the people in this block. Homeopathy (06.25%) and magico-religious (04.46%) treatment are less than other prevalent treatment found among the Lodhas in Keshiary block.

Table-6 Frequency distribution of mode of treatment found among the Lodhas in Keshiary block (n=112)

Mode of treatment	Keshiary
Ethno- medicine man	23.75
Magico-religious practitioner	06.25
Private (Regd.)	18.83
Quack	20.15
Hospitals	31.02

Sources: Field level

Table-6 shows the frequency distribution of mode of treatment found among the Lodhas of the studied block. From this table, researcher also found most of the People(31.02%) are going to hospital for their health treatment. After that second highest (23.75%) of peoples are coming to ethno-medicine man for their good health. Except these a good percentage of Lodhas of Keshiary block i.e 20.15% and 18.83% are coming to quack doctor and private (regd.) doctor respectively for their betterment of ill health. A little percentage (06.25%) of Lodhas are also come to magico-religious practitioner for their health problem.

Table-7 Ethno medical practices against the accidental cases and poisonous bite practiced by the Lodhas of Keshiary block.

1.	Burn	Paste of the bark of demur (*F. glomerata*) plant is applied /paste of leaves is used.
2.	Burn body part	Apply egg/paste of potato and milk/commonSalt/ paste of coconut and lime on burnt area.

3.	Dog bite	Roots of ningush and akan *(Calotropis gigantea Linn)* are applied.
4.	Snake bite	Burk of shyer plant is used /Errand seeds (*Ricinus commnuis*) extracted oil is used.

Suggestions

In view of the above discussion, the following remedial measures about practices and promotion of ethno-medicine were suggested by the researcher under the following:

1. Considering the importance of the ethno-medicinal plants in the life of the indigenous people, natural habitat needs protection from the traders who are meant for marketing and commercialisation of these medicinal plants which has resulted in degradation of natural habitat.
2. Tribal medicine-men play a significant role in catering the healthcare needs of millions of indigenous people. They provide plants centered culturally appropriate personalised health care that meets the needs and expectation of the patients. But due to the promotion of modern health care massive depletion of plant resources etc., their traditional role and status has shown a decaying trend with erosion of local health tradition.
3. Workshop may be organised by government or NGOs for tribal medicine men of different localities and communities to share and improve their knowledge relating to diagnosis and treatment of diseases and collection of materials for the preparation of plant, mineral and anima based medicine.
4. The sources of ethno-medicine and the mechanism of their preparation and application should be documented to protect the indigenous knowledge base of medicine men against pirating of their knowledge.
5. The survival of several medicinal plants is threatened mainly due to deforestation and indiscriminate use as well as unscientific collection of those. In order to conserve the endangered medicinal plant species the tribal people should be motivated for their commercial cultivation through promotion of home herbal gardens and medicinal plant nurseries by forming Self Help Groups (SHGs).
6. The tribal SHGs should be trained on development, management and maintenance of home herbal garden and medicinal plant nurseries. They should be trained on processing storage, packaging and marketing of ethno-medicine.

7. Camps for motivations and awareness generation should be organised for the leaders of the tribal SHGs. The managers of local level Banks should also be oriented for distributing financial assistance for cultivation of medicinal plants and sale of medicines with mutual co-operations.
8. Perfect awareness programme among the Lodhas regarding the medicinal plants and the significant role of the medicine man is more important.
9. There should be encouragement for cultivation and preservation of medicinal plants at least in kitchen garden.
10. To stop the ill effects of continuous and reckless exploitation of natural resources by the external business man.

Due to promotion of modern medical system like allopathic treatment, the ethno-medical treatment is decreased. Because the identification and collection of medicinal plant are a long time consumed process.

The irony of the fact is that although the Govt. of India as well as the World Health Organisation (WHO) recognizes the Indian Traditional System of medicine but so far no suitable measures have been adopted for its revival, sustainability, improvement and wider publicity at large. Any suitable steps to revive the system has wider scope in terms of applications and getting relief from deadly diseases, generating employment, maintenance of natural and social harmony and above all meeting the requirement of down trodden people having their habitation location in remote and isolated places.

References

Ackerknehet Erwin. H., 1946 — "Natural disease and rational treatment" Bulletin of the History of the Primitive Medicine. Vol.19:p.p.467-497.

Ahluwalia, 1974 — "Sociology and Medicine".

Bhowmick, P.K., 1963 — "The Lodhas of West Bengal". Puthi-Pustak.

Bhowmick, P.K., 1976 — "Socio-Cultural Profile of Frontier Bengal". Puthi-Pustak.

Clements, F. E. 1932 — "Primitive Concept of Disease" American Archaeology and Ethnology. Vol.XXXIII, p.p.185-252.

Field, M.J. 1937 — "Religion and Medicine of the Ga People" Oxford University Press, London.

Gonzales, N. S. 1966 — "Health Behaviour in Cross-Cultural Perspective: A Guatemalan Example". Human Organisation, Vol. 25, p.p.122-125.

Gould, H.A. 1957 — "The Implication of Technology Change for Folk and Scientific Medicine". American Anthropologist, Vol.p.p.507-516.

Khare, R.S.1963 Folk Medicine in North Indian Village". Human Organisation, Vol. 22, No,-1, p.p. 36-40.

Lewis, Oscar. 1958 "Village Life in Northern India" New York: Random House.

Marriott, Mackim. 1955 "Western Medicine in a Village of Northern India" in Health Culture and Community. Ed. B.D. Paul, p.p.239-268, Russel Sage Foundation, New York.

Mathur, P.R.G. 1982 "Anthropology of Tribal Medicine: Disease and Curing Techniques among the Tribal's North Wynad (Kerala)".Man in India, Vol. 62, No.-3.

Mead, Margaret. 1964 "Culture, Health and Disease".

Opler, Morries, E., 1963 "The Cultural Definition of Illness in Village India".Human Organisation. Vol. 22.

Rizvi, S.N.H. 1986 "Health Practices of The Jaunsaries: A Socio-Cultural Analysis" in Chaudhuri Buddhadev (Ed.), Tribal Health: Socio-Cultural Dimensions, New Delhi; Inter –India Publications, p.p.223-246.

Development of Tribal Economy and Role of Adivasi Women: A Case Study

Swarup Kumar Jana

Introduction

In the traditional societies which lack market system, the business of everyday living is usually carried on gender division of labour.The division of labour is mainly between herding and agriculture. In all other tasks concerned with life in the village, such as crafts, house building, watermills and work on boundary walls, there is division between men's work and women's work. However the boundaries are not so clearly marked, as there is overlapping and deviations from the rule. There are as well cases where the rule is inflexible and times when change is possible. Major portion of agriculture is done by women who do weeding, hoeing, planting, harvesting and thrashing except ploughing (which are done by men) in the fields adjacent to houses or far off fields. The other activities of women include looking after the house, children and cattle. Food processing and cooking is women's job. It is the women who with the assistance of children are largely responsible for the cattle, water fuel and fodder. This permits them considerable time away from home and the village. When they are away from home, they are free to talk to whom so ever they please, male or female, of any caste or creed. As a consequence, communication among women and between men and women is as high as it is among men. Tribal women are very strong and courageous in the handling of environmental imperatives as can be demonstrated in the trekking and work pattern under the severe limitations of the harsh environment. Several studies dealing with pastoral societies indicate that the position of women in such societies is not very high because the actual care of the livestock and handling of economic affairs is entirely a male domain. Though women do not directly help in handling of livestock, they do look after their husbands during migrations. They cook for them and carry loads.

The sources of subsistence and livelihood are varied so far the Indian tribals are concerned. Starting from the pure and simple parasitic habit of the nomadic hunters and food-gatherers who depend mostly on nature for the sources of subsistence to the settled agriculturists and the group of industrial laborers, we have the views of different economic set-up the Indian tribals.

The tribal population is identified as the aboriginal inhabitants of our country. They are most vulnerable section of our society living in natural and unpolluted surrounding far away from civilisation with their traditional values, customs and beliefs. There has been a long and enduring debate among the social scientists to define a tribe. Not withstanding the academic exercise, for the purpose of development and administration, the definition given by the Constitution serves our objective. The definition is practically an administrative definition. According to the Constitution "*Any tribe or tribal community or part of or group within any tribe or tribal community as deemed under article 342 are Scheduled Tribes for the purpose of the Constitution*".Thus, the groups which are in the Scheduled list of the President of India are defined as Scheduled Tribes. There is a procedure for including tribal groups in the Scheduled list.

In India women are discriminated due to several historical, religious and other reasons. A girl child is suppressed from the movement she is born in terms of personal development. She is made to undergo the feelings of being inferior and feeble. She is denied the prospects for personal expression.There are various hypotheses about why women have relatively high or low status. Thecommon premise is that women status is high when they contribute substantially to primary subsistence activities. Women position is low in the societies where food getting is entirely men'sjob like hunting, herding or intensive agriculture. In the historical times when warfare was essential, men were more esteemed than women. Likewise in the centralised political systems men had high status. Men in most societies contribute more to primary subsistence activities, as women have infant and child care responsibilities. However, women contribute substantially to primary subsistence activities that depend heavily on gathering and horticulture and in which men are away on labour or pastoral duties while subsistence work has to be done. When primary and secondary subsistence activities are counted,women work more than men.

The status of women in a society is asignificant reflection of the level of social justice in that society. Women's status is often described in terms of their level of income, employment, education, health and fertility as well as their roles within thefamily, the community and society. In tribal communities, the role of women is substantial and crucial. They constitute about half the total population but in tribal society women are more important than in other social groups, because they work harder and the family economy and management depends on them. Even after industrialisation and the resultant commercialisation swamped the tribal economy, women continued to play asignificant role. Collection of minor forest produce is done mostly by women and children. Many also work as laborers in industries, households and construction, contributing to their family income. Despite exploitation by contractors and managers, tribals are more sincere and honest than non-tribals.

However, tribal women face problems and challenges in getting a sustainable livelihood and a decent life due to environmental degradation and the interference of outsiders. The strategy for tribal development, and specially women, needs improvement, betterment, development and upliftment to effect their empowerment. Tribal women have adjusted themselves to live a traditional life style in the local environment and follow occupations based on natural resources. Undoubtedly, the programmes, oriented towards the empowerment of tribals, particularly women, have improved their socio-economic conditions ands tatus. However, there are wide variations across regions and tribes in terms of work participation, sex ratio, economic productivity and social life. The impact of development planning needs to be evaluated in terms of desired and unanticipated consequences. The development process should be perceived as an involvement and reorganisation mechanism of not only the socio-economic system but the entire eco-system. Against this backdrop, the present paper reviews the emerging perspective in the context of the socio-economic transition of tribal women and changing paradigms of development.

Study of Literature

Tribal women play a major role in the co-management of their natural, social, economic resources and agricultural development including crop production, livestock production, horticulture and post- harvest operations but they remain backward due to traditional values, illiteracy, superstitions, dominant roles in decision making, social evils and many other cultural factors. The participatory role of tribals in improving their living conditions by fully exploring natural endowments and alternative uses must find an appropriate place in the strategic approach. The social dynamics of tribal welfare and development is such that effective strategies to protect tribals and their livelihood imply negotiating some kind of social consensus about criteria concerning tribal development and values of the society that evolves from such programmes. This also implies a broad social consensus about the basic rights and opportunities that tribals should enjoy and the responsibilities that should be taken by different individual and social groups[TosibAlam, Mohammad Awais&Mohd. Asif, 2009]

There are some entrepreneurial opportunities which are more beneficial for women in rural areas as it enables them to add to the family income while taking care of their own home and increase the standard of living of the rural people. Some of such activities are, Micro enterprise development related to agriculture and allied agricultural activities and bee-keeping; Micro enterprise development related to livestock management activities like dairy farming, poultry farm, livestock feed production and production of using the animal waste; knitting, stitching, weaving and embroidery, create handicraft and handcrafted gift items, embroidery from thread etc.; business opportunities for women folk comprise of using metals, wood, stone and metal like iron, steel to create handicrafts and hand-crafted gift items; floriculture, seed production, mushroom production, processing of milk, dairy products, agro processing, coir work, toy making so on and so fore[Gunajit Sarma.2009,].

The migrant tribal women and girls faced a number of problems immediately after their migration to cities which included difficulty of communication in local language, residential accommodation, employment, education of children, local contacts, adjustment with city life and environment etc. The main causes of financial, physical and sexual exploitation of the migrant tribal women and girls in cities were poverty, lack of employment opportunities, lack of awareness, education, unorganised nature of labour force, misunderstanding of the local people about free sex in tribal's, and lack of community support to victims of sexual exploitation. Besides routine household work, the tribal women work in the agricultural fields, forests for long hours. The overall output if seen in terms of number of hours of work is low. Their schedule of long working hours continues even during pregnancy, natal and postnatal stages. They have a negative energy balance, high morbidity rate, and low child survival rate. They suffer from taboos and superstitions and remain deprived of the benefits from existing development and welfare programmes[GummadiNaresh, 2014,].

Work participation rate among scheduled tribe women were higher in percentage as compared to others. Poor economic condition has a direct bearing on the degree of participation. Scheduled tribe workers are engaged in agricultural sector andin non gainful occupations. Considering the education, economic and health of the tribal women, their positions were not at all satisfactory. A study by Singh and Rajyalaxmi(1993), status of tribal women in terms of their demography, health,education and employment have been discussed. Since independence, various protections have been given to the tribalpopulation by the Constitution of India. The study highlighted some aspects of tribal work; tribal women work equally withtheir male counterparts with lower pay, sexual exploitation. Tribal women don't have property rights, they have lower literacy rate than scheduled caste and general population. Tribal women are not healthy and suffer from mal nutrition and various diseases. The study highlighted the need to improve the status of tribal girl, to bring about change in the status of tribal woman[Pujasree Chatterjee,2014].

Objective of the Study

The studies have so far been made legitimately highlight the fact that the women have a definite role in the socio-economic transition of the tribal families. The scope provided by opening up of economy, if exploited successfully, could bring in definite advantage to the tribal women to engage themselves in newer fields through they can some money to extend support to their male partners in economic upliftment.

Keeping the views arrived at by several researchers, present study has the following objectives:-

(i) To review the change in socio-economic position of the tribal families;

(ii) To analyze the relative role of tribal women in socio-economic change in their families.

Data & Methodology

The present study is based on primary data collected from the families of the village of Belmuri with the help of suitably designed questionnaire. Since the tribal families are not well versed with the method of computation of income a reasonable estimate has been used considering the market price prevailing at the period of study. Socio-economic transition has been measured through access to different facilities-health, education, recreation, electronic devices etc.

There are several classes of tribals living in that village- Oraon, Bhumij, Munda, Santal and Lodha. The village is surrounded by the habitations of these communities. There is a close relationship between these lower caste people and the upper caste communities. So, there is a mutual belief and understandings between all the communities. In this regard, the cultural heritage in this village has always been warm and cordial.

Data collected are presented in simple tabular form to interpret and analyze without using any complicated statistical and mathematical devices. For the purpose of study data have been collected from 100 families of different caste groups as shown in Table-I below. Entire data collected in the year 2014(March to September).

Findings

Table-I

Sl. No.	*Type of Tribal Group Surveyed*	*No of Families Studied*
1.	**Oraon**	22
2.	**Bhumij**	24
3.	**Santal**	19
4.	**Munda**	24
5.	**Lodha**	11
	Total	**100**

Source: Primary Survey

The composition of family has a varied character. There are wide difference in age and sex, earners and non-earners, nature of works engaged in etc. Following are some of such features recorded.

Table-II

Distribution of Families by Number of Members & Composition

Sl.No.	*Type of Tribes*	*No. of Members*			*Composition*		
		Up to 3	*4 to 6*	*7 or more*	*Children*	*Male*	*Female*
1.	Oraon	12	7	3	27	37	21
2.	Bhumij	9	11	4	22	47	45
3.	Santal	10	7	2	24	34	23
4.	Munda	13	6	5	26	48	35
5.	Lodha	6	3	2	11	19	18
	Total	**50**	**34**	**16**	**120**	**185**	**142**

Source: Primary Survey

Table II shows the composition of the families under study. One thing is clear that a large number of families are of small size. Half of the families studied are having total number of members less than or up to 3-34 families are of medium size having 4-6 members. Only 16 families are of large size.

Education is a good indicator for socio-cultural transition of the tribal families. Literacy, level of education and drop-outs are studied among the families. For the sake of comparative assessment and change two period data are considered for 2004 and 2014. There has been change in no of family members due to birth and demise as well.

Table III

Education amongst the family members

Tribes	*Total Members*	*2004*				*2014*			
		Illiterate	*Primary*	*MP or above*	*Drop-out*	*Illiterate*	*Primary*	*MP or above*	*Drop-out*
Oraon	(79)85	45	12	1	21	29	32	12	12
Bhumij	(103)114	53	18	9	23	34	44	20	16
Santal	(74)81	34	15	3	22	23	32	15	11
Munda	(98)109	43	13	4	38	32	29	29	19
Lodha	(41)48	20	11	2	8	11	19	14	4
Total	**(395)437**	**195**	**69**	**19**	**112**	**129**	**156**	**90**	**62**

Source: Primary Survey, Figures in brackets indicate figure for 2004.

Table III shows how the families are getting education or are being more inclined to education. Number of itinerate persons have decreased over the years from 2004 to 2014. It is due to Sarba Siksha Avijan and Saksharata Mission implemented by the central and State Governments. Number of drop-outs has decreased which indicates the increasing conscience for education among the tribal families.

Economic transition can only be achieved only through increased scope for income and employment. The scope for employment is directly related with level of education and skill development. Traditional scope for earnings will help to sustain life but for transition newer avenues are to be explored. Another important matter is the role of women in earning of income and sharing of responsibility with their male partner in the economic development of the family.

A study on the earning scope for both men and women will highlight the respective role played by both of them. Table IV shows the result of the study in this aspect.

Table IV

Distribution of Male & Female members by scope of earnings.

Tribes	*Male*					*Female*			
	Number	*Daily labour*	*Agri-culture*	*Service*	*Other*	*Number*	*Gottery /Piggery*	*Poultry (domestic)*	*Others Including service*
Oraon	**37**	17	18	2	10	**21**	1	2	18(9)
Bhumij	**47**	19	18	1	9	**45**	5	3	37(19)
Santal	**34**	18	11	1	4	**23**	14	Nil	9(6)
Munda	**48**	23	12	Nil	13	**35**	12	11	12(7)
Lodha	**19**	11	4	Nil	4	**18**	6	5	8(5)

Source: Primary Survey.

Table IV indicates he various types of sources of earnings and engagement of the male and female members of tribal families studied. Among the male members daily labour and agricultural labour are the two main sources of earnings. Service is still not dominant source of earnings. Negligible number of people gets service as their source of earnings.

Table V

Distribution of families by Level of Earnings per month(Rs)

Tribes	*Male*				*Female*			
	Number	*≤2000*	*≤5000*	*≤5000*	*Number*	*≤1500*	*≤3000*	*≤3000*
Oraon	**37**	24	11	2	**21**	14	5	2
Bhumij	**47**	31	16	1	**45**	31	9	5
Santal	**34**	29	14	1	**23**	19	3	1
Munda	**48**	31	17	Nil	**35**	23	11	1
Lodha	**19**	11	8	Nil	**18**	10	5	3

Source: Primary Survey.

However, female members have still limited scope for striving out of their house for earning purpose. Still a portion of female members are earning something for the sake of families. Figures in brackets indicate no of female members who are typically housewives having no scope for earnings.

Table V hints about that maximum number of people are belonging to low income category. In case of service holders of any type are able to get a monthly income of Rs 5000 or more. However, in case of female members the number of women earning more than Rs 3000 is very low. But the main point is that out of 142 female members studied 96 women are earning something for their families. This will help them to enjoy some sort of liberty and participation in the family decisions makings.

Another aspect has been studied about the access to modern life. For this purpose access to modern electronic gadgets and other amenities are studied. Table VI shows the result.

Table VI

Distribution of families by access to Modern Accessories

Tribes	*No. families*	*Mobile*	*C/BW TV*	*2Wheeler*	*Internet*	*Freeze*
Oraon	22	**20**	**10**	**2**	**2**	**2**
Bhumij	24	**18**	**8**	**1**	**1**	**1**
Santal	19	**16**	**7**	**1**	**1**	**1**
Munda	24	**19**	**8**	**Nil**	**Nil**	**Nil**
Lodha	11	**10**	**2**	**Nil**	**Nil**	**Nil**

Source: Primary Survey.

Table VI shows most of the families studied have access to mobile phone. On average 20-45% of families have a television (Black & White or Colour) set. But there are very little number of families is having access to two-wheeler or internet or refrigerator.

Another important aspect of modern life is financial inclusion. More and more number of people are expected to participate in the banking network. Thanks to the government policies like Mahatma Gandhi National Rural Employment Guarantee Act. (MGNREGA) of central government, Kanyashrii or Jubashree of the West Bengal State Government have prompted the people to open a bank account. It is then obvious to see to what extent these schemes have laid impact.

Table-VII

Distribution of Male and Female Members having Bank Account

Caste	*No. of male*	*With Bank A/C*	*Without Bank A/C*	*No. of Female*	*With Bank A/C*	*Without Bank A/C*
Oraon	37	26	11	21	5	16
Bhumij	47	37	10	45	18	27
Santal	34	29	5	23	15	8
Munda	48	36	12	35	24	11
Lodha	19	11	8	18	10	8
	185	**1399 (75.13)**	**46 (24.87)**	**142**	**72 (50.70)**	**70 (49.30)**

Source: Primary Survey.

Table VII shows that so far as financial inclusion is concerned, women of the tribal community are lagging behind their male counterpart. It may be a good sign to look into the fact that at least 50% of women are having a bank a/c with them. So, there is still a long way to go in this regard if the women are to be inspired for increased earnings and employment.

Limitations of the study

Since there is not much empirical study on the role of tribal women for economic development of their respective families, the present study is solely based on primary data. The selection of sample area is having a good infrastructural environment. A clear comparison could have been made if another sample area was selected having a slackness so far as infrastructure is concerned. A time dimension could have been introduced in primary data for studying changes in situations with the passage of time. But since tribal men and women both are not well accustomed to recollect data, especially the numeric ones, such data are almost rare to collect.

Conclusions

The study has successfully indicates that there has been a change in the education amongst the families studied. Although a section of tribal women are remaining as housewives content with family work, a good number of them are out in the field to earn something to support their families. Such support helps the families to enjoy access to modern consumer durables. There is a growing interest among the tribal women to open bank a/c. This could open up to start entrepreneurial ventures if proper nourishing is extended. Small and medium enterprises in good number could come up if these women are properly counseled to that direction.

References

1. B. Ezhilarasu,2014, Impact Of Globalisation on Tribals in India, Indian Journal Of Applied Research.
2. Pujasree Chatterjee,2014, Social and Economic status of tribal women in India – The challenges and the Road Ahead, International Journal of Interdisciplinary and Multidisciplinary Studies.
3. GummadiNaresh, 2014, Work Participation of Tribal Women in India: A Development Perspective, IOSR Journal Of Humanities And Social Science.
4. Gunajit Sarma.2009, An Analytical Study on Entrepreneurial Activity as a tool for socio-economic development of Tribal Women in BTAD area of Assam, IOSR Journal of Economics and Finance.
5. TosibAlam, Mohammad Awais&Mohd. Asif, 2009, Socio-Economic Empowerment Of Tribal Women:An Indian Perspective, International Journal of Rural Studies (IJRS).

Tribal Migrant Settlers of Jharkhand in Hassimara of North Bengal: Impact of Tea Industry

Shailendra Prasad Sinha

Introduction

In India, Tribal constitutes a little more than 8.0% of the total population even today since attainment of our Independence. Tribal's are spread though out India but no doubt their large concentration lies in Central and eastern India. They are famously known by their ecological setting and cultural type which make them distinct from the other one. Hence they have developed a distinct style of life best suited to their distinct habitat.

In the Jungle and hilly track of Jharkhand and Santhal Paragana they have sharpened their tools and technology as peasant way of life best suited to the area and climatic condition. Gradually, thus this part of the country was also populated by others since long as well. Towards the close of 19th Century Christian missionaries engineered migration from Lohardagga, Gumla and Ranchi areas to the Tea Garden areas in Assam and North Bengal. Those days Britons were busy in establishing their Tea garden Estates by cleaning forests and planting tea gardens in the areas of Assam and Bengal.

Man is mobile by nature to excel one's condition. Britons were bent upon to trade in tea. So right from clearing the forests to the establishment of the Tea gardens and its all other horticultural activities only the tribal's of this part of the country were best skilled or made to be skilled. They were honest, dutiful and loyal to the Tea garden and its business. Tough Nepalese, Mach, and Rave were there but by dint of their simplicity, honesty, hardworking, sincerity and dutifulness Tribal's of this part of the country excelled and strengthened their position one by one. Gradually, in good number they migrated and thus settled zealously finally in the areas of Jalpaiguri and other parts of North Bengal and Assam only to excel their economic condition. This way they changed their agro-forest economy too exclusively of wage earning.

North Bengal

State of West Bengal is stretched length wise from far away sea-sore of Calcutta to the high hills of Darjeeling dividing thus North and South Bengal or Bengal in high hills in North and plain along with network of rivers meeting sea in South. Extreme northern part of Bengal in hills, foot hills, tarai and plains thereby areas are full of Teagarden and populated mostly by the tribal's of Jharkhand. But, till date they are tribal settlers not the locals one and thus different from others living there.

After experimentation in Calcutta then in Ranchi, the Britons went on large scale establishing Tea gardens such as Santhali, Beaze, Bharnobari etc. in Hassimara Area. Since long the product of these gardens has been exported to different parts of the world as unique example of globalisation by foreigners. Tribal settlers in majority have been laborers.

Within its green heritage this area is surrounded by the hills of Assam, Bhutan, Sikkim, Nepal, Darjeeling and Koch Behar. As such its topography is prized for tea plantation and paddy cultivation.

Hassimara

Hassimara is a part of Kalchini Block of the subdivision of Alipur Duar but lies in the Western Duar of the District of Jalpaiguri. In fact the west to the river Tista was permanently settled by the Zamindars of the area since 1793 under the permanent settlement act but, the areas East of the river Tista - a sub-mountains region of North Bengal known as western Dears went unheeded and remained no man's land for a longer period. This area has been full of water pools here and there which was claimed by the people from Nepal, Bhutan and Raja of Koch Behar. Under the umbrella of British Government at the close of 19th Century a famous Chinchulo agreement came into force in favor of Indians which ultimately went under the control of British Administration. Earlier it was hunting and Bird shooting arena for the Britons. Later on due to unique climatic condition in which temperature used to oscillated between 10° degree to 32° degree Celsius and till date it is like that only in 1960 the government of West Bengal granted Patta (lease of the land) to very few families of settlers and Ravas and Mech on the margin of the forest with twin objectives - one to nurture and protect forest and to save the area from wild attack of elephants and rhinos in plenty in the forest who always invade. This presents two types of tenancy - one of the company ownership and the other of the land lease by the W.B. Govt.

It keeps area moist and humid for the whole year which often invites rain up to seven to eight month with good drainage system served by the two rivers in the area Tista and Turshalar. From Hansh (Duck) mare to Hassimara name of this particular area became popular latter on. This possesses a famous airbase of strategic nature and emerging fast in a small urban centre very close to the phulshing gateway of Bhutan.

Methodology : Present paper is based on the Author's prized opportunity in April, 2006 as Field Supervisor-cum-Prof. in charge of the field work for 46 P.G. students of Dept. of Anthropology, Ranchi University, Ranchi stationed at Hassimara for more than a month. That was an extensive and exhaustive empirical research.

Recently author's interaction with the last month another batch of P.G. Student of Anthropology of Ranchi University who has undergone field work in Hassimara has confirmed many burning problems of Tribal settlers at Hassimara. All standard tool of research were used. Several village clusters of North Satali, Satali and Bharnobari were taken into consideration. Information gathered from few Birjia, many Oraons and Munda families regarding problems faced with which go unheeded by the Tea Company and local administration.

India rich in population but suffers much in abject poverty. To understand fundamentals of problems faced by Jharkhand Tribal settlers in Hassimara it will be better to deal in its Socio-cultural background.

Socio-Cultural Background

To champion the cause of Tea Estate Britons transported tribals from Jharkhand in bulk through the "Sardars" who were the agents (labour contractors) for the tribals mostly from within the tribals. In the name of "Sardar" they were recruited. They were gradually sheltered in free allotted linearly assigned quarters in labour line just located on the boundary of the tea gardens. Thus they were provided 1BHK/2 BHK quarter having water, latrine, electricity, good lanes and roads. In the midst of it health centre for free health problems were made to run properly. They were given transport facility for their children to take them to nearest schools and back. Likewise on subsidized rate they get 2 kg rice per week per labour.

That changed table upside down when in the beginning tribals of subsistence economy eagerly took it as golden opportunity for them and moved to get the first birth. After one's death or retirement the son or the nearest kin was given the job. Females work in garden to pluck tea leaves and weeding. Boys & gents work manual job, supervision and in tea processing factory. As if, Tea garden made them to earn fortune.

This may they passed several generations and now for the last several years it has changed the situation in an atmosphere of fear psychosis with innumerable problems of incurable situation:-

1. Since they are settlers they have been kept at bay from the benefits of the scheduled tribe where as Rava, Mech and Khatri are getting

the benefits. Settlers are, as if, living in a degraded life than the others.

2. Above state of affair has forced them to live hand to month with several restrictions and hiccups.
3. They cannot sale or mortgage or do away with the property for a larger cause of survivals or to excel one's economy due to company's ownership and lease of land within four corners of the law.
4. They are less paid wage earner. They get Rs 46/- per day not that minimum wage of Rs 160 or 180/- per day and the like wise.
5. **Exploitation :** Weighing machine of the company is very old having full of errors. It lies on the dictates of the machine operator. Weighing master plays nefarious game in weighing less the plucked leaves in the bag of the laborer. Per day it ought to be 24 Kg but it is brought to a measure of 18 Kg to 20 kg in many cases putting loss to the garden laborers. This reduces the weekly payment of the laborers.
6. **Complain:** Often it goes unheeded or given a false assurance. In fact, nobody is there to take stock of the situation or listen to complain.
7. Atrocities : It has been irony of the fate of the tribal settlers when they become victim of organised and planned cheating. In fact there are gangs operating in particular area to benefit the settlers specially tea garden workers. At times, news surfaced that just before or after the payment of insurance or retirement benefits or fixed deposit benefit one is murdered. Always there lays ulterior motive either to get the job or the quarter or so on.
8. Also there are people of influence who have kept more than one wife working in the tea gardens or in the company befooling others against the legal and social norms.
9. **Cultural transformation :** Need not to describe much but the process of transformation going on in such a way that the tribal migrant settlers are on the cross-road.

Impact of Tea Industry

They on migration hardly continued their link with the place of orientation but starting finding sufficient cash in hand and other facilities gradually detached them from the areas of Jharkhand by breaking all Socio-cultural links forever.

Naturally, they got uprooted and thus their neighbor/Kith and Keen, other relatives took over all their share of hearth/house and all other properties including land. In large scale, it stands to be a clear case of land alienation.

They are now in a situation whether to go and what to do, as if, there is no way out.

As regards education after eighth class the children are sent to the institutions outside Bengal either in Bokaro or Dhanbad or elsewhere because Bengali or English are only option for medium of education.

Conclusion

In the beginning the Tea garden labour economy brought an alternative/ additional source of employment and income as if a wonder but latter on gradually proved to be a blunder in life and morale with full of bewildered frustration.

- **Marriage** - Bride price has been customary one but inter -cast/inter-tribal marriages have brought some limitations. And thus as a result the girls are advancing more and more in their age as unmarried one. Even for the cause of aged parents the situation is also becoming from bad to the worst when the girls get cheated by the male one and they get trapped in their nefarious games.
- Drug abuse is phenomenal and in good number of cases boys and girls are found serious drug addict.
- Human trafficking is, as if, going on unchecked.
- Taken together drug addict and sex rackets are visible when one can see French leather, used drug packets, while passing through the tea gardens in the garden area they are seen rooming in the bushes- a good shelter. The tea gardens which at times are used as safe place to go for such acts.
- Speech of a distinct nature emerging at Hassimara mixed with Bengali language. Also clothing is reflective of Bengali Style.
- Poor economic condition has forced them to go for a 2nd hand used clothing's - "Saris, Pants, Jackets which they call *Bengali Bastro*" in less price.
- Often master of the company changes and creates a fear psychosis of closure of the company. This forces them to get exploited in many a ways.

All sorts of diseases - curable and incurable as well as perennial one are phenomenal. All sorts of crime are rampant in the area.

Bibliography

1. Bose, K.K. 1865; Political Mission to Bhutan (Account of Bhutan), 1865. Kolkata.
2. Dandaker, V. M & Ratha, 1971; Poverty in India, Economy and Political weekly, 6(1)

3. Grunning 1911; Jalpaiguri District Gazetteer, Jalpaiguri.
4. Kakar, S & Kakar, K. 2007; The Indians Portrait of a people, Penguin Books, India.
5. Max Webbers, 1954: Law in Economy and Society, Cambridge: Harvard University Press.
6. Mitra, 1953; The Tribe and caste of Bengal, Kolkata.
7. Risley. H. H. 1891; Tribes and castes of Bengal, Kokata.
8. Sinha, S.P. 2009; Jharkhand Tribal Migrant Settlers in Hassimara of North Bengal: Human Rights Violation" J.S. R, Vol. 35 : 1 & 2.
9. Sunder, D. 1895; Survey and settlements of Western Duors.
10. Vidyarthi, L.P. & Rai, B. K. 1976; Tribal cultures of India, concept publication, New Delhi.

Impact of Globalisation on Tribal Communities in Jharkhand

Prabhat K. Singh

A number of definitions of globalisation have been given in the last two decades on different aspects in different way. The globalisation started with liberalisation and privatisation. The globalisation has a set of distinct characteristic, such as, emergence of a world order controlled by economically and militarily powerful nations and their allies that exercises its surveillance on all nations of the world; brisk and universal spread of transnational corporations which bring qualitative changes in the lives of the people; and large scale mobility across the nations of goods, commodities, communication, information, products, services and people who need common language, lifestyle, and technology to carry out business and conduct their everyday life.

The globalisation and the term 'neo-liberalism' are, often, used as the synonym and interchangeable. Neo-liberalism promotes exploitation, produces inequality, changes economic and government policies to increase the power of corporations, and a shift to benefit the upper classes, and deregulates the labour market producing casualisation of labour and greater informal employment. It increases the disparities between the rich and poor.

Big houses and corporate sector have been preaching that globalisation is good for all and beneficial for the members of the global community. They say that globalisation has potentials for development and wealth creation. However, overall globalisation has had a devastating effect on developing countries as the problems of unemployment, inequality and poverty have tremendously increased. It has also adversely affected the life and work of people, their families, and their societies, working conditions, income and social protection, security, culture and identity, and the cohesiveness of families and communities.

Globalisation is a multifaceted process with economic, social, political and cultural implications. During this period of globalisation, more and more private institutions are being established. These challenges not only address issues of access, equity, funding and quality but also those of national sovereignty, cultural diversity, poverty and sustainable development.

The first decade of this century witnessed world over large scale and bitter protests from the people at large against the privatisation and commercialisation. General Agreements on trade in Services (GATS) and World Trade Organisation (WTO) are the institutions by the governments. The idea behind WTO- GATS has been the creation of an open, global marketplace where services, can be traded to the highest bidder.

India has undergone major changes since the adoption of neo –liberal economic policies in the beginning of the 1990s. This decade is also known as the start of era of LPG- liberalisation, privatisation, and globalisation. In this regime, one witnesses economic liberalisation, free trade and markets, privatisation and deregulation. Disinvestment of the public sector is increasing, and where greater role of private and corporate sector is taking place.

Change is the universal phenomenon and has been taking place continuously. But, with the advent of this globalisation, changes are taking place with greater pace in all the communities. The tribal communities are also not exceptional; rather the tribal communities are the most and worst affected in this regard. Fortunately or unfortunately the tribal communities are the real custodian of the valuable natural resources by which the development of the world or any nation occurs. The tribal communities' have habitat in the rich natural resource areas. The exploitation of natural resources for maximisation of profits, leads to acquisition of land. Acquisition of land by the state or the corporate house leads to the displacement of the tribal settlements making them vulnerable.

Jharkhand is rich in natural and mineral resources where impact of globalisation through liberalisation and privatisation policies could be seen. **In this paper attempt has been** made to make an understanding of situation of tribal communities in Jharkhand due to globalisation. Exploitation of natural resources, privatisation of public property, alienation of land, displacement due to big projects, such as dams and heavy industrialisation etc. are the things responsible for the poverty of the tribal communities.

Tribal Situation in Jharkhand:

(1) The population of Jharkhand is 32,966,238 with 22.34 decadial growths. The male population is 16,931,688 and 16,034,550 is the number of the female population as per the 2011 census. The sex ratio is 947. Out of the total population of the state, the tribal population is 26.2 percent. About 94 percent tribal population is settled in the rural areas. 66.85 percent are engaged in cultivation and 4.15 percent are engaged in domestic works where as 29 percent are in other works. Jharkhand has a total area of 79,714 sq km in which 23,655 sq km is forest land. Total 37.30% is cultivable land

(30 lakh hectares) and 29.16% is forest land. 1.59 lakh hectares is water resource and 7.17 lakh hectares is waste land.

(2) District wise distribution of ST population shows that Gumla district has the highest proportion of STs (68.4 per cent). The STs constitute more than half of the total population in Lohardaga and Paschimi Singhbhum districts whereas Ranchi and Pakur districts have 41.8-44.6 percent tribal population. Kodarma district (0.8 percent) preceded by Chatra (3.8 per cent) has the lowest proportion of the ST Population.

(3) Out of thirty two (32) Scheduled Tribes notified for the State, Santhal is the most populous tribe having a population of 2,754723, constituting 31.86 per cent of the total ST population of the State. The Santhal,Oraon, Munda and Ho the four largest tribes constitute 76.67 percent of the total ST population of the State.

(4) 'Cultivators' constitute more than half of the total workers and this figure is significantly higher than the national average of 44.7 percent recorded by all STs in this category. 'Agricultural Labourers' account for 31 percent which is less than that recorded for all STs at the national level (36.9 percent). 'Other Workers' form 13.5 percent which is comparable with the national average of 16.3 percent whereas workers engaged in Household Industry (HHI) constitute 3 percent which is marginally higher than that of the national average (2.1 percent).

(5) Among the major tribes, Oraon, Munda and Kharia have 62.71 percent workers engaged as 'Cultivators' followed by Kharwar and Santhal. Bhumij and Lohra have recorded the highest percentage of 'Other Workers' as well as 'HHI' workers in comparison to other major tribes.

(6) The tribes of Jharkhand present several cultural types based on different types of means of production for their livelihood and life. They can be classified under the following cultural types (Vidyarthi, 1976).

(a) Forest hunting (Birhor, Korwa).

(b) Hill cultivation (Sauria Paharia, Saber).

(c) Agriculture (santhal, Munda, Oraon, Ho).

(d) Artisan (Karmali, Lohra, Mahali).

(e) Labour (several tribes).

(f) White collar job (several tribes).

Each cultural type presents specific culture due to specific type of economic system having different type of means of production, products and its relation with the group.

Tribal cultures and Globalisation

Each tribe has its own culture more and less different from the other. There are several factors responsible for its formation and differentiation. The major factors are different geographical distribution, ecological, economical, racial formation and linguistic. Besides these, there are many material and non-material factors for the formation of the culture, which also vary from tribe to tribe, as per the different material and non- material condition of the society.

The culture system can be divided into three sub systems. The most basic one is technology, tools weapons and knowledge of their use. Two other social systems are social structure and ideological or philosophical (for example – marriage, kinship and family and belief, moral, totem, taboo etc.). All these are in a mutually influencing interrelationship. Technology dominates by operating through social structure on ideology. So, we can say that the culture involves adaptation to its surrounding and it cannot be static

Jharkhand is rich in minerals and natural resources which are exploited more in the past for profit alone, without the tribal getting any benefits. So, in the era of globalisation the tribal communities run the risk of greater marginalisation than in the past. The process of marginalisation did not begin with the present form of globalisation. It started with- the first phase of colonialism, the military and political control exercised by European countries over those of global south. The second phase followed with cold-war. This phase is also called as neo-colonialism. During this phase, the countries continued their control over the economics of the south without being physically present. They did it through Aid, and trade such by world Bank etc. Culture was intrinsic to colonialism. The local technology, culture and economy were delegitimized through the new value system. In the third phase, the focus shifted to the imposition of single economy on the world in the name of free market. The WTO Agreement on agriculture- a tool of globalisation includes them in the common domain. A change of culture is basic to the globalised economy, and tool used today is the information technology. Globalisation intensifies individualism which is basic to it with selfishness of the middle class. This changes the form of tribal community into new culture.

Jharkhand: Impact of Globalisation

Jharkhand is known as the abode of Adivasis (the indigenous people, constitutionally they are called as scheduled tribe), the land of struggle and mineral rich state in India. "Jharkhand" literally means 'the land of forests' came into existence as 28th state of the Indian union on 15th of November, 2000 after a long mass struggle, which took place in the 20th century for the realisation of a beautiful dream of the Adivasi heroes – Tilka Manjhi, Sidhu-Kanhu and Birsa Munda. The dream was to form exploitation free, humane and just Jharkhand, where the Adivasis can practice their ownership rights over the natural resources, enjoy autonomy and rule themselves as earlier they used to. The outsiders perceive Jharkhand as the abode of uncivilised, uneducated and the most backward people. The region was mostly neglected in terms of the development but its natural resources were highly exploited. The Adivasis were alienated from their resources, exploited and injustices were done to them in the name of development, civilisation and nationalism.

Jharkhand is witness of unending struggle for mineral resources as the state contains 40 percent of India's precious minerals like Uranium, Mica, Bauxite, Granite, Gold, Silver, Graphite, Magnetite, Dolomite, Fireclay, Quartz, Fieldspar, Coal, Iron and Copper. Forests and woodlands occupy more than 29% of the state which is amongst the highest in India. But unfortunately, the exploitation and injustice are prevalent in the state. Irony is the political leaders of Adivasis do not realize it even today. They have signed 102 MoUs (memorandum of understanding) for establishing steel factories, power plants and mining industries with the estimated investment of Rs 4,67,240 crore, which require approximately 200,000 acres of land, which directly means the displacement of approximately 1 million people.

In Jharkhand, cases of alienation of tribal land have risen despite two laws - Chotanagpur Tenancy Act and Santhal Pargana Tenancy Act to prevent sale of tribal land to non tribals in the state. In addition to these acts, Jharkhand has fifth scheduled areas in fifteen districts out of twenty four districts. Around 5,500 land-related cases of tribals were pending in various district courts in Jharkhand as of March 2007. The government of Jharkhand had an annual budget of Rs 50 lakh to provide legal assistance to poor tribals to pursue their land related cases. However, less than 10 per cent of the total allocated budget was spent over the last six years. Lawyers were unwilling to fight cases on behalf of tribals seeking government assistance. Lack of lawyers to take up land-related cases of the tribals further delayed adjudication. The offer of Rs 5,000 per case was cited as one of the main reasons for pendency of land-related cases in courts.

In February 2007, the Supreme Court allowed a tribal petitioner to file a fresh petition before the Jharkhand High Court for recovery of his land from a mining company. In its order, the Supreme Court held that the Jharkhand High Court was wrong to dismiss the petition of Surendra Dehri, a tribal who alleged that over 10,000 acres of "notified tribal land" had been usurped by mining contractors in connivance with the government officials. The High

Court had dismissed his petition saying that it involved only "private interest". But a bench of Supreme Court comprising Justices B.N. Agarwal and P.P. Naolekar stated that a clear violation of constitutional guarantees given to the tribals could not be held to be related to "private interest".

The tribals of Jharkhand have also been protesting against the implementation of Koel Karo hydroelectric project by National Hydroelectric Corporation over the Koel and Karo rivers. The project, if implemented, would submerge as many as 256 villages involving 50,000 acres of forest area, 40,000 acres of agricultural land and 300 forest groves (considered sacred by the tribals), 175 churches and 120 Hindu temples.

Legal safeguards meant to protect tribal land from being alienated to non-tribal such as the Chotanagpur Tenancy Act (1908), the Santal Parganas Tenancy Act (1949), the Constitutional provisions through the 5th Schedule, the Provisions (Extension to Scheduled Areas) Act (1996), some significant Supreme Court judgements such as the Samata Judgement (1997) were continue to be neatly ignored by the central & state governments in generously awarding vast tracts of land to industrialists at their asking. Over hundred such MOUs were signed during 2001 and 2010. Rough estimates indicate that about 1.4 lakh acres of land have been signed off. Globalisation has accelerated the process of land acquisition in Jharkhand and discontent has raised among the tribes.

Tribals do not want to give their land for the development projects, which can provide them jobs. After the independence, 17,10,787 people were displaced while acquiring 24,15,698 acres of their lands for setting up the Power Plants, Irrigation Projects, Mining Companies, Steel Industries and other development projects in Jharkhand. In every project approximately 80 to 90 percent Adivasis and local people were displaced but merely 25 percent of them were halfway rehabilitated and no one has any idea about the rest 75 percent displaced people. The benefits of these development projects were highly enjoyed by the Landlords, Project Officers, Engineers, Contractors, Bureaucrats, Politicians and outsiders, and those who sacrificed everything for the sake of the "development" are struggling for their survival.

The people were betrayed in the name of rehabilitation, compensation and jobs. The promises were not fulfilled and the jobs were given to the outsiders. In the present era, the technologies are mostly used in the companies therefore job opportunities and job security have declined the corporate. For example, when the Tata steel was producing 1 Mt steel, the work force was 70,000 in 1995. The growth of the Tata steel went up to 7 Mt in 2008 but the workforce declined to 20,000. Similarly, in the Heavy Engineering Corporation, Ranchi there were 23,000 employees at the beginning but it declined to 3000 in 2009.

The Job insecurity can be learnt from the Mittal Company, which is said to provide 1 lakh, jobs to the people. Presently, the company operates in 60 countries and it has plants in 20 countries but the company has been suffering from the economic crisis since 2008. The demand of company's steel went down to10 percent. Consequently, the company cut the production in Canada by 45 percent and axed 9,000 employees. It also cut the job of 1000 employees in lowest cost plant in Poland and shut one out of its two blast furnaces in west Belgium. The company had total workforces of 3, 26,000 which was cut down to 3, 15,867 as a result 10,133 people lost their jobs. The present status shows that the company is totally failure in protection of its employees' rights therefore 2000 employees had attacked the company's headquarter at Lubzumburge.

Tribals had the ownership rights to the natural resources and they judiciously used these resources for their survival. But soon after the East India Company entered into the territory, the Britishers realised the enormous commercial potential of India's natural resources and systematically went about acquiring control over it. In 1793 the "Permanent Settlement Act" was passed, which affected the socio-economic and cultural life of the Adivasis, and their lands slipped into the hands of the Zamindars (landlords). In 1855, the government declared the forests as the government property and the individuals have not right and claim over it. In 1865 the first Forest Act came into force, an avalanche of regulations followed this act. Wherever a loophole was detected in the existing laws a new law would be passed. After the independence, when Indians took over the driving sit they also followed the Britishers' footsteps. The rights over natural resources of the Adivasi were snatched away through the various legislations. The government of India accepts through the Forest Rights Act 2006 that the historical injustice was done on the Adivasi community.

There are numerous laws made for protection of the tribals rights but these laws were never enacted honestly. The Chota Nagpur Tenancy Act 1908 and Santhal Pargana Tenancy Act 1949 prohibit the sale and transfer of Adivasi land to non-Adivasi but the land were illegally snatched away from them. In 1969, the Bihar Scheduled Areas Regulation Act was enforced for prevention and legalisation of illegal land transfer and of Adivasis. A special Area Regulation Court was established and the Deputy Commissioner was given special right regarding the sell and transfer of Adivasis land. When the special court started function, a huge number of cases were registered. According to the government's report, 60,464 cases regarding 85,777.22 acres of illegal transfer of land were registered till 2001-2002. Out of these 34,608 cases of 46,797.36 acres of land were considered for hearing and rest 25,856 cases related to 38,979.86 acres of land were dismissed.

But after the hearing merely 21,445 cases regarding 29,829.7 acres of lands were given possession to the original holders and rest remains with the non-Adivasis. Furthermore 2608 cases of illegal land transfer were registered in 2003-2004, 2657 cases in 2004-2005, 3230 cases in 2005-2006, 3789 cases in 2006-2007 and 5382 cases in 2007-2008, which clearly indicates that the cases of illegal land alienation is increasing rapidly. According to the Annual Report 2004-2005 of the Ministry of Rural Development of the Government of India, Jharkhand topped the list of tribal land alienation in India with 86,291 cases involving 10,48,93 acres of land. Similarly, the constitutional rights, provisions for the sixth scheduled Areas and the Extension of Panchayat Act 1996 were never been implemented with the true spirit in the state. The ruling elites always misused these laws for their benefits.

The government of India was unable to bring a law for the rehabilitation of the affected people even after the 62 years of independence but legislation for the Special Economic Zone (SEZ) was passed immediately. Similarly, when the Jharkhand state was created the first chief minister, Babulal Marandi brought the Industrial Policy but at the same time, the same government was unable to make a rehabilitation policy. This is why the intention of the state was always questioned and the people are resisting against displacement everywhere. The people were displaced from one place to another in the name of development but they were not rehabilitated. Hence they feel that they were betrayed in the welfare state in the name of "development" and "national interest". Therefore, now tribals believe that they can protect their land only through the mass struggle.

The displacement is not just shifting people from one place to another but it is destruction of their livelihood resources, culture and identity which they develop by nourishing for the ages. The life cycle of the tribals is based on the natural resources therefore their co-existence with the nature cannot be questioned. The tribals have lost their faith in the state machinery, constitutional authorities and judiciary therefore they have firmly decided not to allow laying down the foundation of corporate development model over their graves.

Further, in the era of globalisation and after capital formation of Ranchi there are several projects coming to displace and alienate the tribal land which will further uproot the tribals and their culture.

1. Land Alienation

A very conservative estimate indicates that during the last 60 years approximately 2 crores 13 lakhs people have been displaced in the country owing to big projects such as mines, dams, industries, wild life sanctuaries, field firing range etc. of this, at least 40%, approx 65 lakhs are indigenous people/ tribal people. Of all the displaced; only one fourth have been resettled.

The remaining were given some cash compensation arbitrarily fixed by local administration.

Independent studies done during the mid 1990's reveal that in Jharkhand about 15 lakhs acres of land alienated from mainly adivasi people. During the last 15 years, a lot more displacement of people and alienation of land have taken place. Rehabilitation of the displaced was never taken seriously by any government during all these six decades when the process of industrialisation for national development has been in practice. In fact there was no rehabilitation process at all.

People resistance movements against displacement sprang up in different parts of Jharkhand from 2004 onwards. Hardly three-four companies have successful in acquiring land to set-up their industries and started their production. Jharkhand is witnessing of unending struggle for their survival. It is to be noted that 40% of India's precious minerals like uranium, mica, Bauxite, Granite, Gold, Graphite, Magnetite, Coal, Iron, copper etc. Irony is that political leaders of Adivasis do not realize it even today. People are resisting against displacement, attacking the company officials and not allowing them to enter into the villages. Consequently the government is unable to execute the MOUs at the grassroots. There has been turmoil against land alienation in the state. Few cases are such as-

1. On 1st October 2008, the villagers attacked on the Kohinoor Steel Plant near Jamshedpur, seized 70 trucks and stopped the work. They alleged that after acquiring their agricultural land, the Company neither compensated nor gave them jobs as promised.
2. At another case, the villagers attacked three surveyors of Bhushan Steel at Potka of East Singhbhum district. The villagers caught them, painted on their faces with cow dung on 11September 2008.
3. Similarly, the villagers attacked Jupiter Cement Factory, beaten the workers and stopped the factory on 11 September 2008 at Kharsawan alleging for violating the land related laws.
4. Officials of the Steel Gaint Arcelor Mittal Company were not allowed to enter into the villages in Torpa – Kamdera region near Ranchi several times.
5. The people of Tontoposi in Saraikela –Kharswan district are not allowing the Tata steel to acquire land for its Green Field Project.
6. In another case, the Adivasis of Dumka District have imposed Janta Curfew in Kathikund and Sikaripara blocks with the slogan- "we shall give up our lives but not land, against the proposed Power Plant of C E S C Limited. Police firing took place on 6th December, 2008 caused the killing of two activists—Laxman Tudu and Saigat Marandi and another seven were injured.

The people resistances have forced the Tata Steel, Arcelor Mittal Comp, Jindal Steel, Esser Steel and CESE Limited to leave the proposed areas so far. But even to these days displacements and repressions are continuing- recent firing at Keredari in Hazaribagh, Nagri and Torpa firing is the case- and there are many to be resolved.

Interestingly, the corporate houses have not given up their hopes and attempting to enter into the region through the back doors. They are playing tricks and attracting and buying people with the huge monetary for acquiring land. The global steel giant Arcelor Mittal Company is an example to understand how the companies attempt to trick the adivasis. Arcelor signed up MoU on October 8, 2005 for a steel Plant with a capacity of 12 Million tons per annum at an estimated investment of Rs 40,000 Crores. It requires 25,000 acres of land and 20,000 unit water per hour for the Steel Plant. It needs huge water, for it a Mega Dam at Koel Karo which will affected Adivasis of 256 villages.

The people were betrayed in the name of rehabilitation, compensation and jobs. The promises were not fulfilled and jobs were given to the outsiders. Moreover, in the present era, the technologies are mostly used in companies; therefore, job opportunities and job security have declined. For example, when Tata Steel was producing one million tons, the workforce was 70,000 in 1995. The growth of the Tata Steel went up to Seven Million tons in 2008 but the workforce declined to 20,000. Similarly, in HEC, Ranchi there were 23000 employees at the beginning but it declined to 3000 in 2009.

In 1969 when schedule Area Regulation Act came into force, a special area Regulation Court was established and the Deputy Commissioner was given right regarding the sell and transfer of Adivasi Land. Special Court started functioning and a huge number of cases were registered. According to government report 60,646 cases regarding 85,777.22 acres of illegal transfer of land were registered till 2001-02. Out of these 34,608 cases of 46,797.36 acres of land were considered for hearing and rest 25,856 cases related to 38,979.86 acres of land were dismissed. 21,445 cases regarding 29,829.7 acres of lands were given possession to the original holders and rest remains with non-adivasis.

Furthermore, 2608 cases of illegal transfer were registered in 2003-04,; 2657 in 2004-05; 3230 cases in 2005-06; 3789 cases in 2006- 07; 5382 cases in 2007-08 which clearly indicates of illegal alienation is increasing rapidly. Ministry of rural Development of India (Annual Report- 2004-05) - says- Jharkhand topped the list of Adivasi land Alienation in India with 86,291 cases involving 10, 4893 acres of land.

After the formation of Jharkhand state, the first Chief Minister Babulal Marandi brought the Industrial Policy of Jharkhand but could not make the rehabilitation policy. The Industrial Policy marked that along the National High Way- No. 33, the Ranchi –Tata road, 5km stretch both side of the road will be made special economic Zone for the industrialists. People are resisting against the displacement everywhere. The people were displaced from one place to another In the name of development but they were not rehabilitated. Therefore, now adivasis believe that they can protect their land only through the mass struggle.

Further, there is a proposal to acquired land for Greater Ranchi affecting about 587,370 people, acquiring land of about 120,033.63 hectares land from 396 villages from peripheral Blocks of Ranchi such as Ranchi, Ratu, Kanke, Namkum, Burmu, Mandar, Bero, Angara,and Ormanjhi. There is another acquisition of land is taking place for a Ring Road of Ranchi which will affect about 1.39 lakh people of 76 villages and about twenty nine thousand ha land will be acquired. One should understand that the displacement is not just shifting from one place to another but it is destruction of their livelihood resources, culture, and identity which they develop by nourishing for the ages. The life cycle of adivasis is based on the natural resources therefore their coexistence with the nature cannot be questioned. It is need of the hour to rethink on the present development model. The unjust development process cannot be carried on as the Adivasis also have similar rights to life with dignity, freedom, and equality guaranteed by the constitution of India. The Adivasis / Triabal people have lost faith in the state machinery, constitutional authorities and the Judicial. Now the tribal unrest turning towards the militant extremism and very much it has turned towards.

Table: 1

Total Land Acquired for Development Schemes in Jharkhand 1951-95.

Water Resources	507,952.00	34%
Industries	175,730.18	11.7
Thermal Power	6026.87	00.4
Mines	515,124.59	34.4
Defence Estd	112289.11	07.5
Misc. Schemes	178,824.29	12.0
Sub Total	1,495,947.04	100
Missing Scheme	50,000.00	
Grand total	1,545,947.04	

Source: Ekka,A & Ashif M, 2000, 110-11

Table: 2

Proposed Land Acquisition for Greater Ranchi Project

S.N	*Blocks*	*No. of villages*	*Total area in ha*	*Total*
1.	Ranchi Sadar	37	6,206.70	94,713
2.	Ratu	92	23,914.26	125,162
3.	Kanke	86	24,720.71	165,953
4.	Namkum	111	41,993.69	103,886
5.	Burmu	08	2,811.11	12,426
6.	Mandar	08	2,428.13	10,791
7.	Bero	14	4,116.64	25,782
8.	Angara	13	5,701.24	24,381
9.	Ormanjhi	27	8,140.65	27,276
	Total	**396**	**120,033.13**	**587,370**

Source: Prabhat Khabar, Hindi Dainik : 19 Sept. 2005.

Table: 3

Proposed Land Acquisition for the Ring Road in Greater Ranchi

S.N	*Blocks*	*No. of villages*	*Total area in ha*	*Total*
1.	Ratu	8	2,724.74	24,964
2.	Kanke	48	13,620.53	80,413
3.	Namkum	14	9,582.95	20,199
4.	Angara	5	2,928.70	12,876
5.	Ormanjhi	1	104.13	688
	Total	76	28,961.05	139,140

Source; Prabhat Khabar, Hindi Dainik : 19 Sept. 2005

2. Job Loss, Deprivation and Migration

Migration takes place everywhere and is a very old phenomenon. But its nature, pattern, causes and consequences differ from region to region. In Jharkhand, since the early nineteenth century seasonal and permanent out migration was reported this increased as the years passed. The colonial period, 18th century to early twentieth century where imperialist forces started grabbing different parts of the world under its expansion policy. This period, witnessed many violence, wars and famines which put an impact on the people, and forced to migrate from their original settlements.

From Jharkhand, a large number of people out-migrate every year. Several surveys show that highest level of migration is found in Gumla. At least one of the members migrates from 41.3 percent of the families of this district.

Altogether 13.4 percent of the members are found to be migrating. High incidence of out migration from this state is because of the existence of mass poverty and absence of long term productive employment opportunities in the rural areas, as we have seen above. Except the kharif season there is virtually no farm employment available in the villages. The migration is mostly seasonal in nature which is better known as survival migration. Around seventy percent of the households from at least one member migrate for short period in lean season. About three fifth of such families in Gumla and three fourth in Palamau and Dumka reported to be migrating for short period only. Around two third of the migrating persons migrate for short period and only one third for long period. Short period migration is lowest from Gumla (56.6%) and highest from Palamau (78.5%). This is because of socio-economic composition of the districts. Those who are better off mostly migrate for long period and the worse off for short period. Another special feature of the migration from this area is a large number of female out migration.

The magnitude and pattern of migration varies on the basis of socio-economic status of the villages of this region. Migration is higher among the socially and economically weaker sections than those who are better off. The duration of migration also varies on the basis of socio-economic status of the migrants. The socially and economically well offs mostly migrate for long period and those who are worse mostly do so for short period. The reason for migration is also related with duration of migration. Those who go for regular jobs mostly go for long period. The nature of migration also varies with the level of education. The illiterates and the less educated mostly migrate for short period while the more educated among them for long period. While only one tenth of the illiterates and those below primary are migrating, approximately one third of those with educational level of higher secondary and above are doing so. Migration varies on the basis of age also. High incidence of migration is found among the age group 15 to 49 for the males and 15 to 29 for females. For the males 20 to 24 seems to be the prime age for migration.

Another one of the distinctive features of this region is a large scale of female out migration. Female out migration has been reported from 31.8% of those households from where at least one of the members migrates. About one fourth of the total migrants (24 percent) from Gumla area are female. Variation in female out migration is found in different social classes. The high incidence of female migration from the tribes is because of relatively more freedom enjoyed by tribal women than the women of the other social classes. The incidence of female migration is low among those classes which are economically well off. Whatever migration of woman takes place from these classes is mostly for long period.

The rate of migration has increased at a very fast pace over the past 10 years across all social categories. The rate of unemployment in Jharkhand was one of the highest among the Indian States in 1999-2000. As per the 2005 Rural Jharkhand Baseline Survey (RJBS), ten years ago, about 66 percent of rural respondents thought that it was harder to find employment in rural areas. This figure dropped marginally to 62 percent in 2004-05, indicating that the employment situation has improved only marginally since the emergence of the State. In such a situation, a high rate of out migration would be expected. Migration has gone up sharply from 1.5 percent to 5.1 percent according to the baseline data, indicating a threefold increase over a ten-year period. The rate of migration has increased for both poor and non-poor. The rate of the non poor is high compared to the poor. Migration offers upward mobility only for a third of rural migrant households. Baseline survey also suggests that as many as 60 percent of the households have recorded livelihood migration over the 20 year period between 1985 and 2005.

In the name of employment, the girls from Jharkhand are being sent to the metros and other cities. A survey carried out by National Domestic Workers Welfare Trust (NDWWT) has revealed many unbelievable facts. Survey says that in Delhi alone, there are more than two hundred and fifty placement centers. More than forty thousand girls have been deported where they do as the housemaid. The ruthless exploitation takes place of these girls at the placement centres. Many of them are sent to the prostitutions, massage parlours, by the placement centres. After reaching to these points, their lives become hell. In the beginning the girls are kept in these placement centres and that are also in very miserable conditions. It will be surprising to know that these so-called placement centres are run by the Jharkhandis. The owners of these centres have networks in the villages of Jharkhand from where these girls are taken to Delhi by their relatives and friends or better say the agents. Unemployed, uneducated and teen aged girls are generally preferred and taken into net for Delhi. "There are more than 500 such agencies spread all over New Delhi today, and there are tribal girls from Jharkhand in almost every middle and upper middle class home from south extension to defence colony to Vasant Vihar to Pritampura ", says sister Prathiti of Chetanalayaa, National Domestic Worker's Forum (NDWF) with centres in Mumbai and Ranchi.

3. Culture Submergence:

The culture identities in India are formed on the basis of religion, region, ethnicity and languages. The imbalances due to changes and transformations, the cultural identity is under threat. The high influx of people to this region has started the problem. Due to cultural assimilation, new culture and behavior are in the process. Out migration also causing problem where new cultural environment is to be formed. Language which is the mother of the culture is being neglected; own mother tongue or language is not being spoken. Thus, the language which provides a perfect identity to the people is jeopardized. Besides, the modernisation, and globalisation have also started impacts on tribal culture and identity.

4. Unbalanced Development:

In the era of globalistation, rapid changes are taking place where tribal people are unable to maintain the pace. The people, who are from outside the state, are becoming rich and the gap between the tribal and non tribal is widening. The gap between the regional developments is also widening. Industrialisation is growing in and around the Jamshedpur at a greater pace where as in other part of Jharkhand such as in Santhal Pargana area, industrialisation is not taking place.

References

Ekka A, & Asif, M 2000 Development—Induced Displacement and Rehabilitation in Jharkhand; Indian Social institute, New Delhi

Ekka A, 2011 Status of Adivasis / Indigenous Peoples Land Series—4. Aakar Books, Delhi.

Dreze, Jean, etal (ed.), -1997-'The Dam and Nation': Displacement and Resettlement in the Narmada Valley, Oxford.

Fernandez, W., -1990- 'Forest Policy: A Solution to Tribal Deprivation', The Indian Journal ofSocial Work, Vol. II, No. 1, January, 1990.

Fernandez, Walter.-1991- 'Power and Powerlessness: Development Projects and Displacementof Tribals, Social Action', July-Sept. Vol. 41:3, 1991.

Iyer, G R 1993 Tribal Land and Forest Question in Bihar:; The Administration, 38 (April – Jun).

Sharan, R 2005 Alienation and Restoration of Tribal Land in Jharkhand. E P W. Oct, 8.

Singh, S K 2012 inside Jharkhand, Crown Publications, Ranchi.

Singh, K.S., 'Tribal Movements in India', Vol. 2, Manohar Publications, Delhi, 1982.

Sinha, B.K., 1996-'Draft National Policy for Rehabilitation, Objectives and Principles', Economic & Political Weekly, June 1996.

Sinha, S.P., 1981-'Tribal Development Administration': A Historic Overview in L.P.Vidyarthi (ed.) Tribal Development and Its Administration, Concept Publication,New Delhi,

Vidyarthi, L.P. 1969, Cultural Configuration of Ranchi: Study of a Pre-industrial city of tribal Bihar. Book Land Private Ltd, Calcutta.

Vidyarthi, L.P., -1981-Tribal Development and its administration, Concept Publishing Company, New Delhi.

Vidyarthi, L.P., 1976 - Tribal Culture of India, Concept Publishing Company, New Delhi.

Recommendations

The Seminar Committee of International seminar on Globalisation and Tribal, held on 6-7 December 2014 at ISRRA, Bidisa, West Bengal, on this 7th day of December 2014 recommends that-

1. In the globalisation process the Indian tribals are prone to exploitation and have been making vulnerable, the efforts have to be made so that vulnerability would be stopped.
2. Besides the processes of social change like westernisation, modernisations, there is an impact of globalisation by disarticulating and disturbing the tribal social institutions, the efforts of the globalisation are to be directed towards the institution building, social or cohesive bondage, institutional mechanism, value system-based in the tribal social system.
3. Globalisation has been impacting the tribals' subsistence economy in the name of income generation. The international financing system such as World Bank, IMF and the other donor agencies are funding the major or mega projects in the name of sustainable development, which has far reaching results, in the end of day project will be withdrawn leaving the tribal on the verge of destroyed economy. Instead the projects are to be designed in the tribal lands for reducing poverty by producing quality forest and tribal products on bio-resources and bio-diversities based, making value added and to get the market linkages.
4. Due to construction of large-scale irrigation projects, infrastructural establishments, industrial complexes, disruption, displacement and migration of large number of peoples in these mega projects have been taken place. Those affected people are neither compensated nor resettled properly. So rehabilitation-cum- resettlement policies have to be implemented as policy objectives and decisions, specially focussing on indigenous integrated farms and exploring of the perception of the tribal peoples.
5. The globalisation is to be associated with combating climate change with the introduction of the sustainable and clean technologies to

attempt the 'go- zero and zero-emission' with the reduced carbon emissions for ecological sustainability.

6. The promotion of the indigenous knowledge specially indigenous technologies is to be made for the community well being linking electronic technology after the research and development on bench-marking for the local market gaining.
7. In the information and communication technologies e-governance is to be strengthened to disseminate the information of the development opportunities and the identification of the problems and issues.
8. The globalisation requires electricity for production and daily consumption due to up-gradation of the life standards. More emphasis is to be given for producing non-conventional alternative energies like solar, wind or hydro-electricity by providing with electricity and supplying the energy giving materials by cultivating the bio-fuels.
9. The tourism sector has to be developed with development of nature tourism, rural tourism and eco-tourism for bio-diversity management, community livelihood development and imparting environmental education.
10. Ethno-eco tourism site is to be established with the promotion of ethnic foods, ethno-medicines or ethnic dresses in the indigenous lands.
11. The foreign direct investment is to be made towards afforestation and reforestation for the development of livelihoods and income-flow and also mitigating the carbon emission.
12. The utility of mobile phones are to be made by providing the information of the job market and product market.
13. Micro-finance has to be developed to develop small and micro-enterprise development.
14. Globalisation is world-wide drive for domination of the corporation or corporate sector, which is to be mobilised towards accountability in the democratic process with more development of corporate social responsibilities.
15. The human capital development in the tribal areas. is to be strengthened by giving quality education or knowledge management in the ICT sector and also professional management system.
16. There is large impact of industrialisation of modern pharm industries on the tribal health Health care measures are to be taken by introducing of ethno-medicine and follow up health tourism based

making in association with culture and traditions on the natural products. Some diseases like HIV/AID are found prevalent in the tribal belt as the impact of globalisation, which should be removed by developing the awareness.

17. Shift from manufacturing to the service sector encourages weakening at the labour unions and exploiting people in the labour wages.
18. In the globalisation process tribals are subjected to capitalistic exploitation as large section of the tribal population work as unskilled workers and they are forced into low paid labour sections.
19. Union govt. Or state govt. Should ensure through policy and legislations that minimum harm would be taken place as tribals are at the mercy of the employers.
20. The processes of globalisation are to be made on the theme- 'Think globally and act locally'.. So at the local level the civil societies are to be formed into self-help groups at the village levels and subsequent federations from block to the divisions or districts for the entrepreneurial activities and for the community empowerment.